To PAT,
A VERY GOOD
PRINCIPAL. MY F
TO YOU ALWAYS

Coppoo

NO-HITTER
9-2-72

OUT AT HOME

Triumph and Tragedy
in the Life of a
Major Leaguer

by

Milt Pappas

with

Wayne Mausser
&
Larry Names

Introduction by Milton Berle

LKP Group   **Oshkosh, Wisconsin**
                 est. 1999

LKP Group
1521 Columbia Avenue
Oshkosh, WI 54901

ISBN: 0-939995-30-1

Library of Congress Number:

For information, address inquiries to:

LKP Group
1521 Columbia Avenue
Oshkosh, WI 54901

First Printing: February 2000

Printed in USA

Published in association with Angel Press of WI

Table of Contents

Preface   vii

Introduction by Milton Berle   ix

<u>Part One - Detroit</u>
Chapter 1
    Fastball: Welcome to the Majors   1

Chapter 2
    Changeup: Born Greek and Proud   8

Chapter 3
    Single: Alley Ball   13

Chapter 4
    Slide: Safe at Second   17

Chapter 5
    Lead-Off: Not a Bonus Baby   24

<u>Part Two - Baltimore</u>
Chapter 6
    The Hill: "Now Pitching … "   31

Chapter 7
    Bullpen: Just Warming Up   38

Chapter 8
    Grounder: Through the Middle   47

Chapter 9
    Schedule: Home Game   59

Chapter 10
   Slurve: Close But No Cigar   67

Chapter 11
   Intentional Pass: Expansion   77

Chapter 12
   Pop-up: Infield Fly Rule   91

Chapter 13
   Pressure: Two On, Nobody Out   101

Chapter 14
   Liner: Taking It Deep   111

Chapter 15
   Chin Music: High and Tight   123

Chapter 16
   Mound Ace: Flame Thrower   132

Chapter 17
   Teammates: The Players' Union   142

Chapter 18
   Strategy: Conference on the Mound   158

Part Three: Cincinnati & Atlanta
Chapter 19
   Balk: The Trade   167

Chapter 20
   Slider: Toeing the Rubber   179

Chapter 21
   Inside: The Brush Back Pitch   186

Chapter 22
   Split: Divisional Play   197

Chapter 23
   Box Seats: For the Fans   205

Chapter 24
   Pitchout: Caught in a Rundown   212

<u>Part Four: Chicago</u>
Chapter 25
   Road Trip: Traded Again   219

Chapter 26
   Twi-Nighter: In the Gloamin'   231

Chapter 27
   Strike: Painting the Black   243

Chapter 28
   Knuckle-Curve: On the Corner   261

Chapter 29
   Teamwork: Around the Horn   273

Chapter 30
   Swan Song: Bottom of the Ninth   284

<u>Part Five: The Burbs</u>
Chapter 31
   Extra Innings: Pinch-hitters   301

Chapter 32
   Postgame Show: Turn Out the Lights   314

Chapter 33
  Shutout: The Loss Column   **319**

Chapter 34
  Collision: Out at Home   **329**

Chapter 35
  Low Bridge: When to Duck   **338**

Index   **341**

PREFACE

I have given a lot of thought as to why I wrote this book, and I've come to one conclusion. My career and everything that resulted from it could only have happened in America.

My parents were both born in Greece and came to America to achieve a better life. They didn't know the first thing about baseball, but they let me pursue my dream, starting with me being a batboy when I was eight or nine years old.

Some people achieve their dreams, but unfortunately a lot of people don't. I was very fortunate to be able to fulfill my dream, and my parents allowed me to do that. I am forever grateful to them and thank God for my parents. They're both gone, but they did see me play in the Major Leagues, and I know they were extremely proud of their son.

Of course, there were pitfalls along the way, but there were so many fantastic things that happened. I had a chance to travel to many different cities and meet all kinds of people all over the country. I had a long, successful career in the Majors and enjoyed most of my teammates.

Then came the rather dubious opportunity to get involved with the Players Association as a team representative. Later, I would experience the fight with the owners in trying to make a better life for the players. That came about after Marvin Miller came on board and reached its zenith with the 1972 strike. I was able to be in on the groundwork that paved the way for the fantastic conditions the players have today, even though I don't believe many of them care. We did something very important, not only for ourselves but also for the men who played before us and for those who have played since. And because of that work back in the late 1960s and early 1970s, the players were able to pursue free agency and tap into an almost inexhaustible supply of money that the owners have flashed their way.

But like I said there were pitfalls, too. The barriers that I built up as a rookie with the Orioles stayed with me throughout my life and caused me a lot of hardships. The attitude that I had of always being right and that everyone else was wrong cost me dearly in my personal life. It may have been a reason for some of the problems in my first marriage but definitely cost me my second marriage.

When that happened, I finally realized that I may have caused the problems, so I sought help and tried to understand what made Milt Pappas tick. I guess, even though I lost my second marriage, I was still fortunate to realize that I needed help. I feel today that I'm a much better person for it.

Another negative was that being involved with the Players' Association, probably was the main reason why my pitching career ended before I reached the age of 35. But I still believe that even though I haven't gotten much recognition from the Hall of Fame selection Committee, I did have a pretty good career. I'm very proud of it, and no one can take that away from me.

All in all it's been a great life. Even though I've done some things I wished I could have changed, I believe it worked out for the best and will continue to work. I thank God for that and for the opportunity to talk about it. Like I said before, only in America!

Introduction

Milton Pappas met me at Dodger Stadium back in 1962 when I had season tickets for the Angels. The Orioles were in town. Ruthie and I were minding our own business, and this brash kid comes out of the Orioles dugout and asks me for my autograph. He's polite about it, tells me who he is, so I gave it him. Then he gave it to the Angels. Fastballs, I mean. Not my autograph.

I've followed his career ever since. Nice boy for a Greek.

I met his first wife. Carole. A lovely girl. She had a hard time dealing with being the wife of a ballplayer. God rest her soul.

Milton Pappas had a great career as a Major League pitcher. He won 209 games, threw a no-hitter, had 43 shutouts, struck out many more than he walked, and he hit some home runs. Pretty good for a kid from Detroit, the son of immigrants.

The sportswriters never gave him a shot at the Hall of Fame. Why? He had the numbers. He had numbers better than a lot of players in the Hall of Fame. He had a longer career than some of them. He didn't pitch for one team all of his career, and he didn't go out of the game under his own terms. So what? So why isn't he in the Hall of Fame?

Like I said before, he was a brash kid. He offended too many of those sensitive, caring sportswriters. He didn't polish their shoes for them, so they snub him with the Hall of Fame ballot.

So now my good friend is telling his story with the help of a couple of professional writers. He didn't pull his punches, but then again, he didn't bite off anyone's ear. He reviewed his career, and from here, it was a pretty good career. He threw a no-hitter, and he won 209 games. More than Sandy Koufax. More than several others who are in the Hall of Fame.

Read this book, and you decide whether he belongs in the Hall of Fame. I think he had a good career as a player, but that's not all he did for the Game.

Few people realize what he did for the modern players. They don't know that he was instrumental in getting the Players Union going. They don't know how he helped Marvin Miller get the players many of the benefits they now enjoy, how he helped them get free agency, how he helped them get a bigger share of the baseball pie. For this contribution, Milton Pappas belongs in the Hall of Fame.

He was a great player and a great spokesman for the players. He fought their fight, and he won for them. I say for them because by the time they won the biggest battle of all—free agency—his playing career was over. He laid the groundwork for them, and they have reaped all the benefits. For this, he deserves to be in the Hall of Fame. He made his contribution to Baseball just the same as some of those sportswriters and game announcers that are in the Hall.

Read this book, and you'll see what I mean.

Milton Berle
November 1998

OUT AT HOME

To the loving memory of my parents,

Steve and Eva Pappas

And for the love of my children,

Steve, Michelle, and Alexandria

Part One

DETROIT

Fastball:
Welcome to the Majors

T ed Williams.

In my career, I faced a lot of great hitters: Mickey Mantle, Roberto Clemente, Willie McCovey, Willie Mays, Tony Oliva — to name just a few.

But Ted Williams — by far — had to be the greatest pure hitter that I ever saw in my playing years. It was just a pleasure to watch this man hit. During batting practice, the opposing team would come out — almost the whole team — just to watch him take batting practice. It was unbelievable.

The Orioles were in Boston the first time I ever faced Williams. I had him three balls and two strikes when I threw a pitch right down the middle of the plate. The ump didn't say a thing. Williams just stood there. The catcher held the ball where he'd caught it. 10, maybe 15 seconds went by — which seemed like an eternity. Finally, Williams dropped his bat and walked off toward the dugout.

The ump threw up his right arm and shouted: "Strike three." It was the third out.

I walked over to the ump and said, "What would have happened if Williams had gone to first base?"

The umpire said, "It would have been ball four because he's got better eyes than I do."

That was one of my first great lessons in the Major Leagues. It wouldn't be my last.

* * *

W e were playing the New York Yankees, and we were losing, 7-3. In the third inning, Mickey Mantle hit a rocket off the scoreboard in Memorial Stadium, which seemed to me to be about a thousand feet away from the plate. It was the first time that I ever saw the Yankees hitting up close. I had seen them in New York earlier and watched them as a kid in Detroit, but this time I really got close.

Harry Brecheen walked down to the bullpen and told George Zuverink — a relief pitcher we had — and me to go and warm up. So I started to throw the ball, playing catch nonchalantly with a bullpen catcher.

There's 45,000 people in the stands, and it's just a gorgeous evening in Baltimore. I patted George on the back and said, "Go get 'em, George. Hold 'em there, and we'll come back and get you a win." I was also talking to the fans in the stands. I was in seventh heaven, pitching on the mound in the bullpen at Memorial Stadium in Baltimore. It's a dream come true.

Then Harry Brecheen walked up to me and said, "Milt, you're in the game."

My heart sank down to my toes, and I said, "Oh, my lord. Paul Richards wouldn't do this to me."

I was kind of hoping that he'd pitch me against Kansas City or the Washington Senators for my first big league appearance. I didn't think he was going to pitch me against the big, bad New York Yankees. After all, I was just an 18-year-old kid just out of high school!

So I finished my warm-up pitches and walked down to the dugout where I tripped on the dugout stairs. Then, the inning was over, and I walked out to the mound. I was so nervous. The first couple of balls I threw — warm-up pitches — went all the way to the backstop. Gus Triandos was the catcher, and he walked out to the mound and asked me if I was all right. I told him, no, that I was scared to death; and he told me to just relax.

The first hitters I faced in Major League Baseball were Enos Slaughter, Mickey Mantle, Yogi Berra, and Bill Skowron. That was my introduction to the Major Leagues. That's how Paul Richards did things: threw you right into the fire; no salt, no butter, no frying pan; right into the fire.

The first pitch, thank God, was a strike, and I guess that's when history starts as far as Milt Pappas is concerned. I got Slaughter out, but Mickey Mantle got a base hit right back through the middle. I never even saw the ball, he hit it so hard. I looked up to the sky and said, "Lord, please help me." I was scared to death, but I got through it. I managed to get the side out.

I relieved three more innings that night, and my career was begun.

Still, I was a little mad because Mr. Richards didn't break me in against the lowly KC A's or the equally pathetic Washington Senators. Instead, it was against the New York Yankees.

I got my introduction to the Major Leagues, and I was very happy about it. Paul Richards did it, and I thank him for my career. He was a great, great manager who really kept an eye on me.

For that year, my total was nine innings pitched, all in relief. I guess, all in all, it was a great time.

That was my introduction into the Major Leagues.

* * *

We were in New York during my first year in the Majors, and the only teammate of mine who would talk to me at all back then was our shortstop, a really nice guy, Willie Miranda, a Cuban. He was the only one who would really acknowledge that I was there.

Willie asked me to go out and have dinner with him after a night game. I did because I wanted to do something with somebody on my team. So we went out, and all of a sudden, lo and behold, it was about 2:00 in the morning. I said, "Willie, I'm a rookie. It's kind of late. I think we should go back to the hotel."

We did, and by the time we got back it was about 2:30 in the morning. Brooks Robinson was my roommate at that time. He had the room key and was asleep in bed. So I had to go to the front desk to get the night clerk to round up a security guard to let me up into my room.

Just about that time, the Baltimore coaching staff — Paul Richards, Lum Harris, Harry Brecheen, and Jimmy Adair — came walking into the hotel, and they saw me standing there. Mr. Richards, of course, didn't look too happy, and he looked at his pitching coach and said, "Isn't that one of your pitchers?"

Harry Brecheen said, "Yes."

Well, I got into the elevator with them. Mr. Richards was up front. I'm in the back with the coaches, and they're just smiling and laughing, having a great time. Meanwhile, I was scared to death. I didn't say anything to Mr. Richards. I just went to my room and hoped I wasn't in any trouble.

It was kind of hard for me then because all I was doing was throwing batting practice and not pitching in any games. The Orioles were somewhat in the pennant race, so Mr. Richards didn't want to take any heat, I guess, about starting a brash, young rookie. So I was on the sidelines, working out and just pitching a little batting practice.

Our next trip after the incident in New York was to Detroit, my hometown. I had already asked Mr. Richards if I could go home early for the off day we had on Monday before the series began with the Tigers. We were doing all trains back then because Mr. Richards hated to fly. So after the game on Sunday, I caught a plane and flew home to Detroit.

On Monday morning, about 10 o'clock, the phone rang. My mother answered it and said it was Richards.

I said, "Uh-oh."

Mr. Richards said he was sending me down to Knoxville to pitch the remainder of the minor league season, which had about two weeks left. But, he said, as long as I was in Detroit, I could stay with the team for the next couple of days and throw batting practice before going down to Knoxville.

I was kind of upset because I thought I was being punished for staying out late in New York.

It was about the second week in August and a little cool in Detroit. I was throwing batting practice, and I was upset with my teammates because of the way they were treating me. They wouldn't talk to me or do anything with me, so I did a lot of pitching inside, broke a lot of bats, and had a lot teammates screaming at me and yelling at Mr. Richards to get me the hell out of there because I was killing them.

I went down to Baltimore's Knoxville, Tennessee farm team. It was about the middle of August, and even if they were to get into the playoffs, I couldn't pitch for them because I wasn't down there long enough to qualify to be on the playoff roster.

We had a catcher by the name of Walt Hriniak, who later became a very successful batting coach in the Major Leagues. Pitching to him the first couple of times wasn't too bad. For the third game, he bought a new glove, but he couldn't handle me with it. There must have been 15 or 16 passed balls. Walt was so upset with the way he was handling me that after the game he went into the clubhouse and took a butcher knife and sliced up his new catchers glove.

Shortly afterward, I was brought up to Baltimore when Knox-ville's season ended. I was quite thankful for that because I thought maybe the Orioles would just say good-bye and I'd go home to Detroit and my season would be over. But Mr. Richards — again thinking he had something in me — brought me up to Baltimore to finish the season.

* * *

A lthough the "bonus baby rule" was great for young players because it gave them a chance to get to the Major Leagues right away, hardly anyone was ever able to make an impact at that tender age. Players who were 18 years old just didn't have the experience and skill to pitch or play at the major league level.

Although I wasn't a "bonus baby" player, I was no exception. Even though I lobbied for the opportunity to go straight to the Major Leagues, I knew when I got there that I needed seasoning. If I wasn't going to get it in the minor leagues, then I was going to take my lumps for sure whenever I was given the opportunity to pitch with the big club.

It was kind of a "Catch 22" for me — and anyone else during that time who made it as a "bonus baby" player. On the one hand, you wanted to play and prove to your manager and teammates that you could play at their level. On the other hand, you knew that if you got belted around, they would probably get a strange satisfaction out of knowing that you were no better than a minor leaguer. Paying my dues was no bed of roses for me.

It was still a great experience. Here I was, a kid, barely 18 years old and just out of high school, doing what many young men were dreaming about. It didn't matter that it was done under rather difficult circumstances. And it didn't matter that I only pitched nine innings my first year. More importantly, it made me aware of just what being a Major League Baseball player was all about. The home town fans, the road trips, the travel experiences.

That first season was also about getting to know your teammates, no matter how bad of an experience that was for me. Like any other young man, it was also a time to grow up a little; to mature and stare your dream in the face. It would make me realize that I was sampling my dream, and now I would have to work harder to realize my potential. The excitement of what had occurred had to be great, if not a little overwhelming. The excitement of what may lie ahead had to be even more overwhelming. My world as a young athlete would never be the same again.

Just a few short months out of high school, I had signed a Major League Baseball contract and had gotten what I wanted out of that contract. That was, of course, a chance to go into the Major Leagues right away. Even though, I spent a few weeks in the minors that year, it would turn out to be the only time I'd be sent down during my entire professional career.

Then, of course, I had the opportunity to travel and see some of the country, even though it was just seven other major league cities. The American League — which at that time consisted of Baltimore, Boston, Chicago, Cleveland, Detroit, Kansas City, New York, and Washington — would become my home away from home for the next nine seasons. Add Minneapolis-St. Paul and Los Angeles to that list when expansion occurred in 1961. My social world would change. It wouldn't be just hanging out with high school buddies, and in my case, it wouldn't mean hanging out much with teammates that first year either.

But it would signify the end of a somewhat innocent era and

at the same time, an opportunity to perhaps mature a little earlier. It was a chance to think about the future that I had already created, had already entered.

If there was ever a time to be young and feel wonderful, I had that opportunity. If I could throw away those feelings of rejection during that first season, the future looked very promising.

As it turned out, I would be able to disregard the bitterness of those first months in the Majors, at least for awhile. That time would mold me for life, though, and would cause me hardships and problems that would be addressed over 30 years later.

◆2◆

Changeup:
Born Greek and Proud

B orn Milton Steven Pappas May 11, 1939 in Detroit, I was the middle of three sons. If I'd been born in the old country, my name would be Miltiades Stedgios Papastedgios. Is that a mouthful? I was named for a famous general out of ancient Greek history.

My parents were Stedious Papastedgios and Eudoxia Misiakoulis when each of them landed at Ellis Island. By the time each of them departed for Detroit, they were Steve Pappas and Eva Mitchell, their names having been Americanized by some bureaucrat. My mother and father and their respective families came to the United States from Greece to make better lives for themselves.

My dad came over in 1924, alone, as far as I know. He was 24, having been born November 4, 1900, in Greece. But he didn't come directly from the Mediterranean to the U.S. Like so many other young men from many parts of the world, he was drawn to Central America to work on one of the Seven Wonders of the modern world, the Panama Canal.

My mother came over in 1929 with her mother; her father and my uncle having preceded them to America. My mother was 16 when she arrived in this country, having been born April 10, 1913, in Greece.

All of them — my parents, grandparents, and uncles — settled in a mostly Greek section of Detroit.

Back then, the Motor City was a lot different than it is now. Although the neighborhoods were old, they weren't as run down as some are now. There was a certain pride in the people of Detroit, and in the Pappas household, like with many other immigrant families, there was also an ethnic pride in what they had accomplished and what they could still accomplish in a country like the United States.

My grandmother, my mother's mother, lived with us when I was growing up. She was a very lovely woman, and I don't mind saying that I respected her very much as a person. I called her "Ya-Ya." Her real name was Magdeline, and my grandfather's name was John; both having their names Americanized at Ellis Island. My uncle's first name became Tom in the U.S. My grandfather died in 1932, and "Ya-Ya" lived long enough to see me pitch in the Majors, dying in 1971.

Since the household was from the old country, Greek was the language spoken by my parents and grandmother at home. My parents picked up English because they had to learn it in order to survive, but "Ya-Ya" never learned to speak like Americans. She was Greek through and through right up until her death.

Greek was a language that I learned, though not by choice. I attended Greek school for a number of years during the evening, after going to regular public school during the day. Besides the language, I learned Greek history and other aspects of the Greek culture. This was an education that I have been very thankful for in my later years. Greek school afforded me the opportunity to meet other Greek youngsters and develop friendships with them. Although I was born in the United States, it gave me a deep appreciation for and pride in my heritage which has sustained me for all of my life.

All ethnic groups that come to America from another country — whether it's Greece, Poland, China, Mexico, or wherever — tend to congregate in a particular neighborhood or section of whatever city or town they choose for their new home. They do this because nobody speaks the language very well and they aren't well acquainted with the local customs. They feel more comfortable among their own kind. This is a natural thing to do.

My parents were no different. It was very difficult for them when they first came over from Greece. They didn't even know the other existed until they met in Detroit in 1931.

Neither my mom nor my dad ever related their first meeting to me, but I like to imagine it was a romantic moment at one of the many festive parties the Greek community held in those days. He was 13 years older than she was. A dapper, handsome man of 31, suave and sophisticated, filled with confidence for having been in the U.S. for seven years, he must have charmed her off her feet. They courted for a year, then married in Detroit in the church. It was a good marriage.

My father owned and operated his own small business, but not right away. In the early years, he worked for other people. Later, after I was born, he had the store. My mother took care of their three sons and did whatever she could to keep the household together. When we boys were old enough to help out, we did. My dad had the store until he suffered a stroke in 1956. His whole right side was paralyzed. He recovered some, enough to walk again but with a limp. Even so, he had to give up the store, and my mother had to go to work.

My older brother was born in 1935. His Greek name is Kosta; from that, my parents got Gus. Don't ask me how, but Gus he is. My younger brother came along in 1943. His Greek name is Pericles; and from that, my parents came up with Perry.

We lived in "Greek town" in Detroit, which was something of an ethnic community like the one in Chicago where there's a lot of Greek restaurants in a particular section of the city. But the families were pretty much spread all over; for example, my uncle lived about five blocks from us. There weren't a whole lot of Greek families who lived in the immediate vicinity of our house. But there were a lot of Greek families living in Detroit. Although scattered as they were, everybody got together, no matter where they lived, for holiday and "name day" parties. What are "name days?" If someone was named after a saint in the Greek Orthodox Church, you held a party on that saint's day to honor the person and the saint. Everybody jaunted over to someone's house to visit relatives and friends. These were very festive occasions.

Naturally, my family being from Greece, I was baptized in the Greek Orthodox Church. So were my brothers. We went to mass every Sunday, and we celebrated all the holy days. Even so, neither my parents nor my grandmother were what some people might call religious fanatics. They kept the faith, but they weren't devout to the point that religion dominated their lives — or mine.

I guess it took my parents a long time before they learned enough English — which they had to, being in America — so that they could find employment in this country. This might not have been that big of a barrier in good economic times, but in the middle of the "Great Depression" when hundreds of thousands of native-born workers were walking the streets looking for jobs, a poor command of English proved to be a serious road block for them. Still, they made do.

* * *

S chooling to me was simply this: I had to go. No options here, not even when I got into high school. I simply had to go to school. My parents wanted me to get a good education, and at the time, a high school diploma was sufficient for starting a life.

When I applied myself, I was a good student, but I think I only did what I had to do to get through school. We had to maintain a certain average, of course, in order to stay in school and play sports. Otherwise, you wouldn't be able to make the team if you had failing grades. So I would always make sure that my grades were just high enough for me to play baseball.

Besides public school, I went to Greek school at least two hours, three nights a week. There were probably five or six of us that were told we had to go. We were taught the Greek language and Greek history. We learned to speak Greek and also to write it. Class was held at different houses.

One year we had class on Halloween. After the lesson, we went out trick-or-treating. Our neighborhood was racially mixed. As the other kids and I were going by an alley, two black kids came flying by us and ripped off our candy bags. We tried to chase them, but we figured we were better off letting them have the candy while we went home to start all over again.

As for Greek school, I went four or five years. Even though it was tough, now that I look back on it, I'm thankful I had an opportunity to learn a different language, my parents' language, so I could converse with my grandmother, who lived with us.

"Ya-Ya" was a very lovely lady. She taught me love and respect and pride. She wanted me to be proud of my ancestors, proud to be Greek. Now that I think of it, I have to say that she did a lot — maybe more — to mold me into the person that I became. She instilled the good things; she and my mom. So did my dad. He was a good man that I admired as well as loved. I miss them, but they'll always be with me.

◆3◆

Single:
Alley Ball

G rowing up in Detroit, I really didn't think about baseball until I was about nine or 10 years old. My father and mother, coming from Greece, knew absolutely nothing about American sports, especially baseball. The only reason my dad eventually knew anything about the game was because the small grocery store he owned was in the heart of Detroit. Besides canned goods and the like, he sold beer and wine, candy and nuts, and ice cream at a counter where people could sit and enjoy the treat. He was forced to play the radio in the afternoons when the Tigers were playing, so his customers could hear the game. That was probably the first time I ever heard about the Detroit Tigers, in my dad's store.

My childhood friends were basically the kids I played baseball with. When I was growing up, that's all that the kids that I was involved with wanted to do: play baseball. We played baseball from sunup to sundown. My mother would have to come and find me to bring me home for dinner. Wherever we could find a place to play — and many times, it was in the alleys behind our houses — we played. We weren't blessed with the kind of fields that are out there today. It was either Northwestern High, which was almost always taken by the organized teams that played there, or the alleys. Not until we moved to the place on Pacific Street was there any decent place for kids to play baseball. So either we played on a vacant parking lot, if there was a vacant lot, or we played in the alleys.

One alley that we played in, about a block from my house. There was a garage that had close to 30 windows, little tiny windows, and by the time summer was over, there were no windows left in that garage.

Second base was often a beat-up, dirty, smelly garbage can that we'd put in the middle of the alley, with first and third being a telephone pole or a fence post or something of the kind and home being a piece of flat wood or a garbage can lid. This one time I was rounding second on my way to third when I reached out to tag the garbage can base without looking at it. I caught a finger on the jagged metal and nearly lost half the digit. Damn! That really hurt! Blood all over. I wrapped the injury in a rag and kept on playing. That was baseball.

Wherever we could find a place to play, we played. Against the wall of a school or in a vacant lot or a parking lot, wherever we could find the room to put four guys or 10 guys or 18 guys on the "field," we played baseball. Usually in the alleys, we played with a tennis ball, so we wouldn't break a lot of windows in houses and stuff. But in the open areas, we used the real thing. And when the stitches on the ball gave out, we wrapped the ball with tape until somebody came up with another good ball — a good ball being one that still had a cover and all the stitches, whether frayed or not.

After we moved to Marlowe Street, I lived a block away from Cooley High, and we used to go up there and play. There was only one field, of course, so we played wherever we could. If it was up against a building wall, we used a broom handle and a rubber ball; we played stickball. Whatever we had to do to play baseball, we made it work somehow.

It wasn't like it is today. Kids of today have it made. They have little league fields, baseball fields, soccer fields, parks of all kinds with softball diamonds. Everything is out there for kids today. Growing up in Detroit, back in the 1950s, it just wasn't there. Today, everything is almost pristine; idyllic, maybe. It's definitely a lot cleaner and safer than it was on most of our playing fields.

But I wouldn't trade that experience for anything. It gave baseball meaning for us. It gave us an appreciation for grass, dirt, white chalk down the lines, and canvas bases that didn't cut you.

When I was growing up, the dedication was there with youngsters. By that, I mean, that's all we thought about: baseball,

baseball, and more baseball. Today, I just don't see the same dedication. Maybe it's out there still, but I haven't seen it. I wish I could see it again. I wish I could see kids playing baseball on a vacant lot or even on a park diamond; see them playing all day long without an adult there coaching them or in some cases forcing them to play. I'd like to see a group of kids playing day after day all summer long. At least, I'd like to see it in the United States. I know it still exists in places like Puerto Rico, Santo Domingo, Mexico, Venezuela, the Philippines, and lots of other foreign countries.

Maybe it still exists in this country. If it does, I haven't seen it for a lot of years. Not since I was kid in Detroit.

* * *

My mother knew absolutely nothing about the game. Instead of occupying so much of my time with baseball, she wanted me to get a paper route or go help my dad at the store. I wanted to play baseball and be a batboy. She didn't think I'd have time for all three. When I made the Little League team, she took my uniform away. I cried for two days and wouldn't come out of my room. Finally, she realized how much baseball meant to me. I was 11 years old. She gave back my uniform, but said I would still have to find some time to help my dad like both brothers were doing. I found the time, and I got a newspaper route as well.

One of my customers was Jimmy Hoffa, the president of the Teamsters Union. He used to give me a $25-tip. I grew up with Jimmy, Jr.; we went to high school together.

When I was about nine or 10, I had a chance to get a uniform and be a batboy for a semi-pro team in Detroit. I loved it. It got me into the game just that much more. Games were played on Saturdays and Sundays at Northwestern High School, and our team was sponsored by Pepsi-Cola. The players were former minor leaguers or guys who came up short of being professionals. They were all employees of the sponsor during the week, and ballplayers on the weekends.

Later on, I started to play Little League after my stint at being a batboy. I had a lot of fun. I was a shortstop and a pretty good hitter.

This one day, I was about 11 years old and my team was getting beaten, like 21-1, and the coach was running out of pitchers. He asked if anyone wanted to volunteer to pitch, and I said, what the heck and raised my hand. So I went in to pitch and finished out the game and did pretty well. I guess that was the point where I decided I would rather be a pitcher than an infielder.

* * *

L ooking back at my youth, it was a very fun time in my life. It was fun growing up in that era.

Unfortunately, what I see today is a lack of dedication by the kids. I know I've already said this, but it needs repeating. They don't have the same commitment that we had back when I growing up. They have baseball available to them, for certain, as well as other sports. But they also have Nintendo and other video games; they have too much TV; and they have, sad to say, drugs. They have peer pressure to own material things in order to be accepted into their social group. Things like $150-pairs of shoes, jackets that cost as much as a bicycle, earrings and other jewelry that boys didn't wear in the 1950s. To get these things, they have to work or steal or sell drugs. They have little time left for baseball or the other sports. That's so sad.

I repeat: I just don't see the dedication to baseball in American youth today that we had when I was growing up. Baseball was all we thought about. All of us had the aspiration of becoming big leaguers. I don't see that as much today. I think it's unfortunate, but I think our society has changed. Unfortunately, I don't think it's for the good.

Looking back, I'm glad I grew up in the era that I lived through. It was a time when the son of Greek immigrants could grow up and become a big leaguer. It was a good time, a wonderful time.

Slide:
Safe at Second

W orking my way through the system in Detroit — Little League, Babe Ruth League, high school baseball, American Legion ball, and the Federation between my junior and senior years in high school — I was basically a self-taught pitcher. Lou D'Annunzio, the Major League scout, helped me out a little in the later years, but initially, I learned everything about pitching by myself.

Abe Eliowitz was the baseball coach at Cooley High when I went there. He had me splitting time between pitching and playing first base because I was a really good hitter. But again, as far as pitching went, it was just me experimenting on the mound as I was growing up.

As I wrote in the last chapter, my parents knew practically nothing about baseball, and I told the story about my mother, me, and the uniform. But I'm telling it again to make another point.

My mother told me baseball was just a waste of time and that I should work more with my father and not just on weekends. All of us helped out. But this was at a point where Gus, my older brother, was in high school, which meant he had other demands on his time, and Perry, my younger brother, was just getting old enough to help in the store. Gus had done his part, so my mother thought it was my turn to be the big helper in the store, especially after school and in the summer time. Of course, I wanted to play baseball, and this put my mother and me at odds. To enforce her point, she took my Little League uniform away, and I sat for two days and cried and wouldn't come out of my room because I was so upset. Whether it was her decision or my dad's, I don't know, but she finally realized how much baseball meant to me and returned my uniform. Off I went again, playing baseball, happy as a lark because I got my way.

This had two effects on my future. First, I got to play baseball as much as I wanted to and that led to me becoming a big league baseball player. And second, psychologically and subconsciously, I learned a very effective way to manipulate people and situations, something that would serve me well in future years.

Back to being a kid. I spent countless hours playing baseball, from sunup to sunset, finding one guy or two guys or 10 guys, whoever we could find to play a game, whether it be in the alley, the high school field or the grade school playground, wherever we could find a place to play. And I was happy about it.

* * *

It was quite interesting growing up in a household where your family wasn't behind you in your pursuit of a dream. This was only because they knew nothing about the game.

Gus hadn't had much interest in playing baseball while he was growing up. As the oldest son, he was given more responsibilities that kept him from playing as much as he might have liked. First, he had me to look after — in a fashion — when I was born. Then Perry came along four years later to increase that duty of surrogate authority figure. At about the same time as Perry's appearance in this world, Gus began doing more in the store for our dad. And he had school work to tend to. Add all this up and he didn't have time for baseball or sports of any kind. It wasn't that Gus was unaware of sports, because he did have a passing interest and knowledge, but he just didn't have the time to be a participant or a serious fan who reads the sports pages before he reads the comics or who collects trading cards.

At the time we lived in Detroit, the schools had two different school years. Gus was born September 6, 1935. He started school in January. Since I was born in May, I started school in the fall. Gus was a senior when I was just beginning high school, but he graduated in January 1954. Shortly after that, he married his high school sweetheart Nancy Spearman, and within a year of that, he enlisted in the Army. His military experience was shortened because my dad had a heart attack in 1955 and Gus was needed at home to take Dad's place in the store. The Army gave him an honorable discharge for hardship reasons. My mother and Gus worked the store until my parents sold it. After that, Gus got a job as a mechanical draftsman for an oil company. This was back in the days when the skills you learned in high school were actually useful in the working world.

Perry was just turning 10 when I walked into Cooley High for the first time as a freshman. He liked baseball, but we didn't play together because of the difference in our ages. He had his own dream to follow. He had an outstanding high school career of his own at Cooley, then was signed by the Yankees. He received a signing bonus of $15,000, and the Yanks sent him to the Florida State League, a rookie circuit. He played for Johnson City, Tennessee, then was drafted into the Army for two years. When he was discharged, he went back into the Yank farm system and pitched one more year before tearing ligament in his elbow that ended his career. He stayed single for as long as he could, then at age 30 married his lovely wife of 25 years, Joyce Mazzoni.

Now that I think about it, my parents had three different families: Gus, me, then Perry. They loved us all the same, but we were each different from the other two. Each was his own person. We weren't flocked together or paired up two against one as in families with children born closer together. Looking back, I'd have to say we were fortunate to have been born so far apart. Our parents were afforded the opportunity to give each of us the proper attention we needed when we were little. As a parent like most other parents, I know how much time a newborn needs from both mother and father, how much time a toddler requires, and how much time a precocious, active three-year-old demands. I'm no child psychologist, but from my experience as the father of three, I can say that by age four children have begun to settle into their niche in the family and that they are old enough to understand and enjoy the arrival of another sibling.

My mom and dad were good parents. They gave us the love we needed and then some. They treated us fairly and firmly; and they supported us in nearly everything we ever did as long as we contributed to the family as we were expected to do. Mostly, we were expected to be obedient and to do our part within the household, meaning picking up after ourselves and working in the store with our dad. When we worked outside the family for money, like when I had a paper route, we were expected to contribute a little of that money to the family income. We did that without any bitterness or resentment.

But even so, my mother's responsibilities were the traditional duties of a wife and mother in the home, and she helped out in the store some. She didn't have much knowledge of baseball; she had little time to understand it and come watch me play. I can only recall her coming to a few of my high school games and maybe none of my other games, such as Little League or Babe Ruth League.

"Ya-Ya" never came to any games because she never really assimilated into American culture. She had as much knowledge and understanding of baseball as an extra terrestrial would have. All she knew was I was playing a game and not working as much as I should. I don't think she ever really understood that I was preparing for a career in a profession that could be both financially and socially rewarding.

My dad simply didn't have the time to come watch me play. How could he? He had the store to run and a family to support. People who work for themselves have to put in longer hours than the hired help, and in a family-owned business, you have to work all the harder because you can't always afford employees.

I have to say that it was Dad's hard work — his dedication to give us the necessities in life — that gave me the opportunity to play baseball as much as I did. I'll always be grateful that he did that for me. I want Dad to be remembered as a father who so loved his sons that he worked all his life to give them the chance at having better lives themselves.

* * *

inally, I hit high school.

My freshman year I didn't go out for the freshman

football or the freshman basketball team, but I did go out for baseball. I didn't know whether I'd be on the junior varsity or on the varsity. I made the varsity. Naturally, I didn't play much that year. The next year I played a little more, but my junior year I was a regular. We won the Metropolitan League title that year.

Also, my junior year, the basketball coach asked me to come out for the team, so I did. I wasn't much more than adequate as a hoops player. My first shot in a real game was a jumper I went up with the shot, and this huge defender stuffed the ball down my throat, almost literally. Right then and there, I knew basketball wasn't my game.

The last two years in high school, I was All-City and All-State. I also won the Kiki Cuyler Trophy in 1956 for the Most Outstanding Player in the American Legion League. This was the same award that Hal Newhouser, the great Tiger pitcher, had won back in 1937.

But also my last year in high school, I was hobbled because I had hurt my knee the previous winter playing varsity basketball. I tore cartilage in my right knee.

Today when the doctors operate on cartilage in a knee, the patient has a cakewalk compared to how it used to be done. Today, the doctors repair the cartilage instead of removing it like they did to my knee. I thought the pain was terrible when I injured it, but that was nothing compared to the agony I went through after the operation. And when I woke up, man, did that knee hurt. I wanted to touch it, rub it, or scratch it, or something. But I couldn't because I was in a cast from ankle to hip. Thank God for painkillers.

Then there was the therapy after the cast came off. The quadriceps — the muscles above the knee in the front of the thigh — had atrophied; they had shrunk down to practically nothing. The doctor said I had to exercise them and I had to go through therapy for that. I did, and it was absolutely excruciating, too — at first. But as the muscles grew stronger, the pain subsided, and by spring I could move almost normally. At the least, I could play baseball. I wore a brace on the knee, but I played.

Some teams, knowing that I was hurt and playing with a brace, thought I wasn't too mobile, so they tried bunting on me.

I felt like James Stewart in the movie, *The Monte Stratton Story*. He made the play in the end, and so did I.

This one game I belted a monster ball probably about 375 feet. It hit the top of a 20-foot fence at my high school field — almost a home run — bounced back down to the center fielder. He picked it up and swung around to throw to third base, thinking I was going for a triple. He hesitated, then lobbed the ball into second base because I was just rounding first base. Longest single of my life.

After I had signed with the Orioles, the Tigers squawked because they thought the Orioles had paid for my knee operation, which wasn't just totally untrue but was absolutely absurd. The Tigers made a lot of silly complaints back then, but more about that later.

Despite my physical problems, the team succeeded and we had a great year. We won the Metropolitan League championship again.

The championship game my junior season was held — at that time — at Briggs Stadium, now known as Tiger Stadium and soon to be a parking lot. It was quite an experience, even though I had worked out with the Tigers and thrown batting practice there before. But actually playing on the same field where Ty Cobb had played, where Al Kaline was playing then, playing there as a high school kid was a really unique experience. We won the city championship there that day.

The next year I pitched the title game against Cody High, the winner of the other division in the Metropolitan League. We played at Butzel Field because it had lights. I threw a four-hit shutout and struck out a dozen hitters. It capped a really great season for me. I won six games during the regular season without a loss, only gave up a total of 13 hits for the year, throwing two one-hitters and one two-hitter, striking out 54, and walking only six. I also hit .375.

But I wasn't the only Detroit prep player to have a great year. We had some other pretty decent ballplayers in the area as well as me. Many of us played in the Detroit Amateur Baseball Federation (DABF) during the summer. I played on the Arrowsmith team with two high school teammates, Tom Heenan and

Mickey Sinks. This was the next level of baseball after American Legion ball.

Speaking of Legion ball, my team was sponsored by the Internal Revenue Service. We won the city and state championships in 1956. I had a pretty good year. My mound record was a for real 22-4, and I hit a *modest* .571.

I got into one DABF game before signing my contract with the Orioles. I arrived late, warmed up during the bottom of the second, then entered the game in the top of the third with two on, none out, and our guys trailing by a run. I allowed one hit, struck out four, and walked one guy over the five-inning stint. We still lost, 2-1.

There were other guys who were pretty good ballplayers at Cooley. Jerry Lile was a good friend of mine. He was a left-handed pitcher, and we hung out a lot together. Mickey Sinks was our catcher who later on signed with the Philadelphia Phillies. He didn't make it to the Majors. Bob Roman, our shortstop, signed with the Cleveland Indians. He was an excellent athlete, but he didn't make it either. I don't know why neither of them made it. They could have gotten injured or maybe their teams had too many guys at their positions and they got lost in the numbers. And maybe they just weren't good enough. Lots of guys are stars in high school because they play against a lot of mediocre talent. Then when they get into the pros, they find out that everybody else is just as talented as they are. That's when they find out what it takes to separate the men from the boys. Anyway, Mickey and Jerry never made it to the show.

There were other guys that I played with and guys I faced, while growing up in Detroit, who signed with Major League Baseball teams, played in the minors for a while, but never made it to the big show. I can't recall all of them, probably because there were a lot of them. However, I was the only prep player of the 1957 graduating group that actually made it to the Majors.

So for four years, I played varsity baseball and the last two years, we won the city championship. It was a remarkable start of a career for a kid that really didn't know what he was doing.

Lead-Off:
Not a Bonus Baby

High school was a great experience for me. I had fun, and I won a lot of ball games for Cooley High.

A lot of baseball scouts started following my career when I was just a freshman. The most prominent among them was Lou D'Annunzio from the Baltimore Orioles. He spent a lot of time with me. In the winter time, he'd take me bowling and we'd play pool. He was just like a second father to me; maybe more like a favorite uncle who takes you under his wing and shows you the ropes of adulthood. Whatever, we were pals.

After graduation, I had a lot to think about. I had 13 Major League teams pursuing me. Every big league club except Pittsburgh, Brooklyn, and Cincinnati wanted me, and I thought I was something special, a big shot in the vernacular of the time. I can understand why the Dodgers weren't interested; they already had a couple of very young guys named Sandy Koufax and Don Drysdale on their team. As for the Pirates and Reds? I have no idea why they weren't in the chase for my services.

All of those teams that were after me were practically offering me the same thing: $4,000 and an all-expenses paid trip to some rustic bush league town for the summer. This was not exactly what I wanted. Even the Tigers, my hometown team, weren't putting any more than that on the table.

My last couple of years in high school I would go down to Briggs Stadium to work out with the Tigers. They would leave me tickets, and allow me to use the training facilities. When the team was in town, I would get to use the whirlpool and use the clubhouse any time I wanted. I talked to a lot of Tiger ballplayers, and I did a lot of working out with them. So I was quite surprised by their very meager offer. It was just a basic nothing deal that everybody was offered in those days unless you were something very special. Like I said already, I thought I was pretty special. Why else would 13 clubs be talking to me?

A lot of other teams offered me contracts. But the thing I was looking for again was where I could make it to the Majors the fastest. So I told every ball club that scouted me — and made me an offer — that I wanted a Major League contract. None of the teams would go over $4,000 because that meant I would have to stay with the Major League team for over two years. So, then my basic concern was, "Okay, Milt, what happens if you sign a minor league contract? I go to the minor leagues." So I said to the scouts, "All right, guys, I want a Major League contract." In other words, a guarantee to go to spring training with the big team. That's what a Major League contract would do for me. It would put me on the Major League roster and get me a shot at the show the next spring. $4,000 was the money for this kind of contract, so I couldn't go any higher than that. I wanted a Major League contract, not a minor league contract. I thought I made that clear to everybody.

Some of them heard me because nine of the teams dropped out of the bidding at this point. They all said they could not give me a Major League contract and that was that.

I looked at the Yankees at the time. New York had a great pitching staff already that was still relatively young. Although they offered me a contract, I turned it down because I didn't want to spend the next decade in the minors before getting my shot.

This left Boston, Detroit, Baltimore, and Philadelphia in the chase. So, I said, "Well, now it comes down to four teams." My heart was still with Detroit — and Baltimore because of Lou D'Annunzio and Hal Newhouser, the Orioles head scout, who had come to see me, too. Lou had been around since I was a freshman, while Newhouser had just begun paying attention to me during my last two years in high school.

At that particular time there was a bonus rule in effect, which said that if you received anything over $6,000, you had to stay with the Major League team for two years. Al Kaline was probably the most successful player with that kind of contract, but he was the exception and not the usual. So nobody really wanted to offer me a bonus to sign. Other guys who were bonus babies were Lindy McDaniel and his brother Von McDaniel who signed with the Cardinals, and Steve Boros, a third baseman who played a little while with the Tigers, Cubs, and Reds.

So I went to meet with the Detroit Tigers. My high school baseball coach Abe Eliowitz was with me. He was kind of my agent back then, which was unheard of. We sat down in the office with John McHale, the general manager, and Ed Catalinas, the head scout, and I asked them what they were going to do for me. They offered me $4,000. I told them that everyone else was doing the same thing. Then they finished by offering me a minor league contract.

My mouth dropped down to my knees, and I said, "Excuse me. A minor league contract?"

"Yes," they said, "a class "B" or "C" minor league contract."

I said no. I told them everybody else was offering me a Major League contract and that I wouldn't settle for anything less.

"If the money's the same," I said, "I want a Major League contract. If you're not going to give me a bonus, I want a Major League contract."

McHale and Catalinas, feeling that since I grew up in Detroit, believed that I would jump at any opportunity to sign with the Tigers. But, I said no, that I wanted a Major League contract. They said at that point they didn't think they could do it. I then said that we didn't have anything to talk about, so I got up to leave. McHale was in shock that I didn't sign. He told me to make sure that I called him before I did anything. I asked him what that meant, but he just repeated what he said. So I just walked out with Abe.

I looked at Abe and said that I couldn't believe what we had heard. Here I was, I had two or three other teams that offered me Major League contracts and my hometown wouldn't do it. Abe asked me what I was going to do, and I told him that I wasn't going to sign with Detroit but instead would sign with Baltimore.

And I did, and it shocked the hell out of the Tigers that I didn't call them back before signing with Baltimore. Why should I have called them back? I had asked them, right then and there, what their best deal was and they told me it was a minor league contract. They had their chance.

The Baltimore Orioles made me the offer I was looking for. When I signed with them, the Detroit media was totally caught off guard. Paul Preuss of the Detroit *News* reported the signing in the June 27, 1957 edition. When he asked me why I signed with the Orioles, I said, "I figure Baltimore has a pretty old pitching staff. This should help me move up sooner. I hope to be pitching on the Baltimore team within two or three years." Pretty brash stuff for a kid just out of high school, but that was me.

Lou D'Annunzio had more to do with signing me than the offer did. He watched my career pretty much blossom during my early days in Detroit when I was a kid. He watched me in high school and in American Legion Baseball, and I just felt at this particular point that since this man was good to me, then I should be good to him.

Also, right before I made up my mind, the Orioles came to town. Paul Richards, who was the manager, wanted to see me throw. I was throwing on the sidelines to Joe Ginsberg, the back-up catcher, with Harry Brecheen, the pitching coach and Richards watching me. Richards was making his sales pitch as far as me signing with the Orioles when I interrupted him.

"Yeah, Mr. Richards," I said, "I know all about it. Why don't you just save it? I've made up my mind. I want to sign with you guys."

I turned around and walked away, leaving Richards with his mouth hanging open. He was just flabbergasted. That was me, the brash kid.

A lot of the Detroit newspapers were upset that I signed with Baltimore and not Detroit. The Tigers had a habit of letting a lot of their local talent get away. I was kind of hopeful that would be the case with me and I would come back to haunt them.

The Tigers made all kinds of accusations after I signed with Baltimore. They accused me of receiving money under the table, that my parents got money, that the Orioles paid for my knee surgery the winter before. McHale and Catalinas were really stressed about losing me to the Orioles. Everything they charged me and the Orioles with was totally unfounded, totally untrue, even absurd. They made so many accusations that Paul Richards finally had to answer to them in writing. The text of his letter can be found in the Baltimore *Sun* in the May 6, 1958 issue. He categorically denied it all, calling their accusations "bush" and "sour grapes" and just downright petty. I had to agree then and I agree even more so now.

Besides Lou D'Annunzio's treatment of me, I was impressed by the way Hal Newhouser, the one-time great pitcher for the Tigers, who was also scouting for Baltimore, handled me. He had a big hand in my signing with the Orioles.

But most importantly, I signed with Baltimore because the Orioles had a pitching staff that was pretty much up in age. I figured that I had the greatest chance of making it to the Majors the quickest with the Orioles.

As it turned out, I was only right.

Part Two

BALTIMORE

The Hill:
"Now Pitching ..."

I was 18 when I signed my first contract with Baltimore. Initially, I thought I would be sent out to Knoxville in the Class A Sally League, but that's not what happened.

After signing, Hal Newhouser took charge of me. He asked me if I had any good clothes; you know, a suit, sport coat, dress trousers, ties, white shirts, etc. When I said no, he took me out to buy me some clothes. Then he said we were flying to Baltimore, which kind of put me on edge. I had never flown on an airplane, but that didn't bother me. I couldn't figure out why Newhouser was taking me to Baltimore when I thought Lou D'Annunzio should have taken me there. But he was Hal Newhouser, the big name, a big-time pitcher, the head scout. He did all the up-front stuff that the media saw and reported. So off we flew to Baltimore, me and Hal Newhouser, the great pitcher who would be inducted into the Hall of Fame in 1992.

Looking back at Newhouser's career, he won 207 games in his career and lost 150. He had four 20-win seasons, two of them during the Second World War when the level of talent was at an all-time low and two more right after the war when the Majors were full of rookies and players who were trying to resume their careers after stints in the Armed Forces. Of his wins, 118 of them came in those years, 1944-48. He pitched in two World Series and won two games. And he was an All-Star a few times. Of course, he was a nice guy; his nickname was Prince Hal. Being a nice guy with the media is a key factor to getting elected to the Hall of Fame.

Anyway, Newhouser took me to Baltimore to be an Oriole. To make a spot for me on the team's 25-man roster, the O's actually optioned somebody to the minors. Bob Hale, a pretty darn good hitter, paid the price, which he and nearly everybody else on the team resented. I was an 18-year-old kid; I didn't know what was going on. I had no idea how the inner workings of baseball functioned. I was 18, just out of high school, in Baltimore with a Major League contract, and happier than a pig in cool mud on a hot day.

So Bob Hale was optioned out, and I was on the 25-man roster. I don't know why, and I didn't care. I was just there.

* * *

L ooking back now, I'm still not sure why the Orioles kept me in Baltimore instead of shipping me to Knoxville or somewhere else in their farm system right off. I was in Baltimore, and that's all that really mattered to me.

The Orioles weren't exactly in a two-way pennant race with the Yankees at the time I arrived on the scene. The White Sox, Indians, Red Sox, and Tigers were shadowing the Bombers at the end of June, while the O's were right behind the pack. The A's and Senators were playing their usual roles as doormats. The only team that had a chance at replacing the Yanks atop the American League was Chicago. They had pitching, speed, and a super-crafty manager, one of the all-time best, *El Señor*, Al Lopez. The Indians, Tigers, and Red Sox Tigers had talent but no leadership. The O's had leadership, but they also had more gray beards than a Santa Claus convention.

The four regular infielders in Baltimore that summer of 1957 were all 30 or older: Bob Boyd, 31; Billy Gardner, 30; Willie Miranda, 31; and George Kell, 35. Even the utility player, Billy Goodman, was 31. In the outfield, Jim Busby and Bob Nieman were both 30. The third regular outfielder was Al Pilarcik who was 27, and the regular catcher was Gus Triandos, also 27. Brooks Robinson was a mere 20, and Tito Francona was 23.

The pitching staff was much the same as the everyday lineup; getting up in years. Connie Johnson, who had pitched in the Negro Leagues, was the ace of the staff at 34. Ray Moore was 31;

Hal "Skinny" Brown, 32; Bill Wight, 35; George Zuverink, 33. Younger pitchers were Billy Loes, 27; Ken Lehman, 29; and Billy O'Dell, 24. Moore, Loes, and Lehman had all come to Baltimore in trades with the Brooklyn Dodgers. O'Dell was the only original Oriole among the pitchers and a "Bonus Baby" at that, having signed for $12,000.

I looked at these guys and figured that in two or three years only O'Dell, Loes, and Lehman would probably be left on the staff. That meant seven openings, and I felt I had an excellent chance of filling one of them.

Then along came competition. His name was Jerry Walker. Like me, he was only 18, but unlike me, he had signed for a bonus of $20,000, which meant he had to be kept on the Major League roster his first two years. I wondered how we were both going to stay with the Orioles at the same time.

Paul Richards was a very shrewd, cunning man. Probably one of the shrewdest and most cunning men I've ever met in my life. I was with the team about five days and I was throwing batting practice. All of a sudden he walked up to me and said, "Your arm's sore, isn't it?"

I looked at him and said, "What, Paul?" Everybody else called him Mr. Richards, and I called him Paul and got away with it. "What did you say?"

Paul Richards was only a third-string catcher in the 1930s. Then World War II put a lot of has-beens and never-will-be types on big league rosters. He got a shot with the Tigers and had four decent years before his playing days ended. In 1951, he took over the reins of the Chicago White Sox and made winners of them for the next four years before leaving for Baltimore. Before the franchise moved to Maryland, the Orioles were the St. Louis Browns, one of the oldest teams in the Majors. Also, the Browns were a perennial AL doormat with the exception of one season during the World War II when Bill Veeck owned the club and he hired the right has-beens and a little person to win a pennant. When Richards took over as manager, the Orioles were a seventh place team. He was slowly building them into a respectable organization when I came along and started calling him by his first name.

He drawled, "Your arm's a little sore, isn't it?"

"No."

He said, "Your arm's a little sore, isn't it?"

I looked at him a little funny and said, "I guess so." You know, I had no idea why the man was bringing this up to me, saying this to me.

He said, "Okay, tomorrow you're going on the disabled list."

"Why?"

He said, "You just told me. Your arm's a little sore."

"You told me to say that."

He said, "No, your arm's a little sore, isn't it, Milt?"

"Yeah, I guess it is, Paul."

The next day I went on the disabled list, and Jerry Walker was put on the roster.

Now I was on the disabled list, and I was thinking, "Man, this guy is shrewd!" I still didn't know what was going on around me. I was still a really green kid, just out of high school a month.

A couple of days later in Baltimore, I was throwing batting practice and the Tigers were in town. I was out there throwing BB's. I mean, I was throwing 90-95 miles per hour, and I was having a ball. I was throwing batting practice to the Baltimore Orioles, and I was in the Major Leagues. I felt just great!

Two days later, I got called into the office, and Paul said, "We got a problem."

"What's the problem?"

"The Tigers complained that you're on the disabled list."

"Yeah?"

"But you're out there throwing 95 miles an hour, and they figure there's nothing wrong with you. So the commissioner has asked us to take you off the disabled list."

"Okay."

I still didn't know what was going on in this game, but I was starting to feel there were inner workings of baseball that happen that nobody really knows too much about. So now I was thinking, What is he going to do with me? Is he going to send me to the minors or am I going to stay with Baltimore?

At this same time, I found out there were headlines in Detroit that the Orioles paid for my knee operation, that they gave money to my dad under the table, and all kinds of rumors were going around that the Orioles did everything wrong and nothing right.

Baltimore had to answer the charges.

The commissioner's office interviewed me and asked if the Orioles paid for my operation and if they paid my mom or my dad anything. I said, no, that my mother and father paid for my operation. They checked with my parents, and they checked with the hospital.

I was thinking, What am I doing? What is happening here? I just want to play baseball. I don't know anything about this crap that's going on inside the structure of baseball.

Then the commissioner's people went to Baltimore, and they made the Orioles produce my contract. They talked to my dad and asked him if Baltimore had given me any money. They wanted to see my W-2 and my paycheck stubs. The Orioles had to prove everything. This went on for about a month, back and forth, back and forth.

Finally, the Tigers were satisfied that everything was on the up-and-up.

Then I was taken off the disabled list, and Bob Hale went down to the minors again. That poor guy. He couldn't figure out what was going on either.

* * *

I t was the middle of August, and I was just sitting around watching every game and not playing. We were in fourth place at the time, 18 games behind the Yankees. Paul, for some reason, thought we had a good chance at winning the pennant.

This was when the Yankees were really potent, really awesome. They had Mickey Mantle, Moose Skowron, Joe Collins, Hank Bauer, Yogi Berra, Enos Slaughter, Whitey Ford, Bob Turley, and on and on. Everyone in the American League was wondering who would end up second to the Yankees. Basically, that's what it was like throughout the 1950s and early 1960s. But Paul still figured we had a chance at catching them, and I was wondering when I was going to pitch.

Finally, my opportunity came. The Yankees were in town, and we were in a do-or-die series. The date was August 10, a Saturday, and we were playing at night. We had lost the night before, so this game was just that much more important for us to win. Paul started Ray Moore, and the Bombers knocked him down with three in the first. They put up another three in the third, and Bob Turley was throwing bullets. By the eighth, the game was pretty much over with us trailing, 6-2. That's when Paul put me in. I got through the eighth like I said in Chapter 1, and I got through the ninth as well. Mantle singled off me in the eighth, and Jerry Lumpe, a decent hitting third baseman, punched one through the infield in the ninth. I got everybody else out: Slaughter, Berra, Skowron, Bauer, Tony Kubek, and Turley, who was a pretty good hitting pitcher.

A week later we were in New York, and I made my second appearance on a big league mound. We were down, 5-2, and Paul put me in for the eighth inning. I was a little nervous, pitching in Yankee Stadium for the first time in my life. I walked Jerry Coleman to start the inning, then Bobby Shantz bunted him over to second. Slaughter stepped in, and I burned one in on his hands. I heard his bat crack, but that old man muscled it over second for a single. Coleman scored, and my perfect career was over. I retired Joe Collins and Mantle, but we still lost.

The next week I was on my way to Knoxville.

* * *

The Sally League only had two weeks left in the regular season when I got down to Knoxville, so I was ineligible for any playoffs that Knoxville might have. Even so, they kept me there until the playoffs were over.

My catcher in Knoxville was Walt Hriniak, who became a pretty good hitting coach after his playing days were over. One night we were playing Charlotte, and I had such a great fastball going. It was moving all over the place that Hriniak couldn't hold it. Every second pitch was either dropping out of his glove or going back to the screen. Walt was so frustrated that after the game he went into the clubhouse and took a butcher knife to his catcher's glove. He was that mad that he couldn't handle the pitches I was throwing.

My fast ball was moving like crazy. It was sinking and going straight. I finally figured out on my own that I could make the ball rise or sink, so I learned to throw different types of fastballs. That was the difference between being a pitcher and a thrower.

* * *

When the Sally League season was over, I was brought up to Baltimore again to finish the season with the O's. Richards still wouldn't start me. I only pitched two more games, both in relief.

My third appearance was against the Kansas City A's. It was a meaningless game, the opener of a Wednesday twilight doubleheader in Baltimore. The A's jumped on us early with seven runs. I got into the game in the sixth and finished without allowing any more runs. I got to bat in this game for my first Major League plate appearance. I struck out. The date was September 11.

My fourth and final trip to the mound came 10 days later. We were playing out the string, trying to build our stats for the next year. The Senators were in town for a weekend series. Once again I finished up a loss, going the last two innings.

For the year, I got into four games, pitched nine full innings, allowing only one earned run on six hits, while walking three and striking out three.

On the last day of the season, a reporter from the Baltimore *Sun* asked the players what we planned to do in the offseason. I remarked that baseball would come to end some day and I needed something to fall back on. So I said was going back to school to learn drafting at General Motors technical school.

Never happened. I drove my 1957 Chevy Impala back to Detroit, traded it for a new 1958 Chevy Impala, and waited for my contract for the coming year to arrive in the mail. It was a long winter.

Bullpen:
Just Warming Up

My first full year with the Orioles was 1958. I was still only 18 years old when I went to Arizona for spring training. I was still learning the ropes.

Again, the year before, I had pitched only nine innings in relief. But now my teammates in spring training had a little different attitude toward me because I was trying to make the team the same as they were. Now they had to play with me.

Learning how I made the team is something I'll never forget.

Camp had a little over a week left, and of course, I was curious about whether I would be going north with the big club or be assigned to one of the minor league camps. But how to find out, that was the question. I came up with a plan.

I had driven to camp from Detroit. If I was headed down to the minors for the beginning of the season, then my car was no problem; I could drive it to wherever the Orioles assigned me. If I was going to the big show, then I had to find someone to drive my car back to Baltimore because everybody flies out together as a team. I thought I'd ask Paul Richards which way to go. That was the scheme.

"Paul, I've got a problem."

"What kind of problem?"

"Well, I've got my car here."

He looked at me kind of funny and said, "What?"

"I've got my car here."

"So what?"

"Well, I'd like to know if I'm driving out or flying out."

He gave me a quizzical look and said, "Aren't you pitching today?"

"Yes, I am."

"Then why don't you let me worry about managing this team and you go out and pitch?"

"Yes, sir."

I told you he was wise. The old fox saw right through me.

I went out and pitched against the San Francisco Giants that afternoon. To date, I'd made exactly four spring appearances, allowing only one run in nine and a third innings. Not bad for an 18-year-old rookie. Even though I'd walked six guys, I'd struck out four and only allowed four hits. Against the Giants, I threw the first five innings and wound up the loser. Even so, I only surrendered two hits and two walks. Only one of the three runs that Cepeda, Mays, and the rest of the Bay Bombers scored on me was earned, and I managed to strike out five of them before I was pulled. Overall, it was a pretty good outing. At least, I thought so.

After the game, Richards called me into his office and said, "Son, why don't you have somebody drive your car back to Baltimore?"

Was I elated? Like a kid on Christmas morning who finds his first bike under the tree.

"Don't tell anybody," said Richards. He said that because he hadn't made all the final cuts yet and some guys were still on the bubble. I didn't care at the time. I knew I was going to the big show, and I just wanted to tell somebody. I asked if I could call my parents and tell them, and he said okay. The next day he made the formal announcement that I was going back to Baltimore with the team.

That's how I found out I had made the Orioles.

It was good that I did so well against the Giants because in the Cactus League finale I faced the Cubs and wasn't so brilliant. I went seven innings, gave up seven hits and a walk, and allowed four earned runs. The guy who pitched the eighth took the loss, but I didn't care. I was going to Baltimore to start the season.

The car? I got one of the guys being sent down to drive it back to Baltimore for me.

* * *

M y hunch about the Orioles was proving correct. The hunch? The thought that Baltimore had an aging staff and that my best chance to get to the Majors early was with them.

Richards started the youth movement with the O's by moving old guys Bill Wight and Ray Moore. Wight, 35, was put on waivers in December and picked up by Cincinnati; and Moore, 31, was part of the big trade with the White Sox. Baltimore sent Moore, Tito Francona, and Billy Goodman to Chicago for outfielder Larry Doby, pitcher Jack Harshman, outfielder-first baseman Jim Marshall, and Russ Hemon, a minor league pitcher who finally made it to the show with the Indians in 1961. Doby was traded with lefty pitcher Don Ferrarese to Cleveland before the season started for lefty pitcher Bud Daley and outfielders Dick Williams and Gene Woodling. Moore's departure left an opening in the rotation for me. Or so I hoped.

The rest of the staff remained pretty much the same: Billy O'Dell, Connie Johnson, Billy Loes, Hal Brown, Ken Lehman, and George Zuverink. Daley and Harshman were the newcomers. Jerry Walker had to stay because he was a bonus baby. That left one spot: mine.

Our regular lineup consisted of Gus Triandos behind the plate, Bob Boyd at first, Billy Gardner at second, Willie Miranda at shortstop, Brooks Robinson at third, Al Pilarcik, Bob Nieman, and Gene Woodling in the outfield. Dick Williams, Jim Busby, Jim Marshall, and Foster Castleman held down the bench.

We opened the season against the Senators with a win at home on Tuesday, April 15. The mayor of Baltimore threw out the first ball. We had Wednesday off, and I was scheduled to go on Thursday.

Yes, Richards announced that I was starting the second game of the year against the lowly Washington Senators. I couldn't believe it at first. Surprised? You bet I was surprised. I could hardly sleep the night before, but I managed to get through the night and the next day before reporting to the ball park on time.

The year before I'd faced the Yankees for my first two Major League appearances. I told myself that I'd gotten them out, so setting down the downtrodden Senators shouldn't be so difficult.

Right! I warmed up on the side with butterflies in my stomach, then I wobbled out to the mound. I made my warm-up pitches from the hill, then listened to the National Anthem with my knees knocking to the beat. Finally, the music stopped, I put my hat back on, and the umpire yelled out, "Play ball!"

Eagle-eyed Eddie Yost led off for Senators. He played third base and was nicknamed "The Walking Man" because he drew a lot of walks. Over an 18-year career, he led the AL in bases-on-balls six times. But not this day. I got him and nine other outs before I was pulled in the fourth inning. During that span, I gave up a pair of hits in the second inning and a walk to Yost in the third. But in the fourth, I started missing the plate, walking two guys in a row, the same two guys who'd gotten hits off me in the second: Norbert Zauchin (who?) and Lou Berberet (double-who?). Then I uncorked a wild pitch that moved them to second and third, respectively. Richards had seen enough. Always the protecting mother hen, he took me out before I completely lost everything, especially my self-confidence. Jack Harshman, the lefty that we'd picked up from the White Sox over the winter, came in and shut down the Senators the rest of the way.

We were off to a good start, 2-0, and I'd had made my first start in the Major Leagues. I was happy.

Oh, yes. I was involved in an odd play that game. I struck out in the second inning for the third out. Nothing strange with that, except that the Washington catcher, Clint Courtney, trapped the ball. He flipped the ball casually toward the mound as I turned to walk back to the dugout and the rest of the Senators headed for their dugout. Before I took a single step, our bench started yelling for me to run to first base. So I did. And I was safe. Thanks to Courtney's absent-mindedness. But the error made no difference in the game because our lead-off hitter made the last out.

We played the Yankees that weekend, and they brought our good start to an end by sweeping three straight from us. I got into the Saturday game and faced one batter in relief. I got him.

My second start came the next week in Boston against the Red Sox. I went up against Jimmy Piersall for the first time. I'd heard a lot about Piersall, about how crazy he was. For the record, Jimmy Piersall was a great player and a good guy. Before

I played against him, he'd had a nervous breakdown that landed him in a psychiatric hospital. His early life was made into a movie, *Fear Strikes Out*, that starred Anthony Perkins as him and Karl Malden as his father.

Of course, the great Ted Williams was still there in Boston, and so were Jackie Jensen and Frank Malzone in those days.

Anyway, Piersall came up to bat the first time against me, and he was singing: "I've got the whole world in my hands. I've got the whole wide world in my hands."

I was thinking, Oh, my lord. Whatever they said about Jimmy Piersall, I guess they were right. Well, Piersall hit a home run off me, and I was pissed! Besides singing walking up to the plate, he continued to sing while rounding the bases! So I said to myself, Okay, we'll meet again. And we did, two innings later. There were only about three or four thousand people in the ballpark for that day game in Fenway Park. I jammed him really well with an inside fastball that broke his bat. He fisted a weak little grounder back to me, and I threw him out.

Cocky as I was, I then yelled, "Why don't you sing about that, you sonofabitch?"

Of course, everyone in the ball park heard me. Ted Williams started to get on me, calling me a rookie s.o.b. and asking me who in the hell did I think I was. Williams was really, really ragging at me. But he went 0-3 that day against me, so I really didn't feel too bad.

I did feel bad about being taken out after six innings with the game tied, and I felt even worse after we lost in the bottom of the 10th. I was okay with my performance, allowing just two earned runs on four hits and three walks, but I was unhappy with the no-decision. Little did I know then how many no-decisions I would have over my 17-year career, but that was number one because my previous start was less than five innings.

Before I started another game, Richards brought me in to put out a fire against the White Sox. Neither hitter I faced reached base. We went on to win, and Harshman won his third straight.

My next start came on a Sunday afternoon, and as Fate would have it, the opposition was none other than the Detroit Tigers. The date was May 4, 1958, one week before my 19th birthday.

Richards picked me to start the first game of a doubleheader. I was on, and our offense managed to get me three whole runs. I allowed only one earned run on five hits and three walks, while striking out six. We won, 4-3, and I got my first Major League victory. But not without paying a price.

The Tigers had two on and two out in the top of the seventh when Harvey Kuenn — one of the best hitters in the AL, sober or drunk — came to bat. If I didn't get him, I was gone. I reared back and gave him everything I had. I got two strikes on him, then reached back for a little extra. I found it. I blew a vicious slider past him for strike three, and I was out of the inning. I was also out of the game because I felt something give in my elbow on that last pitch. Two days later I went on the injured list for the next two weeks.

* * *

W hen I came off the disabled list, Richards put me right back into the rotation. Big mistake. I started against the A's and failed to get through the first inning. Now the A's that year weren't a bad team. In fact, at the time, they were in second place, one of only three teams above .500 in the AL. I walked two guys and gave up three hits and three runs before Paul pulled me.

That was on May 25. Five days later Richards put me on the mound in relief against the Red Sox for a little mop-up duty. I gave up three hits, but I got out of the inning without anybody scoring. Two days later I finished a game against the Senators, going the last two innings without giving up a hit or a run.

Richards must have figured that I was ready to start again, so he penciled me onto the lineup card to face KC on June 6 — in Baltimore this time. I went out there and threw the best game of my big league career to date. I went the whole way, striking out three, no walks, four hits, and only one run as we beat the A's, 3-1. Not until after the game did I learn about "the plan." If I had not done well against the A's, I was headed to the minors for seasoning. I wonder if I'd been told about "the plan" before the game just how I would have handled the pressure. I guess I'll never really know, but I like to think that I would done okay just the same.

My next outing was against the Indians in Baltimore. I went six innings, gave up one run on seven hits, and got the win, 7-4. The big thing about that game was I got my first hit in the Major Leagues, a single, off the great Bob Lemon. We chased him in the fourth, and Dick "Bones" Tomanek, a lefty who was in his second full year in the Majors, came in to relieve Lemon. He was supposed to put out the fire, but we smacked him around. In the middle of a bunch of hits, I had a sacrifice bunt that he should have fielded and forced the runner at second. Instead, he got me at first. The runner who moved up scored the go-ahead run, and Tomanek took the loss.

The next week Tomanek was traded to Kansas City for Woodie Held and Vic Power. Going with him were Preston Ward and a little known outfielder named Roger Maris. I wonder if the Cleveland management threw Tomanek into the deal because a 19-year-old rookie pitcher had beaten him. Probably not.

My record went to 4-1 with my next start, a 5-3 win against the A's in Kansas City. And guess who the opposing pitcher was that day. Right. Tomanek. I got my second hit, my first extra base hit, a double; and I got my first RBI that game. Tomanek's big league career came to a halt the next year. Gee, do you think I had anything to do with that? Probably not.

My next start was against the Tigers and Paul Foytack. I didn't pitch badly, but Foytack was incredible that day. I found out what it was like to be on the short end of a shutout as we lost, 5-0.

I rebounded to beat the Tribe, 11-6, with my next start, then I faced the Red Sox on the Fourth of July. I got the first four guys out, then Frank Malzone singled off me. Out I came. Why? I don't remember. I wasn't wild; I don't recall being hurt; but it was hot that day. I think it may have gotten to me. That's probably why I can't recollect that game.

Richards held me out for the next five days, then I started against the A's on July 10. I beat them for the third time that year to raise my record to 6-2.

On July 16, I faced the White Sox for the first time in

Baltimore. I lost, 6-1. To make matters worse, I hit my first batter: Sherman Lollar. I didn't know then how slow afoot he was. If I had known, I wouldn't have pitched him inside as close as I did. How slow was he? Lollar was so slow that even Stu Miller wouldn't brush him back for fear that old swifty couldn't get out of the way in time.

Eight days later I got a second chance at the ChiSox, this time at Comiskey Park. What a night that was! I beat the Pale Hose, 7-3, and improved my record to 7-3. More important to me, I also had a big night at the plate. I hit the first home run of my career, and I also had a double for my first two-hit game. The homer came off Gerry Staley, the 37-year-old veteran righthander who was extending his Major League career by becoming an ace out of the bullpen.

The Indians smacked me around my next time out, getting 10 hits off me in six innings. Here we had just gotten over the .500 mark for the first time since April, and I put us right back at even, 47-47, and in third place, 15½ games behind the Yankees.

I lost my next three starts as my teammates could only get me a total of four runs. For all practical purposes, our pennant hopes were down the drain by then. We played for second place for the rest of the year.

* * *

In August, we were chasing the White Sox for second place, and Paul Richards thought we might catch them if we had one more dependable starter. We picked up one, Hoyt Wilhelm, from the Indians. Of course, Wilhelm had always been known as a reliever, but that year he was a starting pitcher for Cleveland under Bobby Bragan and with us.

On a Saturday afternoon late in the year in Baltimore, Wilhelm no-hit the Yankees in just his ninth Major League start on September 20, 1958 on national television. Gus Triandos hit a home run to give the Orioles the win, 1-0. Don Larsen gave up only one hit in six innings. It was a good day for a no-hitter; the game was played in a steady drizzle. I was set to pitch the next day, and I wondered, What do I do for an encore? Well, I didn't throw a no-hitter, but I did beat New York and Tom Sturdivant, 6-2, to complete a sweep of the Bombers. Thank God for Moose Skowron. For some reason, Casey Stengel played him at third base that day, and Moose made two errors that allowed two runs to score. Moose wasn't all that great as a fielder at first base either, which really makes me wonder to this day why the "Ol' Perfessor" put him at the hot corner that game. Whatever the reason, I'll always be grateful.

The next week we went to New York to finish the season. We lost Friday night, then got rained out on Saturday when I was supposed to pitch. Instead, I started the first game of a double-header on Sunday. Sturdivant was the Yankee starter, and this time my guys made the errors. I lost, 6-3, because of four un-earned runs. I guess things have a way of balancing out in base-ball.

That game stands out in my mind because the first time up, Mickey Mantle, batting left-handed, hit a double to left-center field off me. When he was standing on second base, I looked him straight in the eye, and I was pissed.

"Mickey, you don't show me shit."

And he looked at me with surprise and said, "What in the hell did you say?"

"Mickey, you don't show me shit."

"What in the hell is wrong with you, kid?"

By now, I was off the mound, pretending to rub up the ball. "Growing up as a kid and seeing you in Detroit and how strong you are, hitting balls over the roof in Detroit and in Griffith Stadium, and now, man, you can't even pull my best fastball."

I just turned around then and went back up on the hill.

Mickey started talking to the shortstop and second baseman, asking them if this kid is crazy or what. They just laughed.

That ended my first full year in the Majors. I was 10-10 with an ERA of 4.06. I completed three games in 21 starts. Not bad for a teenager. The thing was, I just knew I was better and I was going to prove it to everybody. I had a whole career ahead of me yet.

Grounder:
Through the Middle

Baltimore didn't really have too good of a year in 1958.
Actually, with the exceptions of 1954 and 1959, nobody
in the 1950s had a good year because everybody was chasing the
Yankees all the time.

1958 was particularly tough because the American League
had some real balance for a change — after New York. The
Yanks topped the league with a record of 92-62, and Washington
finished in the basement with a mark of 61-93. In between, the
White Sox, in second place, came in a mere nine games ahead of
seventh place Kansas City. That was only nine games separating
six teams. That's close. If the Orioles had only had a little more
offense to go along with the second best pitching in the AL, we
could have easily finished ahead of Chicago and maybe — just
maybe — we would have challenged the Yankees.

But that's not what happened in 1958.

Or 1959.

When February rolled around that year, I was ready. There
was no question about my spot on the roster. I knew that I had
already made the team, based on my performance in 1958. I was
a veteran now at the age of 19. Although Richards didn't come
right out and say so at the start, I figured I'd be a regular starter,
again based on how I'd done the year before. That was what I
thought before I saw all the competition in camp.

Jack Harshman, Jerry Walker, Hoyt Wilhelm, Billy Loes, Hal
"Skinny" Brown, and Billy O'Dell were still there, and rookies
Jack Fisher, Wes Stock, Chuck Estrada, and Steve Barber were
trying to make the team. The advantage I had over the latter four
was my one good year of experience. Had we all been on equal

footing, I believe I would have made the team — but maybe not.

Our everyday lineup remained much the same as it had been in 1958. Gus Triandos was still the regular catcher, Bob Boyd on first, Billy Gardner at second, Brooks Robinson at third, Bob Nieman and Gene Woodling in the outfield. Willie Tasby was the new centerfielder, having come up from the minors; and Chico Carrasquel was our new shortstop, coming to us in a trade with Kansas City for Dick Williams.

After finishing spring training with the best record for AL teams, we opened the year in Washington against the Senators. Vice-President Richard Nixon threw out the first ball because President Dwight Eisenhower was off playing golf at Augusta, Georgia. Congress and the Supreme Court took the day off because of the game. So did most of the government, but not all the bureaucrats came out to Griffith Stadium. Attendance was a meager 26,850. Pretty poor for Opening Day — even for Washington. We lost, 9-2, as Pete Ramos did a number on us.

That game will be remembered in baseball history forever. The Nats had runners on first and second with no outs in the fifth inning. Washington's catcher, Eddie Fitzgerald, came up. Hoyt Wilhelm was pitching. The runners took off. Fitzgerald hit a liner to Bob Boyd playing first for us. Boyd fired the ball to Chico Carrasquel, our shortstop. Chico stepped on second and rifled the ball back to Boyd to force the runner on first. Triple play! The first one in history on Opening Day.

My first start went very well. We beat the Senators in Baltimore, 4-3, on Gene Woodling's sac-fly in the bottom of the eighth. Next time out I couldn't get through the first inning against Boston. I walked four and gave up two hits and five runs. We came back but still lost, 8-7. That was my last start for two weeks. I picked up a win in relief, then I went up against the Indians in Cleveland and won; my third victory without a loss. I won once more before Gary Bell and the Indians put the hurt on us, 8-3. That started my slump.

Paul Richards knew how to get his team pumped up. I was having my problems as was the whole team. We were playing the A's. Paul Runge was umping behind the plate. I was nipping the corners consistently, and he was calling everything close a ball.

In the third inning, Runge called ball four on a pitch that everybody in the stadium thought was a strike. Whitey Herzog trotted down to first base, and Richards came storming out of the dugout. He screamed at Runge, and Runge gave him the thumb. When play resumed, my catcher, Gus Triandos, put in his two cents, and Runge heaved him out. Ed Hurley was umping at third, and he heard some guys on our bench mouthing off at Runge. Hurley pointed to Bob Hale, Billy Loes, Albie Pearson, and Arnie Portacarrero, then told them to take a shower. Our manager and five players — gone! Did that light up the rest of us? I went the distance, and we won, 6-1.

The next week we played the Indians. I faced them on Thursday and lost, 2-1. Rocky Colavito doubled in the winning run in the eighth inning. I went the distance and considered the game a moral victory because the night before Colavito had belted out four — count 'em! — four homers against us. That Rocky! One of the truly nice guys in the game. Sometimes it was tough striking out a nice guy. I mean, I almost felt bad about it. Almost.

The following Wednesday I went up against Jim Bunning and the Tigers in Baltimore. Bunning was one of the great ones. He was in his third full year in the Majors in 1959. He'd won 20 in 1957 and 14 the next year. He went on to win 224 games over 17 years, retiring after the 1971 season at age 40. The sportswriters inducted him into the Hall of Fame in 1996. He was a congressman then from Kentucky. A really great man and a great pitcher. He was Detroit's ace in 1959. But not this night in Baltimore. I aced him, 4-0, with a two-hitter. The first shutout of my career. June 17, 1959. I gave up singles to Lou Berberet, a lifetime .230-hitter who seemed to hit .600 off me, and Bunning, who was also a great hitter for a pitcher.

To say that I was merely on a roll in June of 1959 would be a gross understatement. I'd beaten KC, 6-1; lost a tight one to Cleveland, 2-1; and shut out the Tigers, 4-0; in three starts. I had another shutout going against the Indians in Cleveland until I gave up a solo home run in the eighth inning. Even so, we won, 5-1, to raise my record for the year to 7-3.

After losing to the Tigers, my next game was on the 4th of

July against the Red Sox in Baltimore. July 4th, the traditional mid-point in the Major League season. And can you believe Ted Williams was only hitting .201 and had been dropped to sixth in the batting order? Well, it was true. The great Ted Williams hitting a pitcher's batting average. Incredible! Of course, he was 40 years old at the time. Still, he was Ted Williams. He hadn't hit his 500th homer yet, but if he hadn't missed three seasons because of World War II and nearly all of the 1952 and 1953 seasons because of the Korean War, he would have had 600, maybe 700 homers by then. He didn't though, and he was hitting a puny .201 on July 4th. We jumped on the Beantowners with nine runs in the first five innings, and I coasted to the win, 11-5. Williams? His season took a turn for the better that day. He had a single and a double off me to put some points on his average. No future Hall of Fame player should have to go through the ignominy of a .200-season.

Five days later we were in Washington for a twilight double-header. I was to go in the first game, and Jerry Walker took the mound for the nightcap. Both of us were on. I got my second career shutout, 8-0; and Jerry mowed down the Senators, 5-0. We were both only 20 years old. Was the future bright for Baltimore?

On July 14, the A's were in town for a doubleheader. We lost the first game, 1-0. I got the call for game two. I won for the 10th time with a five-hitter over Johnny Kucks, who had been a fair pitcher when he was with the Yankees but with KC he struggled due mostly to a lack of support. I mention this game for two reasons: it was my 10th win of the year and an outfielder for the A's spoiled my shutout with a homer, his first ever off me. His name? Roger Maris. Nobody at the time had any idea what he would do in 1961, but that's getting ahead of the story.

My next outing was a rare relief appearance for me, but I saved Skinny Brown's win over the Tigers. Then I lost to Bud Daley and the A's in Kansas City.

We were a game under .500 and nine and a half games out of first when I went up against the White Sox in Chicago in the second game of a doubleheader. Early Wynn, the aging — or should I say, the ageless — master of the knockdown pitch, beat us in the first game, 4-1, with a two-hitter. Wynn was 39 and in the middle of his fourth and final 20-win season. He was near the end of his career, and I was just getting rolling. I rolled on the Sox, 4-0, giving up five hits and three walks with six strikeouts. We were back to .500 and still in the race for the pennant.

A week later we were in Cleveland for another doubleheader. The Indians were fighting the White Sox for first place, and we were in third. We needed a sweep to make a charge at first. We won the first game, 5-4, and I took the hill for the second. For eight innings, I was in total command. We went into the bottom of the ninth, leading, 2-0. I gave up a pair of hits, and Richards brought in Billy O'Dell. Billy got the first guy, then Tito Francona, a left-handed hitter, stepped up. Percentages said plainly that Billy, a southpaw, had the advantage. Not this day. Tito took him deep, and the Tribe won, 3-2. None of us were the same after that.

My good fortune continued through the next week as I beat Cleveland and Washington to raise my record to 13-5. After that, I struggled with Lady Luck and lost. I made an error against the Indians that kept an inning alive, walked a guy, then gave up a grandslam to Woodie Held to lose, 4-2. With my next start, I wasn't sharp against the Red Sox and lost again, 4-1. My record dropped to 13-7.

We went to New York for the first weekend in September. The Yankees and the Orioles still had prayers of winning the pennant. I opened the series on Friday night against Ralph Terry, who had started his big league career with the Yankees in 1956, then was "sent down" to KC for seasoning in 1957 before "returning" to the big time in early 1959. Sportswriters and fans used to joke that the A's were only a minor league team for the Yankees back then. From all the trades the two teams made with each other, it sure seemed that way. Anyway, Terry was just beginning to come into his own at this time, but luck hadn't caught up with him yet. I shut out the Bombers on six hits to halt their winning streak at three games and drive a nail in their pennant drive coffin.

My record was now 14-7, but I was running out of gas. So were the Orioles. So was everybody else except the Indians and White Sox. For a change, the Yankees weren't 10 games out in front on Labor Day; they were fading just like the rest of us. We slipped to sixth place, one game behind the Red Sox in fifth, two games behind the Tigers, and five games in back of the Yanks. For most years in the decade, being five games behind New York would have been a good year, but the Yankees came in third, 10 games behind the second place Indians and 15 games behind the champion White Sox.

I finished with 15 wins against nine losses; had 15 complete games and four shutouts with an ERA of 3.27 and three saves in relief. I also struck out 120 hitters. Not a bad year for a 20-year-old kid just two years out of high school.

* * *

P itching against the Detroit Tigers that year was a great feeling. Obviously, I wanted to beat my hometown team because they didn't give me the contract that they should have. If they had, I would have been playing with the Tigers, instead of the Baltimore Orioles. So it was always a nice, nice feeling when I beat the Tigers. Throughout my career in the American League, I had very, very good success against them, and for some reason, I was also very successful against Al Kaline who was simply a great ballplayer. Kaline had a 22-year career that started when he was only 18 years old and culminated with his induction in the Hall of Fame in 1980.

Of course, visiting other ballparks, like Fenway Park in Boston with its short left field wall — "The Green Monster" — and facing guys like Ted Williams, Jackie Jensen, Frank Malzone, and Jimmy Piersall, always gave me goose bumps. As far as I'm concerned, "Number Nine" (Williams) was the greatest hitter who ever lived.

And then there was my first trip to Yankee Stadium. I was in awe of everything about the "house that Ruth built." A lot of really tremendous ballplayers throughout the decades played for the Yankees: Joe DiMaggio, Lou Gehrig, Babe Ruth, Mickey Mantle, Yogi Berra, Whitey Ford, Bill Dickey, just to name a few. There were just so many great ballplayers, and it was such a great dynasty. It gave me goose bumps when I walked out there and looked at the other side and saw those guys wearing the pinstripes. I remembered as a kid how great the Yankees were, and boy, they were great. They had great pitching and great hitting, and they would beat you by scores of 10-9 or 1-0 and just about everything in between, but they would beat you. When I played against them, they had Ford, Bobby Shantz, Bob Turley, Moose Skowron, Berra, Mantle, Bobby Richardson, Tony Kubek, Elston Howard, to name a few. Some Yankee teams over the years were just incredible, and it never seemed to end.

At that time — the 1950s — Major League Baseball had only 16 teams, eight in each league. In the American League it seemed that everybody was fighting to see who could end up in second place behind the Yankees. From 1949 thru 1964, only two teams beat the Yanks out of the AL pennant; the Cleveland Indians in 1954 and the Chicago White Sox in 1959. Oddly, both of those teams were managed by the great Al Lopez.

* * *

T he players in that era, well, what can you say? That was baseball.

Today, I just don't see the caliber of players that we had when I played. It seemed like every team had great hitters, up and down the lineup. It was pretty darn tough to face any team. Even the Senators were tough.

Baseball has changed so drastically since then. I look at Major League Baseball today, and it's just not the same game. It makes me throw up whenever I think about everything that has happened to the game. I guess what they call it is greed. That's what has happened in baseball today, and it's a shame. It's an absolute shame that this game has changed so much from the time I first started playing in 1957.

There was just a tremendous amount of great ballplayers in that era. Besides all those Yankees I've already mentioned, the Senators had Pedro Ramos, Camilo Pascual, Jim Lemon, Eddie Yost, Roy Sievers, and Harmon Killebrew. Norm Siebern, Roger

Maris, Hector Lopez, Vic Power, Ralph Terry, and Bob Cerv were in Kansas City. The White Sox, with the great team that they had with Nellie Fox, Luis Aparicio, Jim Landis, Sherman Lollar, Al Smith, and that pitching staff: Billy Pierce, Early Wynn, Dick Donovan, Jim Wilson, Turk Lown, and Gerry Staley. Rocky Colavito, Larry Doby, Minnie Minoso, Mudcat Grant, and Gary Bell in Cleveland; Kaline, Kuenn, Jim Bunning, Paul Foytack, Billy Hoeft, and Frank Lary in Detroit; Williams, Piersall, Jensen, Malzone, Pete Runnels, Frank Sullivan, and Ike Delock in Boston. And of course, we had Brooks Robinson, Gene Woodling, Gus Triandos, Billy O'Dell, and Billy Gardner.

I probably left out several guys who deserve mentioning, but the point is the game has just changed so, so drastically.

* * *

A little more on Paul Richards.

Paul took a liking to me, and he didn't mind when I called him by his first name. He took me under his wing. Right away that first year, he told me that when my pitch count reached 90 pitches, I would be taken out of the game; no matter what's happening during the ball game, I'm out. Looking back on that now, that type of handling probably extended my career.

I look at Mark "The Bird" Fidrych as an example of pitchers who were burned out before their time. The Tigers pitched him every fourth day because he was drawing 45,000 to 50,000 people a game, so they were making a lot of money with Mark Fidrych. But they burned that kid out, and in a matter of two or three years, his arm was gone. That's sad.

When I look back at what Paul did for me, taking me out of a ball game when I had thrown 90 pitches, I believe he prolonged my career by five or six years. I never had any real arm problems, and I thank him for it.

I had a shutout going one time. I was winning, 8-0, and it's the eighth inning against Kansas City. I reached 90 pitches, and out he walks. I looked at him and said, "What are you doing?"

"Take a shower."

"Come on, I've got a shutout."

"You're gone. The bullpen is coming in."

I took a shower.

I did throw a few shutouts and wasn't yanked. I had one game where I threw 82 pitches in nine innings and won the game, 6-0. I threw a lot of strikes and didn't walk very many guys.

People ask me about my bad games, but I don't remember too many. I think pitchers kind of block that out of their memory. They only remember the good pitches, the good games we pitched, and the games we won.

* * *

A nother thing I enjoyed doing was hitting. I was a pretty darn good hitter.

In high school my last year, I hit .375 after hitting .571 the previous summer in American Legion ball. But all I ever saw in those years were fast balls. Once they found out in the Major Leagues that you could hit a fast ball, things changed very drastically, very quickly. Anyway, the first pitch to me my first time up was a fast ball. I fouled it off, but I had a good swing at it. However, the next two pitches were curve balls. I had never seen a curve ball in my life, so I was gone.

My first home run was in 1958 at old Comiskey Park off righthander Gerry Staley, and we won the game. My first hit was a single between third and short off Bob Lemon.

I hit 20 home runs in my career, so I hit a few. That's a nice feeling when you're a pitcher. 20 is a lot by a pitcher, and they won me a few ball games.

One game I remember in particular was in Minnesota against the Twins. It was off Pedro Ramos. The day before — I was pitching on a Sunday — I walked up to Ramos and said, "You're a good hitter."

"Thank you," he said in his Cuban accent.

"How about tomorrow, you and me throw each other fast balls?"

"Fast balls?" His eyes got really big. "You throw me fast

balls and I throw you fast balls?"

"Yeah, we'll make a pact."

"Okay. Good deal. We'll throw each other fast balls."

"Fantastic."

I was the first one up. He threw me a fast ball, and I fouled it off. He threw me another one, and I hit it out. I'm winning, 1-0. Pete came up in the second or third inning, and I threw him a couple of fast balls. He hit a rocket to right-center field, and our center fielder made a good catch. I came up the second time, and it's still 1-0 with a man on first base. Richards had me bunting for some reason. So I bunted, but I was still 1-1 with a home run and we're still winning, 1-0. Ramos came up again and hit a rocket to left-center and our center fielder made another good catch. Now I came up for the third time, and it was the seventh inning. The Twins have somebody warming up in the bullpen, and it was still 1-0. The first pitch was a fastball, and I fouled it off. The second pitch was a curve ball! I jumped out of the box as strike two was called. I looked at Ramos, saying to myself, "You dirty s.o.b." He gave me these shrugged shoulders. Then he threw me another curve ball, and I hit it out. Two home runs, and I was running around the bases. He said something to me in Spanish, and I know it wasn't very nice. I couldn't understand him, but he chewed me out the whole time I was rounding the bags. I hit two home runs that day off him and I beat him , 2-0.

To this day, every time I see Pete Ramos, he always says, "You hit two home runs off me! Do you remember?"

"Yes, I do." And I have the biggest smile on my face.

"You made me look very bad that day."

"Yeah, but I won the game too, Pete, didn't I?"

Another homer that stands out came against the Mets when I was with the Cubs. I hit a home run, a double, and a single, and had five RBI's to beat New York, and Jon Matlack, a good left-handed pitcher, 7-2.

Another time against the Red Sox and Don Schwall, a good right-handed pitcher, I hit a homer into the center field bleachers, about 10 rows up, at Fenway Park in Boston.

I hit a few like that, and they always felt good — because a few home runs were hit against me, too.

As a good hitting pitcher, it gave me something of an advantage, but there were a lot of times though when there was a man on third with less than two outs and I was kind of hoping the designated hitter was in place.

But the fans loved it. The fans loved to see the pitcher hit because they were either very bad or they made an attempt. And some guys were pretty good hitters. So the fans loved to see the pitchers hit. Today, with the DH, well, baseball has changed and sometimes for the good and sometimes for the bad. And this time, I don't think we've done very well.

However, in some cases the DH has prolonged some guys' careers. Tommy Davis was in the National League and had a very bad ankle after breaking it. If he would have stayed in the National League, he was done. But he came over to the American League and played another five years, hitting over .300. So the DH helped Tommy Davis. And Paul Molitor. He was still playing — and playing well — after turning 40. It's helped a lot of guys extend their careers by four or five years.

* * *

I faced a lot of great pitchers over the years.

Whitey Ford was one of the best opponents that I ever faced as a starter. I didn't start against the Yankees in 1957, and in 1958, I was opposed by Tom Sturdivant in two late season starts. The first time I pitched against the Yankees Sturdivant beat me, 2-1. Ford beat me — and just about everybody else, for that matter — early in my career. But I got even with Ford later in years. I beat him twice in one season.

Another good pitcher was Billy Pierce. Billy was from Detroit originally, signed by the Tigers, and traded to the White Sox. The Tigers had a history of getting rid of home grown talent. They also had a bad habit of allowing a lot of good ballplayers from the Detroit area escape to play for other teams.

The first three or four years that I faced the White Sox, Billy and I didn't face each other. In the winter time, we'd actually go out hunting together. We used to go up to Dean Chance's place in Wooster, Ohio to go hunting. Billy, me, Chance, Hobie Landrith, and a few others. Also during the winter, we'd work out together. Detroit Edison had a fantastic workout center on the top floor of their building. Al Kaline, Pierce, Landrith, and I — and whoever else was living in town — would work out there.

Billy and I finally faced each other 1962 in Baltimore. It was the seventh inning with the score at 0-0 and a man on first base. My wife, Carole, went to the concession stand to get something, and it took her to the top of the eighth inning. When she came back, the score was 2-0 in favor of the Orioles and she wondered what happened. How did the Orioles get the two runs? She was told her husband hit a two-run homer. She didn't believe it and asked again how we scored the two runs and once again was told that I had hit a two-run homer. She couldn't believe I had hit a home run off Billy Pierce. So we won 2-0, and she was waiting outside the locker room.

"Hi, honey, how are you doing?" I asked.

"How did we get our two runs?"

"I hit a two-run homer."

"Okay, I believe everybody then."

We went back to Chicago; we were playing back-to-back series. I faced Billy again, and I beat him, 2-1. Well, Billy didn't talk to me for about five years! He was so upset with me that not only had I hit a two-run homer to beat him, 2-0, but I go right back and beat him again, 2-1, the following week.

When he was playing, Billy was always a great competitor. He's a nice guy, and I love him. He's still my friend today, and he lives in the Chicago area. Every time I see him, he can't let me forget that I hit that home run off him. Or maybe it's me that can't let him forget it.

Schedule:
Home Game

I was only 18, and I was on my own for the first time in my life. I was a little nervous about it at first, but I got over it in a hurry. I was from Detroit, a bigger, tougher, dirtier city with a much larger working class than smaller, gentler, cleaner, quaint Baltimore. I'd grown up in a neighborhood where you either stood up for yourself if you wanted respect or you hid out in the library if you didn't want to be pushed around by the neighborhood bullies. I could handle Baltimore.

Hal Newhouser, the Orioles' chief of scouting, put me into the Lord Baltimore Hotel when I first got there, but later I moved in with Al Pilarcik, an outfielder on the team, and shared a house with him. That's where I lived that first season of my embryo Major League career.

My personal life was pretty barren for the most part. I didn't have much money, although I did have more than most guys my age. I was too young to drink with the other players, but none of them wanted to hang around with me anyway. So I spent much of my free time watching television in my room, but I did make a friend outside of the team.

Having some money, I wanted a car of my own. I wandered into this used car lot, Johnny's Used Cars, run by handsome Johnny Wilbanks. Johnny became my friend. He was a wheeler-dealer in both new and used cars. He let me hang out at the lot just talking to him and meeting people. He introduced me to Spiro Agnew who was a lawyer then and had yet to get into politics. Maybe having me there was good for Johnny's business because I was a pro ball player, a Baltimore Oriole. I can't say for sure. I was too young to know about jock-sniffers yet. Whether he let me hang around for his own purposes or because he liked me, I don't know. I do know that his friendship, genuine or not, helped me get through that first season.

Johnny did have a purpose for me. He sold me my first car, a 1957 Chevrolet Impala, and he gave me a fair deal on it. I didn't have that car for long because I traded up for a new 1958 when I returned to Detroit once the season was over.

* * *

T he single most memorable event of my first year in professional baseball happened while I was playing for the Knoxville Smokies. It wasn't one of those things that a fellow writes home about, but it was an important rite of passage for an 18-year-old.

I wasn't exactly a high school lothario. Not that I didn't like girls, but baseball was my primary interest. I had exactly two girlfriends in four years. Their names were Carole Tragge and Carol Osterberg. I was dating Carole until she started taking me for granted. So I broke up with her and started dating Carol just to make Carole jealous. Carole and I got back together before graduation, and I went off to Baltimore.

This was back in the days when most guys treated good girls with respect, and good girls saved themselves for "Mr. Right." Carole and I fit into that category. Sure, we did some passionate necking, but that was all until we were married.

While I was in Baltimore, I was lonely. I called home frequently. Home was my mother and Carole. I also wrote letters — almost everyday — to both of them. I could have spent my spare time looking for local girls, but I didn't have a clue about where to find them. So I stayed in my room mostly, and when I did go out, I usually just went to the movies or went by to see Johnny Wilbanks.

But when I was sent down to Knoxville, the situation was different. The Smokies had younger players than the Orioles. Much younger. I was still the youngest guy on the team, but most of the guys were only a few years older than me. So hanging out with them was easier than hanging out with guys in Baltimore.

Near the end of my stay with the Smokies, the team was in Charlotte, North Carolina for a series. After a night game, some of the guys decided to hire a hooker for the night for all of us. To decide who got to be with her first, somebody came up with the idea of playing strip poker. I was the first guy to lose his clothes, so I went first. I was 18, practically without shame thanks to a little alcohol in my system, and totally without experience. I don't know how well I performed that night, but I do know that the rest of guys were constantly trying to sneak a peek at what I was doing with the woman.

This was a one-time experience. I went back to Baltimore soon after that and returned to my celibate ways.

* * *

O ver that first offseason, I lived at home and didn't do much except hang out with old high school buddies and go out with Carole a lot. I didn't work much.

By this time, my parents had sold the store. With my father disabled by a stroke, my mother couldn't work it alone. Hiring help was out of the question because of the extra taxes that would have to be paid for any employees. My brother Gus couldn't help any longer because he was married and working as a draftsman. Perry was still at home, but his first duty was school. And now that I was gone most of the year playing professional baseball, I wasn't much use to them either. So the store became history, and my mom went to work to support the family.

The next two winters went pretty much the same way. I came home, hung out with the guys, went out with Carole, and didn't work much.

Finally, I popped the question to Carole. She accepted, but her parents were opposed to us getting married. Her parents were something else. More about them later.

Anyway, Carole and I were married on February 15, 1960. We went down to the courthouse and said our vows in front of a justice of the peace. Then we left for spring training in Florida.

* * *

When I returned to Baltimore for my second season, I had to find a place to live. I didn't want to live at the Lord Baltimore Hotel again, so I looked around for some other place, a small apartment. Rooming with one of the other guys like I did the year before didn't seem to be a good option.

The first place I found was with a Greek family named Taylor. They lived close to the ball park, so their home was convenient. I didn't stay with them for very long. Why I moved out has been lost in the recesses of my memory, but I do know that it was on friendly terms.

A lady with a couple of teenage kids and a spare room lived in a brownstone house about half a block from Memorial Stadium. Their name was Canelos. Someone told me about them, that they were Greek like me. I called on them, and Mrs. Canelos rented me the room.

Mrs. Canelos was a widow. Her name was Mary. She was a really nice person who treated me very well, always making me feel at home in their house. She came from Greece, and we sometimes spoke to each other in Greek. She passed away in 1986 at almost 80 years old. She was a very wonderful lady.

Her son was just about my age. His name was Jimmy. We became friends, and he and his wife Cathy were godparents for my oldest daughter when she was baptized some years later. Jimmy and his wife owned a pizza restaurant the last time I spoke with them.

Mary's daughter's name was Ann, a very nice girl. She was the sister that I never had. I've lost contact with her over the years. I hope she's happy and well.

The O's made a lot of road-trips by train because Richards hated to fly. Jim Busby, a good outfielder, was my roommate that year. Nice guy, good outfielder; but much older than me as were most of my teammates that year. At the beginning of the season, Ron Hansen, Jerry Walker, and Brooks Robinson were all with the team and under 21. Hansen was sent down early in the year, and Walker was sent down the next month. Robinson turned 21 a week after I turned 19. Being so young didn't leave me with a whole lot of things to do when we were on the road. The other guys couldn't take me into the bars and stuff, so it was kind of a lonely life, really. This left me with a lot of free time.

When we were at home, I found that living with someone else relieved a lot of loneliness. It was only a matter of watching my P's and Q's, especially since I had Carole waiting for me back home in Detroit.

Living with Mary and her children added a lot of joy to my life in Baltimore. They made being away from home and my own family much easier. I will always be grateful to them for their friendship.

* * *

Baseball was a lot of fun back then. Baseball was baseball. It wasn't "walk into the clubhouse with a brief case and a cellphone, talking to your agent and pulling out the business section in the newspaper to see how your stocks are doing." We used to walk in with *The Sporting News* or the *Tribune* sports page or some other newspaper sports page, depending on what town we were in. The players have changed drastically.

Another drastic change has been the money.

During those first couple of years, during the off season, I lived at home with my folks and really had no obligations, so I didn't need a job. But when I got married in 1960, that changed; I needed more income to support Carole and me and then the kids when they came along.

A lot of guys had to work in the winter time. We didn't make enough from baseball to make ends meet. Minimum salary was only $6,000 a season. After taxes and spreading it over the six months of the regular season, a guy was only taking home about $800 a month. Divide that in half for the other six months of the year, and you can see why a guy had to work at another job in the offseason. Even when the minimum salary was raised to $7,500, it still wasn't enough to live on for the whole year.

Of course, after being in the Majors a few years, your salary went up. Mine increased to $8,000 in 1959 and $10,000 in 1960. Those weren't bad raises, but the money still wasn't enough for a couple to live on. Let me back up and elaborate on that.

Most baseball players don't play for a team in their hometown. I was from Detroit and played in Baltimore. I had to pay for a residence in both cities after Carole and I were married. Of course, I didn't have to pay for both places at the same time, but I did because Carole sometimes went home when I was on a long road-trip with the Orioles. And then there was spring training. Carole went to Florida with me, so we had to rent a place there. We had a lot of living expenses, and when the kids came along, the bills got bigger. Also, after the kids were born and growing, they had to go to school, which meant we either lived the year round in the city where I played or we had to keep two homes: one for the school year and one for the summer months.

The only benefit of being a ballplayer was the notoriety. Players had the opportunity to earn extra money by making endorsements. I made some, but they weren't all that lucrative at first. The extra money helped, but it didn't exactly make you a millionaire.

Travel those early years was an experience. Most of us had to watch our money. I forget what kind of meal money we made when I first broke in. Maybe it was eight dollars a day. I think today it's up to $80 or $90 dollars a day. When I retired in 1974, I think it was up to $20 a day. A lot of guys came home with more money than they started with. They ate at a White Castle or some other fast food place where the food wasn't very expensive.

The first three years I was in the Majors I couldn't go to bars and drink because I was under age, so I went to a lot of movies. I would see two movies a day, if we played night games. I'd start around 11:00 in the morning in cities like New York. My lunch was popcorn and a coke. I'd spend a dollar or a couple of dollars for the movie and a dollar for the popcorn and that was my dinner. Then after the game, in most places, they had food spread out for us in the clubhouse. Mostly, they were hot dogs cooked in water. That was supper.

Brooks Robinson was one of my roommates in those early

years that I was in baseball. Most of the time the pitchers would hang out together, and the infielders would hang out together, and the outfielders would hang out together, unless there were cliques. Later on in my baseball career, with most every team I was with, there were cliques. Brooks, an infielder, and I, a pitcher, rooming together was the exception.

Nobody recognized us in the different cities that we went to. The name recognition wasn't quite there yet. Television didn't have the exposure with satellite service like it does today, so the only place that you were really known was in your hometown. However, it was kind of funny because wherever we were staying on the road people knew where we were staying because there were a lot of kids all over the place. They would ask for autographs when you were getting off the bus. They would wait for hours to get autographs all the time. I signed my first autograph in New York. That was my first road trip. I remember the team bus came into the hotel we were staying at, and there were a few kids out there waiting to get autographs. I didn't have a baseball card then. That didn't come out till 1958. When I did sign my name, guys would look at it and say, "Who are you?" I would tell them I was a rookie. But it was nice that people even asked me for my autograph.

* * *

My first media interview was when I came to Baltimore upon joining the team. A couple of the local newspapers sent reporters around, and they came into the clubhouse and interviewed me. They asked me what an 18-year-old kid thought about making it to the Major Leagues right out of high school. They asked me how I thought I would do in the Majors. I really didn't know how to answer their questions, so I just told them I felt that I was good enough to be in the Majors; that was why I was given a contract. I also told them that I wanted to thank Paul Richards for giving me the opportunity and that I would make the very best of the situation that was given to me.

My first radio interview wasn't until the following year, after

I won my first ball game. I was on the "Lead Off Man" the very next day. For doing the show at that time, the ballplayers were given a dress shirt, and that was it. I took my gift certificate and picked up my shirt; I needed it.

The reporter who questioned me for the newspaper article was John Stedman, and the radio interview was done by Ernie Harwell. Ernie and Herb Carneil were the radio announcers for the Orioles back then. Two years later, Ernie left and went to the Tigers where he became a legend in his own time. One of the all-time great baseball announcers: Ernie Harwell.

Television wasn't big at that time. Home games were never televised locally. Only road games and then maybe only 10 or 15 games a year. But as television money became more plentiful, stations and networks paid the baseball teams more for the right to televise, which made television more and more prominent.

My first network game was broadcast by CBS, which was doing the "Game of the Week." Dizzy Dean did the play-by-play with Pee Wee Reese. Dizzy interviewed me before a national audience before the game, and my folks were happy because they got a chance to see me. I was still a teenager. Dizzy interviewed me because of my age, a kid really, who was pitching in the Major Leagues.

Over my career, I was 14-0 on national television! In my last year, NBC was doing the games then, and I used to go on a lot with Curt Gowdy. Even Howard Cosell was involved with the "Game of the Week" for a while. I was a ham. I just loved going on national television because the whole world was watching me, and I knew I was going to win.

Later, Joe Garagiola and Tony Kubek were doing the games. They did some research and asked me if I knew that I was undefeated on national television. I told them I wasn't surprised. Every time they came into the town, the first question they would ask would be, "Who's pitching Saturday?" If they were told Pappas, the announcers knew I was going to win. I was just on my whole career when it came to Saturdays and national television.

I was a big ham — and hot dog! I just loved it. I still do.

Slurve:
Close But No Cigar

In the early 1960s, the Orioles had so many good young players on the roster who had a lot of promise that the competition to make the team forced all of us to step up our games.

Chuck Estrada was a good right-handed pitcher who was a year older than me when he joined the staff in 1960. He was a hard thrower, blessed with a great fastball. He didn't last too long in the Major Leagues, but the time he spent in Baltimore was pretty good. He won 18 games his rookie year and was named Rookie of the Year in the American League.

Of course, Brooks Robinson was special. I saw a lot of good third basemen in my career. I didn't see Honus Wagner or some of those older guys play, but Brooks, as far as I'm concerned, was the greatest third baseman that I ever saw play the game of baseball. He was a great teammate, the nicest guy in the world.

In 1960, Marv Breeding was our second baseman. He had a good year, but it was his only year as a regular because Jerry Adair came along the next season.

Jim Gentile was at first base that year. He was a rookie. A big Italian kid who could hit the ball a mile — and often. He had a short career in the Majors which was probably due to his life off the field.

As for catchers, we had three. Gus Triandos was my first catcher, and he was the number one catcher for a number of years with Baltimore, until being traded to Detroit in 1963. He was slow, but big and strong. He caught me for my first five years. Joe Ginsberg was a back-up catcher. Joe didn't play very much. We also had Clint Courtney, who was around for Paul Richards, basically. Paul just loved Clint Courtney. Here was a guy that had very limited ability, but he had a lot of heart and soul. He would go through a brick wall to catch a ball. That man would do anything in the world you asked him to do. If Paul Richards would have asked him to put a broom up his butt and sweep the floor at the same time he was catching, he would have tried.

Ronnie Hansen was a good ballplayer. He was tall, lanky, and covered a lot of ground in the field. He wasn't a very good hitter then, but he made himself into a decent one. He was not a Louie Aparicio at shortstop, but then I don't know of many shortstops back then who were like Louie. But Ronnie made himself into a good shortstop. He was like Ernie Banks was when he broke in, and he gave everything he had to every game. He played the game well and made good plays. He was a good guy to have behind you. He had a lot of back problems and that ended his career prematurely.

Steve Barber was also a rookie that year. He was a southpaw who could throw hard, but he had lousy control. He was tough to hit against, but he often beat himself with walks.

With guys like these, we were ready for the 1960 season.

* * *

I n 1960 we started fighting the Yankees for real, giving them a run for their money. We figured we had a pretty decent ball club at that time. Our pitching staff was getting better, and we had Hoyt Wilhelm at that point. We were similar to the Atlanta Braves of the 1990s. We never had a really long losing streak because one of us would always come out and pitch a good ball game in every round of the rotation. So we felt in 1960 that we had a legitimate shot at the pennant.

The season opened at home, and our first opponent was lowly Washington; you know, "Washington, first in the nation, first in the hearts of his countrymen, last in the American League." I was slated to start, but Richards went with Jack Fisher instead. We won. A good beginning to any season.

My first start was the next night against the Senators. I

wasn't sharp. Washington nailed me for 10 hits, and I gave up three walks. The result: seven runs — all earned — and no decision. I even gave up a homer to Harmon Killebrew. We lost, but I wasn't charged with the defeat.

When my turn came again, the Orioles had lost five straight. We drove up to Washington to face the Senators. Jim Gentile homered with two aboard in the first inning, and I made that hold up as we broke the losing streak, 3-2. I went the distance, giving up just five hits. None of them were collected by Bob Allison who came into the game with a seven-game hitting streak. I rather enjoyed stopping him.

The Yankees were back in 1960. I took the mound against them the following Saturday, and they hammered me and the bullpen. I lasted all of an inning and two-thirds, and they scored six runs off me. Roger Maris had come over to them in a trade with the A's, and he slammed me for the first time as a Bronx Bomber. I'd gotten Kubek to start the game, then walked Gil McDougald and Mickey Mantle. Yogi Berra stepped up to the plate and slapped out a single. More about Yogi later. Roger came up, and one swing later I was trailing, 4-0. We lost, 16-0. Not our night.

My next outing wasn't any better. The Indians touched me for four runs on four hits and three walks in four innings. We lost again, 11-5. If you judged the Orioles by my performances, you'd think we weren't doing well. We were doing fine. I was the one having the problems.

Richards put me in the bullpen because of my two poor outings. I didn't like it, but I wasn't in charge. Richards knew what he was doing. I won in relief over KC. Five days later we slipped into first place, a half game ahead of the White Sox.

Richards gave me another shot at starting on May 17. I was excited, but my arm wasn't there yet. I couldn't find the plate as I walked eight A's in seven innings. I also gave up six hits and four runs, three earned. To make matters worse, I committed a balk and a throwing error. We lost, 4-2.

Things went from bad to worse for me. Richards brought me in to save Hoyt Wilhelm's game against the Tigers. Wilhelm walked Frank Bolling and Norm Cash to start the bottom of the ninth. We were ahead, 3-1. I couldn't find the plate either. I issued passes to Rocky Colavito and Red Wilson to force in a run. I got the next guy out, then Charlie Maxwell came in as a pinch-hitter. He drove one deep to right that stayed in the park for a sacrifice fly. The relay throw from Walt Dropo hit Colavito, and the winning run scored on an error. I lost again. My record was down to 2-4.

The Yankees were in town for a weekend series at the end of May with a doubleheader on Sunday. Wilhelm won the opener with Clint Courtney using the oversized catcher's mitt for the first time. No passed balls that night. In the twin bill, I got into the second game in relief, and our guys pulled out a win in the bottom of the ninth for the sweep. I picked up a win.

Richards gave me a start the next week, and I was hammered again, this time by Washington. I gave up 10 hits, five walks, and all four runs as we lost to Hal Woodeshick. It was old Hal's first complete game in two years. It was my fifth loss.

My next start went just as badly. The Tigers reached me for seven hits and five runs in six innings. I also surrendered five walks. Only a rally in the bottom of the sixth to tie the score saved me from a loss. We still lost, 7-5, but Arnie Portacarrerro suffered the defeat.

Despite my ineffectiveness, we moved back into first place on Saturday June 11 with a 10-inning win over KC, 6-5. It didn't last as we dropped two the next day to fall back into second place, but we won on Tuesday at Cleveland. I still stunk, but our offense managed to carry me to a 7-4 victory. I was still all over the plate with three walks, 12 hits, a wild pitch, and a hit batter. The victory put us a half game ahead of the Tribe for first place.

The win put some confidence in me. We went to Detroit and faced them in a doubleheader. Wilhelm started game one and shut out the Tigers, 2-0. I got the call for game two, and I was on. I also shut out the Tigers, 1-0, despite walking six. My record was now even at 5-5, and we were a half game ahead of the Yankees for first place.

When I beat KC, 11-2, in my next start, I thought I was on my way to a big year and the Orioles were on their way to the pennant. I was only half right.

Billy Pierce was my mound opponent for my next outing. The White Sox came to town, and it was July 1. I threw another shutout, holding the Pale Hose to five hits and walking three. But better than my pitching was my hitting. I slammed a two-run homer off Pierce for my first hit of the season. I was on a cloud with a four-game winning streak of my own going.

One more outing for me before the All-Star game. It was against the Yankees. My teammates spotted me to a 3-0 lead through four innings. Then I gave up a two-run shot to Bob Cerv in the fifth and a solo shot to Bobby Richardson in the seventh. Richards kept me in for the eighth, and the Yankees stroked four singles to send me to the showers. We lost, I lost, 6-3. We were now in third place, four games out of first.

After the All-Star game, we went to Chicago. I faced Pierce again, and again, I beat him, this time, 5-2. I got another hit and scored a run. My record was now 8-6. Brooks Robinson hit for the cycle. That was Friday night. We lost on Saturday and Sunday and fell into fourth place behind the Yankees, Indians, and White Sox. We were in a really close race at only three games out.

I wasn't sharp in my next start as I lost to KC, 4-3, and luck was against me in the start after that. The A's were in Baltimore, and Johnny Kucks was my opponent. He was on, and so was I, only giving up one hit in the first six innings. We led, 1-0. Then Fortune frowned. Jerry Lumpe doubled and Whitey Herzog singled to tie the game in the seventh. I got the first two hitters in the eighth before the eighth man in the KC lineup singled. Kucks came up, and he singled. Bill Tuttle topped a slow roller to third, and he beat it out to load the bases. Lumpe hit another dribbler to second and beat the throw to first. The runner scored, and we lost, 2-1.

The White Sox were my patsies that year. They came to town to start the month of August, and I went up against Herb Score who was trying to make a comeback. He was good that night, but I was better. We won, 2-1, and my record went back over .500. Richards was ejected in the eighth inning, his fifth thumbing of the year.

We were 60-46 at this time, a half game behind the White

Sox and only two games behind the Yankees. We continued our winning ways until we were 65-46, tied with the Yankees for first, and a trip to New York just two days away. We lost on August 14, but so did the Yankees. Monday morning we were tied with Chicago for first with the Bombers only a half game back.

Jerry Walker opened the series in New York. Art Ditmar beat him, 4-3, on the strength of Mantle's two homers. Chuck Estrada faced Ford in game two, and Whitey came on out on top, 1-0. It was Ford's second shutout in three days, having three-hit the Senators before doing likewise to us. We went home with our tails between our legs, and the Senators extended our losing streak to four on Wednesday, leaving us two and a half games behind the Yankees.

My turn in the rotation came on Thursday. I wasn't sharp, but the guys hit behind me. We won, 10-8. My record was now 11-8, but more important than that, we'd broken the losing streak.

We lost my next start, 5-3, in 11 innings against the Tigers. I had them through the first eight innings, 3-1, then got the first man out in the ninth. Charlie Maxwell, who seemed to have my number, singled, and Al Kaline doubled. Richards brought in Wilhelm, and Rocky Colavito singled off him to drive in the tying runs. Maxwell smacked a two-run homer in the top of the 11th to win the game. Despite the loss, we remained close to the Yanks and White Sox.

The Bombers put Cleveland out of their misery for the year the following weekend by sweeping a pair of doubleheaders on Friday and Saturday. We swept KC on Friday in a twi-night affair, but the A's got the better of us on Saturday. We trailed by two and a half games.

My patsies came to town on Sunday, and I got the start. I had complete command through seven innings, leading, 3-0. Then in the eighth I was blowing it when big Ted Kluszewski stepped into the batter's box with two on and one in already. It was then that an umpire saved my bacon.

Big Klu had the most massive biceps in baseball; he was as strong as a bull elephant. In his prime, he could hit a ball out of any stadium in baseball. His best years were in the early 1950s when he belted out 181 homers over a four-year period while playing first base for the Cincinnati Reds. It was once said that the Reds designed their sleeveless uniforms just to show off Big Klu's arms. The White Sox picked up Kluszewski the year before to help them with their pennant drive. He made some major contributions to help them get to the World Series.

Anyway, Big Klu stepped into the box with a pair of runners on base. I served up a gopher ball. Just as I let go of the pitch, umpire Ed Hurley called for time and declared: "No pitch!" Big Klu didn't hear Hurley, and he slammed the ball into the right field stands. Hurley waved off the homer. Al Lopez, the Chicago manager, burst out of the dugout and charged Hurley. The ump explained that he was calling time to tell Earl Torgeson and Floyd Robinson of Chicago that they were warming up in the wrong area and had to move. The homer was reversed, and I got big Ted. Lopez protested the game, but it was later denied. Wilhelm relieved me in the ninth with one out and the bases loaded. He got Torgeson on strikes and Aparicio on a fly ball. My record improved to 12-8.

By the end of August, the Orioles held on to second place, one game out, and we were scheduled to play the Yankees. In Baltimore. And I was slated to take the hill against none other than Whitey Ford. This was our big chance to take control of the race, and it was my big opportunity to attain stardom once and for all. Was I up for the game? Yes! Was I up to the challenge? Yes! I shut down the Yankees on three measly singles; two by Tony Kubek and one by Clete Boyer. Maris, Mantle, Berra, Skowron? The killers? Rubber bats that night. I struck out nine and walked nobody. We won, 5-0, and I was now 13-8. More importantly, we were tied for first.

Jack Fisher was set to go on Saturday against Art Ditmar. Fat Jack shot down the Bombers, 2-0, just like I did, and we moved into first all by ourselves. Ditmar had a seven-game winning streak going into that game.

On Sunday, Chuck Estrada beat Bill Stafford, 6-2, and we had a two-game lead on the Yankees. Better than that, we were four games up on New York in the loss column. The pennant was ours for the taking. All we had to do was hold on.

On Labor Day, we split with the Senators in a doubleheader, while the Yankees were sweeping the Red Sox. Hector Harold "Hal" Brown won our night cap game after Steve Barber lost the opener. The White Sox lost a single game that day to fall four games behind us.

We had Tuesday off, but while we were traveling to Cleveland, the Yankees and White Sox were losing. All we had to do was keep winning, and I was scheduled to pitch the opener against the Tribe.

Jim Perry was my mound opponent. He was having a good year and was Cleveland's ace. I wasn't sharp in the first inning, and the Indians touched me for two runs. I settled down after that, but we couldn't do anything with Perry until the seventh. Even then, we could only get one run. They got that back in the eighth, and we scored once more in the ninth. Too little too late. We lost, 3-2. We had a chance to tie the game, but the rally ended when Dave Philley was picked off first by Perry with Gene Stephenson on second.

Besides us losing, the Yankees beat the White Sox the same day to cut our lead to a half game. We bounced back the next night, and so did the White Sox. Then it was our turn to face the White Sox. We lost to them twice, while the Yankees were taking two from the Tigers. We were now a half game out and two down in the loss column. On Sunday, we moved on to Kansas City, and the Yankees traveled to Cleveland with the White Sox hosting the Red Sox. We won a single game, while the Yankees and Pale Hose were sweeping doubleheaders. We all had a day of rest on Monday. We were a game out with the White Sox three behind New York.

The Orioles moved on to Detroit; Yankees to KC; and the White Sox entertained the Senators. I went up against Jim Bunning again. This time he was the better pitcher. We lost. The Yankees lost. Chicago won. On Wednesday, we won, New York lost, and the White Sox lost. No games on Thursday. Tied with the Yankees for first, we headed to New York with pennant in the balance.

Steve Barber faced off with Whitey Ford in the opener on Friday night. Maris and Hector Lopez homered to lift the Yanks to a 4-2 win. Chuck Estrada and Bob Turley were matched up on Saturday. Chuck went the distance but still lost, 5-3, as Mantle and Berra homered off him. Now two games behind New York we played a doubleheader on Sunday. Jack Fisher opposed Art Ditmar in the opener, and Ralph Terry was my opponent in the nightcap. We both lost. Fisher lasted just two innings in a 7-3 defeat, and I got absolutely no support as Terry shut us out, 2-0. We were now four back, and for all practical purposes, the season was over.

* * *

W hen we were playing the Yankees, the one guy that I didn't want to see come up in the seventh, eighth, and ninth innings was Yogi Berra. That man hit anything you threw. If the ball was eye high, he'd smack it for a base hit. If the pitch was a one hopper up to the plate, he'd get a base hit. Yogi was the greatest clutch hitter and bad ball hitter that I ever had to pitch against. I did not like to face Yogi Berra late in a ball game. He would almost always beat you.

Another notorious bad ball hitter was the Twins' Tony Oliva. Just like Yogi, he could hit just about anything thrown at him.

But if I just threw and didn't try to get cute with them, I could get Yogi and Tony out. I actually had pretty good success against both of them. I'd just throw the ball right down the middle, and I'd get them out. The rest of the other pitchers on the team just couldn't understand that. They would almost always beat you in the late innings. But not me.

* * *

G oing back to Ted Williams, in his final Major League season, 1960. Jack Fisher was pitching against Ted in the last game he was playing. So I asked Jack what he was going to do with Williams?

"Well, I'm going to try and get him out."

"Really? This is his last time in Fenway Park. Let him go out with a bang."

"What do you mean?

"Let him hit one out."

"Nah, I can't do that."

"Okay."

So the game progressed, and then it was Williams's last time at bat. Jack grooved him a nice, easy fastball, and Ted hit it out. Williams came out of the dugout and acknowledged the crowd, which was strange because he didn't normally do things like that. But he came out this time.

After the game, I went up to Jack and said, "Well, you did it, huh?"

"Yeah. Why not?" He laughed.

Was that wrong? I guess in some people's eyes it was, what Jack Fisher did with Ted Williams — and which I did later on with Roger Maris, but more about that in a future chapter. Throwing them a fastball down the middle wasn't a guarantee that they would hit it out, but we did give them a pitch that they could hit out. I don't think what we did was wrong. I think that's the way baseball is.

My image of baseball, with guys like Ted Williams, Mickey Mantle, Roberto Clemente and others, was that these men were great athletes. I look back on my career, and then I look at what I see today. I just remember baseball as being a lot of fun. It was a bunch of grownups playing a kids game and having fun at it. Not today. Sadly.

Intentional Pass:
Expansion

J im Gentile was his own worst enemy. For a big man, he was a heck of a hitter. In 1961, he hit 46 home runs, including two grand slams in one game against Minnesota, and he drove in 141 runs that year.

But Jim was his own worst enemy. I mean, he would go on a hot streak with a lot of home runs and RBIs with a couple of hits a game and he'd come into the clubhouse, sit down at his locker and say, "Man, I'm going too good. God, I wonder when the slump is gonna come." And I'd ask him to think about what he was saying, then tell him just to get his butt out there and keep hitting. Would he listen? No. He would literally talk himself into a slump and go out the next day and go 0-4.

Jim was a good looking guy who played around a little bit — off the field. He and I and Brooks Robinson made the All-Star team in 1964 in Chicago. That year there were two games, one in Washington and one in Chicago. Wrigley Field, of course, didn't have lights in those days, so we were playing a day game. The three of us scheduled a nine o'clock flight home to Baltimore. It was the only flight we could get. We'd be arriving around midnight. I don't recall how we did it, but we got an earlier flight and got back to Baltimore around 6:00.

When we landed in Baltimore, Jim said, "Hey, let's go out. The wives won't be expecting us to be home until midnight. We can go out and have a good time." Brooks was a good guy, a straight laced guy; he said he was going straight home. I told him to make sure he didn't say anything to his wife that we all got in early, just that he got in early.

So Jim and I went out, and we partied. We went to Greek

town. We went everywhere, and when I got home around 1:00 in the morning, my wife was in the living room, with the light on.

"Where have you been?"

"I just got in. We had a late flight out of Chicago."

She looked at me with a very puzzled look on her face.

"What's the matter?"

"Well, Connie Robinson called and said you guys got in around 7:30."

"Uh-oh." I knew I was in trouble.

I got by that incident. But Jim?

Gentile had a girl friend on the side. This one time he went out to the airport to pick her up, totally unaware that his wife was following him. Jim and the other woman went to a motel. Before they could get settled in, his wife knocked on the door. The other woman answered it. The wife pulled Jim outside and told him he was coming home with her.

Their marriage didn't last.

Jim had his fun, but he would talk himself into a slump. I wonder if there's any kind of correlation between his love-life and his baseball career. Weird, huh?

* * *

1961 was an expansion year. The American League put a new team in Washington and ventured to the West Coast with a team in Los Angeles. The new Senators were necessary because the old Senators had moved to Minnesota to become the Twins. Also, Congress threatened to remove Major League Baseball's anti-trust exemption if a new team wasn't put back into the nation's capital.

The AL came up with a format for stocking the new teams. League officials decided to hold a draft of players from the existing franchises. Each team was allowed to protect 15 players initially, then after one was taken, they could protect two more until another was taken when they could protect two more, and so on.

The Orioles put me on their protected list. I felt very honored that the Orioles thought enough of me to protect me.

Expansion created a lot of jobs in baseball. Besides adding two more teams to the AL, a dozen farm clubs stayed in business. Back in the days before television, just about every town with a level place to play had a professional minor league team or a semi-pro team. Mickey Mantle played for a team in Joplin, Missouri when he started out in pro ball. Towns like Terre Haute, Indiana; Holdredge, Nebraska; and Paris, Texas had minor league teams. Television put those teams out of business, and it would have put more out of baseball if not for expansion.

We lost Gene Woodling in the draft. Of course, he was near the end of a career that had begun in 1943, so losing him wasn't that big of a deal. The Senators took him, and he had a decent season in Washington, hitting .313 with 10 homers and 57 RBIs in 110 games. Not bad for an overweight guy pushing 40 real hard. Shows you how talented he was.

* * *

T he Orioles came home from spring training with a new attitude and a new slogan: "It can be done in '61." About 700 fans turned out to have brunch with us in a downtown hotel, and the city gave us a parade that lasted two hours and was witnessed by an estimated 200,000 people. We felt appreciated, and we were ready to get after the Yankees for the pennant.

Baltimore had the privilege of playing host to the new Los Angeles Angels to open the season. I got the nod to take the hill for the Orioles, which makes me a trivia question in Angels history. I was the first pitcher to face them in a regular season game. I was ready, but so were the Angels. Big Ted Kluzsewki belted out two homers, and Bob Cerv hit one. Eli Grba threw a six-hitter against us, and we lost, 7-2. I couldn't get through the second inning. I took the loss.

My second decision was also a loss. I pitched better, but a grand slam homer in the fifth gave the Indians the win, 5-1. I gave up all five Cleveland runs in that inning. That's all it takes to lose a game; one bad inning. You can be perfect for 12 innings like Harvey Haddix did against the Braves once, then make one mistake in the 13th and come away the loser. That's baseball.

My next start was a six-hit shutout against Washington. The win raised the club record to .500 for the first time that year.

On May 4, I went up against the Angels in California. I lasted eight innings, but I didn't get the decision. The bullpen blew my lead, but we went into extra innings to win and raise our record to 10-9. We were in fourth place, three games behind the Yanks and Tigers. Cleveland was a half game ahead of us in third.

On May 6, I went on the disabled list for the next month. I had a little tendinitis in my right arm. The rest did me a lot of good. I came back on June 6 to lose again, but my arm felt better. I didn't win another game until June 17 when I went six innings against the Indians at home. I only gave up one run in that game, and the victory brought us back to .500 again at 31-31. We were tied with Boston for fourth place, nine games behind the Tigers. It was becoming clear that we had to make a move soon or face the reality of finishing as also-rans again.

We beat the Twins in Minnesota, 8-2, with my next start. I went the distance, and Gus Triandos had a big game, driving in five runs with a single and two doubles. My record was even now at 3-3. My personal winning streak increased to five in a row with wins over KC, Cleveland, and KC again. The team was hot, too. We had won 15 of 19 and had moved into a third place tie with the Indians at the All-Star game break. We were poised to make a run at the Yankees and Tigers.

We started the second half of the season against the Boston Red Sox. Richards tabbed me to start against Don Schwall. This was Don Schwall at his best. He was a 25-year-old rookie with lousy control, which made him dangerous to hitters. He beat me, 3-2, to end my winning streak.

The Yankees came to town next, and I faced Whitey Ford in the first game of a doubleheader. Whitey was Whitey that day, and although I was decent, I wasn't good enough to beat him. He ran his record to 17-2 on the season, and I slipped to 6-5.

By the end of the third week in July, it was becoming clear that the American League pennant race would be between the Tigers and Yankees. Detroit was in first, a half game ahead of

New York, and we were in third, nine full games away. Catch one team from that distance? Possible. Catch two teams from that far out? Not too damn likely.

My patsies of the year before, the White Sox, extended my personal losing streak to three games. They took advantage of every hit and walk to score seven runs on me in less than two innings. I was humiliated.

We went to New York for a weekend series. Things looked really grim. We were still in third place, but now we were 10½ games out of first. To make matters worse, the Tigers were slumping. Not that I felt sorry for them or anything like that. It's just that the Yankees of that era were like sharks; when they smelled blood, they moved in for the kill. Going into the Big Apple, we felt like the main course.

Hal "Skinny" Brown pitched the Friday night game for us, and he was on. He shut out those damn Yankees, 4-0, on a six-hitter. All right! Reason to celebrate! But only for one night. Ford was matched up with Hoyt Wilhelm for Saturday's TV affair. Once again, Whitey was Whitey, and we came out on the short end of the final, 6-4. Whitey had 19 wins, and it was still July.

We had a doubleheader scheduled for Sunday. Steve Barber was set to go in game one, and I was pencilled in for game two. A split wouldn't have been a bad thing because we would have left New York in the same shape as we had come in. A sweep by the Yankees would have put the nails in the coffin of our pennant hopes. The only thing we could do after that would be to play out the string and watch the Tigers chase the Yanks in vain.

But, lo and behold! Barber was sharp as he clipped the Yankees, 4-0, in the opener, and I was on in the second game, nipping the Bombers, 2-1. A sweep! In New York! Who would have thought that possible? Well, we did. And although it only brought us back to eight and a half out, it was a statement that we were a quality team with backbone.

Over the next two weeks, we played decent ball, but the Yanks were incredible — as usual. Evidently, losing that twinbill at home put some fire in them. We lost four games in the standings, and the Tigers slipped to three out. The Bombers were alive and well and on the prowl.

My next start after beating the Yanks was a no-decision with the Angels. Then I faced Kansas City at home and shut them down, 8-0. It was my third shutout of the year and the 16th for the Baltimore staff. The big highlight of the game was Dave Philley collecting his 21st pinch hit of the season to break the record set by Ed Coleman of the St. Louis Browns in 1936. Guys were always doing things like that when I was pitching. Breaking records of some kind, I mean. I was always happy for them, but it always took the shine off my game, especially on a day like I had against Kansas City.

My next start had a direct bearing on the pennant race. We were in Detroit, and the Tigers were struggling to stay alive. I got some great support that night as Jackie Brandt, Brooks Robinson, and Jim Gentile hit homers. My control was lousy as I walked nine, but the Tigers couldn't hit me as I only gave up a pair of safeties to win, 8-2. Richards was thrown out of the game, his seventh tossing of the year, and Detroit's manager, Bob Sheffing, played the game under protest because Norm Cash, his first baseman, tripped over Earl Robinson's foot when Cash was trying to catch a foul ball and Robinson was running. The play stood up, and I had my ninth win of the year.

After losing my next start in 10 innings to KC, I threw my fourth shutout of the year, a two-hitter. This was the game where Pete Ramos and I made a pact to throw each other fastballs. I connected for a homer twice, and he hit for spit. I beat the Twins with 11 strikeouts. My second homer of the game was the 124th of the year for the Orioles. This set a new team record for the franchise in Baltimore.

Four days later, Paul Richards resigned as manager and Lum Harris was named interim manager. Lum had been the pitching coach. We lost his first game as boss, then I won his second, 3-2, to raise my record to 11-7. I scored the winning run that day.

My next start was a win over the Washington Senators, but then my personal winning streak came to halt in Boston. Gene Conley, the very tall righthander who also played professional basketball for the NBA Boston Celtics, beat me, 3-2. Carl Yazstremski hit a homer off me to win it.

Although we weren't mathematically eliminated, the season

was over for us and the Tigers. We were 14 games behind the Yanks with just over two weeks to play, and Detroit was 10½ back. The Tigers had lost Al Kaline to injury a few weeks earlier, and that put a real damper on their pennant drive. Al was a prime cog in their baseball machine. Besides being a great hitter, he was also a great fielder. His glove saved a lot of games for the Detroit pitching staff. As a pitcher, when you have great fielders behind you, you pitch with more comfort, knowing that a ball put into fair play has a better chance of being an out than a hit with good glove men behind you. Kaline's absence from the order put a little more pressure on the centerfielder and on the pitchers. Pressure usually produces losses, not wins. Detroit folded without Kaline.

I only had two more decisions that year to finish at 13-9 for the year. We came in a distant third, 14 games out. Detroit held on to second, eight behind. The Yankees, of course, won the flag again, their 11th in 13 years. Remarkable!

* * *

Everyone always asks me how I did against Mickey Mantle and Roger Maris, especially in 1961.

Well, Mickey only hit two homers off me in my career and one was in relief. Every time I saw Mickey in later years before he died, he would tell me that he just couldn't hit me. It's a good thing for baseball that Mickey didn't have to face me every day. Or maybe it was good for me. If he had, he probably would have figured out how to take my pitches deep on a regular basis.

Roger Maris was one of the best streak hitters that I ever saw. 1961 was a phenomenal year for Roger. When he got on his streak that year, it didn't make any difference where you threw the baseball; he'd hit it for a home run. I had never seen a man that hot. He was incredible.

Mantle and Maris pursued Babe Ruth's home run record all year, and they pursued each other as well. They were nip and tuck most of the time with Roger usually a homer or three ahead in the race, but with Mickey taking the lead on occasion.

Near the end of the season, the Yanks came to Baltimore for a mid-week series. Roger had 58 homers, and Mickey had 53.

Just a short time earlier, Roger was told by Commissioner Ford Frick that unless he tied or broke Babe Ruth's record in 154 games, there would be an asterisk by his name if he tied or broke the record in games 155 thru 162. What a nice thing to tell a guy. In so many words, Frick was telling Roger that his achievement wasn't worth full recognition and he, Roger Maris, wasn't as good as the great Babe Ruth. What a crappy thing to do to a nice guy like Roger. Frick had a lot of shortcomings as commissioner, and this was the lousiest of them all.

Anyway, the Yanks were playing games 153, 154, and 155 with us in Baltimore. The night before game 154, just as I was leaving the clubhouse, Roger and Mickey walked by, and I called Roger over.

"I think it's really horse shit that the commissioner has to come out and say this with the year you're having. Tomorrow night, I'm pitching, and I'm going to throw you nothing but fast balls. I want to see you break the damn record."

Roger looked at me with this total expression of disbelief and said, "What?"

"I'm going to throw you nothing but fastballs. I want to see you break the record. So if I'm shaking my head, I'm calling off either a slider or a changeup. I'm throwing nothing but fastballs."

He still didn't believe me. "Are you serious?"

"Damn right, Roger. I want to see you break the record."

Roger was stunned, and Mickey, who'd heard what I'd said to Roger, just looked at me with equal disbelief. They shook their heads, then walked off.

The next night, his first time up, I threw Roger a fastball, and he hit a line drive to right field. He didn't get under it though, and the rightfielder caught it against the wall. The second time up, I shook my head a couple of times, so he knew I'm going to throw a fastball. He hit it out for his 59th of the year. I was taken out of the game, losing, 5-2. Dick Hall came in and got Roger twice, then Hoyt Wilhelm replaced him late in the game. He tapped out on a knuckleball his last time up. That was the end of Roger's attempt to equal Ruth's record in 154 games.

The next week we went to New York, and Roger hit his 60th home run off Jack Fisher. He hit his 61st off Boston's Tracy Stallard in the last game of the season at Yankee Stadium. He had an incredible year, but Ford Frick (and you know what that rhymes with) took the shine off it with his decree that Roger's record would always carry an asterisk with it. Thanks to Mark McGwire and Sammy Sosa, the asterisk is now gone from Roger's record. It shouldn't have ever been there in the first place. Roger had an incredible season, and he deserved better treatment from the commissioner.

* * *

With a month to go in the 1961 season, the Orioles and I lost Paul Richards to the Houston Colt .45s, one of the two National League expansion teams that would begin play in 1962. Paul was from Waxahachie, Texas, and he loved the fact that he was returning to Texas to be with a new franchise that he could mold his way as general manager.

Paul's departure left me devastated. This man had made my career. Whatever I did to that point, I owed to Paul Richards.

Luman Harris took over as manager when Paul left. Lum was a decent guy, a nice guy. But he was no Paul Richards. After Harris, we had Billy Hitchcock and Hank Bauer. Then after I left, Earl Weaver came on board.

But getting back to Paul Richards, he was my man. He took me under his wing like his own child, nurtured me the first year with the 80- and 90-pitch rule to keep me from hurting myself. I owe my whole career to Paul Richards.

His leaving did not affect my pitching, but it was another change in my life and in my career. It was hard to take, but the adjustment had to be made because we had to go out and play baseball. Did I like it? No, but I accepted it after the first two or three games. When Paul was no longer there and Lum Harris was the new manager, I realized that I still had to go out and just play.

* * *

E xpansion had to come to baseball eventually. But it had its drawbacks. Teams were thrown together from lists of players that were mostly past their prime or were at best second-teamers or minor leaguers. This made it difficult for the expansion teams to win many games.

Besides all the new players that expansion brought into the game, there was a new stadium to visit: Wrigley Field. Not the one in Chicago; the one in LA. That's right. Los Angeles.

When the Dodgers moved to LA in 1958, they played at the Coliseum. They were still playing there in 1961, and they didn't want to share their place with the expansion Angels. They were the Los Angeles Angels those first few years before they built their own stadium in Anaheim and Gene Autry renamed them the California Angels. The only place available for the Angels in 1961 was old Wrigley Field where the old minor league LA Angels team played when it belonged to the Wrigley family.

Wrigley Field was pretty much a nightmare for pitchers — home or visiting pitchers. LA's Wrigley Field was more of a bandbox than the one in Chicago, and it wasn't even as pretty. The power alleys were only five feet deeper than the foul lines. It was a joke, like playing in a little league park. The Angels had five guys who hit 20 or more homers that year, and as a team, they finished second to the Yankees in home runs for the season.

We had to play nine games in Wrigley Field. All of them were real nightmares, but the one that really still stands out in my mind came late in the season. I remember this game because of the umpire that night.

Ed Hurley was a terrible ump. He had the quickest thumb in baseball. He would throw anyone out of a game for any excuse that he could think of at the moment, and then laugh about it. Worse than that, he hated Paul Richards, and Paul hated him just as much. For some reason, these guys never got along. I guess it was because Hurley was such a bad umpire, and Paul hated bad umpiring. And Hurley hated Richards because he knew he was a bad ump but wouldn't ever admit it, instead choosing to throw out guys who caught him making major mistakes on the field.

Anyway, while we were in Los Angeles to face the Angels

for the last time that year, Paul announced that he was leaving the Orioles to take the front office reins at Houston. In the game that night, Hurley was umping behind the plate. Word had it that he had made up his mind to throw Paul out of his last game in the American League. He was just going to throw him out for the hell of it. That's the kind of jerk that Hurley was.

Jack Fisher was pitching that night. He walked 14 guys, and many of those pitches that were called balls were really strikes! Every time Hurley called a ball, he looked at our dugout. *Ball one!* He looked at the dugout. *Ball two!* He looked again at the dugout. This went on for all nine innings. Fisher didn't deserve to walk 14 guys!

The Angels were over in their dugout, laughing their heads off. They just walked up to the plate. Strike? No, it was a ball. They knew those pitches were strikes, but they finally figured that Hurley was waiting for Richards to come charging out of the dugout so Hurley could throw him out of the game! Hurley apparently wanted the distinction of being the last umpire to throw Paul Richards out of a ball game in the AL. Richards never came out. We were all just laughing our heads off. It was just so comical to see this umpire making an idiot out of himself. And Fisher was out there, just frustrated as hell. Every time he threw a strike, Hurley called it a ball. Fisher just glared at him, and Hurley looked at Fisher, then turned around to look at Richards. He just wanted him to come out of that dugout!

Richards did come out of the dugout once, and Hurley went storming to the mound, hoping Richards would turn around to chew his butt. But halfway to the hill, Paul turned and walked back to the dugout. Another time Richards started toward Hurley, and I said, "Here it comes." Just before Paul reached him, he turned back to the dugout. And was Hurley ever pissed! Paul had just made him look like the fool that he was. Hurley was so mad at Paul that he couldn't see straight. What a jerk!

Paul survived his last AL game that year, and Ed Hurley kept throwing guys out of games for little if any reason at all.

* * *

A s for the media during that time, I really didn't have a lot of respect for some of the print guys. Most were decent, but unfortunately some were idiots.

That's the way it is with any media, really. It's the good guys and the bad guys. The bad guys would write what they wanted to write without even bothering to ask what the story was all about.

A good example of that was when negotiations between the players association and the owners were going on. The players were always labeled the bad guys when there was a lockout or a strike threatened or if negotiations weren't going too well. The owners would be at the meetings with their chests stuck out, saying the players were all pampered babies and that they were trying to get everything in the world. That was a bunch of baloney. We were trying to get things done, and the owners were telling the media that they were losing money. The reporters printed that, which would just burn the players and the player-reps. We didn't know how they could take a story like that and run with it and do it consistently. But it always happened. Every time we had negotiations, the owners would always bitch and moan that they never made any money. We challenged the print media to ask the owners if they could see their accounting books. We'd asked, and the owners turned us down flat. We said if they could prove that some of the teams were losing money, then we'd have a third party look at the books and if the judgment was made that certain teams really were having problems, then the players association would have to take a different view in negotiations.

Unfortunately, when it came to the owners, these guys would write everything the owners would say, no matter what it was. They'd print it without asking for any proof, and that was very disturbing.

Did they ever print what we had to say? Of course not; that never happened because the print media printed what the owners wanted them to print, which led the fans to believe that the owners were the good guys and the players were the bad guys. It was absolutely ridiculous.

The majority of the media were decent guys. They'd come in to get quotes after a ball game from the different players or the manager. They'd ask the typical questions reporters ask. But you had some guys who were strictly looking for dirt, or something that had changed the complexion of the ball game so they could write about it. These guys were the ones you had to be really careful with because they were the type you knew, that no matter what you said, it wouldn't come out the same way you said it. They'd change what you said to make it come out the way they wanted it to come out, to make it look like something was wrong as opposed to something that was right. It really was a tough situation for both the writers and the players. You really had to know who you were talking to because some of the writers were just total cutthroats.

As time has passed, the attitude of the writers has become a little different than when I broke in. I blame the escalation of player salaries for that. I don't know what kind of money these latter-day sportswriters make, but obviously the athletes that they cover make a hell of a lot more. Considering that most writers look down their intellectual noses at the players, I'd say they're jealous and resentful that some rookie who can hit a ball 400 feet or who can throw a ball 95 miles per hour makes five, six, maybe seven or eight times as much money in starting salary for playing a children's game as a college-educated reporter with 10 years experience earns writing stories for a newspaper.

And what about having to deal with players who make 20 times more than they do? Those writers who slam the superstars on a regular basis are probably all frustrated want-to-be-ballplayers who would rather be the guy in the limelight than the guy aiming the spotlight. They never had the talent to play, so they became sports writers.

And yet the writers have to travel with the players all of the time. It was a difficult situation when I was playing. It must be downright hell now.

Howard Cosell, before he broke into the football situation, was doing sports on a local New York TV station. Howard would manufacture things to put on his program, whether they were right, wrong, factual or whatever. He did this without any conscience whatsoever. Thank God, there weren't a lot of those guys like Cosell.

For the most part, I always felt that I got along decently with the press. I've always been a free thinker, so I get in trouble a lot of times because I say what's on my mind instead of what's politically correct or what's proper for polite society.

When I was with the Cubs, WGN-TV had "The Lead Off Man" with Jack Brickhouse. What a great guy! He would try to get every Cub on at least once during the year along with the coaches and the manager. Being the talker that I am, Jack would get me on an average six or seven times every year I was with the Cubs. He knew that I liked being on and that I always had something to say. Plus, by that time, I think we got fifty bucks and a gift certificate either to a restaurant or for a pair of Florsheim shoes for appearing on the show. I had really progressed over a period of 16 years. I had gone from a polo shirt for a radio show in Baltimore to fifty bucks and a pair of shoes for a TV show in Chicago. I have no idea what players get now, but I'm sure it's a lot more than fifty bucks.

But I enjoyed it. I liked talking to the press. But a lot of times they would irritate me. If I'd had a bad game, they would come down and asked me, "What happened?" Then I'd say, "Well, didn't you watch the same game I did? You saw what happened. I got my ass kicked. I don't have any excuses. I got hit and I got hit hard." They would often ask dumb questions. I couldn't figure out why these guys, who were professionals, were asking such dumb questions. Not many of them were very innovative at all. At least not that I can remember.

The media that was the toughest when I was playing were the New York writers and the Boston writers. The Boston reporters were the worst of all of them. They were just cutthroats. You had to be extremely careful in Boston of what you said because ninety percent of the time, it wasn't going to come out the way you said it. That's one of the reasons why Ted Williams wouldn't talk to them very much. He insisted on being quoted accurately. Could you blame him? Not me. But maybe if you're a sports writer, you could.

◆12◆

Pop-up:
Infield Fly Rule

J ack Fisher was another teammate. "Fat Jack" was what we called him. Jack was on the heavier side. He always had a gut, but he was a real competitor. He had good control, a good curve, and a good changeup. He was one of those guys — perhaps not quite in the class of Stu Miller — who didn't throw really hard but who had great command of his pitches. After facing Estrada, Barber, and me in a series, teams hitting against Jack Fisher or Jerry Walker had a tendency to be frustrated at the plate.

Then there was Hoyt Wilhelm, another unique guy. Hoyt had a long career in the Major Leagues and is best remembered for that incredible knuckleball of his. He was very, very successful with it. He fought in World War II, was wounded, and was decorated with the Purple Heart. He didn't get to the Majors with the New York Giants until 1952 when he was 28 years old. That's kind of old for a rookie. Usually, organizations give up on guys by the time they reach that age. He pitched in 71 games that year, all in relief, and won 15 with 11 saves. He also hit a home run his first time up to bat. He never hit another in a career that spanned 21 years. He was a reliever for most of his career except for the first few years he was with the Orioles. Hoyt threw just so effortlessly. He would just throw the knuckleball all game long and wouldn't even break a sweat. He was very cunning, too. He'd get two strikes on a hitter, then the hitter would look for the knuckleball. Just about then he'd slip a 65-m.p.h. "fast ball" past the batter for strike three or a lazy grounder or pop-up, if the hitter reacted in time. He was a great pitcher. He more than deserves his place in the Hall of Fame.

Gus Triandos was a heck of a catcher. He was strong, hit well, could hit for power, and he had a good arm for keeping runners from stealing too much on us. He was a very good defensive catcher as well. What hurt Gus was Wilhelm. Once Hoyt came to the Orioles, it seemed like Gus's career began to unfold and go the other way because Hoyt just drove him crazy — literally. Hoyt would throw the knuckleball, and it would go back to the screen. Gus would have to chase it. It seemed like every five out of 10 pitches would have Gus running to the backstop to pick up Wilhelm's knuckleball. Finally, Paul Richards came up with the innovative idea of a huge catcher's glove. I don't know how much it helped, but Gus always kept up a sense of humor about it, saying that if the hitters couldn't hit it, how could anyone expect him to catch it. That was his line. Makes sense to me. Gus came up with a bad back from catching Wilhelm. It put his career on a down slide, which was sad to see.

Boog Powell was strong, a very good defensive first baseman, hit for a lot of power, and wasn't bad with the average, hitting as high as .304 one year. He played left field mostly in his first few years with the Orioles because Jim Gentile was our regular first baseman. When Jim was traded, Boog took over at first and became a fixture there for the next 10 years. Boog was fun to watch. He was big with a big belly on him, but boy, he could hit the ball a mile. I liked playing with Boog Powell. He was a heck of a nice guy, and he was a very large addition to our lineup in 1962.

* * *

Luman Harris kept the tag of interim manager for the last month of the 1961 season. Over the winter, the Orioles hired Billy Hitchcock to be the regular manager in 1962.

We opened the year with the determination that we could catch the Yankees and win the pennant. We had a first class starting rotation with me, Chuck Estrada, Steve Barber, Jack Fisher, and Robin Roberts, whom the Orioles had purchased from the Phillies after the 1961 season. In case we faltered, we had a great bullpen filled with guys like Hoyt Wilhelm, Dick Hall, Billy Hoeft, and Hal "Skinny" Brown. Our regular lineup was pretty solid, too. Gus Triandos behind the plate, Jim Gentile at first, Marv Breeding at second, Jerry Adair at short, Brooks Robinson at third, Boog Powell in left, Jackie Brandt in center, and Russ Snyder in right. On the bench, we had some great veterans in Johnny Temple, Whitey Herzog, Charlie Lau, Dick Williams, and Hobie Landrith. We had all the right components for a title run.

Spring training went terribly for me. I was just getting into good shape when I came down with appendicitis on March 12. I went to the trainer because I felt really sick to my stomach, was running a fever, and my side hurt like someone was sticking a knife in me in the area of my appendix. He poked me there. I yelped. He said I should be seen by a doctor, so they rushed me to the hospital in an ambulance. The doctor ordered some tests on me. My white blood cell count was sky-high, which was a solid indication that I had appendicitis. The doctor told me I wasn't going anywhere for a little while because I needed to go into surgery immediately. They wouldn't even let me call my wife. Someone else did that for me. By the time she got to the hospital, I was already feeling the effects of the pain shot. The doctor operated, and I survived. He cut me in such a way that I healed fast, and in three weeks or so, I was back working out. Not really hard at first, but it was easier than it would have been if I hadn't been in training before the operation. I was almost back to 100% when we headed north for Opening Day.

We had a real chance to get off to a great start in 1962 because two of our first three series were against the Yankees, first in New York. All we had to do was take two from the Bombers at Yankee Stadium, and we'd be off and running. Someone forgot to tell the "M&M Boys": Mickey Mantle and Roger Maris. They tripped us up, 7-6, Opening Day with a homer each. We lost three of our first five, including a one-run loss to the Red Sox in the second game of a doubleheader in Baltimore. I got in for one inning. That was my first appearance for the year because I'd missed much of spring training.

The Yankees came to Baltimore the second week of the

season. This was another opportunity for us to make an early move toward the pennant. We lost the first game on Tuesday. Afterwards, John Stedman, a writer from one of the Baltimore papers, and another reporter came into the clubhouse to interview some of the guys. The game was over, and we had gotten our asses kicked. None of us was in a good mood. Stedman came up to me and said, "Milt, you're pitching tomorrow."

"Thank you, John. You're a very astute sportswriter." I knew that I was being a smart-ass, but I had to talk to him. "What can I do for you? It's 11:30, and I want to go home."

"Well, what are you going to do tomorrow?"

"What do you mean? I'm going to come out and pitch."

"Yeah, but how do you stop these Yankees?"

Very much annoyed, I cracked, "Well, you throw a shutout, and you hit a home run."

I just wanted to go home, so I got dressed and did just that.

Well, it was an afternoon newspaper and Stedman had a big column on the Yankees. In the middle of the column, Stedman wrote that I told him that the easiest way to beat the Yankees was to shut them out and hit a home run. That night I lasted six innings. Of course, the Yankees failed to score on me. Then they failed to score on Hoyt Wilhelm who pitched the last three innings. We shut them out and won, 1-0! The one run? I hit a homer off Bill Stafford in the fifth inning. John Stedman made me look like a prophet.

I rode the good feeling of that first win for about a week before I took the hill again. I wasn't sharp this time. I gave up four earned runs on eight hits and three walks, going the distance, but my teammates bailed me out by scoring four runs in the bottom of the ninth to pull out a win, 5-4. I was 2-0 for the year and floating on a cloud.

The cloud darkened in my next start, but I escaped without a decision. That luck didn't hold. After the no-decision, I faced the Twins, and they banged me around but good in less than three innings. I gave up three homers up in Bloomington, the big blow being a grand slam by Don Mincher. That brought me back down to earth.

The A's came to Baltimore, and I faced them in the middle

of the week. The heater was working that night as I fanned 13 batters on my way to a 6-3 complete game win. I was so strong that I retired the last 16 hitters in a row. I was 3-1, but the team was 11-12 and in seventh place. Still, we weren't worried. We were a good team, and we knew we'd make a run at the flag sometime during the year.

Boog Powell gave me all the support I needed for my next win as he connected for a pair of two-run homers against the Angels in Baltimore. I went the distance for the third time that year, gaining my fourth victory against a loss. I also struck out 10 hitters. We were now 15-13 and had moved up to fourth place.

My next start was another catastrophe. I couldn't get loose in the early going, and the White Sox shelled me for four runs and five hits in an inning and two-thirds. I took the loss in the first game of a doubleheader that we lost by identical scores of 8-3. Despite this twin killing by Chicago, we were still in third place at 18-16, just two and a half games back.

Figuring I hadn't thrown much on Sunday, Billy Hitchcock brought me back to pitch on Tuesday against the Indians. I was ready that night in Cleveland. I hit a two-run homer in the fifth inning to break up a scoreless game. Jim Gentile hit a solo shot in the sixth and another in the eighth. I ran out of gas in the seventh and gave up a run before Hoyt Wilhelm came in to save the game.

Hitchcock thought I was the ace of the staff so far as I had won five of seven decisions, so he saved me to face Jim Bunning in Detroit on the following Monday. I wish he hadn't done that. I couldn't get loose again, and the Tigers slapped me around for five runs on five hits and four walks in three and a third innings. I can take solace in the fact that the only way I could've won that game was to throw a shutout because Bunning threw a three-hitter to beat us, 5-1. Rocky Colavito had my number that day as he crushed a two-run homer and an RBI double off me. Such a nice guy until he had a bat in his hands.

Two weeks went by before I got another decision. We were in the Big Apple for a weekend series with the Yankees. They took the first two games to extend their modest winning streak to five games. Then Hitchcock picked me to stop their skein in the first game of a doubleheader. I rose to the challenge this time and beat those guys, 5-1. Then Hal Brown won the second game, 7-2. Our sweep of the Yanks raised our record to 27-29 for the year and lifted us into seventh place past Kansas City which was swept by Los Angeles. We were in seventh, but we were still only six games behind the Yankees and Twins who were tied for first. We had two-thirds of the season yet to play, so there was still reason to hope.

The American League race was so tight in the middle of June that when I won my next start and our record improved to 30-31 it put us in fourth place, just five games behind New York, Minnesota, and Cleveland who were in a three-way tie for first.

My next decision was a real gem. I threw a four-hitter at the White Sox at home to beat them, 1-0. We didn't score until the bottom of the ninth when Charlie Lau hit a little dribbler about 30 feet to score Dave Nicholson who was pinch-running for Boog Powell. Charlie Lau. The guy couldn't hit squat himself, but he became one of the all-time great hitting instructors when his playing days were over. Nice guy, too. Sadly, he died way before his time at the age of 50. I'll always remember him for winning that game for me.

My record was now 8-3, and Hitchcock had me throwing every fourth day. I was okay with that. I was now 23 and in my fifth full year in the Majors. I figured I had the stamina to go that often, so why shouldn't I start every fourth day. That way Robin Roberts, who was 35, could get more rest between starts.

So my next time out was on June 30 against the Tigers at home. I was perfect — for three innings. I struck out six of the nine men I faced. Then I crumbled in the top of the fourth. I couldn't get anybody out. I gave up five hits and a walk before Hitchcock pulled me. And that nice Rocky Colavito — what a guy! — even touched me for another two-run homer. We lost, and my record slipped to 8-4. It wasn't the end of the world, but how do you explain being perfect for three innings then crumbing in the fourth? I can't. I can only say, "Well, that's baseball."

On July 4th, I started the first game of a doubleheader against the White Sox. I wasn't sharp, but my teammates carried me to a win. I gave up all three Chicago runs, but the guys got seven tallies for me to raise my record to 9-4. While I was beginning to think that I might win 20 that year, we lost the second game to even our team record at 40-40, but we were still only five and a half games behind the first place Angels. Yes, the Angels. The expansion team from the year before had a half-game lead on the Yankees and Indians and a two-game jump on the Twins. The Tigers were in fifth place, four and a half back, then us. What a race!

Four days later we were in Detroit for another twinbill. This was our big chance to make a move, and we did. Straight downhill. The Tigers swept us, including beating me in the first game, 5-1. I couldn't get past the second frame, giving up all five runs.

My next start resulted in a no-decision, then I got beat by a nobody named Bob Giggie. With a name like that, he should have been a back-up outfielder. He'd pitched briefly with the Milwaukee Braves in 1959 and 1960 before they traded him to Kansas City. He'd never started a game in the Majors before this night that he faced me, and he'd never done anything spectacular in any of his 26 relief appearances. He was 29 years old and had been in Organized Baseball for a dozen years. On the night he faced me, he was Cy Young, Walter Johnson, and Christy Mathewson all rolled into one. I pitched decently, giving up nine hits and a walk, and I allowed only three runs, one unearned. But this guy goes eight and a third innings and holds us to two runs to beat us, 3-2. He got one more start after that, then passed into history. I wish he'd had his big shining moment in the Majors against Whitey Ford or Ralph Terry and the Yankees instead of against me and the Orioles.

After another no-decision, this one in LA, I missed my turn in the rotation because my arm was a little tired. In a 10-day stretch, I made only one relief appearance in Chuck Estrada's 12th loss of the year. Poor Estrada. He'd been AL Rookie Pitcher of the Year in 1960, winning 18 games, then he won 15 more in 1961. Now he couldn't buy a win. He was a hard thrower, and his arm was going. He was hard to hit, but he walked a lot of guys and threw more than his share of wild pitches. In a few years, his career in the Majors would be over.

When I started again, I beat the Angels in Baltimore, 6-3. The date was August 3. I hadn't won a game since the 4th of July. If I was going to win 20 that year, I'd have to be nearly perfect the rest of that season. The Yankees put that notion aside five days later when Bill Stafford bested me, 3-2, in the first game of a doubleheader. Then the Red Sox took me down after that. My record was now 10-8, and we only had seven weeks to play. Now I had to be more than perfect; I had to be lucky as well.

I was neither. I beat the Indians and Dick Donovan, 5-2, for my 11th win, then had a no-decision when the White Sox knocked me out of the game in the fifth inning. My arm was tired again, so Hitchcock took me out of the rotation for 10 days. When I came back, I beat the Indians again, 4-1, in the first game of a doubleheader that we swept. It didn't do us much good as the Yankees were only a few victories away from winning the pennant again.

* * *

Remember Tom Cheney? I do. After yet another start without getting a decision, I was matched up with Cheney when he was with the expansion Washington Senators in a game that meant absolutely nothing to either team.

In that game, Washington's second baseman, a late-season call-up named Ronald Roy Stillwell, who will be best recalled for being the father of a Major Leaguer, Curt Stillwell, collected one of his eight — count 'em, eight — career hits in the Majors. It was an infield single with one out in the top of the first. Outfielder Chuck Hinton followed with a double to put men on second and third. Then up came Marion Sylvester "Bud" Zipfel, Washington's first baseman. He grounded out, but Stillwell scored. That was the only run I gave up in seven pretty good innings.

In the meantime, Cheney held us scoreless until the bottom of the seventh when Charlie Lau, hitting for me, drove in the tying run. I watched the rest of the game from the bench. It lasted nine more innings. *Nine more!* A whole game more. Talk about long nights.

I was out of the game, but Cheney kept pitching.

Dick Hall took over for me in the eighth and held the Senators without a run for the next eight innings. Then Bud Zipfel — a guy who owed his chance in the Majors to expansion — a guy with a name that sounded like it belonged on a Vaudeville marquee just below the dog act — Bud Zipfel, a trivia question answer — Bud Zipfel homered off Hall in the top of the 16th to give Washington the lead and the game, 2-1.

Cheney took the mound in the bottom of the inning. He'd gone the whole game. All 15 innings so far. He'd been brilliant. He'd already broken the record for strikeouts in a Major League game when he struck out Marv Breeding in the 14th inning. That was Number 19 for the game, a record at the time. Then he struck out Russ Snyder in the 15th to raise the record to 20. Now in the 16th inning he got the first two guys out on routine plays before nailing Dick Williams with a called third strike to end the game.

What a performance! Tom Cheney! A guy whose only claim to fame was that one shining night in 1962. Tom Cheney! A guy who won all of 19 games in his Major League career that spanned a whole 115 appearances scattered over parts of eight years. Tom Cheney! A guy who usually couldn't find the plate in broad daylight with a pack of bloodhounds struck out 21 Baltimore Orioles in one game. And I was the opposing pitcher.

That game was Tom Cheney's claim to fame, his 15 minutes of fame, his spot in the record book, his page in the history books. Because of his performance that night, nobody remembers Bud Zipfel. Cheney robbed poor Bud of his 15 minutes of fame.

* * *

W hat a year I had!

First my appendix had to come out in spring training, forcing me to miss my first two starts. Twice I was rested because my arm tired and I missed two more starts. I had 11 no-decisions in 32 starts. I finished the year with a record of 12-10 with nine complete games and one shutout.

But that's just the half of it. The other half was the

experience of contributing to history. Not my history but that of others.

First there was the great Bob Giggie; he beat me. Then that incredible, unforgettable, unforgivable trio of Ron Stillwell, Bud Zipfel, and Tom Cheney had their all-time career-best games in the very same game — against me. All four of those guys had their greatest moments in the Majors against me.

And to think, at the All-Star break I thought I might be a 20-game winner. That was before I faced those four guys, those nobodies. Win 20 games? When you have to pitch against guys like Giggie, Stillwell, Zipfel, and Cheney? Not a bleepin' chance.

Pressure:
Two On, Nobody Out

O n August 2, 1961, Carole and I became parents. Our son, Steven John Pappas, made his first appearance in the world. Carole had a lengthy labor that began early the day before and ended after midnight. She had the pain, and I had the waiting.

There's some old saying about a child making a man out of the father and a kid out of the grandfather. I don't know how much truth there was to that line when it came to me because I was a grown man still playing a kid's game for a living. But I was proud to be a father.

* * *

A fter we were married, Carole and I left immediately for Florida. We had our honeymoon on the drive to Miami. When we arrived there, we rented a furnished apartment for the duration of spring training. I had to go to the field every day for practice. Carole came out when I was scheduled to throw a few innings, but the rest of the time she went to the beach or just stayed home and watched television. She made a few friends with the wives of other players and occasionally did things with them. For the most part, she was alone when I wasn't at home.

When spring training ended and the team went north, Carole and I set up housekeeping in an apartment in Lutherville, a suburb of Baltimore. Our life was pretty basic back then. I went out and played ball, and she kept house. She always came to home games when I was slated to pitch, but when I wasn't starting, she rarely attended. Some of the friendships she had made that spring continued through the summer of 1960, and she made a few more friends among the other players' wives and with some of the neighbors in the apartment complex where we lived. Carole and I would go out when the team was in town and had a day off or when we had an afternoon game. When the team was on the road, Carole usually spent her free time with her friends. I would call her every day from whatever city the team was playing in. She'd tell me what she'd done that day, and I'd tell her what I'd done. And of course, we spoke the usual words that young married couples say to each other when they're separated from each other like we were. She was lonely when I was away, and I tried to make up for it when I was home. For the most part, Carole's life centered around me that whole summer.

Once the season concluded I wanted to move back to Detroit for the winter, but Carole opposed this idea. She had new friends in Baltimore, and she had no desire to be near her parents. That sounds strange, I'm sure, but you had to know her parents and Carole's troubled relationship with them.

* * *

Carole's parents were Oliver and Helen Tragge. They owned a tool and die business in Detroit. I worked part-time for them one winter before Carole and I were married. I swept up the metal shavings. They didn't think a whole lot of me because I was a ballplayer. That's part of the reason why Carole and I got married by a justice of the peace in the courthouse.

Oliver ran the shop, and Helen did the books in the office. Their primary interest in life was making money. Having gone through the Great Depression, a lot of people were like them: money first and everything else a very distant second. Oliver used to brag that he never changed the oil in his car in order to save money. He'd buy a new Ford every seven years or so and drive it back and forth to work until it seized up and died on him. Helen drove a Cadillac. With both of them, though, money was always the key. That was the other part of the reason for Carole and me being married by a civil servant instead of having a church ceremony. They were too tight to spend the money on a lavish wedding.

Carole grew up as an only child and a lonely child. Before becoming pregnant with Carole, her mother had a miscarriage and lost hearing in one ear at the same time. The doctor told her that the hearing loss was due to the miscarriage. Whether that can happen or not, I don't know; I'm not a doctor. A doctor did tell me that the miscarriage was probably caused by some other ailment that also caused the hearing loss. But Carole's mother thought she would lose the hearing in her other ear because she was pregnant again. I'm sure if abortions had been legal back then, that she would have gotten one and Carole would never have been born. So even before she came into this world, Carole had one strike against her: her mother resented her.

After she came into this world, Carole's parents lavished her with gifts every single Christmas. No child ever got as much for Christmas as she did. She wanted for nothing — on Christmas Day. But for the remaining 364 days of the year, they ignored her. They never showed Carole any love or affection. She never received any of the normal nurturing that a child needs of its young life. That was strike two.

Strike three came a lot later.

* * *

W hile I was living in Baltimore before Carole and I were married, I dated a couple of girls. I can't remember their names now, not that they're important. But with one of them, the relationship was only a little more than platonic, while the other one and I went all the way on more than one occasion. My interest in both of those girls wasn't serious. The one was just a casual companion, while the other was strictly for fun. Neither one stirred my emotions like Carole did.

When the team was on the road during those two years before Carole and I were married, I didn't chase around like some of my teammates did. I was too young to go into the bars with the guys, and that's where most of them picked up women. That first summer after we were married I was old enough to go into the bars with the guys, but I didn't fool around because Carole and I were still in the honeymoon stage of our marriage. The next year — 1961 — that all changed.

The doctor confirmed that Carole was pregnant with our first child soon after Thanksgiving. I guess the news was sort of my Christmas present that year. We didn't go back to Detroit for the holidays to tell our families about Carole's condition. We just called them. My parents were absolutely ecstatic about the news and very, very happy for us, but Carole's mother and father were less than enthusiastic. Her mother still had that old fear about pregnancies, and she thought what had happened to her would happen to Carole.

When we left for training camp in Florida, Carole was just about four months along. She started showing when we were in Miami, and as the baby started to grow inside her, she started losing interest in sex. I suppose this was only natural, but I didn't understand it at the time. All I knew was I was sleeping next to a woman and getting nothing for it. By the time the regular season rolled around, I was really beginning to feel the strain of not having sex with Carole.

It's been so long ago now that I can't recall exactly which road-trip was the first one where I strayed from the path of fidelity. We started the year off in Baltimore, then made a few short trips before flying off for a series against the Angels in Los Angeles. If I was anybody else but me and had to bet on which trip it was that I first cheated on Carole, it would be that one. However, it wasn't that one. It was the first trip north to New York and Boston. I met a stewardess on the plane who took a liking to me. I can't remember her name, but we first got together in Boston. So that's what I'll call her. I was on the disabled list with tendinitis, so I had more time on my hands than usual. "Boston" was accustomed to one-night stands. This was something new for me, but it soon became something of a habit.

"Boston" and I had a few more interludes together that summer. Then just after Steve was born I received a note from her congratulating us on our first child. She also mentioned the facts that I had neglected to tell her that I was married and that my wife was pregnant. She was nice about it, but it was the last I saw or heard of her.

There were others over the years. Most of them — nearly all of them — were one-nighters or single road-trippers. It depended on whether the woman was a flight attendant or a cocktail server or whatever. I'll use the more politically correct terms here instead of those in use at the time, although it seems easier to me to call a flight attendant a stewardess in this context because now men can be flight attendants and I don't want anybody to get the wrong idea about my sexual orientation. Anyway, many of the flight attendants I knew were usually stopping over for one night in the city where we were playing, so they only had the opportunity for one-nighters. Some of them were based in those cities, which made seeing them more than once convenient.

Women who lived and worked in the cities where we were playing were a different matter. They sometimes went up to my room with me for a casual one-nighter, and sometimes they came back the next night. That would usually be the end of it, however. I wasn't a sailor looking for a regular girl in every port. I was a ballplayer looking for a little action to occupy some of the down time I had on my hands on every road trip.

I'd meet a woman flight attendant on the plane to Chicago, let's say. We'd hit it off. I'd ask her if she was based in Chicago. If she said yes, then I'd ask her if she was flying out again immediately. If she said no, then I'd ask her out to dinner. Dinner would lead to my hotel room or her apartment, depending on whether she shared her home with another attendant, and even then that sometimes didn't make a difference whether we went to her place or mine.

If the flight attendant wasn't based in the city where the team was playing, then I'd ask if she was laying over there for a while. If she said yes, then I asked her to dinner. That led to her hotel room or mine.

If I didn't have any success with flight attendants, then I'd meet a woman in a bar. It seemed there were always nice looking women looking for action in hotel bars. It was never hard to make a connection. I'd usually order a drink and nurse it for an hour or two before either having one more or going up to my room with the woman or to her room, if she was staying there, too.

I was ballplayer and making some decent money for a young guy. My room was paid for by the team, and I had my meal money on top of a few dollars of my own. Most ballplayers are clothes hounds. I was no different. I usually dressed well. I was tall, thin, well dressed, flush with money, and I was a ballplayer in the Majors. If these things weren't enough to turn on most young women looking for action, then I don't know what else I would have needed to succeed with them.

Casual sex on the road was easy to come by, and I had my share and maybe then some. Except for one woman later in my career, I never had what anybody could call a steady or regular relationship with any woman in any of the cities where we played. If a woman gave me any indication that she wanted any-thing more than an evening out and a casual fling in bed, I didn't even bother to say, "Thank you, but no thanks." I just avoided seeing her again. I didn't want any entanglements. I was married and very happy with it.

However, I knew a few flight attendants who weren't looking for a man to call their own. They were seeing other guys just like me on the same basis. I'd call them before leaving Baltimore or wherever I was playing and try to set up a date before arriving in their city. Those few women would be the closest things anybody could calls regulars for me. I'd get settled into my hotel, then meet them for dinner and a drink before going back to my room or to their apartment.

Like I said before, except for the one woman that I had a real affair with, I was merely looking for casual sex with women who wanted the same thing. I didn't consider any of these one-nighters or semi-regulars to be anything any more serious than going to the movies or playing miniature golf or enjoying a ride at an amusement park. They were something to do on the road and nothing more than that.

The moral considerations? I wasn't very religious then any more than I'm religious now. I never worried about burning in Hell for fooling around with other women, but I did consider Carole. She was the reason why I only had the one affair. I loved my wife and wanted to be with her all the time. But being a ballplayer and being away half the time with little to do, well, sex was just something to do.

When I was home, I did everything with Carole, and after Steve was born, I was more intent than ever on being a good husband and father. This desire was given added strength when our daughter, Michelle Anne Pappas, was born January 13, 1963. As both kids grew, I worked harder and harder at being the best father and husband that I could be.

But what about my infidelity, some might ask? Well, what about it? Would I live like that again? I think not. Because I know now where it led. But back in the early 1960s, I didn't have a clue what the future held. All I knew was I was having a good time; I was having my cake and eating it, too. I was young. I was a ballplayer. I was married to a wonderful woman, and I was the father of two beautiful children. I was leading a double life and getting away with it. Everything was just about perfect. If I'd only seen where I was headed with that life …

To hell with that. Hindsight is 20-20. Let's just say, if I have one great regret, it's what I did that led to the greatest tragedy of my life, and if I could go back and change it, I would. I can't do that, but I can reveal it. By doing that, maybe I can help just one other guy. Maybe some other guy will learn from my mistake and keep from making the same error with his life.

* * *

S ex was easily and readily available when I was playing. It still is, from what some of the younger guys have told me.

When we were chasing women on the road, we had a lot less to worry about when we caught them than players today have to be concerned with. We didn't have the big one — AIDS — to think about when we were making it with a woman. Sure, there were some venereal diseases such as gonorrhea and syphilis, but except for some places around the Majors, guys didn't have to worry about it. I don't recall ever hearing about a guy who contracted a dose of the clap from any woman.

Players today practically have to ask a woman for a health

certificate before jumping into bed with them. AIDS and herpes of all different types can be contracted in a lot of different ways. Guys don't have to have sex with women to get them. The idiot players who are doing drugs can catch those diseases from a dirty needle.

As if venereal diseases weren't enough to worry about, guys today really have to concern themselves with the consequences of their actions. When I was playing around, you and the woman — usually a woman with some smarts and certainly with some cautious wisdom who didn't want any complications any more than you did — took care not to get caught. Most of the women were taking birth control pills or they had a device of some kind, an I.U.D., if you will, to prevent pregnancy. She didn't want any kids to mess up her life, and you certainly didn't want any paternity suits. So you took precautions.

Today, women are different. And so are the players. Why? The money. Today's players make so much money that many of them don't care if they get some woman pregnant and have to pay her child support for the next 18 years. And the women? Some of them get pregnant intentionally just to get a piece of a player's incredibly high salary. That's bad enough, but there are worse.

Two stories to illustrate my point. Both involve football players, but they apply to baseball and basketball players just as well.

A wide receiver in the NFL back in the 1980s had a penchant for casual sex. Nice looking guy and really well paid. He met a woman in a bar, bought her a drink, made a lewd suggestion, and she picked up on it. They went out, found a dark corner in a stairwell, and she proceeded to perform oral sex on him. When she finished, she demanded money for her services. He refused to pay her. She called the police and stated that he'd forced her to commit the act. The cops and district attorney — who are always eager to bust a high-profile guy like a pro athlete — believed her and arrested him for it. He was later cleared of the charge, but that's not the point. The point is: she tried to shake him down. She failed, but a lot of other women have succeeded in doing the same thing to a lot of other professional athletes.

The second tale of woe is about another NFL wide receiver

who has been known to get himself in trouble with the law because of sex and drugs. This guy is presently paying for a college girl's education because when he had sex with her she was under 18. He bought off her parents and the girl with the education money. This was much to the chagrin of the local district attorney who wanted in the worst way to bust this player.

These are but two examples that I know of. There are others.

It's a real minefield out there for pro athletes today. They can contract a deadly venereal disease if they aren't careful or they can have their lives ruined by some conniving people who just want their money.

It's these situations that make me glad that I played when I did, but on the other hand, I wonder how much money I could earn today with my pitching abilities. It's a tough call.

* * *

Before the 1961 season, Carole and I moved into an apartment in Baltimore. I'd earned extra money that winter by doing speaking engagements for the Orioles. With a new baby on the way, I knew the next winter that I'd need to do more than that pay the bills.

As a kid, I fell in love with bowling. I got a part-time job as a pin boy. For those younger readers of this book, bowling alleys didn't always have automated pin spotters. They used to have kids at the end of the alley who picked up the pins and fed them into a spotter by hand, then set the pins on the alley with the manual machine. It was one of the jobs available to boys that has disappeared because of automation. Another one is being a caddy on a golf course. But automation didn't do away with caddies. Greed did that. Golf courses don't make any money from caddies, but they do make money from renting power golf carts and hand-pulled carts.

Anyway, I was a pin boy when I was a kid. I earned a little money, and I got to bowl for free. I bowled a lot. I loved the game. I still do. And I was good at it. I'm still decent. I think I would have become a professional bowler if I hadn't been a baseball player. I bowled almost every chance I got. Lou D'Annunzio knew that I liked to bowl, so he got himself on my good side by taking me bowling during the winter when he was scouting me for the Orioles.

This love for bowling served me well after the 1961 season. I was hired by Fair Lanes, Inc., to teach bowling in the Baltimore area.

What a life I was having! I was being paid thousands of dollars in the summer to play a kids game, and in the winter I was being paid to teach people what I liked doing best with my free time. I thought I had it all, and I was only 22 years old. Was I ever wrong.

◆14◆

Liner:
Taking It Deep

U mpires are not my favorite people as a group. They never have been, and they never will be. They're a rare breed. Mostly an off brand, if you like to put labels on people. They can favor the good pitchers as well as the good hitters. Sometimes they can even cost a team some big games. One hurt me big time, and he did it so well that I'm not going to tell that story here. But it's in the book. You'll know it when you read it.

The butt of that tale is a real jerk named Bruce Froemming. He's the exception and not the rule among umpires. Many that I knew were very straight-laced. Jocko Conlon, Eddie Vargo, Ed Hurley, Paul Runge, to name a few, were among the best. They were the exceptional umps, but on the opposite end of the scale from Froemming.

Paul Runge was a darn good umpire. He was Italian, but for some reason, he did not like Rocky Colavito, also Italian. To the best of my knowledge, Rocky never said anything negative to anybody. He was one of the nicest guys you'd ever want to meet. He had a great arm, was a good hitter, hit with power, and would go across the street in rush hour traffic to avoid getting into a fight. He was just a placid, easy going guy. But for some reason, Runge didn't like Colavito, and I knew it.

The night before I pitched, Rocky hit four home runs in one game against us. The sportswriters came in afterwards and asked him what he was going to do the next day. If he hit five in a row, Rocky would set a record. Then the writers asked me about it because I was the scheduled starter the next day. I said, "So what? If he does, he does." I went on to tell them that I couldn't predict that night what Rocky Colavito might do the next day.

The next game Runge was behind the plate, and again I knew he didn't like Colavito. The first time up I threw Rocky a slider about eight inches outside, and Runge called it strike one. Okay. The next pitch was a slider that was about 12 inches outside. Strike two. Rocky was just fuming, and he was looking at Runge. He wanted to say something, but he didn't. The next pitch was another slider about a foot outside. Strike three! There weren't going to be five home runs hit in a row and the chance at the record was gone. Poor Rocky turned around and walked back to the dugout. That night, I struck him out four times, and not one pitch was a legitimate strike.

To this day, I don't know what it was with Runge and Colavito, but when Runge was behind the plate, you could always get Rocky out and never have to throw him a strike.

Some umpires would tell you face to face, "I'll give you the first two, but you have to earn the third one." Obviously, you'd love to get ahead of a hitter 0-2. That's great for a pitcher because now you have four chances to work your best pitch to get the guy out. God, I would love the umpire who would give me the first two strikes. But I also knew that to get a guy out, or if I was going to strike him out, I'd have to throw him a legitimate strike.

Actually, consistency with an umpire is more important than the guy who gives you the outside corner but won't give you the inside corner. That's just frustrating. He'll give you the low pitch, but won't give you the high pitch. You just don't know what to do with this guy. And the same with the hitter. He's also frustrated. There were a lot of umpires like that when I was playing, and they're still like that today. Umpires today, I feel, protect the hitters more than they do the pitchers.

As for the strike zone, that's another mystery. When I broke into the AL, umpires had that huge, big balloon, chest protector, so they'd have to stand up over the catcher to look at the ball. With the AL umpires, you'd get a lot of high called strikes because that was the ball they could see. But they couldn't see the low pitches decently, and a pitcher would get frustrated because you would know it was a strike and they would call it a ball.

In the NL, umpires had the inside chest protector, so they'd stand on the inside of the catcher, next to his ear. They could see the inside pitch and you would get a lot of inside called strikes, but they couldn't see the outside corner. So you would throw the ball on the outside corner, and it would be a guess for the umpire. Half the time they're right and half the time they're wrong.

Since AL umpires copied NL umpires by going to the inside chest protectors, they all have the same problem. They can see the inside corner very well but not the outside corner.

So umpires were frustrating as hell to me. If you said something to them, they usually took offense. And, boy, you had to be pinpoint accurate from that point on to get a strike.

The men in blue also hold grudges, which carry over for years. Witness the war between Jocko Conlon and Leo Durocher. Just the mere mention of Leo would cause Jocko to reach for his heart pills.

And some umps were real characters.

One year on May 11, my birthday, I was sitting on the edge of the dugout with my feet hanging over onto the field. Ed Hurley was umpiring at first base. I looked across the field, pointed my finger at him, and said, "Hey, Ed!" It was just a friendly greeting; nothing more.

He pointed back at me and said, "You're outta here!"

He was all the way over at first base, and I was at third base, sitting in the dugout! I said, "What do you mean?"

He repeated, "You're outta here." He came charging over and said, "Pappas, you're gone. Go take a shower!"

"What the hell did I do?"

"You don't have to do anything. You're outta here. You're gone!"

"Are you serious?"

Paul Richards asked, "What do you mean? He was just sitting here and didn't do anything."

Hurley then pointed his finger at me and said, "By the way, happy birthday! You're outta here." He didn't write me up, but he threw me out of the game. What a character!

When you get thrown out, some teams will pay your fine, depending on what happened. Once when I was with the Cubs, one of my teammates got hit by a pitch, and I threw at one of the Giants hitters in retaliation. A bench-clearing fight ensued. I got tossed out for precipitating the brawl. The Cubs paid that fine. But if it was something really stupid, like being thrown out for arguing a call, then I usually ended up paying it.

Umpires are far from perfect. They know it, but they won't admit it. They absolutely refuse to reverse a decision. Case in point, Jim Honochick, 1963. This was classic umpiring.

The Orioles were adding an upper deck along the foul lines that would add a lot of seats to the stadium's capacity. The construction crews actually worked while we played day games during the week. They didn't hinder us that much, and of course, they didn't work at all when we played night games. Down the right field line, the contractor had put up a big metal sign with the company name on it. The thing must have been about six feet by six feet square and was very prominent down the right field line. Most of important of all, it was about 15 feet into foul territory.

In the first game of a twilight doubleheader, Dick Stuart of the Red Sox came to bat against me with two men on base. Stuart hit a line drive down the right field line. High and deep. I held my breath until the ball hit the construction company's sign with a resounding "*Bong*!" I exhaled with relief. Honochick, who was umpiring at first, put up his right arm, waved it in a circle, and called Stuart's drive a home run. I was nearly nuts. "How in the hell can you call that a fair ball? Shit, the ball was 10 feet foul."

"Well, it was fair the last time I saw it."

"What do you mean the last time you saw it? Didn't you follow it all the way into the seats? My lord, the ball was foul. It hit the damn sign. Didn't you hear the gong? What do you have, bells in your head, that you didn't hear the ball hit the sign?"

Everybody was laughing at him, even the Red Sox. The bullpen guys were just roaring. The ball was hit so far foul. It was plainly a foul ball to everybody — except Honochick. He called it a homer, and he would not reverse his call. He wouldn't even ask another umpire for help. It was an unbelievable situation. He was one stubborn s.o.b. Fortunately, I also hit a three-run homer, and we won the game, 6-4.

* * *

S tu Miller was a great relief pitcher for the Orioles. He had three speeds for his pitches: slow, slower, and slowest. He had a phenomenal career for a guy that couldn't break a pane of glass with his fastball. He would just frustrate the hell out of the hitters. His best fastball was probably about 45 miles per hour, and then it got worse. But he had a change-up curve, a regular change-up, a change-up off his fastball, and a change-up off that fast ball. He would just totally frustrate hitters.

Stu had a herky-jerky wind-up, too. He would wobble his head back and forth before releasing the ball. If the hitter was watching him, the poor schmuck didn't have a chance of hitting the ball. If the batter was watching the release of the ball, he had somewhat of a chance to hit it. But most of the time the guys would just walk up to the plate frustrated before they stepped into the box. They would gear up for a fast ball, and that thing would come in at 35 miles per hour. Hitters would double-hitch twice before they could even get the bat out over the plate. It was really comical to see this guy pitch. I remember that one All-Star Game in San Francisco when he got blown off the mound by a big gust of wind. That's how small he was.

Luis Aparicio was one of the greatest shortstops I ever saw. Little Louie was not a big man, but he just knew how to play the hitters. If there was a ground ball in the hole, past Brooksie, Louie would be there to make the play. He just knew the game and the hitters very well. He had really outstanding instincts and knew where to play the hitters. He also knew what the pitchers were throwing. If you were throwing a fastball, Louie knew how to position himself. He'd move back and forth according to the pitch. He was just a tremendous shortstop.

Both Miller and Aparicio came to the Orioles for the 1963 season in trades.

With Aparicio, we figured we had a first class lead-off man and the best glove in the business at short. But to get him, the Orioles had to give up Hoyt Wilhelm, our ace in the bullpen. We also traded shortstop Ron Hansen, outfielder Dave Nicholson, and a promising young third baseman, Pete Ward. Coming with Aparicio from the White Sox was outfielder Al Smith. He was in the twilight of his career, but he still had some pop in his bat and his defense was among the best. Besides playing the outfield, he could play first and third, which made him all the more valuable to a team.

To replace Wilhelm, the Orioles sent pitchers Jack Fisher and Billy Hoeft and Jimmie Coker, a little used backup catcher that the team had purchased from the Phillies after the 1962 season, to the San Francisco Giants for Miller, left-handed pitcher Mike McCormick and backup catcher John Orsino. McCormick would replace Hoeft, and Orsino would take over most of the catching duties for Gus Triandos who had been traded to Detroit with Whitey Herzog for catcher Dick Brown.

Mike McCormick was a bonus baby. The Giants had signed him in 1956; he only played a little with them that year. He got more time in 1957, then became a regular in the rotation when the Giants moved to San Francisco in 1958. He won 51 games over the next four years, then fell into the nagging injury category in 1962. Billy Pierce became the new left-handed ace in San Francisco. That made McCormick expendable.

Besides the additions through trades, the Orioles brought up lefty Dave McNally from the minors. McNally had good stuff, and the organization expected big things from him. He was only 21 that year, but he had a live arm.

So now we had a rotation of me, McCormick, Robin Roberts, Steve Barber, and Chuck Estrada. Our everyday lineup had Brown behind the plate, Jim Gentile at first, Jerry Adair at second, Aparicio at short, Brooks Robinson at third, Boog Powell in left, Jackie Brandt in center, and Smith in right. Great defense and speed up the middle, power on the corners and in left and right: the traditional formula for winning a pennant. All things considered we thought we just might have enough to catch the Yankees this year.

* * *

My friend Larry Names, the author of several sports books and a lot of novels and a big baseball fan, has this theory about what it takes to win 300 games in a Major League career. According to him, a guy has to win at least 50 games before he turns 26 years old. Then over the next 10 years he has to win 200 more. After that, he has to have enough left in him to win another 50. That's 300 wins and a sure bet to be elected to the Hall of Fame.

At the start of the 1963 season, I already had 65 wins to my name and I was only 23 years old. I had five full seasons in the Majors, and I was healthy. I was just coming into my own, as the expression goes. With a few breaks and some decent support, I felt that I should win 20 games that year and every year after that. Just a few breaks and some decent support. That's all I needed.

I got both in my first start of 1963. We'd opened with a win over Washington as Steve Barber picked up his first win of the year, then beat the Senators again before moving on to New York where I was slated to face Whitey Ford in the Yankees' home opener. It was chilly that day, and only 30,000 fans showed up to watch, once again proving that Yankee fans are fair weather followers. I gave up a homer to Mickey Mantle in the fourth inning, but it was my only mistake of the day. My teammates got to Ford for three runs in five innings, and I went the distance, giving up only five hits. We were undefeated and in first place. What a feeling!

My second start didn't go well. Looking back, the long lay-off between assignments might have had something to do with it. I missed my second turn in the rotation due to a postponement. I'd beaten the Yanks on April 11, then didn't go again for eight days on the 19th when I took the hill against the Indians at home. I was okay for five innings, then lost it in the sixth, giving up three runs. We came back to win, 8-5, but I had a no-decision.

Four days later I shut out the Twins, 1-0, with a five-hitter. I struck out eight and didn't walk anyone. I was 2-0 and felt sure those 20 wins were in the bag.

The Orioles, whom many figured would be the best bet to overtake the Yankees for the flag, were now 8-4 on the year and in first place. Kansas City trailed us by half a game, but they were hardly a threat to win the pennant. The Yanks and the White Sox were tied for third, just a game back. They were the real competition for the title. We still had 150 games to play, and the A's had yet to form the team that would dominate the American League and win three straight World Series in the 1970s.

* * *

I t's amazing how much difference an inch makes in so many things, especially in sports.

A drive down the line with the bases loaded and the game on the line, if it misses the chalk by an inch, it's a foul instead of a three-run double. The referee puts a football down after a bone-crunching play, and the chain gang comes out for a measurement. The ball is a chain link short of being a first down, and the defense holds on for a victory. Tennis, golf, bowling, basketball, hockey, soccer, curling. All games of inches.

It's the same with injuries. How many times have you heard the war stories about a guy being shot in the chest and living or dying? If the bullet had been just an inch to the left, it would have missed his heart and he would have lived. Or an inch to the right and it would have hit his heart and killed him.

In sports, it's the same thing. Take Ron Cey, for instance. Goose Gossage beaned him in the 1978 World Series. Cey's helmet took the brunt of the shot, but if the ball had hit his head just an inch lower, Cey might have had his career and possibly his life ended tragically just like Ray Chapman, the Cleveland Indians shortstop who died from a beaning in 1920.

A tragedy that might have been avoided happened in pro football not too many years ago. Jack Tatum clothes-lined Daryl Stingley, broke Stingley's neck, ended his career, and disabled him for life. It wasn't Tatum's intention to do all this to Stingley, but the blow he delivered hit the exact right spot to do the damage. An inch or two higher or lower, and Stingley would have suffered little more than a sore neck for a week or so.

My own close call with a potentially career-ending tragedy came in 1963 in Los Angeles. It was a weekend series in late April against the Angels. As usual, I was matched up against the other team's ace; in this case, Dean Chance. He was younger than

I was and in his second full year in the Majors after winning 14 games as a rookie. We squared off on a Sunday afternoon. We went an inning and a half without anyone scoring. In the bottom of the second, I gave up a hit just before big Ed Kirkpatrick came to the plate. He hit a grounder to Gentile who fired to Aparicio for the force at second. At the same time, I ran over to cover first base. I got there ahead of Kirkpatrick — barely. My foot landed on the bag, then his foot landed on mine. His cleats tore into my ankle, but I didn't seem to notice at the exact moment that it happened. I caught Aparicio's throw, and the umpire called Kirkpatrick out. Two down, and I headed back to the mound. Just then, someone noticed blood seeping through my sanitary stocking and pointed it out to me. I have no idea who it was because I was evidently in some sort of shock. I recall being led off the field and being taken into the clubhouse where the doctor used five stitches to close up the wound in my ankle. He told me that I was a very lucky young man.

"An inch closer and he would have severed your Achilles tendon and your playing career would be over."

I heard that.

This was 1963. Re-attaching a severed Achilles tendon was still a relatively new procedure in medicine. A friend told me about his older brother having an Achilles tendon re-attached after an accident involving a storm window. He said that it was one of the first ever done and that was in 1953. Since people don't sever their Achilles tendons every day, it was still a rare operation in 1963 and success was far from guaranteed yet.

Big Ed Kirkpatrick could have ended my Major League pitching career right there at first base in Dodger Stadium on April 28, 1963. Only an inch closer and — I shudder to think about it.

* * *

A lmost two weeks went by before I pitched again, and that was a relief appearance against the Yankees at home. We got clobbered, 13-1. I was touched for four hits, but one of them was a homer by Mantle, his second off me that year.

My next start came on May 15 against the Senators. I went the route, throwing a three-hitter and allowing only one run. I got two hits and scored a run, so it was a big day for me. We were only two games out and in third place. The season was still young.

For the rest of May, I won one and lost one with a no-decision. My record on June 1 was 4-1, but how I was doing was unimportant. The team was doing great. We had a nine-game winning streak that the A's snapped on May 29 when they beat us, 5-4, in 11 innings. At that time, we had a three-game lead on New York. When I lost on the last day of the month to the Angels, the Yankees moved into a tie with us for first. The season still had four months to go.

The first week in June we had a big series with the Yankees in Baltimore. Steve Barber won the first game to put us a game and a half up on New York. I squared off with Whitey Ford in the second game. I was good enough to win, but Whitey was a shade better that day. We lost, 4-3, on an unearned run. The good news for us and bad news for the Yankees that day was Mickey Mantle broke his foot and would be out for a month. Now nobody likes to see another player get hurt, especially a great guy like Mickey, but the reality of the situation was without him the Yankees were no better than the rest of us. Or so we thought.

The Red Sox were up next for me. I had no decision again, but I pitched well, going five-plus and allowing just one run on six hits and four walks, while striking out six. We lost in 14 innings to drop out of first place, a half game behind the White Sox but still a game ahead of the Yankees.

My next start was against the Red Sox in Boston. Dick Stuart hit a homer off me that was measured at 500 feet. Roman Mejias also took me out, then I retaliated by hitting their shortstop, Eddie Bressoud, with a pitch. I was gone in the sixth, and we lost, 5-1. I was now 4-3, and the Orioles were two games behind the White Sox and one behind New York. The Twins were tied with us, and the Red Sox were only a game behind us. What a race! Five teams within three games of each other on June 14. We had the sense that this season would go down to the wire.

I got back on track against the Indians in Cleveland. I had a two-hitter going into the seventh when Tito Francona homered off me. I still completed the game, and we won, 6-2.

June was not our month. When the Twins hammered me in Bloomington, 6-4, we dropped to six and a half games out of first into sixth place.

July was better. I managed to win two games before the All-Star break, beating KC, 3-2, and the Angels, 3-1, going the route both times. I held the Twins to three runs over eight innings, and we won in the 10th to climb into a three-way tie for third with Boston and Minnesota. We were six games behind New York which was five games ahead of Chicago. The Yankees had stepped up their game to compensate for the loss of Mantle. What a team they had!

After the All-Star Game, I beat the Tigers, lost to KC, then beat the White Sox and Tigers with back-to-back complete game shutouts on only seven hits. I was 10-5 with an outside shot at winning 20.

August started out the hard way. I lost to the Yankees in New York when I gave up two solo homers to John Blanchard and threw a wild pitch that allowed the winning run to score in the eighth. The loss left us nine games out, but we were still in third place. The White Sox were in second, seven and a half out, and the Yanks were on top.

My next start was another loss due to a lack of support. I pitched well, but Mudcat Grant was better. We lost, 4-1, as he held us to five hits. I only gave up three runs, but we couldn't get to Grant.

The Senators were the right item on the menu for me. I beat them with my bat as I hit a two-run homer in the third inning. I was decent on the mound, too. I held Washington to two runs over seven innings before Stu Miller took over for me. Stu kept them scoreless, and he hit a bases loaded triple in the top of the ninth to seal the win, 7-2.

How I hated to pitch in Minnesota. The Twins rocked me again for five runs in less than three innings, and we took it on the chin, 13-3. I got even with them the next week, going the distance in a 14-4 win. We swept them that day, but despite winning a doubleheader, we were still 11 games behind the Yanks.

I wound up August with one more win, 3-1, over the A's. My record was now 13-8, and I realized that my chance of winning 20 was out the window again.

We lost a doubleheader on Labor Day to the Red Sox in Boston. I took the loss in the first game, getting beaten by Bill Monbouquette who was their ace in those early years of the 1960s. He won 20 in 1963, his best year in the Majors. Four days later in Baltimore, I beat him for my 14th win of the year. I won two more games that month, and lost my last decision to finish the year at 16-10. In my last win, I had the distinction of bunting into a triple play against the Tigers. With the runners on first and third on the move, I squared around and lined the ball straight to Norm Cash. He wheeled a throw to third to Dick McAuliffe for the second out, and McAuliffe fired to Don Wert, the second baseman, who was covering first for the third out. Eh! I still won the game.

The O's finished 10 games over .500, but the Yanks ran away with the pennant, only to lose to the Bums in four straight in the World Series. I started looking toward the next season with hopes of winning 20 games and a pennant. Not necessarily in that order.

◆ 15 ◆

Chin Music:
High and Tight

The Orioles had five new faces on the 1964 roster. One old, one worn, one stern, one fresh, and one with peach fuzz. All five made an impact on the team.

The old face belonged to Hank Bauer, our new manager. He was a funny man with a great sense of humor. He was usually smiling and upbeat. Hank was a big change from Billy Hitchcock, who was a very nice man but a bit on the stern side.

Hank was a heck of a ballplayer. He reminded me a lot of jolly Clint Courtney, except he was a much better ballplayer than Courtney. Hank made himself into a darn good ballplayer. He didn't have the really great ability of Mantle or DiMaggio, but he worked hard at his trade. He was a good outfielder who hustled all the time and did whatever it took to beat you. He was that kind of guy. He would just keep banging on you and banging on you and banging on you. He played rightfield most of the time during his career that spanned 16 years, the first 14 with New York and the last two with the A's.

One of Hank's many claims to fame was the one trade he was involved in. He'd been the regular rightfielder for the Yanks for years, but in 1959 he was getting old for a ballplayer at the age of 37. New York sent him to Kansas City along with Don Larsen, Norm Siebern, and Marv Throneberry for Kent Hadley, Joe De Maestri, and a younger rightfielder named Roger Maris. Hank Bauer was to Roger Maris what Wally Pipp was to Lou Gehrig; the successor exceeded the predecessor.

In his tenure with the Yankees, Hank often batted leadoff, especially against lefties. He didn't hit for power very much, but he could beat you with a homer. When he was swinging for the fences, his average suffered. He hit .300 only twice, and in those years, he hit 10 and 13 homers. When he hit 26 homers in 1956, his batting average was a mere .241. He had a good arm, but he didn't need it in Yankee Stadium, where right field wasn't much bigger than on a high school field in those days.

About a third of the way into the 1961 season, Hank became the player-manager for the A's. He didn't help much as Kansas City finished in ninth place. The Athletics weren't any better in 1962, so Hank was sent packing. His combined record in KC was 107-167 for a worse than poor winning percentage of .391.

Why did Lee McPhail, the O's general manager, hire him? Who the hell knows? He must have seen something in Hank that nobody else saw because Hank Bauer was just the right medicine that the Baltimore Orioles needed in 1964.

During the offseason, the Orioles purchased ageless Harvey Haddix from the Pittsburgh Pirates. Nicknamed "The Kitten" because of his strong resemblance to my first pitching coach, Harry "The Cat" Brecheen, he had seen his best years in the NL by the time he came to the O's. He came up to the Cardinals in late 1952 as a 27-year-old rookie. The next year he won 20 games and finished second in the balloting for Rookie of the Year behind Junior Gilliam of Brooklyn. He had some good years after that, but he is still best remembered for pitching 12 perfect innings against the Milwaukee Braves in 1959 then losing the game on an error, a walk, and a Joe Adcock homer that was ruled a double when Adcock passed Hank Aaron on the basepaths. He finished with the longest one-hitter in the history of baseball.

In a deal with KC, McPhail sent Jim Gentile and a wad of cash to the A's for Norm Siebern. Some people whined because Gentile was a big power hitter, but he was a liability in the field and such a flake off the field that McPhail thought he was disruptive to the chemistry of the team. Siebern had a better glove, giving us the best defensive infield in the American League. Coming from a loser in Kansas City to a winner in Baltimore put some new life in Norm.

In a late season call-up the year before, Sam Bowens had shown that he could handle Major League pitching. He was a pretty good outfielder, too. He could hit for power and run the bases well. He got his chance when Russ Snyder came up lame early in the year.

At the end of the 1963 season, McPhail brought up a kid named Wally Bunker, and he was a kid, only 18. Bauer kept him on the roster for the 1964 season. It seemed the Orioles now had a tradition of bringing up kid pitchers. First me and Jerry Walker. Then Chuck Estrada and Steve Barber. Now Bunker. And it wouldn't stop with him. Don't forget Jim Palmer.

* * *

W ith the rest of our roster basically intact, we headed into the 1964 season with high hopes again. The starting pitching staff was almost the same as the year before. Me, Robin Roberts, Steve Barber, and Dave McNally were back. The bullpen was still in the capable hands of Stu Miller and Dick Hall. Bunker and Haddix made our staff that much better. With the exception of Siebern at first and Bowens in right, our every-day lineup was unchanged. Dick Brown and John Orsino shared the catching duties, Jerry Adair at second, Luis Aparicio at short, Brooks Robinson at third, Boog Powell in left, and Jackie Brandt in center.

I was 24 years old, and in terms of service, I was the senior man on the staff. Only Robinson, who was on the team when I signed in 1957, had more time with the Orioles than I did.

Bauer tabbed me to pitch the opener in Chicago. I went five innings but didn't get the decision as we won, 5-3. My next start was our first loss of the year. The Yankees and lefty Bud Daley beat me in Baltimore, 5-3. My arm stiffened up in the fourth, so I came out of the game and didn't pitch again for more than two weeks. My next opponent? The Yankees, of course, in New York. Jim Bouton shut us out, 4-0. I was 0-2 for the first time in my life.

My first win of the year came on May 10, more than a month into the season. Winning 20 that year? It sure didn't look like it then, but I reeled off four straight wins, including a shutout of the Angels. I hit LA's catcher, Ed Kirkpatrick, with a pitch in that game, and his batterymate, Dan Osinski, nailed me in retaliation. I finished May with a 4-2 record and thought all I had to do was win four games a month to make 20. That was doable. Yeah, right.

After getting off to a good start in April, the Orioles were still going well in May. We stayed on or near the top of the standings for the entire month, and on the first of June, we were tied with Chicago for the league lead.

I really hated pitching in Bloomington. The Twins pounded me for five hits and four runs in the first inning as I could only get one guy out before Bauer sent me to the showers. I rebounded with a win in Chicago before the White Sox returned the favor in Baltimore behind Juan Pizarro who threw a three-hit shutout at us. My next two starts were wins over the Red Sox and the Senators. I finished the month with a record of 7-4, but it was a short month, only 30 days long. I still had time to get my 20 wins.

We ended the month on a losing note. A loss to the Twins in Baltimore snapped our seven-game winning streak. Even so, we'd built a three-game lead on the Yanks, and we were playing the best baseball I'd seen us play in my career there to date.

July was really disappointing for me. My first three starts ended in disappointing no-decisions. When I pitched lousy, we scored runs. When I pitched up to my capabilities, we couldn't buy a run. The Angels roughed me up for four runs in five innings; I left with the lead, then Willie Smith hit a grand slam in the top of the ninth to beat us, 10-6. I held the Indians to a run over seven innings in the second game of a doubleheader, but we could only score once in that same time. I held the Yankees to three runs in six innings, then we lost in the ninth, 4-3. I was not a happy camper, although we were still in first place in the middle of the month.

Finally, I earned a decision. I beat the Tigers at home, 6-1, in the first game of a twinbill that we split. I was 8-4, and 20 wins were now out of the question, although mathematically still possible. More important than my record was the team was still in first place by a full game over the Yanks.

My next start was forgettable as I gave up seven runs to the Indians to lose, 7-4. We were 8-9 as a team since the All-Star

Game, and the Yankees had taken over first place by a game.

Knowing that I hated pitching in Minnesota, Bauer pulled me after five innings in my last start of the month, which was up in Bloomington against the powerful Twins. We were leading when I left the game, and we held on to win, 4-3, as Haddix and Miller held off Killebrew and company. I was 9-5, but we were a game behind the Yankees even though we were winning again.

August started well. I won my 10th game of the year, beating the Angels in California, 7-0. The win put us a half game ahead of the Yanks, but we were a percentage point behind them in the standings. Our record was 66-40 for a percentage of .623, and they were 63-38 for a percentage of .624. We were in heck of a race as we headed to New York for a four-game weekend series.

Steve Barber won the first game of the New York series, 2-0, and that put us up by a game on the Yankees. I went up against Whitey Ford in the second game, but neither of us got a decision as the Orioles won in 10 innings, 6-5. That put us up by two on New York and a game and a half on the White Sox, a team that refused to go away and leave the race to the Yanks and us. We split a Sunday doubleheader, and we felt great that we'd taken three of four from the Yankees in New York.

My next start was great. I shut out Boston, 7-0, in Baltimore to increase our lead over Chicago to two full games and three and a half over New York. I was hot, and so was the team. The Yanks were coming to Baltimore, and we were ready for them.

We split the first two games of the series, and I was slated to go against a rookie named Mel Stottlemyre in the rubber game on Sunday. Mel was another of those Yankee live arms. He was already 1-0 when we met. I held the Yanks scoreless through six innings before my right shoulder stiffened up. Barber relieved me in the seventh, and the Yanks scored a pair of runs off him. We lost, 3-1. If I'd been able to finish that game, maybe I could have held them and we might have won. In the final scheme of the season, that one game made a big difference.

We slipped some more that week and fell into a tie with the White Sox for first. Then we went to Chicago for another key weekend series. I held the Sox to two runs over seven and a third, but Haddix wound up winning it. We were back in first place by a game over Chicago and four games over New York, and the White Sox were coming to Baltimore the following weekend.

After yet another no-decision with the Indians, I squared off against Juan Pizarro and the ChiSox on Saturday night. Pizarro was 17-6 at the time. He was on top of his game. So was I. For the month, I'd only allowed six runs in 44⅓ innings. This would be my last start of the month. I made the most of it. I shut down the White Sox, 5-0, to increase our lead to a game and half over Chicago and four over New York. One month to go in the season, and we were ready for a strong finish.

But we were headed to Minnesota to play the Twins, and I really hated pitching in Bloomington. Not this time, I told myself. As good as the Twins were at the plate, I wasn't going to let them get to me this time. And I didn't. I held the Twins hitless for seven and two-thirds innings before Zoilo Versalles singled off me. I got the next hitter and retired the side in order in the ninth for a one-hit shutout, 2-0. The win kept us a half game ahead of the White Sox and three in front of the Yanks.

The Angels were my next victims. I shut them down, 2-0, in LA to raise my record to 14-5. I was determined to lead us to the pennant, and that was that. We were a half game behind Chicago now but still two ahead of the Yankees. What a race!

We climbed back on top before my next start which was against the Senators in Washington. I wasn't sharp, but I didn't have to be. Our guys scored a dozen runs in the first six innings, and I coasted home, 12-5. I was 15-5, and we were still holding on to first place.

The Twins came to Baltimore for a weekday series in the middle of September. I faced them on Monday. We won, but I didn't get the decision. I held them scoreless for six innings before Don Mincher hit a pinch-hit, two-run homer off me to put them up, 2-1. We tied the score in bottom of the seventh on a homer by Sam Bowens, but Jimmie Hall nailed a round-tripper off me in the top of the eighth. With me now out of the game, we tied the score again in the bottom of the inning, then won it in the bottom of the ninth.

We were a game and a half ahead of the Yankees and two ahead of the White Sox with 15 games to play. The problem was the Yankees had 20 games to play. We could win all 15 and New York win all 20, and the Yankees would win the pennant by a full game. We did the math and figured that we had to have help to win the flag.

For some reason, Bauer started me against the Angels with only two days rest. I was okay for four innings, leading 5-2, going into the fifth. Then the roof caved in. I couldn't get anybody out. Bauer yanked me after the first three guys reached, and the Angels went on to score six runs in the inning. We came back, however, and won the game, which only kept us in a tie with the Yankees for first. We were down to 12 games to play, and they had 16 remaining.

After my normal rest period of three days between starts, I faced the Tigers in Detroit. Al Kaline hit a two-run dinger off me in the first inning, and righthander Ed Rakow — another nobody who had a 36-47 record over seven years in the Majors — made it stand up as I suffered my first loss in more than six weeks, 2-1. We dropped to two and a half games behind the Yankees who didn't seem like they would ever lose again.

I beat the Tribe in my next start, 5-3, to raise my record for the year to 16-6, but the Yankees won their 11th straight that day to hold their four-game lead over us and Chicago. The season had eight days left, and the clouds were suddenly very dark.

* * *

W hile we were running with the Yankees and the White Sox, the National League was having one of its greatest finishes ever in 1964. Those baseball fans who are old enough to remember it will agree that it was a total surprise ending.

The Philadelphia Phillies had been leading that NL since April, and with three weeks left in the season, they looked like a sure lock to make it to the World Series. They had a double-digit lead in the standings when the roof caved in on them.

At the same time, the St. Louis Cardinals and Cincinnati Reds turned on the after-burners. With a week to go, the Reds and Cards had both caught the Phillies, and the NL had a three-team race to the wire.

In the meantime, the Yankees were busy being the New York Yankees. They had their winning streak snapped by the Senators, then they won a twinbill from the Tigers in New York on the last Wednesday of the season. Even though Wally Bunker beat the Senators in the first game of our doubleheader that same night, the Orioles were only two losses or two Yankee wins away from being eliminated. Unfortunately, I couldn't make it a sweep of the doubleheader with the Senators. We were now only one game away from being also-rans again.

The next night the Yanks lost two to Detroit, while Steve Barber shut out Washington to keep us alive for one more day. New York beat Cleveland on Friday night, and we were out of it. The White Sox were still holding on by their fingernails, but on Saturday the Yankees finished off the Indians to win the pennant. We wound up two games out, and the White Sox were only one game out in the final standings. What a race!

Back in the NL, the Cardinals and Reds went into the final day of the season tied for first place. The Phillies were just one game behind them. St. Louis was scheduled to play the Mets, while Cincinnati and Philadelphia squared off against each other. A three-way tie was very possible, if Philadelphia beat Cincinnati and St. Louis lost to New York.

That didn't happen. The Cards pounded the Mets, while the Phillies did the same to the Reds. St. Louis won the flag by a single game over both Philadelphia and Cincinnati. What a race!

* * *

W hat a year for me! I finished the season with a better than decent record of 16-7. Seven of my wins were complete game shutouts. My ERA was my best ever to date at 2.97. I pitched a total 251⅓ innings with 36 starts, the latter a career high for me. I also had a career best 157 strikeouts with only 48 walks allowed.

Those were the good numbers.

On the disappointing side, I had a total of 13 no-decision

games. Of these "sister-kissing" games, I had pitched well enough to have won eight of them, if only the bullpen had held onto the lead for me, or if we could have scored just one more run in the game while I was still the pitcher of record.

Looking back on 1964, I feel that I should have won at least 20 games. I was good enough for it, but that's not what happened.

When the season ended and I looked back of the campaign, I thought, Well, maybe next year I can win 20 and we can win the pennant. Yeah, and maybe Hell will freeze over and the Cubs will win the World Series from the Yankees.

◆16◆

Mound Ace:
Flame Thrower

T he 1965 season came, and at the time, I didn't know that it would be my last year with the Baltimore Orioles.

As a team, the Orioles made no major changes in the way of trades, but Hank Bauer saw fit to bring up two rookie outfielders and a rookie pitcher. All three of them would play very big roles in the future fortunes of the Baltimore Orioles.

Curt Blefary was originally signed by the Yankees, then sold to the Orioles while still in the minors. He played left because he was a lousy fielder; the guys nicknamed him "Clank" because of his iron glove. But he could hit, and that was why he was in our lineup on an everyday basis as a rookie. He had power, and we needed it.

Paul Blair was an intuitive outfielder whose speed going away from the infield allowed him to play unusually shallow. Intuitive outfielder? Blair had that rare ability to know when and where a hit ball was going coming right off the bat. This made his defense more valuable to a team than his hitting. He'd had a cup of coffee with the Orioles in 1964, and he was slated for spot duty in 1965 as a late inning defensive replacement and an occasional starter. He liked to talk a lot and really fast, so the guys gave him the nickname "Motormouth."

Ever since signing me and Jerry Walker in 1957 and putting us on the big league roster right away, the Baltimore organization had developed the reputation for bringing up very young pitchers to the Majors with little or no minor league playing time. After Walker and me, there was Jack Fisher, Chuck Estrada, Steve Barber, Dave McNally, and Wally Bunker. All of us barely shaving on a regular basis when we joined the big club. For 1965,

Bauer kept a kid from Arizona on the roster. His name was Jim Palmer. Handsome, smart, and cocky. But he came to play, I'll say that much for him. He was a competitor.

* * *

T he schedule makers couldn't wait to put us in the fire of the pennant race. We opened against the White Sox in Baltimore. Steve Barber got the call over me because I had a sore elbow at the time we left training camp and Bauer wanted to let it rest just one more day before putting me on the hill. Chicago won the opener, but I shut them out the next day, 6-0, on only six hits and no walks. I was really pumped for that game.

My next two outings weren't so good. The adrenalin wasn't there, I guess. I went five innings in Chicago and gave up only one run on four hits and a walk. We lost the game, 7-2, but I had a no-decision. I was lucky against the Red Sox the next week because they clobbered me for five hits and scored three runs off me in only a third of the first inning. Bauer yanked me quick. We caught them and tied the score, so I wasn't saddled with the loss. As it turned out, my knee was giving me trouble, so I spent two weeks on the bench nursing it.

When I returned to the rotation, the Tigers were in town for a weekend series, including a Sunday doubleheader. Bauer sent me out to pitch the opener, and I responded with a complete game, 7-1. It was my 99th career win. We won the second game, too, which helped us get into the pennant race.

The pressure was on me the next time I took the mound because I was going after my 100th win. Everybody knew it, including the Indians. I had some decent command of my pitches that night, and Boog Powell hit a game-winning homer for us. I got the victory, 3-2, and we moved into fourth place, just two and a half out of first.

* * *

W hitey Ford and the Yankees had finally gotten old. He was 36; Mantle, 33; Maris, 30; Elston Howard, 36; and so on. And the young guys they were bringing up weren't quite as good as the stars they had in the 1950s. They'd won the pennant the year before with Yogi Berra as their manager, but the Cardinals had beaten them in seven games in the World Series. Yogi was fired, and the new management team in New York hired Johnny Keane to replace him because Keane had managed the Cardinals to the top the year before.

What those suits in the Big Apple didn't understand was Keane made only one move that made a difference in 1964. He gave Lou Brock the "green light" on the base paths. Brock, a young and very speedy outfielder, came to the Cards from the Cubs in June of 1964 in what Chicago fans still call "The Trade." In Chicago, Brock had been held back by the "rotating head coaches" who were running the team on the field. In St. Louis, Keane told him to steal bases whenever he felt like going. Brock ran, the Cardinals caught fire, and Keane took the credit. Keane went to New York, and Brock went on to a Hall of Fame career.

Whitey was old now, and although he was still among the best in the Majors, he was no longer at the pinnacle of the game. His fast ball was a shade slower; his slider and curve didn't break as much; his control was off an inch or so from its previous pinpoint accuracy. He couldn't get a strikeout every time he needed one. Retirement was peeking at him over the horizon. But he was still Whitey Ford, and he was still wearing Yankee pinstripes. And I had to face him at home — again.

When the Yanks came to town in mid-May, Ford had a losing record at 2-4. This was the first time I'd ever known of Whitey being on the underside of .500 a month into the season. The closest he'd ever come to a losing season was in 1960 when he went 12-9. His career mark at this time was 218 wins against only 88 losses. And I had to face him at home — again.

Having Bauer, who had played most of his career with Ford, as our manager was a definite advantage for us. He knew that the only way to get to Whitey was with right-handed hitters. The only lefty in our lineup that night was Boog Powell. It paid off.

YOUNG AND BRASH — TO SAY THE LEAST. Just look at that face. It's easy to see why some people thought of me as being brash, conceited, and arrogant instead of merely full of self-confidence in my abilities as a baseball player and in myself as a young man who thought he knew what and who he was. I was very young, and I was in the Major Leagues with the Baltimore Orioles. I was living my boyhood dream of becoming a big league player. Why shouldn't I have been full of confidence? Or even full of myself? I had the world by the tail, and I wasn't about to let it go.   *Family Photo*

STEVE AND EVA PAPPAS. This picture was taken not too long after
my parents were married in 1932.   *Family Photo*

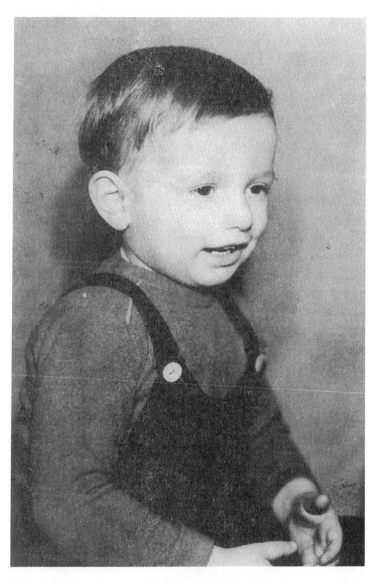

LITTLE MILT. I was only two years old when this photo was taken. Even then, I had my jaw flappin'. You know I was talking here. Just look at my hands. Obviously, I'm gesturing something as I speak to someone while the picture was being taken. Greeks are very expressive people. *Family Photo*

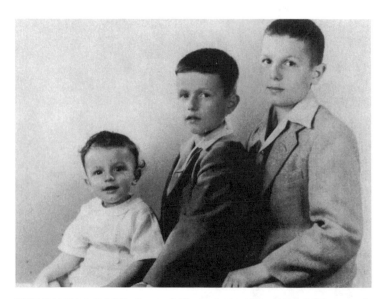

THE PAPPAS BOYS. Perry, Milt, and Gus. We were about two, six and 10 in this picture. *Family Photo*

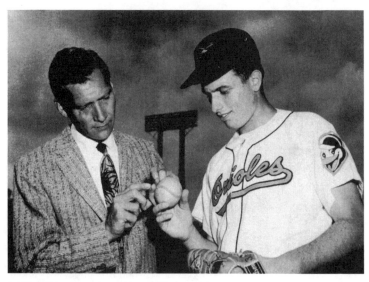

THE SCOUT AND THE KID. Hal Newhouser was given credit for signing me, but Lou D'Annunzio actually did all the work of scouting me for the Orioles. *Author's Photo*

HERB SCORE. After only two years in the Majors, Herb Score seemed destined for the Hall of Fame. Then Fate intervened. A line drive to his face in 1957 eventually ended his career. He was proof that tragedy can strike at any time; a lesson not lost on me. *Author's Photo*

THE VEEP ON OPENING DAY. Vice-President Richard Nixon signed the first ball thrown out at Opening Day, 1959. He threw it from the stands and I caught it. That's why I'm in the picture. I don't recall who the Washington pitcher was. Does anybody? *Photo by Don Wingfield*

THE PITCHING COACH. Behind me is my first pitching coach, Harry "The Cat" Brecheen. He was the first lefty to win three games in a World Series when he pitched for the St. Louis Cardinals against the Boston Red Sox in 1946. He got his nickname from his "cat-like" grace when he fielded bunts. World War II helped him get to the Majors at the age of 30, but he proved that he belonged by winning 20 games in 1947 and leading the NL in winning percentage (.741), ERA (2.24), strikeouts (147), and shutouts (7). He was one of 61 players to play for both the St. Louis Cardinals and the St. Louis Browns.   *Photo by Don Wingfield*

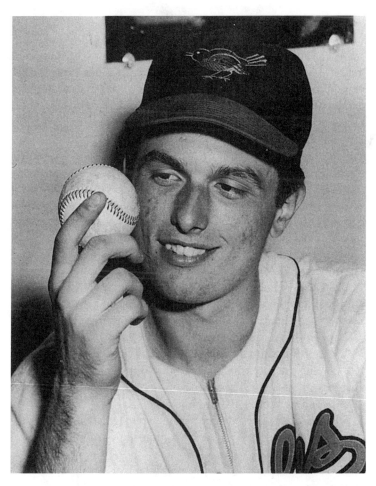

THIS IS THE BALL THAT MILT HIT. This ball was my first hit in the Major Leagues. I got it off the great Bob Lemon of the Cleveland Indians, June 11, 1958. We won the that day, 7-4, and I got my third win of the year. We chased Lemon in the fourth, then picked up a few runs on his replacement, Dick "Bones" Tomanek, who was the actual losing pitcher. Lemon was in the twilight of his career in 1957. In fact, this was his last Major League start. His playing career came to an end a few weeks later, while mine was just beginning. Tomanek was traded the next week to the Kansas City A's, and I beat him again when I faced him in KC in my next start.

Photo Courtesy of Baltimore News-Post and Sunday American

YANKEE KILLER: This was one of my many good days against the New York Yankees. I mowed them down, 5-0, September 2, 1960, with a three-hitter, striking out nine and walking none. Winning that day put the Orioles into a virtual tie with the Yankees for the American League pennant. Much to our disappointment, we couldn't keep with them after that. They went on to win the flag, and we watched on television as the Pirates beat them in the World Series.   *Author's Photo*

A BRIDE AND A raise will make this a week Milt Pappas long shall remember . The former Cooley High athlete, who won 15 games for Baltimore last season, is pictured here with Carole Tragge, taking out a marriage license. They are to be married Thursday. Monday Pappas signed his 1960 contract with the Orioles for a reported $13,000.

SLOW NEWS DAY IN DETROIT. The Detroit papers always gave me decent coverage. Carole and I were married in a civil ceremony because her parents opposed our marriage and they were too cheap to pay for a real wedding with lots of guests. Sadly, I had no family there either.

NEWLYWEDS. Here we are in Florida, Carole and me, spring training, 1960. We'd been there a while when this picture was taken. Just look at how tan she is.   *Author's Photo*

PAPPAS AND SON. Stevie was about three when this picture was taken during one of the many "Father and Son" days that I enjoyed during my career.

Author's Photo

PARTNERS. My one-time partner Don Hurwitz and his lovely wife Dorothy with Carole and me in our restaurant in Baltimore. Don was a good guy, but he couldn't deal with the failure of our business. Sadly, he took his own life over it. *Photo by W.M. Clinton*

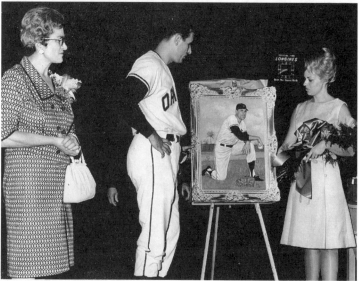

BIG NIGHT. I was the first Baltimore Oriole pitcher to win 100 games, so my friends feted me for it at the ball park. For once, my in-laws showed up. Left to right on top, Helen Tragge, my mom Eva Pappas, Carole, Oliver Tragge, me, Michele, and Stevie. You can see that the kids were really impressed with daddy's accomplishment. In the bottom picture, my mom, Carole, and I admire the portrait that was done from a photograph of me by Joseph Hudson. The portrait now hangs in my living room. *Author's Photos*

OUR LITTLE FAMILY. We were still in Baltimore when the upper photograph was taken. At the time, neither Carole nor I thought we would ever leave there. See how happy we were. Compare the looks in our eyes with the lower picture. I had just been traded to the Cubs, and we were moving to Chicago. We were living proof that life has no guarantees. *Author's Photos*

A HANDSOME TRIO. That's Gus on the left and Perry on the right: my brothers. *Photo by Barney A. Sterling*

OUR LITTLE FAMILY GROWN UP. We were at a game at old Comiskey Park in1980. This was the last photo taken of us together.
Photo by George Brace

THE GOLDBERGS AND ME. Harriett and Elliott Goldberg are my best friends in life. Seated between me and their lovely daughter Kathy, Harriett and Carole were so close that they were almost sisters. When I was with Orioles, we did everything together the year round. Our friendship grew after I was traded to the Reds, and they stuck by me and Carole through our marriage difficulties. Harriett and Elliott did more to keep Carole and me together than anybody. They saved our marriage. When Carole disappeared in 1982, Harriett did everything she could to find her. That's their son Jon seated next to Elliott.

Photo Courtesy of Harriett Goldberg

MY SECOND FAMILY. After Carole disappeared and I gave up hope of her ever coming back, I met and fell in love with Judi. Because I couldn't have Carole declared legally dead until she'd been gone for seven years, Judi and I lived together as husband and wife, and we had Alexandria. Soon after Carole's body was found, Judi and I were married. *Author's Photo*

The game started poorly for me. I walked Horace Clarke who led off the first inning. Bobby Richardson followed with a single before I could get Tom Tresh out. Then I walked Mantle to load the bases. Joe Pepitone stepped in and singled in Clarke and Richardson, and I was on the ropes. For sure, I thought I was just a single hitter away from an early shower when up to the plate came Raymond "Buddy" Barker, a nobody — another nobody — looking to have the highlight of his career against me. Well, not tonight, Buddy. I beared down on him, got him and nearly every Yankee hitter after that. I gave up three more hits and walked only one more for the rest of the game. In the meantime, our guys matched the two runs the Yankees got off me in the first, and we got an unearned run in the fourth to take the lead. You know the old joke? What does Ford stand for? Found on road dead? Well, Whitey's motor gave out in the fifth. He walked Aparicio to lead off the inning. Jackie Brandt doubled, then Bob Johnson and John Orsino singled. Out came Whitey, and we went on to win, 9-2.

My record was now 4-0, and I was feeling pretty good about myself and my chances of winning 20. When I beat the Tigers four days later to up my mark to 5-0, I felt even better. Even missing another win against the A's by one out didn't depress me because I had smacked a bases loaded triple in the second and we won the game, 6-3. If I'd only gotten the last guy out in the fifth, I would have won that game and been 6-0. But that didn't happen because the A's were pounding me — nine hits and two walks in four and two-thirds innings.

In 1964, the Angels were my patsies. I shut them out four times, and entering the 1965 season, I had a five-game winning streak going against them. I owned those guys. At least, I did until Fred Newman beat me in Baltimore, 3-1. I pitched decently, holding them to three runs — two earned — on just five hits and a walk over seven innings, but Freddie and Bob Lee were just a little bit better. To make matters worse, I lost to the Angels again the following week out in LA. Five wins in a row including four shutouts. Now two straight losses. That's the way of baseball.

So far I had five wins, two losses, and three no-decisions, and I had missed three starts because of injury. All total, I should have had 13 chances to win and only had five W's. Give me back those three missed starts, and I would have won one of them, maybe two. Winning 20 was still in sight, but if my season continued in the same vein, I knew I would miss the brass ring again. I focused on improving.

The Senators were still just another bad team in 1965, although Gil Hodges, their manager, was slowly turning them respectable. The rest of the league could no longer look at them as mere doormats. They were now competitive, and they gave us all we could handle every time out. I held them to two runs over nine innings, but their pitchers did likewise to us. I left the game, and Stu Miller took over in the 10th. He gave up a run, and we lost. No decision for me again. I'd gone four straight starts without a win. I was not a happy bird.

We went north to play the Red Sox in the middle of June. It was Friday the 13th. Not really. It was Sunday the 13th. I was superb for eight innings, but my teammates could only get me one run. I gave up a pair of hits and got one out before Stu Miller relieved me again. Tony Conigliaro stepped to the plate, and I was sure he'd take Stu deep. That was the kind of luck I was having. Well, not that day. Miller threw one pitch, and the game was over. Tony bounced into a double play, and I had a win. Hey, I thought, maybe things were changing for me.

My next outing was in Washington. I went the distance, making only one bad pitch all day. Jim King, a good fielding outfielder who occasionally displayed some power, hit one out on me. I struck out 10 and gave up only one walk. I was 7-2 and feeling confident.

The Red Sox came to Baltimore, and I faced them in the last game of a three-game set. I was on again. We won, 4-1, and I went the distance. This was our 12th win in 14 games. We were hot, but so was everybody else it seemed. The Twins were in first with Chicago and Cleveland only a half-game back. Then us at one game out. Detroit was only two games out and in fifth place. This was a tight race, and furthermore, the Yankees were always lurking in the weeds.

The Tigers came to town at the end of the month. We won when I started against them, but I had another no-decision. I went seven innings and gave up only a pair of runs on five hits, but it wasn't enough because we couldn't score on them until late.

Some sloppy fielding cost me my next decision on July 4th. I went eight innings, and we lost, 4-2, on two unearned runs. Ralph Terry beat me. Him, and Leon Wagner who smacked the first and only pitch I threw to him for a two-run homer in the bottom of the eighth.

My last start before the All-Star Game was against the White Sox in Baltimore. I was on a high because I'd been selected to the American League All-Star team. Al Lopez, who was picked to be the manager of the All-Star team because Yogi Berra was no longer managing the Yankees, not only chose me for the team but also to start the game.

But back to the White Sox. Having been picked by Lopez, I strutted my best stuff against Chicago and shut them out, 1-0. This was my 25th career shutout, and I was only 26 years old. I was 9-3 and certain that I could win 20 games that year.

* * *

The 1965 All-Star Game was played at Metropolitan Stadium in Bloomington, Minnesota, the home of the Twins who were leading the American League at the break. I started for the AL, and Juan Marichal of the San Francisco Giants started for the NL. Juan was in the middle of his third straight 20-win season. This was my third All-Star Game, having pitched the ninth inning of both games in 1962. I got a save in the second game that year despite giving up a homer to John Roseboro who was the catcher for the Dodgers.

With all the hoopla of the annual mid-summer classic, I was late getting in my warmups before the game. I rushed my pitches and hurt my arm. Of course, I didn't tell anybody because I wanted to pitch, so out to the mound I went to start the game.

Willie Mays was the lead-off hitter for the NL. He fouled off my first pitch, then parked the second one in the left-centerfield stands, 400 feet away. That was a real homer. I got Hank Aaron to fly out, then Willie Stargell, who was just beginning to strike terror in right-handed pitchers in the NL, singled to center. Richie Allen, as he was known then instead of Dick as he would be called later in his career, popped out to shortstop. I was breathing better as Joe Torre stepped in. I got him to hit a high fly to left. The only problem was that it hit the foul pole before going out of play. A cheap homer. After giving up another hit and a walk, I got out of the inning.

I also got out of the game.

Jim "Mudcat" Grant started the second inning. He had two out when Stargell smacked him for a two-run shot. Marichal was mowing down our guys in the meantime. After three innings, the NL led, 5-0. Pete Richert, who was pitching for the Senators then and having a good year, pitched the fourth and fifth innings for us, and Jim Maloney took over for Marichal. We got a run off Maloney in the fourth, then Dick McAuliffe, the Tigers shortstop, and Harmon Killebrew homered in the fifth. Those Minnesota fans went nuts when "Killer" hit his out to tie the game.

Sam McDowell from Cleveland pitched the sixth and seventh innings for us, and Sandy Koufax pitched the sixth for the NL. Those two were the pitchers of record when Ron Santo of the Cubs singled in the winning run in the top of the seventh.

I hadn't pitched well in the game, but it really didn't matter. I was there, and I played. I'd started. That was all that mattered. It was a great thrill. A feeling that I wanted to repeat again and again and again. Much to my disappointment, I never had that experience again until long after my playing career was over.

* * *

With the All-Star Game behind me, it was time to get back to work. At the top of my list of priorities was an American League pennant.

At the break, we were five games behind the Twins, tied with the Indians for second place. The White Sox, always dangerous as long as Al Lopez was managing them, were close behind in fourth. Everybody else was fading fast, although we could never count out the Yankees, not with their talent.

My first start after the break was in Detroit. I only went three innings before my arm stiffened up; it was still hurting from the All-Star Game. No decision there. But the next week I faced the A's at home shut them out for seven innings before giving way to Dick Hall who put up two more goose eggs to save my 1-0 win. We won the second game of that doubleheader to bring us within three and a half of the Twins. We had a good feeling that we could overhaul Minnesota and win the flag for the first time in our history since the club moved to Baltimore from St. Louis.

Some lousy fielding by our guys and some timely hitting by the Twins put me in the loss column in my next start. I gave up eight runs, but only half of them were earned. Don Mincher and Harmon Killebrew tagged me for homers. I only gave up six hits and three walks in seven innings, and we lost, 8-2. Going into that game, I had an ERA of 1.67. It didn't help. We lost to Minnesota again the next night, and this really hurt our chances to catch them.

Then we went to Minnesota for the weekend. The Twins won the first two games before Bauer sent me out to face them on Sunday. I didn't have it. They scored three runs on me in four innings on four hits and a walk. Boog Powell hit a three-run homer in the ninth to pull out the win for us, 7-6. This victory kept us alive, but we were now five back on August 2. The road was getting harder to travel every game.

We went to Kansas City, and I was still off my game. The A's rocked me for five runs in three innings on eight hits. I took another loss to drop my record to 10-5. Since the All-Star Game, I had one win, two losses, and two no-decisions. Win 20? Not likely. But the pennant was still a visible goal. I focused on that.

The Red Sox roughed me up in Boston on August 10. Roughed me up? Hell, they roughed up the whole staff. I left in the fifth inning with one out, having given up four runs on eight hits. After me, the Red Sox scored eight more times, and we lost, 15-5. We won the second game, 12-4. We were still in second place, but now we were eight and a half games behind the Twins with seven weeks to go in the season. The prognosis didn't look good.

I suffered another no-decision against the Senators at home, once again because of shabby fielding by my teammates. The Nats scored three unearned runs off me in the first inning, then an earned run in the second. I left the game after six innings, and we won in the bottom of the 11th, 8-5.

Jack Cullen. Ever hear of him? Maybe if you're a true-blue Yankee fan, you've heard of him. This guy pitched in two games in 1963, 12 in 1965, and five in 1966. He had a lifetime record of 4-4 with nine starts and two complete games. He threw one shut-out. One shutout! Just one. And guess who the opposing pitcher was. Yep. Me. It was August 20, 1965 in Baltimore. He threw a three-hitter. I only allowed the Yankees six hits in eight innings, but one of them just happened to be Tom Tresh's 19th homer of the year. I lost, 1-0. I was now 10-6. I'd tried six times to get my 11th win of the year. I was beginning to feel like a pregnant hooker driving an Edsel with a Nixon sticker on the rear bumper.

My next start was in Chicago against Gary Peters. Al Lopez had tried to get Peters onto his staff for years, but Gary just couldn't quite make it until 1963. Then he won 19 games and Rookie of the Year honors. He won 20 in 1964, but he was having his problems in 1965. I was one of them. I beat him that night, 2-1. I went the distance, giving up just four hits and a walk.

I was finally off the dime. It didn't last. The next week the White Sox touched me for four runs on five hits and a pair of walks in just three innings. I also hit Moose Skowron with a pitch. I can't recall whether I did it on purpose. Probably I did. What the hell! He probably deserved it. Yeah, he did. He called me "a five-inning pitcher." So, Moose, how did I throw 43 complete game shutouts in my career if I could only go five innings? He deserved to be hit.

We went to New York for a Labor Day doubleheader. I drew the assignment to start the first game. And my mound opponent? Who else? Whitey Ford. Whitey had rebounded from his poor start. He was now 14-9, and I was 11-7. Funny about those numbers. I started out 5-0, and he was 2-5 at the same time. He'd gone 12-4 since then, and I had only won six games against seven losses. Still, I had Whitey's number. Through five innings, we led, 2-1. I came out to pitch in the sixth, threw some warmups, then called time. I was unsteady on my feet. The trainer came out and waved some smelling salts under my nose. I threw two more warmups, said I was okay, and got ready to pitch to Tom Tresh. I looked into the plate, saw Babe Ruth standing there, and called time again. Out came the trainer again, and he led me back to the dugout and into the clubhouse. I was done for the day. And the night. The whole night. The heat had gotten to me. Still, we won. I won. And Whitey's 10-game winning streak at Yankee Stadium was ended.

For all practical purposes, the season was over for us and for me. I had no chance of winning 20 games, and we had no chance of catching the Twins. I did manage to win once more, but I lost two more games and had another pair of no-decisions. It was a tale of two seasons for me: 9-3 before the All-Star Game, and 4-6 after it. I started 34 games, completed nine with three shutouts, but only had 22 decisions. I had 12 no-decisions. Oh, yeah. My ERA. It was 2.60.

The recipe for 20 wins in a season. All I needed was some better fielding and some better hitting by my teammates. If only we could make a trade that would bring that one great hitter to Baltimore.

◆17◆

Teammates:
The Players' Union

Hank Aaron was one of the greatest players to ever play the game of baseball. He was also one of the nicest guys to ever play the game.

When I was with the Atlanta Braves, he came up to me on a couple of occasions and asked me to do a few things for him or the team. He sometimes wanted me to take issues to management. When that happened, I would look at him and start laughing.

"What are you laughing at?" he asked.

"Hank, you're a superstar. If anybody has any pull with this team, it's you. Why don't you go upstairs and tell them what you want? Hell, you can get in trouble instead of me."

He'd always get a big kick out of that. "Well, that's your job."

"I understand that, believe me."

I was the team's union representative. It was my job.

* * *

As for the Major League Baseball Players Association (MLBPA), I really didn't know that much about it when I broke in. In those early years of my career (1957-1964), we had player-representatives on the Orioles. Three of them were outfielders Bob Nieman and Gene Woodling, and pitcher Mike McCormick.

As the seasons went by, I tried to learn as much as I could about the MLBPA and its workings. After all, I was from Detroit, a blue collar city, where unions ruled and one of my closest high school friends was Jimmy Hoffa, Jr. I was steeped in unionism and its benefits, but I didn't know that much about how they worked.

In those early days, players paid two dollars a day in dues to fund the Players' Association and to pay for the MLBPA office and other expenses, including the salaries of our officers and their staff. Judge Robert Cannon ran our organization at that time. I'm calling it an organization instead of a union because under Judge Cannon the MLBPA didn't behave like any union that I'd ever heard of, but more about that later.

In talking with player-reps, I learned more about the MLBPA each year. I talked to them to find out how negotiations with the owners for more meal money, better rooms, and better hotels were going. I learned nothing really about contracts because at that time in baseball the owners had the reserve clause firmly in effect, which really limited the ability of the Players' Association to bargain for them. In fact, all a guy could do was negotiate with the team that had him under contract and if he didn't sign with that team, he went home as a holdout or a retiree. Either that or he'd get lucky and get traded to a team that would meet his price. The only other option was to be released. Then you had some freedom to negotiate with any team that would deal with you. The problem with that was hardly any team would negotiate with a player who was considered to be a real troublemaker.

Sign. Hold out. Retire. Trade. Release. That was the limit. Not a whole heck of a lot you could do, and a lot of the guys were not happy with that kind of setup. We had no voice really, and not much power at that time.

The negotiation meetings were conducted in the off season with the presidents of the two leagues and their attorneys. They would rehash a lot of things. Many of our requests were very minor, like putting a pad up against a wire fence so the player couldn't get his foot caught underneath, padding the walls, making sure there were whirlpools in every dressing room, and other requests like that. They were really just little, rinky-dink things, but that's really all the Players Association could do then. Again, anything pertaining to our contracts or going to a different team, you had to just forget about it.

I didn't have a whole lot of confrontations early in my career with managers or team management about the MLBPA. The managers and coaches pretty much went along with the owners because they were being paid by the owners to do that. The only thing we started to get vocal about was that the managers and coaches were in the players' pension plan and we didn't feel that was right for two reasons. One, they were being paid by management, and two, they weren't members of the MLBPA. We felt the teams that they played for should have them in their own pension plans and be excluded from ours. The managers and coaches did not belong in our union because they were essentially front office personnel. They didn't even follow the guidelines of the contract, such as minimum salary. We had coaches in the Major Leagues, believe it or not, who were getting less than the minimum salary of a player. For some of them, they were only coaching to accrue pension time. But again there wasn't a whole of a lot we could do, as far as the association was concerned, to change things and make them better. We had to do with whatever we could get through negotiations, but again that wasn't much.

Excuse me while I digress, but in order to understand my involvement in the union a little background on the labor movement in Major League Baseball is necessary.

* * *

When professional baseball began back in the 1870s, every player was a free agent as soon as one season ended. He was free to sign with the club of his choosing. The owners called this freedom of movement "revolving" because the players often "revolved" from team "A" to team "B" one year and back to team "A" the next. Sometimes there was a team "C" involved in a player's revolving.

In 1879, William Hulbert, president of the National League and owner of the Chicago team, invented the "reserve clause" for player contracts. He and other owners decided that five players on each team would be put on a list of "protected" players that the other owners would respect; i.e., the other owners wouldn't tamper with these players by offering them contracts at the season's conclusion. This would allow the present team to retain the services of these five players for the next year. A year later the reserve list was increased, and eventually it led to the reserve clause as it was known in the 20th Century.

Naturally, the players resented the reserve clause. Before the owners instituted it, players were free to move about, to sell their services to the highest bidder every year. Salaries began jumping from $500 a season to $1,000 to $2,000 by the late 1870s.

The owners complained bitterly about this inflation. They weren't making all the money; they were being forced to share it with the players. Ticket prices in the National League were set by the league office at 50 cents each in order to keep the "shadier" elements out of the ball parks. At this time, 50 cents was a quarter of a day's pay for a working man. Crowds averaged about 3,000 "kranks" per game for the better teams and a lot less for the poorer clubs.

The Chicago franchise was the most successful club in the early days of baseball, drawing the best attendance in the NL in 1876 with about 110,000 paying spectators in the stands for the year. With a roster of 15 players, it cost Hulbert about $20,000 a year to pay his players. In 1876, his team grossed over $55,000. After other expenses, he was left with a profit of about $20,000. This wasn't enough for him. It was only 30 times as much as the averaging working man, but it wasn't enough for him. Big Bill Hulbert wanted more especially the next year when attendance went down and salaries went up and he made less.

How to get more? was the question. He decided to control the salaries of players, and to do that, he had to control their movement. Thus, the reserve clause.

The players fought back by jumping to a rival league, the American Association. The pay was less in the AA, but they still had the freedom of movement. Eventually, the owners in the AA joined their brethren in the NL and smaller circuits in an agreement that led to the formation of a new entity that was known as Organized Baseball. Signers to this compact agreed to respect the reserve clauses of other teams.

This led to a new league that was "player-friendly" called the

Union Association. In the UA, the players were free again. The problem was that their freedom led to the destruction of the UA.

The players didn't give up. They formed the National Brotherhood of Professional Baseball Players in 1885, and this led to yet another league being formed, this one called the Players League. The owners in this circuit agreed to pay players large salaries and to share the profits with them. They problem was there were no profits, and after two seasons, the PL folded. Unfortunately, the PL took the AA down with it, which not only gave the National League more power over the players but it cut the number of decent paying jobs for players.

The formation of the American League brought new hope to the players in 1900. When the NL owners refused to recognize the new circuit as a major league on a par with the senior loop, the AL owners declared war and started signing NL players to serious money contracts. The NL surrendered a year later and peace was restored. So was the reserve clause.

Over the decades, the players made more attempts to group themselves into some sort of organization to combat the owners. There was the League Protective Players' Association (1900-1902); the Baseball Players' Fraternity (1912-1918); and the American Baseball Guild (1946). All of these failed. The last of these might have succeeded if the founder of it, Robert Murphy, hadn't made one fatal blunder; he threatened to have the players strike before actually taking a strike vote.

Murphy was a Boston lawyer who had worked as a field examiner for the National Labor Relations Board. He chose the Pittsburgh Pirates as the team to organize first because Steeltown is a blue collar city with a strong labor movement. He had a list of items on his collective bargaining agenda. These included:

1. Putting an end to the hated reserve clause.
2. Arbitration over salaries and all other player-owner disputes.
3. Guaranteeing players a share in their purchase price.
4. The institution of Spring Training pay.
5. A minimum salary of $7,500 per season.
6. A more equitable contractual arrangement than the

one then in use, where owners could cancel contracts on
10 days notice while dissatisfied players had no similar
mechanism that they could employ.

For 1946, these were pretty reasonable demands. Murphy's problem was he threatened to strike without having the Pittsburgh players solidly behind him. When he took a vote, the players voted 20-16 to strike, but they needed 24 yes votes in order to do it. Murphy's attempt to organize them into a union faded into history, but it did achieve some of its goals.

The owners recognized quickly that the players were disgruntled with the way things were, so they authorized their commissioner, A.B. "Happy" Chandler, to choose a player-rep from each of the 16 Major League clubs to discuss working conditions with the owners. They talked about travels arrangements and money, exhibition game pay, and a pension plan. The owners made concessions to placate the players. They instituted a pension plan, modified the waiver rule, and started paying players for spring training games, a practice that became known as "Murphy money" in remembrance of the man who tried in vain to organize them into a union.

At this same time, the owners also established another system whereby the players in each league elected a player to represent them on Major League Baseball's ruling body, the Executive Council. These players had no voting power, but they could submit grievances and other proposals to the committee through the commissioner. The Council would then discuss them at their regular sessions.

These two systems of representation were steps in the right direction for the players and decent concessions by the owners, but they weren't enough. Not yet.

The representation system worked rather well for several years. The players were happy, and the owners were happy. Things were getting done — slowly — very slowly. The players griped, and the owners listened — and sometimes they acted on the complaints and requests. Despite this congenial relationship, the players still didn't have a collective bargaining unit.

The players gradually became dissatisfied with the system,

and in 1953, they hired J. Norman Lewis to be their legal advisor. The owners responded with fits of anger that ranged from naive bewilderment to angry suspicion that the players were contemplating the formation of a union. The player-reps avowed that Lewis was merely there to consult with them on the legalities of various issues; he was not their representative. Some owners knew better.

In the short time that he was working for the players, Lewis made one major contribution to the players' lives. He helped them develop a revised pension plan that actually was beneficial to the retired players.

The owners decided that the players were right; they did need a legal advisor. They had the commissioner bring in Judge Robert Cannon to fill this need once Lewis was gone. Cannon held that position for a decade until the players figured out that he was a Judas in the camp.

Finally, the Major League Baseball Players' Association was born at a meeting of the player-representatives during the All-Star break in Cleveland. The date was July 12, 1954. The players insisted that their new organization was not then and never would become a union. They described it as a players' social or fraternal order.

And it was until I became actively involved with MLBPA.

* * *

As my playing years went on, I became more and more involved with the MLBPA.

My first experience as a team player-representative was in 1964 with the Baltimore Orioles. Mike McCormick was the O's player-rep at that time, and I was the alternate. When he was traded August 4, 1965 to the Washington Senators, I inherited the job automatically. Then the players voted for me to finish McCormick's term that year.

At that time, there was a grass routes movement led by Jim Bunning, Robin Roberts and some of the veteran ballplayers, to find a strong leader to head the Players' Association. Judge

Cannon was the early frontrunner, but we later found out that he was working both sides of the street, so to speak. Cannon was supposed to be working for our benefit, but he was actually doing the owners' bidding by keeping the MLBPA as nothing more than what it was in its original form and purpose. This double-dipping on his part disqualified him. He was taken off our list.

I was on the search committee for the MLBPA. Some of the people that came up as potentially strong leaders were senators and congressmen. Others were lawyers and businessmen. We went over and over a lot of names, and the one name that kept popping up was that of Marvin Miller, who at that time was a union negotiator. We did a lot of research on Marvin, and we finally hired him in 1966 to head the Players' Association.

In getting to know Marvin over the years, I found him to be just one tremendous individual, both personally and profession-ally. He was frustrated with the owners and the way they negotiated. I felt so sorry for this guy when he took the job. He had no idea what he was getting himself into, but the job he subsequently did was simply masterful.

Before Marvin came aboard, we kept asking and negotiating for better accommodations in baseball. I've already mentioned these situations when we wanted extra meal money and better hotels and different things, but for the most part traveling was okay.

Travel in the Majors wasn't like the minor leagues where there were some really nasty hotels. I thank God that I only played a few weeks in the minors because I saw what it was like, and after being in the Majors first for two months and then going to the minors, I appreciated the Majors a whole lot more. We stayed at the better hotels. The ball club would pay for your room, then give you meal money on the road. But out of that per diem, you'd have to tip the clubhouse man after you were done with a series. The laundry would come out of that and other in-cidentals like telephone calls. And a lot of the guys did a lot of drinking, so the liquor came out of that, too. I was not one of those guys who was in a bar every night. I spent my money on movies and popcorn and probably spent more money than anyone else in baseball on those two things.

Again, when I started back in 1957, I believe we were getting eight dollars a day for meal money. It started to go up as time went on, especially when the better television contracts started to occur. That led to better equipment in the clubhouse and whatever else we felt we needed to better ourselves. The MLBPA brought up these matters whenever we negotiated new contracts with the owners. And whatever we agreed upon was usually locked in for two, three or four years; whatever the contract was for. Those early years, of course, we had longer contracts. The team locked you in whether you wanted to or not. Again, they controlled your life and your career with those contracts. There really wasn't a whole lot we could do about it until later, when the union got stronger.

Back to the meal money. When I got out of the game in 1974, we were up to $20 a day. Now it's close to $90 a day. As if these guys playing today and making a heck of a lot of money really need all that meal money. I know it costs a heck of a lot more today to eat and eat well, but $90 is a lot of money for three meals a day. I don't think they need all that meal money to live on, but again, it's a different game today and with all that money out there, the owners can afford to pay it.

I still say it's ridiculous. You know, the whole game of baseball, from the meal money to the clubhouses to the parks, it's all drastically changed, and unfortunately, I don't think it's changed for the better.

* * *

A s time went on, things progressed for the MLBPA A lot of people called it a union, but it really wasn't a regular union. We weren't affiliated with the A.F.L.-C.I.O. or anyone else. It was just the ballplayers. and we had to — on our own — do what we could to better ourselves.

As I stated earlier, when I first got into baseball, I really didn't know a heck of a lot about the Players' Association and how it operated until I got involved as a player-rep and tried to solve the problems that came up between a ballplayer and the team. That's how I learned about the real inner workings of baseball. I had a firsthand opportunity to get to know the players involved and also management. Most of the time, a situation was ironed out long before it became too serious simply by bringing it to the attention of management. But if the problem wasn't solved that easily, then we'd have to deal with the front office directly to get the matter resolved. If that didn't get the problem solved, then we'd have to take it to the director of the Players' Association, who at that time was Judge Cannon.

My first manager in baseball was Paul Richards. He hated to fly, so the Orioles took a lot of train trips, which I absolutely hated, because most of our opponents were within an overnight train ride away from Baltimore. I don't think anybody on the team really liked them. It was even worse for me because, as a rookie, I would have to sleep over the wheels of the damn train. You talk about some tough times trying to get some sleep! It was absolutely ridiculous because we'd ride 12-14 hours on a trip, and I'd have to listen to that damn clickety-clack, clickety-clack of the wheels hitting the breaks in the rails which was always louder over the wheels. It was just terrible.

The players who voted for their own player-rep expected them to do the job for them, but usually there wasn't much thanks given to the rep by the players after he solved a problem for them. It was basically a totally thankless job.

As a player, I really wasn't impatient with the MLBPA because it seemed like we could only get so much at a time from the owners. It was frustrating, but that's the way it was. The player-rep would come back to the rest of the players after negotiating with the owners and either have good news or not. Mostly, we would be told that it was a never-ending battle with the owners to get what we wanted. I think for the most part, my teammates understood.

Progress was slow back then. It was a heck of a lot slower than it is today, where it seems the players have almost more power than the owners. Or their agents do.

My teammates knew that the owners basically dumped on us when they had the chance, which was most of the time. Whenever they did give you something, they thought they were doing you such a big favor, and usually it was just a pittance as to what they could have done for us.

That would change with Marvin Miller, but it even took a while with him. Hell, the owners never even showed up at the meetings when contract negotiations came up. It was the two league president. Joe Cronin was American League president, and Warren Giles was National League president. Of course, each league president had an attorney present, and that was it. The owners didn't even give a damn enough to be there. They knew they didn't have to be. They were in control at that time, and nothing else mattered enough to them. No owners ever showed up at the meetings, even though we, the player-reps, asked them to be there.

It was a very frustrating time, and it led to a search committee where we screened a lot of men and eventually settled on Marvin Miller. He was the best choice we could have made.

* * *

One of the most prominent player-reps in my early years was Jim Bunning. After leaving baseball, he became a congressman, then a United States Senator from Kentucky. He was a big man in the Players' Association and did what he could to make things better for the players.

Robin Roberts was another as was Yogi Berra of the Yanks. Some of the games other big stars, like Willie Mays and Hank Aaron, were never player-reps, for whatever reason. But we had some damn good people, and thank God for these guys who had enough foresight to realize that we needed good representation to see if we could get something better than we were getting from the owners.

When I took the player-rep job for the O's, I was only 26 years old, but I was a veteran at that point, having been in the Major Leagues since I was 18. When I inherited the job from Mike McCormick, I really got involved with the activities of the Players' Association. I wanted to find out what really made it tick and how we could do things to better ourselves.

It was a very exasperating experience, getting the crumbs off the table while the owners continued to screw us and do very well for themselves. We thought we were dealing with fair people, but they had no feeling for us. Even though the owners put money in our pension plan, they made it seem like they thought they were doing us a favor. Anytime they ever gave us anything, they always made us feel like that. That just made me very angry because the players were really the ones who were responsible for baseball being the game that it was. It was still considered the national pastime then. We put ourselves on the field and were responsible for drawing the fans into the park but the owners were getting all of the fruits of our labor and we were just their as pawns. It was really sad.

The owners thought of me as a maverick and a total union man. I thought that was unfair. The owners, in their own way of thinking, thought I was against baseball and that I only thought of myself, which was totally untrue. Whatever I did was not for me, but for the players and for the good of baseball. But I was stuck with that label with every team I was on. I worked hard for the teammates and for my employers, the owners of my respective teams. I tried to solve as many problems as I could without taking them up to the front office and management. I would try to settle the issue in the clubhouse, and I would wager a guess that I did that probably 95% of the time. But again, it was a very thankless job. If you did your job, that was what you were supposed to do and you're teammates never even said thank you. Of course, the owners didn't like player-reps, and a lot of them, including myself, were traded because of the job we held.

Looking back on it, I don't give a damn what they thought of me. I did what I had to do for the players and for the game of baseball during my era. Unfortunately, what we did then set the stage for what is going on now, and even more unfortunately, the ballplayers of today don't give a damn about what happened over 30 years ago. And that's what really upsets me, and at the same time makes me very sad. We set the table for what is happening today. It was our blood, sweat, and tears that went into making the MLBPA what it is today, a very powerful organization that has done much for the present day ballplayer. The tragedy is the

MLBPA is now a union that overall cares nothing about us, the people that made it all possible for them.

Just what should today's union do for us? Well, one thing would be to up our pension. There are some of the old-timers — guys who played before my era even — who are only drawing $300-$400, maybe $500 a month. Some of those players are really having a hard time financially. Pensions for today's players — those who have retired in the last two decades or so — are forever escalating, and right now some are over $140,000 a year. The present-day ballplayer — unless he's an idiot who blew all that big money he made as a player — doesn't need this kind of money to retire on. The guys from my era and before my time really need a little more. We need the present-day player to take some time and think about his situation today and just exactly the circumstances that made it possible for him to make the kind of living he's making playing a kid's game — and that's what it really is, isn't it? It's a game, but a game that is a very big business. It's the same game that has been played for more than 100 years. It's the same game that the ball-players in the late 1950s and 1960s were playing, only for much less. We are not asking for the kind of money the players are making now, but we want some recognition and some of the financial rewards for what we did because of the sacrifices that we made. It's just a sin that today's ballplayers can't take care of their own. That means us, the guys who made it possible for them to live like kings.

* * *

To put things in perspective, the first contract I signed out of high school in 1957 with the Orioles was for $4,000. Anything over that amount at that time in baseball called for the player to stay with that team for two years. So everybody who scouted me offered me the same money, $4,000, and that's what I ended up signing for. In my first full year with the Orioles, in 1958, I was 10-10. The minimum salary was $6,000, and that's what I made my first full year. The following year, 1959, I jumped up to $8,000, and I won 15 games. Then I finally made

$10,000 a year.

It was funny that I got that kind of increase in pay each year because a player had to fight for a raise of $2,000 a year. Not just the younger players or the average players that had been around for a few years. This even applied to some of the stars of the game. Granted, they got their money, but it sometimes came after a lot of haggling. As an example, Sandy Koufax and Don Drysdale threatened not to play in the mid-1960s unless they received what they thought they should get. They finally did. Good for them! But that's how hard it was before the Players' Association got strong.

When I was first traded, I was making $25,000 a year, but that was after nine years in the Majors, counting that rookie season when I only made four grand. I was winning almost 15 games a year at that point, and I still had to battle and almost threaten to quit before I was given a lousy $5,000-raise. That would equate to $4- or $5-million dollars today! I made $30,000 that year and in 1967 received a $2,000-raise. That year I won 16 games which got me a $5,000-raise. When I went to the Braves during the 1968 season, I ended up winning 10 games and got an $8,000-raise, if I remember correctly. So I was up to roughly $45,000 a year. The next year I made $50,000. Then my contract was sold again, and I won 10 games in a half year to get another raise of $5,000 to put me at $55,000. I won 17 games two years in a row and was rewarded with a $5,000-raise each year to put me at $65,000 for my last year in baseball. After a bad season, I took a pay cut, which I never got because I was released before the season started, but that's another story.

Contracts were pretty much black and white back then. For example, in 1963, I had one incentive clause in my contract. I had a chance to pick up an extra $5,000 because Baltimore general manager Lee McPhail and I had an impasse with my contract. Of course back then, you either signed or you went home and didn't get paid. McPhail didn't want me to be a holdout, so he put a $5,000 incentive clause in my contract that stated, if I would conduct myself off the field in a gentlemanly manner, then I would collect the bonus. In other words, I couldn't get into any fights in a bar or get stopped by the police or whatever. It was just an idiotic thing that we both agreed on for me to make an extra $5,000. Why he didn't want to put it in my contract to begin with is beyond me. But it was left up to the discretion of the manager whether I fulfilled my end of the deal or not.

Billy Hitchcock managed the O's in 1963. When the last day of the season came around, I felt I deserved the money because nothing had happened during the course of the year. I never got into trouble with anybody for anything. But before I could meet with Hitchcock about the clause in my contract, he was fired! So I was thinking, Oh, man! Now I have to ask him if I deserve the $5,000. I knew he wouldn't be in a good frame of mind to talk about something like this, so I was at his mercy when I walked into his office.

"Billy, I just heard the news, and I'm sorry."

"Yeah, I know," he said. "I feel bad."

"By the way, I have that clause in my contract that says, if I was a good guy during the season, I would get an extra $5,000."

"Well, do you think you deserve it?"

"Well, Billy, I'll tell you what. I know you're going through a tough time right now, but you know this means a lot to me. However, I'm just going to walk out right now and just forget this conversation ever took place. It's just not worth it."

So I started to walk out of the office, and he called me back. "I'm sorry, Milt. There won't be any problem."

So I got the $5,000, but to be at somebody else's discretion as to whether or not I deserved the money was just ridiculous.

I'm not a big fan of incentive clauses. I can't see a guy, if he makes $3 or $4-million dollars a year, having a $50,000 incentive clause if he makes the All-Star Team or $25,000 more if he gets up to bat 500 times. Hell, these guys can go to a baseball card show and make that kind of money. I don't like incentive clauses.

* * *

When we negotiated back then, it was a lot different than it is today. Some teams, if they had fast ball pitchers, would raise the height of the pitching mound. I'll use the Dodgers as an example, whose staff consisted of predominantly fastball pitchers. Their mound would be probably 10 inches higher than the Giants, who had mostly breaking ball pitchers. Their mound would be very low, because it would benefit them. Dodger Stadium was very unique. The Dodgers had a lot of switch-hitting speedsters like Maury Wills, Wes Parker, Jim Lefebvre, and maybe a few others who bunted a lot and beat out grounders into the holes. The Dodgers would fix the infield foul lines, making them a little higher so that when they bunted the ball would stay fair instead of rolling foul. What they did, was turn the foul lines in to help their team. They would also water the hell out of the area around the plate, so that when they hit or bunted, the chance of them getting on base was a lot better than the visiting team that came in, only because the Dodgers knew about it.

These were some of the things the MLBPA felt it had to get resolved in negotiations. We wanted to make the pitching mound standard with every team. We didn't want a team to be able to alter its field so that the home team had a definite advantage. There were really a lot of games that were being played back then by different teams to get an advantage. I'm sure some of that is still going on today, but back then, it wasn't watched as closely as it is today. The home field advantage meant a lot.

The Dodgers of that time were built on speed. They would water the rest of the infield to make it very hard so that ground balls would skip into the outfield. Of course, you could say that both teams could play that same game, but it was an advantage for the Dodgers. Their hitters knew ahead of time what the infield conditions were. They would slap the ball on the ground, and it would go through the infield for a base hit. On the other side, a lot of teams who would have power hitters, would soak the heck out of the grass to keep the ball from shooting through the infield, giving their infielders a better chance to throw out hitters.

It was just amazing, the different techniques that were used by different clubs to help themselves or to hinder the visiting team. It was just amazing that every team was doing something like that. So a lot of times we were negotiating for that, to standardize the playing field. Now if we could only standardized the pension for the old-timers …

Strategy:
Conference on the Mound

Marvin Miller was an unbelievable negotiator. He was poker-faced and never raised his voice as he brought up points on matters that we needed to know and get done. He very seldom ever backed off, but after meetings, he would say that he had never experienced the kind of negotiations like those going on in baseball back then. When it came down to the major points like contracts and how ballplayers could improve their working conditions, the talk just fell on deaf ears. If the owners of today were to look back at the minutes of the meetings between the union and the two league presidents, they might be astounded by them because some of the things we proposed in the late 1960s could have prevented the chaos that abounds in baseball today.

We put free agency on the table. It was free agency in something of a restricted form. If after five years in the Majors, a player was, let's say, the number four outfielder or the number 11 pitcher on a team and he believed he could play every day with another team, then we proposed that he should be allowed to sell his services elsewhere. Also, the ball club losing him would have the first right of refusal on any deal he made with another team. For example, if I was the 11th pitcher for the O's and felt I wasn't being given the opportunity I deserved and wanted to go to the Yankees to be a starting pitcher, the Yanks could negotiate with me, but the Orioles had the first right of refusal. If they matched what the Yankees wanted to give me, then I'd have to stay in Baltimore. This was only one form of free agency we proposed.

Another proposal was that a 10-year player, if he played the last five years with the same team, could be free to go where he wanted to, which essentially was the right to become a free agent. The ball club that the player came from would have to relinquish a player or a draft choice, the latter because the draft was becoming more of a tool in our negotiations with the owners.

But no matter what we brought up, the owners always told us to go to Hell. We thought we had the reserve clause in our favor with this proposal because the owners would still retain control of player movement, which would continue to stabilize the game. But the owners were exempt from anti-trust laws, so they never gave our proposals any consideration. This was why the first few years with Marvin Miller at the helm of the MLBPA were still so very frustrating.

Another example concerned meal money. We walked in on the first day of the meeting one year and proposed increasing per diem from $18 to $20 a day. The attorneys for both leagues said that was acceptable and we went on to talk about other things. This was a Monday. The next day we walked in, and the first thing out of the attorneys' mouths was that they were taking the $2-meal money increase back. The owners decided they didn't want to approve the increase. That was a load of fertilizer.

There was still really no negotiating like normal companies and their unions take part in. With the Major League owners, it wasn't even close to being that way. We'd accept things one day, and they'd take it away the next. It was just so frustrating for years trying to get something done with the owners that made sense. With the real meat and potato issues, the owners would just look at us and tell us to forget about it because they didn't want to talk about it. They had the reserve clause, so we couldn't do anything; and if we didn't like the way things were, it was tough cookies or go home. And as far as the commissioner's part in matters, he was never involved in any of the talks and was therefore a non-factor.

* * *

fter we hired Marvin Miller and he went to a couple of negotiating sessions with the league presidents and their two attorneys, he'd come out of meetings shaking his head. He'd say in all the years that he'd been a mediator-negotiator that he'd never been a part of anything like those meetings. He was just flabbergasted by the way the owners negotiated. They'd give you something on Monday, take it away on Tuesday, give it back on Wednesday, then modify it on Thursday. They were absolutely ridiculous, and Marvin found out that you could never really take their word for anything. He was finding out in a hurry what the rest of us knew all along.

The small things would really be a hassle. The big issues? The owners — or I should say, their attorneys — didn't even want to discuss them. Free agency was out as far as they were concerned. Upping salaries or raising the minimum salary was something they didn't want to consider. Any issue that was major, they would just tell us politely to go to Hell. That was really a shame because if they'd have listened to us back then — in the late 1960s and early 1970s — if they'd listened to what we were proposing, it would have prevented a lot of the crap that is still happening in baseball today. I don't say that because I'm pro-union as opposed to pro-management. It's just too damn bad that there wasn't more cooperation. A lot of problems could have prevented. But it's hard to break bad habits, and the owners had a lot of them. It caught up with them. I don't believe any of the player-reps — or Marvin Miller — wanted to go through all the bull we did. But we couldn't tell management anything because the owners knew it all. That's all right, I guess. I'm not involved any more. But back then, things could have been so much different if the owners wouldn't have been so nearsighted. With a little vision, I really believe, we could have not only made things better for us, but we could have made it better for future generations of Major League Baseball players.

But the owners remained in charge. They didn't want to change. They refused to acknowledge our demands to make any changes. But their time would come, though, when radical things, like strikes would occur which would force them to do some serious re-evaluating.

* * *

O ne of the big issues, other than free agency and more money and a few other bones of contention that we wanted to change, was playing so many doubleheaders. Playing two might have been great for Ernie Banks, but I think even he would tell you that they were a great big pain in the ass.

A couple of teams — the Boston Red Sox and the Houston Astros — would even play day-night doubleheaders, which were truly ridiculous. You'd have to get to the ballpark at 10:00 o'clock in the morning to play the day game, then sit around in the clubhouse for two or three hours, waiting for the second game preparations to begin. The fans would come in, usually around 7:00 in the evening, and the game would start at 8:00. The second game would end around 10:30 to 11:00, if it only went nine innings. If it was extra innings, we might be at the park until 1:00 or 2:00 in the morning. That's 12- to 16-hour workday. Now how many regular working guys would put up that without some kind of compensation or other consideration?

And regular doubleheaders on Sundays, for instance? If they were being played at Wrigley Field, we'd have to report at 9:00 a.m. because game time was at noon. They would go anywhere from six to seven hours, if both games finished in nine innings and the Cubs won both of them in low-scoring pitchers' battles. But if the visiting team won both and the Cubs and their opponents were scoring a lot, which meant a lot of pitching changes, then we could be at the park until after sundown, which could be around 9:00 o'clock.. That would be another 12-hour workday. How long would the UAW put up with those hours?

Not only did it make sense to the players not to play doubleheaders, but it made a lot of sense financially to the owners. They could make more money if they scheduled more single games.

The Dodgers were the first to recognize this fact that it would be better for them not to schedule doubleheaders and that it sure as Hell would be better for their players. Of course, their management didn't think of this before they did it. It didn't dawn on them that playing single games instead of doubleheaders was better for the team's treasury and the team's won-lost record until after they had been doing it for a few years. Then they figured it out by accident.

The Dodgers began life in Los Angeles much the same as they had been doing in Brooklyn. Night games during the week with an occasional twi-night doubleheader, and regular doubleheaders on Sundays. Gradually, they went away from this sort of scheduling. By the time they moved into Dodger Stadium in 1962, they began noticing that attendance was on the rise and that their players played better when they didn't play so many doubleheaders in the daylight. When they won it all in 1963, they put two and two together and came up with the idea that doubleheaders were bad for the bottom line and this motivated them to keep doubleheaders off the home schedule.

Players on other teams realized that playing so many doubleheaders was wearing them down as the season wore on and that playing fewer doubleheaders would save them a little more energy for the pennant chase in September. We told this to the owners. It fell on deaf ears at first, but finally the owners phased out the day-night doubleheaders. The owners listened a little more as time went on and realized they could make more money just scheduling single games. Now teams only play doubleheaders when they have a game to make up to complete the championship season schedule.

It's kind of funny now because there are some fans of the game who would like to see more doubleheaders today to sort of revitalize the interest in baseball. That's a lot of nostalgia crap as far as I'm concerned. Baseball can probably do a lot of other things to make it more attractive to the fans which would make them want to come out in greater numbers to the ball parks around the Major Leagues.

* * *

T he owners would not budge on the reserve clause. They would not budge on free agency or any of the other issues that we proposed so the ballplayer would gain a little more freedom or make a little more money. The owners just flat out refused anything major that we wanted.

Of course, Marvin Miller kept working hard for us. He kept pushing ahead and got very frustrated. I loved the guy, but to the owners, he was just a big pain in the neck. But we finally had someone who would stand up to the them and keep moving forward.

In 1957, when I broke in, there were only 16 teams in Major League Baseball compared to 30 in 1999, which is absolutely ludicrous. Back then, most of the teams were owned by one man who had all the stock in a team or a huge majority of it as opposed to today's owners which consist of ownership groups and large corporations.

I recall owners like Tom Yawkey of the Boston Red Sox and Philip K. Wrigley of the Chicago Cubs. Wrigley was a powerful owner, who was very sympathetic to the players — as long as you didn't try and show him up or talk about him. Yawkey was something of a bigot as witnessed by the Red Sox being one of the last two teams to integrate racially.

Peter O'Malley of the Dodgers was one of the power-houses. He saw the money light and moved the team to Los Angeles where he made nothing but money.

Mr. Galbreath of the Pittsburgh Pirates owned a lot of race horses, which was fine for the owners to have but not for the players.

Then there was Cal Griffith of the Washington Senators and later the Minnesota Twins. He was very, very cheap. He didn't want to pay his players anything.

Spike Briggs owned the Detroit Tigers at that time. He was like Tom Yawkey of Boston in that he was something of bigot.

Horace Stoneham held ownership of the New York-then-San Francisco Giants. Stoneham was not a bad guy, but he was an alcoholic.

Larry McPhail controlled the New York Yankees, then they became the first team to be owned by a major corporation when the Columbia Broadcasting System (CBS) bought the franchise in the early 1960s.

Ownership of the Chicago White Sox was a family affair, passed down from the founding father, Charles Comiskey, Sr. The Comiskeys learned their lessons well from the "Old Roman" who stinginess was a prime cause for his players throwing in with gamblers who bribed them to blow the 1919 World Series.

Then there was old Charley Finley with A's in Kansas City then later in Oakland. He was a true maverick in baseball, but he was also very cheap. Sounds like a pattern, doesn't it? Anyway, Finley didn't want to pay his players anything, even after they won the World Series three times in a row. Finley was extremely tight with the dollar, and he had so much ego that he had to show everybody that he was the boss. He really made enemies of all his players. Finley was very innovative though, but he was, quite unfortunately, way before his time, just like Bill Veeck, Jr., was with the White Sox.

Bill Veeck, Jr., took the Sox over from the Comiskeys in the late 1950s. He was one of the nicest men I've ever met. He did a lot for the game. Unfortunately, the other owners saw him as somewhat of a maverick with crazy ideas. Time has proven that he was a sly fox when it came to promoting baseball because now just about everybody is doing the crazy things that he did to get people into the ballpark and to spread the good news about baseball. Veeck came from a true baseball family as his father was a long-time general manager of the Chicago Cubs. The Veecks helped to plant the ivy at Wrigley Field.

August Busch of the St. Louis Cardinals was very strong within the owners group and very vocal. A beer baron first, a baseball owner second. He treated his brewers better than his batters.

Bill DeWitt was top man with the Cincinnati Reds. He dealt Frank Robinson to the Orioles for me, one of the most famous trades in baseball. He was cheap, offering me only a measly $2,000-raise after trading for me.

The reserve clause in baseball at that time was the most powerful thing the owners had. When you signed your contract, the club ended up owning you lock, stock, and barrel. That was something that we had to correct. It was a big challenge, but all of us associated with the union felt we could do it. We had to. Otherwise, the owners would just continue to run everything and the players would essentially continue to be their puppets. It would and continues to be a heck of a fight.

Part Three

CINCINNATI

&

ATLANTA

Balk:
The Trade

T he Orioles were coming back from the last road trip of 1965. General manager Lee McPhail was with us. During the flight from California, Steve Barber came up to the front of the plane, where I happened to be at the time. He confronted McPhail and manager Hank Bauer with a demand to be traded as soon as possible after the season was over. He said that he didn't want to stay with Baltimore any longer, that he didn't like the team, that he didn't like the city, and that he didn't like the fans. He really wanted out of Baltimore.

That pretty much summed up the whole conversation Barber had with Bauer and McPhail. For those of us who heard their exchange, it was pretty much felt that Steve would be gone by the next season. I know I thought he was sure to be gone. Why would you want to keep someone with no desire at all to be a member of the team?

During the course of the next few months, trade rumors popped up about this player and that player, and especially about Barber. Nothing much was being said, except that the Orioles said they were looking to do something, if they could.

Then came December and the players' union meetings in Miami. I was the player-rep for the Orioles, so I was there. I'd planned to spend the first couple of days by myself before my wife Carole would join me when the meetings were concluded. We wanted to go to Key Biscayne to rent a home, if we could, for spring training. She had called me a couple of nights before she was to come down to Florida to tell me that she'd read a lot of rumors in the newspapers, claiming that I would be traded. I figured I wouldn't be traded because Barber had shot his mouth off on the plane back in September and he'd be the one to go. Even so, I asked Carole where the rumors said I would be traded, and she said the San Francisco Giants. I told her I'd see her in a couple of days and to keep me informed of what was going on.

The player-reps were staying at the Fountain Blue Hotel. The owners and general managers were also meeting at this time. That night I as I was leaving the hotel to go out for dinner, I met Bauer and McPhail as they were walking in. I went up to them and said, "Hey, guys, I just heard from wife, and she said there are a lot of rumors that I'm going to be traded. You know, I really don't want to be traded. I like it in Baltimore. Steve Barber is the one who said he wants to be traded and he said it very vehemently."

"Don't you worry about a thing," McPhail said. "You're the mainstay of our pitching staff, and there's no way that we're going to trade you."

I felt a lot better at that point and went out for dinner.

Carole came down a couple of days later, and we looked at houses in Key Biscayne for spring training. One morning it was really rainy in Miami, so we decided to go to a movie. We saw *The Cincinnati Kid* starring Steve McQueen. The following day we returned to Baltimore.

The day after I got back, Harry Dalton, who would be taking over as general manager for McPhail, called me. He said that I had been traded to the Cincinnati Reds. I was just dumbfounded and very upset. I had just been told a couple of days earlier that I wouldn't be going anywhere, that I was the cornerstone of the pitching staff. I didn't like it, but that was baseball.

But why me and not Barber? I honestly don't know. I can speculate that it was because I was the player-rep and I was just beginning to stir the cauldron of player-owner relations, but that was never mentioned to me in any conversation I had with the Baltimore or the Cincinnati front office people. More than likely, the Reds wanted me because of my history as a pitcher was better than Barber's. As for the Orioles letting me go? In baseball, if you want a superstar in a trade, then you have to give up a superstar or at least two potential superstars in exchange. Robinson for me was considered an even trade at the time it was made.

The trade was basically a one-for-one deal, involving Frank

Robinson and me. Relief pitcher Jack Baldschun and utility guy Dick Simpson were also involved, but Robinson and I were the principals. It's a funny thing about that trade. Just a week earlier, the Orioles had shipped Norm Siebern to the Angels for Simpson, and a few days later, Jackie Brandt and Darold Knowles were sent to Philadelphia for Baldschun. Then they were packaged with me for Robinson. But that's baseball.

Obviously, getting traded for a player of Robinson's caliber made me feel a little better. Not a whole lot better, but a little. So I was flown to Cincinnati about a month later to meet the press and to talk to everybody. I didn't like the city. I guess I was just bitter about the trade, and at that point, I didn't like anything about Cincinnati or anyone with the Reds management. I spent a couple of days there, and I just didn't care for it. I went home. Back to Baltimore. And waited.

The contract finally came from the Reds. They offered me the same money I'd made the year before. What a crock! The Reds had just traded superstar Frank Robinson for me. The same money? That really made me mad. I told the Reds that since they'd traded Robinson for me, then they must really want me. But now they were offering me the same money that I'd made the year before with Baltimore. I sent the contract back with a nasty note that I wouldn't accept their terms and that they should re-evaluate their offer, then get back to me. About a week later, I got another contract with a raise of $2,000. That was just another slap in the face as far as I was concerned. After more negotiating, we finally agreed on a raise.

At that time, Major League Baseball had no free agency, no arbitration, no nothing. A player either signed a contract or he stayed home and held out. Considering the pay scale back then, getting five grand more wasn't all that bad of a deal. Considering, of course, that I didn't have an agent to bargain for me.

* * *

The Reds trained in Tampa, while the Orioles still trained in Miami. The first time the O's came to Tampa, a newspaperman asked me if I would mind having my picture taken with Frank Robinson for the AP wire. I told him that it would be okay with me. Hell, the trade was done and I had to go on with business. About a half hour later, the same guy came back to me with a sheepish look on his face. He told me that Robinson didn't want to be in a photograph with me. That incident really soured me on Robinson. Who in the hell did he think he was? I did get even with him a few years later. But that's another story.

All and all, Cincinnati was not very friendly to me until I received a letter from George and Stella Batsakes, a Greek couple who lived in Cincinnati. They told me if I ever needed anything that they would be more than happy to help me. They offered to show me around Cincinnati. I thought that was very, very nice. I did take them up on their offer, and we became very good friends. They really helped out there because I had absolutely no one else to turn to.

The fans weren't very friendly to me because I had been traded for their hero, Frank Robinson. It was extremely unfair of them to treat me that way because it wasn't my fault, but every time I walked out to the mound in Cincinnati, they booed me. I thought that was really lousy. Fans are supposed to support the home team, but those fans were totally against me.

The Reds had won the pennant in 1961 and had been over .500 every year since. In 1965, Jim Maloney and Sammy Ellis were 20-game winners, but the rest of the staff was mediocre at best. Offensively, the Reds were explosive, scoring a league-leading 825 runs and banging out 183 homers, while topping the National League with a team batting average of .273. The everyday lineup for the Reds consisted of Johnny Edwards behind the plate; an infield of Tony Perez, first base, Pete Rose, second base, Leo Cardenas, shortstop, and Tommy Helms, third base; and an outfield of Deron Johnson, Vada Pinson, and Tommy Harper. With all that firepower, Cincinnati's management figured they could spare an aging outfielder if they could get a topnotch starter in return who could put them over the top in the pennant race. Robinson was the old guy at 30, and I was the arm they figured would do the job for them.

Robinson wasn't the only old face to depart Cincinnati after

1965. The Reds replaced manager Dick Sisler with Don Heffner. Sisler had been a winner and was at the helm when the Reds went to the wire with the St. Louis Cardinals and Philadelphia Phillies in 1964. Heffner was an old-timer who was nicknamed "The Jeep" because of the way he was built, but he had no Major League managing experience.

The weather delayed the start of our season by four days. My NL debut was also put off. I finally got my chance to strut my stuff on April 21 against the Pirates. Of course, I faced their ace who happened to be Bob Veale, a really nice guy who was also a really tough competitor. He out-dueled me, 2-1, as the Pirates scored the winning run on a squeeze bunt in the sixth.

Six days later I went up against the Giants in San Francisco. I was cruising along through four innings with a 6-0 lead when the roof fell in. I gave up one run before Willie McCovey cleared the bases with a grand slam homer. Out I came after four and two-thirds for a no-decision. We held on to win, but it only raised our team record to 3-8. By the numbers, it was already looking like a very long season for the team and for me.

The Dodgers had one of most potent rotations in baseball in the mid-1960s. Sandy Koufax, Don Drysdale, Claude Osteen, Johnny Podres. For 1966, they added a kid named Don Sutton. At 21 years old, he reminded me a lot of me. Brash, good fast ball, and more than willing to knock down a hitter whenever the occasion called for it. He was my mound opponent the first time I ever faced the Dodgers. I gave up four hits and three walks in seven innings. Sutton was just as tough. The difference was he scattered our five hits, while I gave up three of their hits and a walk in the same inning. The result was an LA win, 3-0.

That loss dropped our record to 4-11. We were only a half game ahead of the absolutely pathetic Chicago Cubs.

As if the Reds starting poorly wasn't bad enough, the Orioles were 12-1 and tearing up the American League. Robinson was off to a hot season.

I wasn't.

The Reds went home to Cincinnati, and the boo-birds came out in droves to see me pitch against the Dodgers the following week. Those fans pissed me off so much that I really beared down on LA. I gave up eight hits, but the Dodgers could only score once on me. In the meantime, Sutton fell apart. We rocked him for seven runs, and I had my first win in the NL. The date was May 6, 1966.

Four days later I shut out the Braves in Atlanta, 8-0. Our record was now 8-14, and we were headed to Chicago to play the hapless Cubs.

The Cubs hired Leo "The Lip" Durocher the previous winter to be the "head coach" of Chicago's so-called "College of Coaches" failure, but at the press conference, old Leo let the media know that he was the manager, not a head coach; this was baseball, not football. He also said the Cubs were "not a eighth place team." He was only right. They were a 10th place team.

When I faced Leo's "Lovable Losers" for the first time, Ron Santo hit a homer off me. I still beat the Cubbies, 3-2, going the distance to record my third straight win in as many games. I was on a roll, and so were the Reds. Or so it seemed.

I missed my next scheduled start because I wasn't feeling well, but when I did pitch again, I beat the Braves in Cincinnati, 6-2, for my fourth win and fourth straight complete game. Now at 4-2, I was beginning to show the stuff that the Reds wanted from me. I was envisioning a 20-win season for me and a pennant for the Reds. Then the Giants brought me back down to earth.

Willie McCovey hit me like he owned me. That guy was a gentle giant — literally — at six-foot-four. Man, could he hit. Fast ball, curve, slider, change-up. You name it. Put the ball anywhere near his wheelhouse and it was gone. He belongs in the Hall of Fame.

And then there was Willie Mays. He owned me, too. Of course, Mays could hit just about any pitcher he wanted to hit. Facing those guys back-to-back was often my worst nightmare.

When they came to Cincinnati for the first time in 1966, they rocked me for seven runs in three and a third innings. I was gone, and we lost.

That shelling must have taken something out of me because when the Cubs came to town the next weekend they worked me over, too. I gave up five runs in five and two-thirds to them. We came back to win because Joe Nuxhall held them down and

Chicago had zilch for a bullpen that year. Well, not exactly zilch. They did have Ferguson Jenkins, but he was just a kid then. More about him later.

The Phillies were an excellent team in those middle years of the 1960s. Their ace was Jim Bunning. I'd squared off against him when he was with the Tigers, so I knew my work was cut out for me when I faced him in Philadelphia for the first time. I gave up 10 hits and five runs in seven innings, while he was striking 14 of our guys and allowing only one run. We lost, 5-1.

From Philadelphia, we went to New York. The Mets had been the doormat of the National League for the first four years of their existence, having won no more than 53 games in any one season under the tutelage of the "Ol' Perfessor" Casey Stengel. But now Wes Westrum was managing the New Yorkers, and they were beginning to become a respectable team. I helped their cause, losing my first appearance at Shea Stadium, 4-0. I didn't pitch as poorly as I had the previous three games, but when your guys don't score, it doesn't make any difference how you pitch.

My next start was another no-decision as the Phillies rocked me at home. We managed to come back and win the game to bail me out of the loss. We also won the second game of that twi-night doubleheader. Over my last five starts, I was 0-3 with two no-decisions. Winning 20 was beginning to look a little difficult.

The Mets came to town, and I got the nod in the first game of a Sunday doubleheader. I was on; the Mets weren't. I allowed seven hits, but no runs for my second NL shutout and fifth win. We won the second game as well, but our record was only 29-34. The season still had a long way to go, but we couldn't seem to make any headway in the standings.

My next start was against the Pirates at home, and I beat them this time, 5-3. I hit a home run, my first in the National League and 12th of my career. Don Cardwell grooved a fastball for me. This was our fifth straight win, and we were now 32-34 and in sixth place. The first division was becoming a distinct possibility now.

The Dodgers came to Cincinnati at the tail end of June, and I pitched the opening game of the series. I was cruising along for seven innings, holding a small lead. Then in the eighth I hurt my leg covering first base on an infield hit by Junior Gilliam. Bill McCool came in and finished my win, 3-1. With my record now at 7-5, I was beginning to think that 20 wins were still quite possible. I just needed a little luck to go with my skills.

After another no-decision, we went west to play the Dodgers. I drew Claude Osteen this time. We matched pitches for seven innings as neither team could score. Then in the bottom of the eighth, John Kennedy led off for LA. Kennedy was no magician with a bat. He could field with the best of them, but at the plate, he was usually a sure out. Not this night. He doubled to lead off the inning. Then Osteen — a good-hitting pitcher with a lifetime batting average of .188 with eight homers — came up and singled in Kennedy. I was pulled, and the Dodgers won, 1-0. That one hurt to lose. It was the third time that year our guys were shut out when I was pitching. I was wondering what had happened to all that offense of the year before. Then I realized that a large portion of it was currently playing in Baltimore.

My next start was in San Francisco. I determined that I wouldn't let Mays and McCovey maul me again. They didn't, and I beat the Giants, 2-1, with a complete game. It was the end of a long, sad road trip. Don Heffner, our manager, was rumored to be headed for the door, and it affected our play. Right after we got home, he was fired and replaced by Dave Bristol and his constant big wad of chewing tobacco.

The Cardinals came to town that week, and they clobbered me in the second game of a twi-night doubleheader. I gave up eight hits, a pair of walks, and seven runs in just two and a third innings. I stunk. My next game was no better. The Braves pounded me for eight hits and six runs in four innings. We lost. I deserved a loss, but I had another no-decision.

Bristol figured I was tired, so he skipped me when my next turn to start came around. It didn't help much because the Cubs came to town and took a turn dancing on my head. They scored five runs on six hits in five innings off me. Thank God, they had no bullpen as we pulled out a win, 8-6. I didn't deserve a win, and I didn't get one.

My stuff got better with my next outing, which was against the Astros in Cincinnati. I only gave up six hits and two walks in seven innings, but Houston scored three times. My guys didn't score for me at all, and I lost for the eighth time, 3-0, the fourth shut out against me that year.

I won my next start which was at Pittsburgh. It was our 16th win in 19 games. We were finally over .500 at 55-53. I was 9-8 with a mathematical chance at winning 20, but in all likelihood, I'd be doing well to win 15.

The Giants came to town again, and I got the call. I was sharp in the early going, then gave up a tying run in the fifth. We scored in the bottom of the inning on a single by Pete Rose that drove in Leo Cardenas who had singled. In between them, I got hit in the right arm by a pitch from Bobby Bolin. I gave up two hits in the top of the sixth and got two out before my elbow started hurting more than I could stand. Bristol pulled me out and brought in Sammy Ellis. Sammy walked two guys and forced in the tying run. There went my win. I got a no-decision, and Sammy got the win.

My next two starts were no-decisions although I gave up only one run in one game and three in the other. I pitched decently in both games, but the bullpen lost them for us.

We went west again, and I drew Juan Marichal when we played the Giants. I got roughed up, and Juan won his 18th of the year. It was our sixth loss in a row. We weren't giving up yet, but the odds of us finishing like the 1964 Reds were getting slimmer every day.

We returned home to face the Phillies in a Saturday twinbill. I took the mound for the second game after we'd won the first, 14-7. I held the Phils to four runs in seven innings and left with the lead. The bullpen blew my game, but we still won, 8-7.

On the first day of September, I faced the Cubs, the last place Cubs, the totally pathetic Cubs. I couldn't find the plate, walking four in five innings while giving up six hits. Some shabby fielding behind me, and the Cubs scored four runs off me. I left the game trailing, and the bullpen was even worse. Chicago clubbed us, 11-3.

On Labor Day, we were in New York for a doubleheader. I started the first game and won, 8-2. We won the second game, too, but the season was practically over for us. We were only a game over .500 and a dozen games out of first. The Dodgers, Giants, and Pirates were in a three-way fight for the flag, while the rest of us were struggling to finish in the first division.

* * *

I t was not a good year for most of us in Cincinnati. Don Heffner was fired as manager in early July. Dave Bristol didn't fare any better over the last few months of the season than Heffner had. Guys who had big years in 1965 weren't nearly as good in 1966. I had the second best record on the staff at 12-11 and only walked 39 batters in 210 innings pitched. But as a team, we finished seventh, 18 games behind the first place Dodgers.

My arm was okay, and I felt I did my job even if the fans didn't. The unfortunate part of it all was that Frank Robinson won the Triple Crown in the American League and the Orioles went on to beat the Dodgers four straight in the World Series.

As far as adjusting to the National League, I thought I would be more successful there than in the American League, even though after a few times around, I thought the NL had better hitters.

It was a good experience for me because the National League umpires wore the inside chest protector, while the American League umps still employed the big balloon chest protector. The AL blues had a lot of trouble seeing the low pitches, but I was getting a lot of low strikes in the National League. Obviously, if a pitcher kept the ball down, he had a better chance of getting ground balls and double plays, as opposed to fly balls and home runs. So it wasn't so bad adjusting to the National League. I just had to go out there and pitch.

* * *

D ave Bristol was a rather strange man. He would have a meeting every single day of the season, on the road or at home. Every day, every day, every day, he would go over the same things, like play well and play hard. It got to the point one time where I took a tape recorder and taped his meeting. Then when he came back to do the meeting the next day, I said, "Dave, hey wait a minute. Save yourself the trouble." I turned on the tape from the day before and got a few laughs. Of course, he got very, very upset with me. I was just having some fun with him, but he didn't think it was too funny.

One thing about Dave Bristol was he could be a little nasty. We were playing the San Francisco Giants, and I had given up a home run to Willie McCovey that was hit pretty well. I mean, really well. I was having breakfast the next morning and reading the paper. Bristol had made some comments after the game. He said my pitch to McCovey ended up sinking a battleship in San Francisco Bay. I wasn't too thrilled with Bristol after that. I was kind of upset that my manager was talking about the home run and making it sound like I was a lousy pitcher.

After the game that day, we were walking out of the clubhouse through the groundskeeper's room. I waited there until Bristol was coming out of the locker room to make sure he was behind me. The groundskeeper's room had a real heavy door, and when it opened, it automatically closed itself. When he walked up to the door, I let it go, and it came back and hit him. His sunglasses were broken, and he glared at me and started swearing.

"David, what are you doing? Why are you yelling at me?"

"Well, you did that on purpose."

"No, I didn't."

"Oh, yes, you did."

"Well, maybe if you stop talking about your pitchers in the paper about how far they threw a home run ball, geez, maybe that accident could have been avoided."

I thought it was funny, but he didn't.

* * *

As far as the 1966 season goes, I thought I did as well as I could with the team we had. I was over .500 as a pitcher for a team that was under 500. We had some pretty good pitchers on our team. Jim Maloney, lefthander Joe Nuxhall, Sammy Ellis. Some great everyday players in Deron Johnson, Pete Rose, Leo Cardenas, Vada Pinson, and others. We had a pretty damn good ball club, even though we didn't gel. We just couldn't put it all together.

I lived in Baltimore during the off season, and all I heard was how the Orioles had won the World Series and how Frank Robinson had won the Triple Crown. Everybody thanked me for making it possible, and I felt like telling everybody to go to Hell. I opened up a restaurant in Baltimore that winter and a lot of people came in just to say thank you for helping the Orioles win the championship. I ended up getting a lot of extra customers because of it.

The Robinson trade really did shake me up as far as me realizing the business side of baseball. The fact that the Reds didn't initially want to reward me with a good contract — after they had traded Robinson, essentially for me — really burned me up, and it stayed with me.

Some people in the Reds organization said Robinson had lost his skills at the ripe old age of 30. But that was baloney. He was a heck of a player, and the Orioles knew it. They got a superstar.

At the same time, both teams must have realized my value, otherwise the trade wouldn't have been made. But when it was completed, the Reds didn't want to recognize my ability with a decent contract. They were lousy about it, and that really got me to thinking about how the real game of baseball was played. The game upstairs, where management could screw with your life and your career, and you didn't have a damn thing to say about it. It was just ridiculous.

To sum up 1966, it was a year of disappointment, frustration, learning, and realizing that baseball was continuing to change. I saw it more as a business, and I realized that probably more trades would happen down the road, and at the same time, I hoped I would be able to survive. That's really what it was coming down to. Surviving.

So far, so good.

◆20◆

Slider:
Toeing the Rubber

T he National League had some great pitchers at the time I joined the Reds. Bob Gibson, Sandy Koufax, Don Drysdale, Juan Marichal, Gaylord Perry, and Steve Carlton; just to name a few. Ferguson Jenkins and Tom Seaver were just kids then.

Obviously, whenever you faced the Dodgers, you didn't want to come up against Koufax or Drysdale; neither did you want to face Gibson when you played the Cardinals. But if you had to, you had to.

The only time I ever had the misfortune to oppose Koufax he was absolutely unbelievable. He had such a great fastball and an even better curve. But even with Sandy, it took him five or six years before he found his control after coming to the big leagues. As great as he was, there's no telling how good he may have been if he had been throwing strikes when he came up to the Major Leagues or if arthritis hadn't shortened his career. He might have been the greatest lefty in the history of the game, but that honor still belongs to Warren Spahn.

Don Drysdale and I had a few matchups during our careers. He was a good pitcher and kept the ball down. I'm not taking anything away from him as far as being a good pitcher, but I am upset about one thing. Don Drysdale is in the Hall of Fame after winning 209 games and losing 166. I won 209 games and lost 164, and I've only been on a Hall of Fame ballot once but only because I bitched about it. That upsets me, and it makes me wonder about the Hall of Fame balloting. I guess it's politics in baseball just like business and life in general.

Besides great pitchers, the National League had more than its

share of great hitters. Willie McCovey, Willie Mays, Jim Ray
Hart, Orlando Cepeda; the Alou brothers: Felipe, Matty, and
Jesus; Roberto Clemente, Willie Stargell, Dick Allen, Johnny
Callison, Ernie Banks, Ron Santo, Billy Williams, Hank Aaron,
Tony Gonzalez, Rico Carty, Joe Morgan, Jimmy Wynn, Rusty
Staub. And more.

The Dodgers didn't have a lot of home run hitters, but they
had guys like Tommy Davis, Maury Wills, and Ron Fairly. It
seemed like every guy in LA's lineup could hit. They had a lot of
switch-hitters, which made it a little rougher to pitch against the
Dodgers. With their great pitching, you always knew you were
going to be in for a battle. There were a lot of 1-0, 2-1, 3-2 games
with them, so you had to be on your game. They were just Punch-
and-Judy hitters, but every now and then they would hit a home
run. But most of the time it was a walk or a base hit to get a man
aboard, then a stolen base, a ground out to the right side, and a
sacrifice fly, and all of a sudden, you're down, 1-0.

In the NL, if they couldn't beat you with a home run, they
beat you with speed. Maury Wills, Lou Brock, Joe Morgan.
Those guys could run. You hated to see them lead off and reach.
A walk or a single by one of them was almost the same as a
double. Brock and Morgan could beat you with the long ball, too.

It was really a different league.

* * *

We had a lot of talent in Cincinnati when I arrived, but it
wouldn't really mature for a few more years. Jim
Maloney was the established ace of the staff. Sammy Ellis, Joey
Jay, Billy McCool, and Joe Nuxhall were the veterans. We had
a couple of good catchers in Johnny Edwards and Don Pavletich.
Our infielders were Gordy Coleman at first base, Tommy Helms
at second, Leo Cardenas at shortstop, Deron Johnson at third and
later Tony Perez. In the outfield, we had Tommy Harper, Vada
Pinson, Pete Rose, and Mel Queen, who later became a pitcher,
along with Art Shamsky. Not a bad ball club. Unfortunately, we
didn't win.

Dave Bristol changed the face of the Reds only slightly for the 1967 season. The front office picked up a veteran reliever, and Bristol kept two young guys in particular on the squad when we headed north.

The bullpen vet was Ted Abernathy, the submarining righty who had been with the Braves and Cubs in 1966. He had a great year in 1965, making 84 appearances and posting an ERA of 2.57 in relief for the Cubs. More phenomenal than that, he saved 31 games for a eighth place team. Leo Durocher traded Ted to Atlanta because he was over 30, and Leo was trying to build a young team in his own image. He also traded Larry Jackson and Bob Buhl to the Phillies, but he got Ferguson Jenkins in return in that deal. The Braves released Ted between seasons, and the Reds signed him.

Lee May put Gordy Coleman out of a job. Lee had come up near the end of the previous season and had shown a lot of promise. He was big, strong, and young. He could hit for power, and with Deron Johnson's skills on the decline, the Reds needed a big bat in the lineup.

Gary Nolan was just a baby. He was only 18 years old when the season started. He reminded me of me. He had a great fastball and a lot of poise for a kid.

Bristol made one other great move. He converted outfielder Mel Queen into a pitcher. Mel had begun pitching the year before, but now it was a permanent move. Bristol also rearranged the everyday lineup. He moved Tony Perez to third base, Tommy Helms to second, Pete Rose to left, and Tommy Harper to right. With Doc Edwards and Don Paveletich behind the plate and Vada Pinson still in center field, we had a pretty solid team.

* * *

W e opened at home against the Dodgers and won. My first start was against the Astros at home. I left the game in the seventh with the lead, and the bullpen held it for me. I wasn't really sharp, but I was good enough to win. That was enough for me.

The next week on the West Coast I pitched a Wednesday night game in LA. I was pulled after seven, trailing, 3-2. The Dodgers had touched me for eight hits and a pair of walks, but I kept us in the game. The bullpen didn't as LA scored four runs in the eighth to put the game away, 7-2.

After beating the Astros again, this time in Houston, I missed my turn in the rotation because of the weather. When my spot came up again, we were in St. Louis. I faced Ray Washburn. Ray had been a bonus baby in 1961, receiving $50,000 to sign with the Cardinals. He was worth it. He won 12 games in 1962, losing nine, and posting an ERA of 4.10. He tore a muscle in his shoulder in 1963 and missed most of that year and good portions of the years that followed. Word had it that he was finally well and had gotten back the stuff he'd shown in 1962. The rumor proved true as he two-hit us, 2-0. I threw fairly well, only giving up five hits and a walk over seven innings.

We went to New York to play the Mets the next week. I was off my game, but we won anyway, 7-4. I gave up 11 hits in six and two-thirds innings. The win raised our hot start to 18-9, and we were in first place. I was 3-2. Could this be the year for a pennant and me winning 20? I had my hopes up.

I had two no-decisions in my next two starts. Against the Pirates, I was lousy, but we won. Against the Phillies, I was brilliant over seven innings, giving up only one run on five hits. But we lost, 2-1, in 18 innings.

My next start was at home against the Pirates. I made one bad pitch. Or at least, Roberto Clemente made me look bad with it. He hit out. But it was the only run I surrendered in a complete game win, 6-1. I was now 4-2, and we were still in first.

By this time, I was beginning to build some hostility toward Dave Bristol. I wasn't starting every fourth day or even every fourth game. My starts were five, six, even seven days apart: April 13, April 19, April 23, May 3, May 10, May 15, May 21, May 27, May 31. Through the first two months, we had played 48 games, and I had had only nine starts when I should have had at least 11, probably 12 or even 13. I felt fine. So why was Bristol holding me back? Who knew? Maybe it had something to do with that door incident the year before. Maybe.

Dave Bristol thought of himself as a combination of Walter Alston, Paul Richards, and Vince Lombardi all rolled into one man. He was none of the above, even in part. He should have just been himself, and he'd have been a lot better off.

After losing to the Cubs at the end of May, I won a game in relief on June 2, then beat the Giants, 3-2, at home on June 6. My next start was June 11 in the first game of a double-header against the Astros. They smacked me around, and I lost, going only four-plus innings. My next appearance was in the second game of that doubleheader. I threw one inning of shutout ball, which was good enough to get the win. My record was now 7-4.

Just as I was about to bitch at Bristol for not letting me start regularly, I made five straight starts in the rotation: June 17, June 21, June 25, June 29, and July 3. I lost to Drysdale in LA, 7-5; had a no-decision in Houston; lost to Pittsburgh at home; then shut out LA and Drysdale at home, 14-0; before getting bombed by the Cardinals in the first inning at St. Louis. I gave up six runs on six hits. My record had dropped to 8-7, and we had slipped into second place, five games behind the Cardinals. Winning 20 was still possible, but not likely as my arm started giving me trouble. I didn't start again for nearly three weeks which also included the All-Star Game break.

When I came back into the rotation, I beat the Phillies, 2-1, going seven and a third innings and giving up only two hits and one run. I followed up with a no-decision with the Cubs. I went nine innings, but it took us 10 to beat Chicago. That closed out July for me. I was 9-7, and the way Bristol was handling the rotation, I didn't think I would even get a shot at winning 20. I probably wouldn't get more than 14 or 15 starts and I'd have to win 11 of them. The chances of that, based on my past, weren't very good.

August started well as I won three straight, including a pair of shutouts. I beat the Braves, 7-3; the Astros, 5-0; and the Dodgers, 4-0. That was my second straight shut out of LA, and the blanking I gave the Astros was a two-hitter. I was now 12-7. The season had 49 days left. That meant 11 maybe 12 starts for me. Or so I thought. Bristol had other ideas.

I lost a tough one to the Giants and Ray Sadecki in San

Francisco with my next start. Sadecki had come up with the Cardinals in 1960 and had some good years with them, including a 20-win season in 1964 when St. Louis won the World Series. He bombed in 1965, winning only five and losing 15, so the Cardinals traded him to the Giants in early 1966. The move didn't help him until 1967 when he seemed to be returning to top form. I held his Giants to two runs in seven innings, but he held us to one in going the distance.

We went down to LA for our next series, and I drew Drysdale again. I went the distance. He lasted four innings. We won, 7-1. Now I was 13-8, and with two probable starts left in August and seven in September, I still had an outside shot at winning 20. Those odds got worse after I lost my next start. Then I closed out August with a win over the Phillies, 2-1. I got all but the last out. Ted Abernathy got that, and my record climbed to 14-9. That was the good news. The bad news was we were 10 games out of first place, and the Cardinals were showing no signs of faltering.

Looking ahead at the schedule, I figured I would get five starts at home and two on the road. In order to win 20, I estimated that I would have to win all five at home and one of the two on the road. That theory was shattered when I lost to the Giants — and Ray Sadecki — again, 4-0. I won the road game, 3-1, at Philadelphia to raise my record to 15-10, but with only five starts left, I had no margin for error.

We couldn't score enough runs in seven innings for me to get the win against the Pirates, but we did in nine innings. I was left with four starts, and no chance at winning 20. I was disappointed but not without the determination to have the best season of my career. Winning 19 or 18 or even 17 was still better than any year I'd had with Baltimore. I looked to the future with that in mind. Then Ray Washburn beat me again, 4-1. I was down to three starts.

At the beginning of the month, the Reds brought up a rookie catcher, a 19-year-old kid named Johnny Bench. He caught 26 games. He was my catcher for all seven of my starts in September. On September 20, we played the Braves in Atlanta. We won, 9-4. I got the win, although I only lasted five innings.

Bench hit his first Major League homer that game. I was 16-11 now with hopes of winning just one more game. Two would have been better, but I was willing to settle for one, which would give me my best year yet for victories.

The Braves came to Cincinnati to start the last week of the campaign. We were still fighting the Cubs for third place. The Cardinals had locked up the pennant and were practicing to meet the Red Sox, Tigers, Twins, or White Sox in the World Series. The Giants were in second and not likely to give up their place to us or the Cubs. I started against the Braves on Tuesday, and I hit a homer, my only one for the year. Still, we lost, 4-3.

Very appropriately we hosted the Cubs for the final weekend of the season. I took the hill for the Saturday game, still clinging to the hope and prayer that I could win my 17th game of the year. I didn't have it that day. I got two guys out, but seven other guys reached on me, and all of them scored. We lost the game and third place, 9-4.

I finished with a record of 16-13. I was better than the previous year, but I was still disappointed with my performance. I was still determined. I was still only 28 years old. I hadn't even reached my prime yet.

There was always next year.

Inside:
The Brush Back Pitch

I n baseball, as in life, you pick your friends. As time went on with the Reds, I was gradually accepted by most of my teammates. Only one guy in particular do I recall as never being very friendly to me.

Joe Nuxhall was always very critical of me. I didn't care for him that much either. He came up to the Majors during World War II when a lot of ballplayers were in the Army or Navy. He was a mere 15 years old when the Reds put him in a game in 1944. He pitched two-thirds of an inning, gave up two hits, and walked five, allowing five earned runs. He didn't step onto a big league mound in a regular season game again until 1952 when he was 23. He had some decent years in the mid-1950s, then faded before returning to form in the 1960s. His last year was 1966. He stayed in the game, becoming a radio announcer for the Reds.

Sammy Ellis, another pitcher, became a good friend. Sammy and I hung out together. He made playing for the Reds an easier transition for me.

The Reds had a few cliques just like any other team I played on. It's something that goes on today, too. There's really nothing wrong with it, unless it causes dissension.

Occasionally, the militant black players brought their politics to the park. Once with the Reds in spring training, a black player went to the clubhouse man and actually made him integrate the locker room. At that time, a lot of white guys shared a locker next to each other and the black guys would locker next to each other. Nobody ever thought anything of it as far as I know, but this certain player walked up and told the clubhouse man that he wanted some whites next to blacks. I don't know if he was with the N.A.A.C.P. or what, but it was kind of a different situation. We didn't have many guys like that, and I'm glad we didn't. It was tough enough to go out and fight the enemy on the field without having somebody like that in your clubhouse.

For the most part, teammates were acquaintances more than friends. At the end of a season, everyone would take off and go back to their homes, wherever that might be. The same could be said for the players' wives. I told Carole that one of the worst things she could do would be to get close to the other wives. I didn't mean that sarcastically. But if she became good friends with another wife and her husband was traded, then her friend was gone, too. That was a shame, but that's the way it happens in baseball. It's not that players and their wives didn't get together and be friendly, but in the back of your mind, you knew it could change in a hurry. Anybody could be playing with a different team the very next day. That happened with Carole. She became friends with Jack Fisher's wife, Judy, when we were with the Orioles. They became such great friends that when Jack was traded Carole was devastated by it. So it was tough.

Plus, some of the stars' wives thought they were a little better than the wives of the guys who didn't play every day. It was like a social climbing situation. I really didn't care for that either, but again, that's the way it was and probably still is.

* * *

In 1968, I was again voted the player-rep for the Reds. We had some problems there, but that's putting the cart before horse again. First, the season.

In the offseason, the front office made a few trades to improve the team. Tommy Harper went to Cleveland for pitcher George Culver and outfielder Freddie Whitfield, and outfielder Alex Johnson came over from St. Louis. The deal I didn't like was the one where Sammy Ellis was traded to the Angels for Bill Kelso and another pitcher who never even made our club.

Bristol turned Jerry Arrigo into a regular starter to replace Ellis, and Culver replaced Mel Queen in the rotation after Mel was injured. I was back, and so were Jim Maloney and Gary Nolan. Ted Abernathy and Ted Davidson manned the bullpen.

The only changes in our everyday lineup were the addition of Johnson in left field to replace Harper and Johnny Bench as the regular catcher.

The assassination of the Reverend Martin Luther King, Jr., put a pall over baseball just as much as it did over much of the country. I heard some guys make crude racial remarks, but for the most part, we were saddened by his death, especially the black players. Many of them looked at white players with jaundiced eyes after that, and frankly, I couldn't blame them. The greatest man ever to lead the civil rights movement had been murdered. I remembered how I felt when President John Kennedy was assassinated, and I was very sympathetic to them.

Reverend King's funeral delayed the beginning of the Major League Baseball season by two days. I pitched the opener against the Cubs in Cincinnati, and we won, 9-4. I went five and a third innings for the victory. I didn't pitch again until the following Wednesday against the Cardinals. I went seven innings, but the game took 12 to finish. No decision for me that day. I lost to the Braves, 5-2, the next week, then on Saturday, beat the Mets, 5-3, coming one out away from throwing a complete game. I was 2-1 in four starts, and I was feeling good. Maybe this would be the year I'd finally win 20. All I had to do was get 40 starts and win half of them. Not bloody likely, as the British say.

After two no-decisions, I lost to the Phils, Mets, and Astros in succession. Bristol took me out of the rotation for one turn, and I made a rare relief appearance against the Pirates. When I did start again, I lasted a mere two and a third innings against the Dodgers. I avoided losing when we rallied to catch them. The next game I wasn't so lucky. The Phillies beat the hell out of me in the first inning. I gave up four runs on five hits and only got two outs as we were clobbered, 12-0. That dropped my record to 2-5, but the season was less than a third over. I could bounce back and win 20. Yeah, right. Two more no-decisions and all thoughts of winning 20 were out of my head for the year.

* * *

S enator Robert Kennedy was assassinated in California on Tuesday June 5 at the Ambassador Hotel in Los Angeles. Much of the nation mourned, and so did baseball.

A directive came from the office of Commissioner Bowie Kuhn that no game would start until Senator Kennedy's body reached Washington, D.C., by train from New York. It was a Saturday, and we were in Cincinnati, hosting the Cardinals in front of a sellout crowd.

General Manager Bob Howsam of the Reds, assistant GM Dick Wagner, and Dave Bristol told me that the game would have to be played because a lot of people were there and the front office didn't want the fans to be disappointed. As player-rep on the Cincinnati club, I told them, no, the game would be delayed or postponed because of the commissioner's order. They told me to take a team vote, but I replied I didn't have to do that and that I didn't want to do it. Then they asked me nicely if I would do it. So I asked the players to vote, and they voted against playing and in favor of the commissioner's order. I left the dugout to tell the Cardinals and the umpires of our decision, and they told me they would abide with whatever we had voted on. When I returned to the dugout, Bristol and Howsam were addressing the team in the clubhouse. This pissed me off. I asked the two of them politely to remove themselves, and they responded testily, wanting to know who I thought I was, as if they didn't know. I made it clear to them that I was the player-rep and told them not to come in to the clubhouse threatening my guys by telling them they're going to lose their pay if they don't go out and play the game. Bristol and Howsam asked for another vote. Just to show them up, I took one, and again the players voted not to play.

I then went back out to talk to the umpires and Cardinals again. Dick Wagner stopped me on the field in front of the St. Louis dugout and started to put his finger on my shoulder as if he were some kind of tough guy. He was one of those short guys who was mad at God for making him short, so he had this enormous chip on his shoulder. I looked him in the eye and said, "If that finger reaches my shoulder, I'm going to break it." I meant it, and he knew it.

Wagner didn't touch me, but he kept telling me that I had to get my teammates to play the game. I told him to get the hell out of my face. We had a huge argument in front of the fans. When I went back to the locker room, some of the players were dressing to go out on the field to play. That was it. I blew up at them.

"You don't need me, you need a zookeeper! If you guys want to play, go ahead. I'm going home." I changed and went home.

The game was played. I came back the next day and pitched the second game of a doubleheader.

The following week we had another hassle, this one involving team travel accommodations.

The Reds did not fly charter. We flew on regularly scheduled flights. The manager, coaches, and front office personnel who traveled with us would sit in first class with the press people. Whatever seats remained in that section would be taken by players, and the rest of the team would sit in the coach seats right behind first class so the whole team could be seated together.

I was getting a lot of flack from the other players as to why the media was sitting up front in the nice seats, while they went out and played nine innings and then had to sit in regular coach seating. So I filed a grievance against the Cincinnati Reds with Marvin Miller, the head of the union. Marvin filed my complaint with the National League office, then he set up a meeting with the local press corps in Cincinnati in an attempt to resolve the situation. He came to town the night before, and we talked about how to solve the problem. The meeting was set for 10:00 a.m. the next morning. We had a noon game, so I asked if I had to be there. Marvin said, no, that not even Reds management would be there. It was strictly between him and the press.

Later that day, I found out that Dick Wagner and Bob Howsam did attend the meeting, which they weren't supposed to. So after the game, I called Howsam and told him exactly what I thought of him, of how low-handed he was and that Wagner was the same way. I was extremely upset because it made me look real bad. I wasn't able to be at the meeting to defend myself and my teammates as to why the grievance was filed.

The end result was that three days later, I was traded to the Atlanta Braves.

To summarize my stay in Cincinnati, it was absolutely horrible, but it was all behind me.

* * *

A tlanta was better than Cincinnati — in the beginning. The manager was Lum Harris, my first pitching coach back in Baltimore. It was almost like going home, pitching for him again. But you know what they say about going home.

The Reds also sent Bob Johnson, a utility infielder, and Ted Davidson, a relief pitcher to Atlanta in exchange for Tony Cloninger, Woody Woodward, and Clay Carroll. Cloninger was to replace me in the rotation, while Carroll replaced Davidson in the bullpen and Woodward took Johnson's place on the bench.

Cloninger had developed some arm trouble the year before, and he had a problem with his vision due to a viral infection. The Reds hoped he would rebound to the level he had achieved when the Braves were still in Milwaukee. He won 57 games over the three seasons, 1964-66, including a 24-win season in 1965. Besides being a pretty fair country pitcher, Tony could hit. He belted two grand slams against the Giants in 1966 in the same game. He's the only pitcher who's ever done that. On the mound, he was less than so-so after coming to the Reds.

Clay Carroll, on the other hand, had the best years of his career in Cincinnati. He was a healthy addition to the bullpen. He was a big part of the Reds' success while he was there.

Woodward provided some excellent defensive help for the Reds over the next three seasons.

Davidson pitched in four games, then his Major League career came to an end. Johnson finished the season, then moved on to play two more years before he hung up his cleats. Me?

My 29th birthday was only a month earlier, and I already had 10 full years in the Majors. I figured I had another 10 years ahead of me. I was in my prime.

The trade was made June 11. The Braves put me to work on June 15 against the Cardinals. I went seven innings, gave up only four hits and a walk, and allowed two runs, one earned. The game went 10 innings, and we won. No decision for me.

Five days later the Reds were in Atlanta, and I got the call. I couldn't have been happier. I wanted to beat those guys in the worst way. I did. I only went five and two-thirds, but I got the win, 3-1. My first in nearly two months.

After making a rare relief appearance, my next start was delayed to June 28 in LA. I drew Mike Kekich, a lefty who had a so-so career. I beat him, 3-0, to raise my record to 4-5. Since coming to the Braves, I had been in four games and had given up only three runs over 23⅓ innings. I still wasn't getting much support, but at least, I was winning.

We went up the Coast to Frisco for a three-game series the next week. My start was on Wednesday, and I was up for it. I shut down Mays, McCovey, and company for seven innings, then Claude Raymond, who had come to the Braves from the Astros just four days after I did, pitched the last two innings. Together we shut out the Giants, 2-0. I was now 5-5 and riding a streak of 21⅔ straight scoreless innings. I was on top of my game.

Then we went home to face the Astros in a weekend series just before the All-Star Game break. I drew the Sunday assignment. It wasn't my day. Norm Miller — another nobody — led off with a homer, one of his career 24. Joe Morgan and Rusty Staub followed with singles, then Jimmy Wynn homered. Four batters, four hits, four runs. I was gone. We wound up losing in spite of Hank Aaron hitting two home runs for us. I took the loss.

After the break, I came down with a serious case of the flu. It weakened me so much that was unable to pitch for a week, and when I did make an appearance in relief, I had no zip in my fastball. I started against the Pirates on July 21 but could only go two innings before tiring. I gave up four runs, and we lost, 6-0.

Finally, I felt better, so Harris started me in the second game of a doubleheader in Philly. I went six innings; we won. I was now 6-7 for the season, 4-2 with the Braves. With just over two months left in the season, I set my goal at 15 wins for the year.

Harris started me in New York on July 31. My hill opponent was Jerry Koosman, a rookie. Some rookie. He was 14-5 when we matched up. He went the distance. I lasted seven and a third. Claude Raymond picked up for me and finished the game, saving my win, 3-2. I was now 7-7 and confident that I could win 15.

We returned to Atlanta, and I started against the Cubs in the first game of the series. Chicago was on a roll, having won six straight. They were due to cool off, and I was the guy to throw ice water on their parade. I went the distance, giving up just six hits and one run, a homer by Ernie Banks. I had a big lead when he hit it out. I could afford to be generous. Besides, I hit a three-run homer myself that game. After Banks's round-tripper, I retired the last 10 Cubs in a row. I was now 8-7, and 15 wins were looking better all the time.

The Cardinals were the reigning World Champions, and they were on their way to another National League pennant in 1968. We were a good team, but not as good as St. Louis. They were tough. I held them to two runs over seven innings and left the game trailing, 2-1. The Cards put the game away with five runs in the ninth, and I suffered the loss. That was in Atlanta. The next week in St. Louis, I was a little better and so was our offense. I went eight and two-thirds, giving up only one unearned run on four hits, while the guys were scoring five runs to support me. We won. I was now 9-9, having lost in relief to the Mets earlier in the week. With six weeks left in the season, getting 15 wins suddenly wasn't looking so good any more.

In Chicago, I pitched well, but Lum pulled me for a pinch-hitter in the sixth. No decision for me. We came home to play the Pirates. I lost to Steve Blass, 4-0. Then I beat the Phillies to even my record at 10-10. We had the whole month of September to play, and although I figured to get at least six starts, I no longer thought I could win 15.

The Mets beat me, 4-3, in New York, with me going seven innings. Then I beat the Astros, 4-1, in Atlanta, pitching a complete game. The Dodgers beat me, 3-0, in LA before I beat Houston again, 4-1. My record was now a decent 12-12, and all I wanted was a winning season. Tom Seaver kept me from that goal by shutting us out, 3-0. What a finish. I lost four of my last seven decisions, three of them by shutouts. It was like I'd never left Cincinnati.

* * *

While in Cincinnati, Johnny Edwards was the starting catcher before Johnny Bench. One year Edwards had a sore arm for a while, and when he came back, he had a problem doing something I've never seen a catcher have a problem with before. He couldn't throw the ball back to the pitcher! John would cock his arm and try to throw the ball and couldn't get it back to the mound. Again and again, he'd try to throw the ball, and in the process, he'd drive the pitcher absolutely batty, along with the umpire and everybody else. He was afraid to let the ball go because he thought it would go into centerfield — or wherever.

It was weird, but if a guy tried to steal a base, he had no problems. Then John would gun it. But when it came to throwing the ball back to the pitcher, he had all sorts of problems.

The coaches would work on it with him. It seemed like it took forever, but finally after about a month, John was able to throw the ball back to the pitcher. It was the funniest, damn, irritating thing you ever saw.

* * *

Was there any illegal drug use when I played? Well, some players took pep pills, but that was prevalent at that time.

Pete Rose did, and I did, too. But it wasn't abuse. If the pills were used, it was during the summer when it was very hot and we had 13 or 14 games in a row without a day off. We'd begin to run down, and we'd be very, very tired. So we'd take a "greeny" or pep pill. I took the lowest dosage because I couldn't sleep the night after the game if I took a big dose. After a game, I was physically and mentally drained, so I wanted to get some rest.

The pills contained amphetamines — uppers, and they would keep you going when you needed that little extra boost. But I stress that usage of the pills was never a problem for me.

It's hard to say if these drugs affected the performance of the players taking them. Unfortunately, most of the guys who took them got hooked on them, only because they were so easy to get. I can't really prove that, but I'll bet there's a lot of guys who can corroborate this statement as a true fact of baseball life back then. Just being a professional baseball player, most of the time you didn't even need a prescription. If you knew your local druggist you could walk in and buy them from the guy, which was obviously against the law. Or there were guys who would find them for us without any problem.

The one reason I can see why it was even started was because we were playing in a very hot, summer time climate and the season was 162 games long and there are some stretches in the summer time when you play maybe 10 or 12 straight games without having a day off. That takes a lot out of you. A lot of guys would start taking them for that reason only; just to get them up for that day because they just got through playing three or four or five straight days in very hot weather. They were tired, sometimes actually exhausted. To get up for the game they would start taking these greenies.

One drug was called "The Sox." I saw a few of guys in Cincinnati drinking it. It came in a liquid as well as a pill, and boy, that stuff got in your blood stream really fast. Even Pete Rose took it on occasion. I saw Rose and Jim Maloney taking some once, so I tried it one time. Whoa! It was just way too powerful for me. The medical name for it was Disoxin, but we called it red juice. That stuff would immediately get into you, and you were just flying sky high.

Pat Jarvis, when I was with the Atlanta Braves, would take what he called a "black beauty" when he pitched. This thing was like 25 milligrams. We would almost have to pretend to shoot him down out of the sky to get him back on the ground.

Was drug abuse really prevalent? Not really, but it was there. Some guys took the pills, some guys didn't take the pills. Again, the players took them to get up for a day, to get through the game.

Guys like Joe Pepitone, I think unfortunately, abused it. He was a playboy. Joe would stay out until all hours of the morning. I was with the Cubs at that time, and we played a lot of day games. He'd come to the park in the morning at 8:30 or 9:00 a.m., and he'd looked like death warmed over. He looked like he was just getting in from a night out, and sometimes he was. When he tried to sleep that night, he would take a downer, then come to the ball park the next day looking like death warmed over again. So he would take another upper. Joe would do this everyday, it seemed. He would take these pills everyday. That was real abuse.

My biggest concern was the after-effects. What does that do to your system? A guy would get so used to taking pills that his body would become dependent on them. Fortunately, we had about five months between the end of one season and the beginning of spring training the next year. So a lot of that stuff would get out of a guy's system. I never heard of anybody taking them in the offseason, so I don't think it was a thing where you got hooked on them. I don't remember anybody really having a problem where they would continually take the pills when the season was over. It was just basically during the season.

The managers and coaches were well aware of the pill usage, but they never said anything. Again, I can't prove this, but if you ask those guys, they could corroborate this statement as the truth.

The trainer, by law, could not dispense them, which he didn't. So guys would have their friends, who were doctors or pharmacists, get the drugs for us. We had absolutely no problem getting all the pills we wanted. Every team I was on, guys were taking them. So, it wasn't just an isolated case of one team.

As for Pete Rose, he took quite a bit of the red juice. I don't know why he took it because he always gave 110 percent. Obviously, if you look at Pete's career, it didn't bother him that much. It couldn't have for him to come out with the records that he did, to play as long as he did, hit the way he did, and run the way he did. But sometimes Pete would still take the red juice.

Today, cocaine is probably used more than speed or pep pills. You hear more and more about players who are into drugs, which I think is very sad. Most of the other sports have drug testing, but not baseball. It's still the only major sport that doesn't. Maybe there should be some mandatory testing.

The Players' Association has fought testing all along, so it's never been implemented. I think those guys should quit fighting it and clean up the game a little. That probably won't ever happen as long as the druggies keep running the union.

◆22◆

Split:
Divisional Play

O ver the winter of 1968-69, I was really looking forward to the new season in Atlanta. We had a good team from top to bottom, and I felt we had a good chance of taking first in the new West Division of the National League.

Yes, West Division. The Major Leagues had expanded again. This time in both leagues at the same time. The American League added Seattle and Kansas City, putting both of them in their West Division with Chicago, Minnesota, California, and Oakland. The AL East Division consisted of New York, Boston, Detroit, Cleveland, Baltimore, and Washington, which was now managed by the old "Splendid Splinter" Ted Williams. The powers-that-be placed the Braves and Reds in the NL West Division with the Dodgers, Giants, Astros, and the new San Diego Padres. The men with the pull to do this were the owners of the Cubs and Cards: Philip K. Wrigley and August Busch. They didn't want to play so many games on the West Coast because those three teams played a lot of night games which wouldn't be aired on radio or television back in Chicago and St. Louis until 10:00 p.m. This meant smaller listening and viewing audiences, which translated into lower advertising revenues for the radio and television flagship stations broadcasting and telecasting the games of the two clubs. Less advertising money for the stations meant smaller radio and television rights deals with the two teams. Wrigley and Busch weren't about to have that, so the Cubs and Cardinals were put in the East Division with Pittsburgh, Philadelphia, New York, and the expansion franchise in Canada, the Montreal Expos.

* * *

Based on the performances of the 1968 teams, the Braves would be in a tight race with San Francisco and Cincinnati for the first division title. As it turned out, that's exactly what happened.

Our roster was loaded with talent. Old and new.

Lum Harris was once again the manager, having taken over for Billy Hitchcock near the end of the 1967 season. Hitchcock had replaced Bobby Bragan midway through the 1966 campaign. Ironically, Hitchcock had replaced Harris in Baltimore after Harris had taken over for Paul Richards when he resigned to become general manager of the Houston Astros. That's called the "good ol' boy network."

A lot of owners and general managers don't really care if their teams win, so they bring in a guy whose managed before and failed so they can blame him when the team doesn't win. Why else would guys like Bragan, Hitchcock, and Harris keep getting managing jobs? How about Dave Bristol? He managed 11 years in the Majors for four different teams and only had one team that finished as high as third place. How about Jimmy Dykes? After managing the Chicago White Sox for 12-plus years and never finishing any higher than third, he got jobs with the Philadelphia A's, Baltimore, Cincinnati, Detroit, and Cleveland, and he never finished higher than fourth with any of them. The "good ol' boy network" will keep you in baseball as long as you lick the right boots.

But back to the 1969 Atlanta Braves.

Our starting rotation had Phil Niekro, Pat Jarvis, Ron Reed, and me with Jim Britton, who had shown flashes of brilliance the year before as a rookie, for a fifth starter. In the bullpen, we had Cecil Upshaw and George Stone.

In the regular lineup, we had Bob Didier and Bob Tillman to split catching duty, Orlando Cepeda at first base, Felix Millan at second, Sonny Jackson and Gil Garrido sharing shortstop, Clete Boyer at third, Rico Carty and Tony Gonzalez sharing left field, Felipe Alou in center, and Hank Aaron in right. On the bench, we had Tito Francona, Mike Lum, and Bob Aspromonte. Veterans and youth, but all talented.

We started the season with a pair of wins over the Giants at home before it was my turn to pitch. I went six innings, giving up only one run in the first inning. I retired 14 straight hitters at one stretch. We won, 4-1, and I got my first win. Only 19 more to go.

My next start was a loss to the Astros in Houston, 4-2. I gave up all four of their runs, only three being earned, in seven and a third innings. No support and I was 1-1. I still had 19 to go.

I missed my next start because my arm was tight. Then we went out to the West Coast. I faced the Giants again, and I threw well, going seven innings and giving up only two runs. The bullpen couldn't hold them in the eighth, and we lost, 5-1. No support and another loss for me. One win and holding.

I faced the Astros again, this time at home, and beat them myself, 2-1. Almost. I pitched seven innings and only allowed the one run, but I also drove in a run with a single. My record was even at 2-2. The countdown to 20 resumed.

By this time, it became apparent that Harris was going with a three-man rotation of Niekro, Reed, and Jarvis, with a fourth and fifth starter when needed. I was the fourth and Britton the fifth when he was healthy. When Jim wasn't well, Stone started. Harris would pitch Niekro, Reed, and Jarvis on successive days, then pitch me on the fourth day, if we had a game. If not, he went back to Niekro because he was a knuckleball pitcher who could throw every fourth day without too much stress to his pitching arm. I didn't like this arrangement because I felt I was a better pitcher than either Jarvis or Reed. But I wasn't the manager. So I just went out and did the best I could.

My first start in May was against the Dodgers at home. I held them to three hits and one run over six innings, and came away with a win, 3-2. This raised our team record to 17-8. We were in first place, two games ahead of the Dodgers. I was one closer to 20, but I was wondering already if I would get enough starts to win that many.

My next start wasn't for another week. I went seven and two-thirds against the Phillies and gave up three runs. No decision for me in that game or the next, which was against the Expos. Unable to get into any kind of rhythm, I lost three straight games: to the Phillies at home, then the Cards at home and in St. Louis. I didn't pitch well in any of those games. My record dropped to 3-5 before I finally won again, a 4-3 victory over the Pirates in the second game of a doubleheader at home. I helped myself that game with a homer and two RBIs. My record was now 4-5, but at this rate, I'd be lucky to win 15.

The following Friday night Harris gave me the call against the Pirates in Pittsburgh. I was sharp for nine innings, holding the Bucs to just one run before we lost it in the 10th. I put the winning runner on before Harris pulled me. Again, no support and another defeat.

Harris pulled me after four innings of my next start which was against the Astros at home. I'd only given up three runs on six hits, but he was the manager and we were in first place. What was I to say? We won the game, but it was a no-decision for me.

The next outing for me was the first game of a doubleheader with the Giants in Atlanta. I lost the opener, 5-1, to drop my record to 4-7. Again, no support.

That afternoon, just before the second game was about to begin, Harris looked down the bench to see if the starters were ready to take the field. When he didn't see Orlando Cepeda who was in the starting lineup, he looked at me and said, "Milt, go find Cepeda." So I went into the clubhouse to find him and tell him it was game time. I looked high and low for him and couldn't find him. I checked the toilets and everything. Nowhere. Then I looked toward the training room and saw that the door was closed. I opened it, and man, I got hit with some heavy smoke. There was Cepeda and another guy that I can't recall at this time, smoking a little marijuana and getting higher than a kite.

"Hey, guys, three minutes to game time."

They somehow got to the field just in time for the game to start. Oh, yeah. We won the game, 7-5. Those Sunday double-headers could be long days at the office.

My next start was in Frisco 12 days later on July 4th. I threw six effective innings, holding the Giants to two runs on three hits and as many walks. The bullpen blew it, and we lost, 7-6. Another lousy no-decision for me, but we were still in first place a game ahead of the Dodgers.

Four days later I started against the Dodgers in LA, and they hammered me for nine hits, a walk, and five runs, three earned, in just three and two-thirds innings. I took the loss to drop my record to 4-8. I was having a lousy year, and it didn't look like it would get any better as we moved into the All-Star Game break. I gave up on winning 20 and set my sights on winning a mere 10.

When we came back from the break, my arm was bothering me, my knee was bothering, my shoulder was bothering me, my head was bothering me. I was a mess. Lum Harris sat me down for two weeks in hopes that the rest would get me going again. The truth of the matter was I was having domestic problems that were putting a lot of stress on me. That's covered in another chapter, so I won't go into it here. Let's just say that my head was all messed up and that it was affecting my pitching health.

When I did start again, I faced the Phillies in the City of Brotherly Love. I went five innings and won, 6-3. I gave up two runs, but I won. Then I had a no-decision with the Mets in New York, although I pitched just as well as I had in Philly. I pitched even better against the Mets in Atlanta, allowing only a single run in eight innings, but our guys couldn't score until the bottom of the ninth after the Mets had touched our bullpen for three more runs in the top of the inning. I took the loss, 4-1. I was now 5-9 and learning what it was like to be on the bottom of the barrel.

I beat the Phillies in the first game of a twilight doubleheader on August 13, then I lost to the Cardinals the following Sunday. That was my last decision of the year. My record was 6-10. I started two more games in September, but neither meant much to me. I got a few relief chances, but I didn't care. I was miserable on the field and off, but more about the latter in a later chapter.

We won the NL West Division, and we prepared to face the Mets in the first ever National League Championship Series. We were licking our chops, thinking there was no way the Mets could beat us three games out of five. We had a damn good team. The Mets had good pitching, but they were only a little above average everywhere else. They had been good enough to overtake the Cubs who had looked like sure-fire winners of the East Division back on the first of August, but the Cubs managed to play a little less than .500 ball over the last two months, while the Mets were winning like the Yankees of the 1950s. The Mets were hot, but we didn't care. We had the better team. We had the loaded line-up, pitching and hitting. We had tradition and history. But it didn't mean a thing because those amazing Mets had destiny on their side. They bounced us three games in a row. I got into one game and got roughed up for four runs in less than three innings. I went home to Baltimore after that and saw Brooks Robinson. Ironically, the Mets and Orioles were matched up in the World Series, and I spoke to Robinson about it.

"Brooksie, my friend. You're going to get your butts kicked."

He looked at me and laughed.

The Orioles were loaded with pitching, hitting, and defense. They had won their division by a full 19 games over a very good Detroit team that had won it all in 1968. The O's had it all. The whole enchilada. Everything except what the Mets had. Destiny.

The Mets won the Series in five games.

Some astrologer did some figuring on the star charts of the Mets and Orioles; the New York Knicks and Baltimore Bullets; the New York Jets and Baltimore Colts; and the cities of New York and Baltimore. Whoever this person was came to the con-clusion that it was in the stars that the Jets should beat the Colts in the 1969 Super Bowl, that the Knicks should beat the Bullets in the 1969 National Basketball Association Playoffs, and the Mets should beat the Orioles in the World Series.

I don't know about the stars, but that's what happened.

Oh, yes. All three New York teams were heavy underdogs. Go figure.

* * *

B ack to our series with the Mets.

In the first game, Aaron disappeared down the dugout runway for a while every time he came off the field. Curious about what was going on, I followed him one inning and found him with the team trainer. Aaron was just removing a batting glove, which he never wore to hit. That was strange in itself, but not as strange as the long gash in his hand that was sewn closed with about two dozen stitches. I watched as the trainer injected the injury with Novocain to kill the pain.

Aaron was having problems with his wife. When he went home the night before, he discovered that she had locked him out. Not to be kept out of his own home, he busted the window by the door to get in. In the process, he sliced his hand but good.

Much to his credit, Aaron hit the ball as hard as he ever did every time up. I never saw anything like that in all my life. He hit line drives like I'd never seen any human being hit before in my entire life. Every time up he hit the ball hard.

In spring training the next year, I told him to get his butt in the training room and start injecting his hand with Novocain because he could break every hitting record in baseball! We both had a good laugh over that.

* * *

W hen I was with the Braves, we had a traveling secretary named Donald Davidson, who was diminutive. A little person, I believe is the politically correct term for someone who was as vertically challenged as he was.

Every time the team went on the road Donald would always book our hotel rooms on the lower floors because he couldn't reach the elevator buttons for the higher floors. One time I called ahead and talked to the hotel manager, whom I knew fairly well, and who also knew Donald. I suggested that we pull a little joke on Donald. I told him next time the team comes to town to have a fake list of our room assignments that would put all of us, including Donald, on the highest floors of the hotel. My pal agreed to do this.

When we got to the hotel, the manager gave Donald the list to check over, then stood back. Donald went absolutely bonkers. He was yelling, swearing, and threatening, kind of like Yosemite Sam, the cartoon character, when he loses his temper. He was furious. He threatened to change hotels. He told the manager that he didn't want the high floors but wanted the low floors. My buddy played the role. He apologized profusely and said there was nothing he could do about it. Donald went into another tirade that was something akin to Donald Duck throwing a fit. Finally, the hotel manager started laughing and the jig was up. Of course, Donald wasn't too thrilled about being the butt of this joke. But he finally settled down and had a few laughs about it as well.

We players did a few other things to him, too. We'd hang him up on door hooks when he would get angry with us for something. He really got mad then, and we'd crack up while he was having a fit. Then we'd let him down.

All in all, Donald was a good-natured guy, a good person with a big heart, and I really liked him. Looking back now, I can't say that I'm exactly proud of the treatment we gave him sometimes. He deserved better from us. All I can say is, we were ballplayers with too much time on our hands. That's no excuse, but it explains our lack of consideration for a nice guy like Donald.

* * *

I n 1969, I appeared in 26 games, starting 24. I only went 6-10 for the season. I wished I could have contributed more, but that's the way it goes in baseball.

Niekro won 23 games for us, and Reed contributed 18 wins. Stone and Jarvis each won 13. Aaron smashed 44 homers at the age of 35, and Carty, despite being injured and playing in only 104 games, hit .342. Joe Torre had been traded to the Cardinals before the season began, but Didier and Tillman filled in. Their offense wasn't as productive as Torre's, but they did do a good job of handling the pitching staff. We had good relief pitching from Upshaw, who appeared in 62 games, saving 27 of them. He was 6-4 with a 2.91 ERA. Even my old teammate from my Oriole days, Hoyt Wilhelm, got into the act. He got into eight games, won two, and picked up four saves. He was still amazing.

But it didn't matter in the end as the Mets dashed our hopes of getting to the World Series. But it still was a pretty good season for the Braves, if not for me. All I could do was look forward to the next season. It had to be better than 1969.

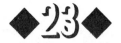

Box Seats:
For the Fans

Getting fan recognition is part of being a pro athlete.

It's funny when you become a Major League player. You're pounding your chest and you think you're a major star. It's not like being a movie star where everyone knows who you are when you walk out in public. It takes quite a while for fans to recognize who you are when you walk on the street.

That was kind of a bummer for me for a while, but it changed when television became more involved with baseball. Television brought a lot more exposure than newspapers or radio. I thought it was great that people recognized me. I was tickled to death that people knew who I was back then. Even today, when I walk into a place and someone recognizes me, I get a kick out of it. It's good to be remembered.

Of course, there were times, like eating dinner at a restaurant, when it could be a real hassle. But I always tried to be as very courteous as I could, unless the guy was belligerent or drunk and became a nuisance. At that point, I just had to tell the guy as politely as I could to take a hike.

As someone once said, "Fame and Fortune? I'll take the fortune, but you can take the fame and shove it."

* * *

Lee McPhail was the general manager of the Orioles after Paul Richards relinquished the job to be just the field manager. I was the top winner that year. When I received my first contract from Lee, I was quite disgusted with the size of the raise.

So I immediately tore up my contract into about a million pieces and sent them back to him. A few days later he called me on the phone and told me that I couldn't rip up contracts because it was illegal and all that bullshit.

"Why is it illegal for me to tear up my contract? That's how I felt about it because of the ridiculous raise you offered me. I was the top winner on the team, and I feel I deserve a lot more money."

"Okay, but don't tear up the contracts anymore."

"Yes, sir."

A couple of weeks went by, and I received another contract from him. He upped the ante a little bit, but I sent it back to him — unsigned.

About a week later, I was at Memorial Stadium to pick up my fan mail, and I happened to walk by his office. Someone was inside, so I just looked in, just out of curiosity. It was McPhail.

"Hi, Lee."

"Is everything all right, Milt?"

"Yeah, Lee, everything's fine." I continued to walk on.

Two days later my contract came back with the same money in it that was on the previous contract I had sent back. What the hell kind of a game was this?

Finally, I called him and asked if we could sit down and take care of it. He said to come in and we'd work things out. I went.

"Lee, why would you send me the same contract for the same money that I just sent back to you?"

"Well, that one day when I saw you walk by the office, I asked you if everything was all right and you said yes."

"With me saying yes, you thought I was agreeing on my contract! I don't believe what I'm hearing."

That's the kind of mentality we had to endure.

We worked out a deal that satisfied me, if not him.

* * *

s for baseball cards, Topps was the biggest card company doing it — actually the only one — when I broke into baseball in 1957. For a few years before that, the Bowman company had been in competition with Topps, but Topps bought them out. That was too bad because the Bowman people put out some really great cards, especially the television screen cards in 1955.

In the early 1960s, the Fleer company put out a set of cards, and a food company put out sets of cards on the backs of cereal boxes. During this time, the Topps people had an exclusive deal with Major League Baseball to produce collector cards of players, managers, and anybody else in Major League Baseball, including the commissioner. Then in 1981 the market opened up to all sorts of companies that wanted to get into the business of making collector cards.

My first card — No. 457 — came out in 1958. My memory isn't the best here, but I think they took the picture at Yankee Stadium in New York the previous year. The photographers for the Topps company usually took our pictures in spring training, and sometimes they took them during the regular season, especially if we'd been traded early in the year. I'm wearing a Baltimore uniform in the cards from 1958 thru 1966. Yes, thru 1966, even though I had been traded to Cincinnati the previous winter. My card number was 105, which put it in the earliest set to be released. Evidently, the Topps people thought my job with the Orioles was safe.

In all but two years, I'm wearing a hat in the picture on my cards. I refused to wear a hat when I was with the Braves in 1969, and I was without a hat in one of my cards with the Cubs. I don't remember why I wasn't wearing a hat, but I do recall how pissed the photographer was about it. The Topps people wanted every player to be in full uniform, including the hat, when they took the pictures for the baseball cards.

As for reimbursement, in the early years, we had our choice of either $125 or a gift from a gift catalog. That changed when Marvin Miller became head of the Players' Association. We started getting royalties on the baseball cards at that time because it was a small concession that the owners could give us. The last year that I played I received a check for $400 during spring training, and I thought that was fantastic. I didn't tell my wife about it because that was my rat hole money. Recently, I heard that players today are getting checks in the range of $90,000 a year. Either we were getting screwed back then or the business has grown that much over the last 25 years.

* * *

T he most money I ever made in a season came near the end of my career with the Cubs when I signed a contract for $65,000. But that didn't include any outside endorsements. Not that those were all that great in those days.

I did have get some endorsements over the years. I smoked, so I got one with Camel cigarettes and another was with Philly cigars. When John F. Kennedy became President, he put a halt to athletes endorsing liquor and tobacco. The money wasn't too bad, maybe a thousand dollars and a carton of cigarettes or a box of cigars. That was pretty good money back then. I didn't like cigars, so I always gave them away. I once got $500 for doing a television commercial in Baltimore, and there were a few others along the way.

* * *

S igning autographs was something I really enjoyed doing when I was a player. I still like doing it, but for a slightly different reason now.

When the Orioles signed me, I felt like a million dollars. I was cocky about it, to say the least. That was at first, but after getting to Baltimore and meeting all those guys that I'd only read about in the newspapers, I came down to earth pretty quick. I was the low man on the totem pole, as the expression goes, but I was still a big leaguer. That set me above a lot of people in baseball and some in regular life, too. Even so, I didn't let it go to my head.

The first time someone asked for my autograph I was honored by the request, and without hesitation, I signed. That set the tone for me. I signed every time someone asked me for an autograph. I signed balls, collector cards, photographs, autograph books; the usual stuff. I've heard about some guys signing a woman's breasts or a cheek of her derriere, but I never did any of that. Not that I wouldn't have done it, but no woman ever offered — or I should say — asked me to do that. I guess I didn't have the same sex appeal as some other guys.

Once when I was with the Cubs something unusual did occur. I don't remember which year it was, but the day was May 11, my birthday. How do I remember that? My wife Carole bought me a new custom made belt as a present, and I wore it to the park that day. After the game, I showered, dressed, and headed out to my car just like I did after every game. Back then, the players parking lot wasn't fenced in like it is now, so we had to work our way through the fans that were waiting there to get autographs from the players. That day there must have been 200 people mobbing me. I signed and walked and signed and walked. The fans kept bumping against me, but I kept signing and moving closer to my car with every autograph. I finally got to it, opened the door, made some lame excuse about having to leave to the people who were still asking for a signature, crawled into the car, and drove home. When I reached home and got out of the car, my pants felt loose. I went to tighten my belt and discovered it was gone. My first thought was that I had left it in my locker, but then I realized that I never took my belt out of my pants when changing into my uniform. Finally, I concluded that someone in the crowd had taken my belt right off me while I was wearing it. When I told Carole about it, she just shook her head with amazement, but she believed me. To this day, I still don't know how that fan got that belt off me without me knowing it.

There's no way that would happen to a player today. Not in any sport. They don't let the fans get that close to them in the first place, and most of them won't even consider signing their name without getting a check — or cash — first.

Players today are unfairly rude to the fans. They don't seem to realize if ticket and merchandise sales and television and radio ratings dropped — all of which come directly from the fans — then their phenomenal salaries would drop as well. Then see how friendly they become to the fans.

Of course, I can also see the modern player's point of view. How's he to know which one of those eager fans doesn't have a gun or a knife in his pocket and is crazy enough to use it on him? Who's to know when the next Mark David Chapman (the guy who killed John Lennon) will show up and shoot some player for some insane reason? That really happened, and it was long before so many idiots started shooting each other on our streets and in our schools.

Eddie Waitkus, who was National League Rookie of the Year in 1946, was traded from the Cubs to the Phillies in 1948. The first time the Phils visited Chicago in 1949 Waitkus was shot in the stomach by an obsessed fan named Ruth Ann Steinhagen. She went up to his hotel room and knocked on the door. When Eddie opened it, she shot him in the gut with a .22-caliber pistol. He survived to play again but not until the following year.

The fictional character, Roy Hobbs, the hero of the movie *The Natural*, was based on Waitkus. Or at least that particular incident in the life of Eddie Waitkus was. In the film, Robert Redford, playing Hobbs, was shot in the stomach by Harriet Byrd, played by Barbara Hershey. Harriet jumped out of the hotel window, but Ruth Ann Steinhagen stood trial and was sent to prison for attempted murder.

It's incidents like the murder of Lennon and the attempted murder of Eddie Waitkus that some players fear will happen to them if they allow themselves to get too close to the public. I said, some players. For the most part, today's players are just full of themselves and think they're too good to meet the fans. For others, it's just greed. They want money for their signature or they won't give it. It's those guys that I really resent because they're already making a ton of money and don't really need the extra cash. Some of them say that they only ask for money just to keep the fans away from them. I think that stinks just as much. The fact is plain and simple. Today's players — most of them — are just jerks who don't give two cents for the very people who make those high salaries of theirs possible.

You might ask me about charging for my autograph when I do a signing now, and I'd like to address just that point.

Most of the guys from my era aren't making very much from their pensions. Doing signings at card shows and such events like them is the only way some of us can still trade on our playing careers. Not all of us are big time broadcasters like Ron Santo, Joe Nuxhall, or Tim McCarver. Some of us still have to work for a living at jobs outside baseball and all the glamour of professional sports. For those guys like Santo, I say more power to them for landing a good paying job in broadcasting. Unfortunately, they represent a very small minority of former players. The majority of us need those extra dollars for doing signings at card shows and the such. I won't apologize to those fans who resent having to pay for our autographs. A signature is just about the only thing of value that we still own, and we're just trying to earn some money with it — money that we really need just to live a decent life. Why would anyone resent us for that? Beats the hell out of me.

◆24◆

Pitchout:
Caught in a Rundown

When Michelle was born in 1963, Carole and I figured we would be permanent fixtures in Baltimore. We had friends and a good home. The Pappas family of Baltimore had grown to four: me and Carole, our son Stevie, and our daughter Michelle. We had put down roots. This was our home.

Carole and I bought our first house in 1962. It was a three-bedroom ranch style located at 2119 Eastham Road in the suburb of Timonium. Brooks Robinson, Gus Triandos, Dick Hall, Jack Fisher, and Jim Gentile also lived in the same area. Considering the fact that I was only 23 that year, it was quite a move upward for us.

The house was actually a modest place. It didn't have air-conditioning or a garage. The lack of a garage was no big deal, but not having any air-conditioning was because we lived in Maryland, which is very warm and humid in the summer. We made purchasing a window unit for our bedroom a major priority. Why? So I could get a decent night's sleep, especially the night before I was scheduled to pitch.

Air-conditioning or not, the house in Timonium was ours, and we loved it. At the time, we thought we'd be raising both of children there. The neighborhood was quiet with good schools. We expected Stevie and Michelle to grow up there and eventually graduate from the local high school. Even after I was traded to the Reds, we thought that. Even after I was traded to the Braves, we thought that. Baltimore would be home, no matter what. Our home would be at 2119 Eastham Road for some time to come. At least, that's what we thought until the last time I was traded. Then we made a new choice. But that's getting ahead of things.

We were so confident that I'd never be traded by the Orioles that I started getting involved in local affairs. Nothing big, just a benefit now and then, or some promotion for the Orioles.

My confidence in not getting traded was increased when the O's had a night for me at the stadium. Actually, the event was sponsored by a committee made up of some of my friends. They gave me a night because of my 100 victories as an Oriole. I was the first Baltimore pitcher to reach that mark. Johnny Wilbanks, the car dealer I wrote about earlier, finagled a Cadillac out of some other dealer to give to me that night, which was June 22, 1965. A couple of the other gifts were 100 hours of free baby-sitting from a neighbor of ours and 100 lollipops for the kids. My teammates gave me a pewter plate with all their names inscribed on it, and I received a plaque from "The Birds Nest" fan club at the Maryland state penitentiary.

Among those friends on that committee was Stanley Scherr, a lawyer that I had met through Johnny Wilbanks. Stan was one of the finest men I've ever known. He invited me to dinner at his house, and I met his family. Sylvia, his wife, was a wonderful lady who treated me like I was a member of their family. She helped make living alone in Baltimore a very positive experience for me. Stan and Sylvia had two children: Harriett and Bobby.

A frequent visitor to the Scherr home was Harriett's boyfriend, Elliott Goldberg. He and I became good friends, and now we are the closest of friends. Elliott became a lawyer and still has a practice in Baltimore.

Bobby Scherr also became a lawyer, but when he was young, he was a batboy for the Orioles.

Carole entered this circle of friends soon after we married and settled in Baltimore. We went to a dinner at the Scherrs' home with Jim Gentile and his wife and Gus Triandos and his wife. That's when Harriett and Carole first met. They became instant friends, more like sisters because they shared everything from that moment on. As Elliott once put it, "They became attached at the hip."

Elliott and Harriett were married in 1964. The day was August 16; a Sunday. I started against the Yankees that afternoon and went six innings, holding them scoreless. I told our manager,

Billy Hitchcock, that my arm had stiffened up, so he took me out
of the game. The truth was I was eager to get to the wedding. The
game started at 1:00 p.m. Harriett and Elliott were married at
2:00 p.m. As soon as Hitchcock told me to take a shower, I took
a quick one and rushed off to the reception, getting there by 4:00.
It was a great party. The only negative for the day was the bullpen blew my 1-0 lead and lost the game, 3-1. But who cared?
Harriett and Elliott were wed, and that was a happy memory that
completely outweighed everything else.

* * *

As my salary increased each year that I was in Baltimore,
Carole and I began thinking about the future as well as
the present. We felt sure that I'd play out my career in Baltimore,
but I couldn't go on giving bowling lessons in the offseason for
a second job. And what about the time when my playing days
were over? What would I do for a primary job then? These were
good questions. I asked my friends to advise me on what to do.

The best advice I received came from Stan Scherr. He introduced me to Mack Snyder, a restauranteur in Baltimore. Mack
owned a place known as Punch & Judy's, and he was rather successful at it. Stan thought Mack and I would make good partners
because Mack had knowledge and experience in food handling
and I had the name, being a Baltimore Oriole. We decided to call
the business "Milt Pappas' Scotch & Sirloin."

Mack and I found a building in downtown Baltimore near the
Civic Center, where the NBA Bullets and IHL Clippers played
basketball and hockey in the winter. Before we bought it, the
two-story structure housed Meyer & Thalheimer, a toy store;
therefore, we had a lot of remodeling to do which would take
some time. We started our venture in 1965, neither of us sus-
pecting that I would be traded by the end of the year. Our plan
was to be open by the following fall because we felt certain that
the Orioles would be in World Series and because the basketball
and hockey seasons started in October. The idea was if the O's
were in the Series, then we could trade off my name as a player.

It was a good plan that worked except for that thing about trading on my name as an Oriole. Right from the start, business was good. Mack and I worked well together, each of us taking a turn at running the place through the working day. We had a bar and restaurant on the first floor and a large banquet room upstairs. Business was brisk, especially on game nights, which averaged five nights a week between the two teams.

Just before I was to leave for Florida the next spring, Elliott's father, Wilbert Goldberg, took Elliott and me to his Knights of Pythias lodge meeting over on Belvedere Avenue. After the meeting, we went separate ways. Elliott went home, and when he got there, Harriett was on the phone talking to Carole. In the next minute or so, an operator broke in with an emergency call. The restaurant was on fire. The fire department was trying to locate me, but I wasn't there. Carole was stressed, and so was Harriett.

Stan Scherr was president of the Baltimore City Fire Board. A limousine picked him up to take him to the fire, and he swung by the Goldbergs to pick up Elliott. Why? Because Carole didn't know where I was and she was afraid I was at the restaurant and maybe in the fire. Stan and Elliott volunteered to find me. They found me. On the sidewalk watching the fire. I was in a daze. My memory of that night isn't all that good, so I've had to rely on Harriett and Elliott for details in telling about it.

When the fire was finished doing its dirty work, the building was a total loss. We had insurance, but that didn't ease the pain of losing a thriving business. The investigators figured the cause of the fire was faulty wiring in the second floor banquet area.

Financially, we came out okay, but the emotional beating we took from the fire was hard on us. It only added to the horrible feeling I had about playing in Cincinnati. These two factors only slopped more grease on the slippery road I was traveling in my personal life.

* * *

 few years later I went back into the restaurant business in Baltimore with a new partner, Donald Hurwitz, an attorney. Don was a really outgoing guy. He was connected with just about every political type you could name. He convinced me we could make a go of it.

We leased a building from Max Cohen next to the Lyric Theater in downtown Baltimore not too far from the ball park. The Lyric was an old opera house that hosted stage plays. We thought our building would be a good spot for a restaurant because of its locality to the ball park and the Lyric. We had to remodel it, then we named it "The Meeting Place." We opened in the fall of 1969. Don and I ran the restaurant together, each of us working different shifts. When the theater was running a show, business was good for us, but when the marquee lights were off, very few people met at The Meeting Place. But as far as I knew, we were getting by.

Not long before I was to leave for Puerto Rico for the Major League Baseball Players' Association meetings in December, Don took Carole and me to sign the lease with Max Cohen. I didn't think anything of it at the time, but in the passing of the years, I've wondered why he chose that particular time to have us do it. You see, about two weeks after that, we closed the restaurant doors for good because it had failed. About 10 days later I was in Puerto Rico at the player-rep meetings when I got a call from Harriett who told me that Don had committed suicide. What a shock that was! We lost our restaurant, and now I had lost another friend.

All sorts of rumors cropped up about why Don took his own life, and none of them proved to be true. I want that much known about Don. He was a decent and honest guy who couldn't deal with failure. That's all there was to it. The stories about him taking money from the till and other similar tales were proven to be totally untrue and without foundation when the auditors went over the books and Don's finances as well. The restaurant just didn't make it because we didn't get enough business on nights when the Lyric was closed.

To this day, I still don't think failing at business is a reason to take your own life. I wish Don hadn't. I still feel sad about it whenever I think about him. He was a decent guy who deserved a better ending to his story.

Part Four

CHICAGO

◆25◆

Road-trip:
Traded Again

1970 started off really weird with an incident that involved Cecil Upshaw, a good relief pitcher.

The Braves were in San Diego for the opening series of the season. After the first game, a group of us went to dinner. We left the restaurant to return to the hotel. Along the way, Cecil was pretending to dunk a basketball by jumping up and touching the top of a bus stop sign, which was probably about eight or nine feet high. A few blocks from the restaurant, he went up to dunk, and when he came down, he was missing a digit from his hand. He'd hit the top of the sign and cut off his finger. It was not a pleasant sight to see after just eating dinner.

We found the finger on the sidewalk and wrapped it and Cecil's hand as best as we could to stop the bleeding. Then we jumped into a taxi cab and went back to the hotel where we found the team trainer. I put the finger on ice, and the team flew Cecil and the finger to a hospital outside of San Francisco immediately.

The doctors there sewed his finger back on. Of course, he was lost to the team for the year, but he came back the following season and to pitch again. It was just phenomenal that he was able to come back at all. He not only came back, he was still an effective pitcher, winning 18 more games and collecting 31 more saves over the balance of his career.

It was really sickening to see his finger lying on the ground and to have one of your buddies hurt, but we dealt with it. Queasy stomachs and all.

* * *

T he Braves were hoping to build on the success of the 1969 season in 1970. Atlanta's everyday lineup was mostly unchanged with Orlando Cepeda, Felix Millan, Sonny Jackson, Clete Boyer, Hank Aaron, and Tony Gonzalez being joined by Rico Carty and Bob Tillman. The pitching staff was much the same with the very large exception of Upshaw being on the disabled list and with the addition of Jim Nash who had come to the club in a winter trade with Oakland for Felipe Alou. Upshaw's role as closer was taken by Hoyt Wilhelm.

The acquisition of Nash didn't bode well for me. The rotation already had Phil Niekro, Pat Jarvis, Ron Reed, and George Stone. That left me and Nash. He was younger than me by six years, but he already had four years experience with the A's. In his rookie year, he was called up in mid-season and won 12 games while only losing once. Big things were expected from him, but when he didn't even come close to that kind of performance again in the next three full years, the A's shipped him to Atlanta. He took what should have been my spot in the rotation.

Lum Harris put me in the bullpen to start the season, and I pretty much stayed there. I made all of two relief appearances in the month of April. In May, I witnessed Hoyt Wilhelm pitch in his 1,000th game, then I saw Ernie Banks hit his 500th homer. In the meantime, I made a few more appearances in relief, and I got two starts. By the middle of June, it was becoming clear that I was the proverbial fifth wheel on the Atlanta pitching machine. I had a 2-2 record in 11 games, of which three were starts and eight were in mop up duty. My ERA was a really lousy 6.00 as I had given up 44 hits in just 36 innings. My control was still good; I only walked seven hitters, while striking out 25.

I was unhappy with my situation. I wanted out, and the Braves obliged me. The move was due more to a friend of mine intervening on my behalf than it was Atlanta trying to do me a favor. The friend was Blake Cullen, traveling secretary for the Cubs. He put the bug in Chicago general manager John Holland's ear to buy my contract from the Braves. More about Blake later.

* * *

W ell, it was time to move on again. The Braves peddled me to the Cubs who were in the midst of fighting for the pennant for the second year in a row. They needed a fourth starter to go along with that great trio of Ferguson Jenkins, Ken Holtzman, and Bill Hands.

I drove my car to Baltimore, intending to fly to wherever the Cubs were at the time. That night at home in Baltimore I received a call from Rick Tally, a Chicago sportswriter. He introduced himself, then asked, "So, what are you going to do for the Cubs?"

Without remarking that it was a stupid question, I replied, "I'm going to try to win ball games."

"Well, you know, I don't think you're going to do a very good job here."

Surprised by this remark, I said, "Excuse me? Who are you?"

"My name's Rick Tally."

Now I'm getting a little testy. "What can I do for you?"

"Well, I'm introducing myself to you and welcoming you to Chicago."

Yeah, right. Now I was hot inside, but I kept my cool outside. "That's the way you welcome me to Chicago? Telling me I'm not going to do very well? Mr. Tally, I think there's something wrong with you." I paused to let him respond to that, but when he didn't, I went on, saying, "Obviously with Atlanta, I wasn't doing too well, but I still have a lot of time left in me. So I'm going to go out and win some games."

"Well, I don't think you're going to really help the Cubs."

My shot. "That's one man's opinion, but I don't really care what you think."

End of conversation.

He wrote the piece on me, and I felt the hatchet in my skull. What an idiot! But Rick Tally ripped the hell out of everybody. Of course, he wasn't the only sportswriter who took delight in tearing into players.

The worst press was in Boston. Beantown writers back then were just horrible. They ripped anybody anytime they could. New York was pretty bad too because a ton of writers covered baseball at that time. Chicago writers, with the exception of Tally, were great. Jerry Holtzman, Bob Verdi, and others. They were great then and still are. Baltimore writers were extremely gracious. Most of them anyway. Some were jerks like Tally, but most of them were all right.

Some newspaper writers were and still are jealous of ballplayers because we're out there playing a kids game and making decent money and they aren't. They have to cover us, and they resent seeing us having a good time playing a game and getting paid well for it. Newspaper writers made baseball the national pastime by building up the early players as heroes and "men of the stick." Those early writers never envisioned salaries getting to where they are today. If they had, maybe they wouldn't have written such glowing stories about players like Cap Anson, Mike Kelly, George Wright, John Clarkson, and hundreds of others who gave baseball its start.

But they wrote those stories, and it appears that some writers today are trying to counter their predecessors' mistakes. Many radio and television sportscasters are the same way, but most are decent guys just doing a job. The ones I dislike are the frustrated jocks who never made it into the game. They seem to have a bigger axe to grind than the guys who played the games.

A few writers I know should get the same respect and admiration that professional athletes receive from the public, but for some odd reason, the public idolizes people of great physical prowess more than the people with exceptional intelligence and mental talents. Why is that? I'm not sure, but it boggles my mind that more kids know more about Babe Ruth than they know about Thomas Edison. Or how about Mark McGwire and Bill Gates? I'll bet if you asked a kid five questions about McGwire he'd get at least three right, but if you asked him five questions about Gates, he'd be lucky to get one right.

Let's weigh their accomplishments. The Babe and Mark hit homers for a living. Who benefitted from that? Edison improved and made practical all sorts of things from the light bulb to the phonograph to the motion picture camera. Bill Gates has written some incredible software that has made life easier for nearly everybody on the planet. So why do we build up jocks and not the people who make our lives better? I don't have the complete answer, but I think it has something to do with entertainment. That's why everybody remembers the actor, but only a small minority can tell you who wrote the play or the movie or the television show. Funny thing about that. If a play, a movie, or a TV show is bad, nobody blames the actors or the director for it. But the writer? The writer gets the shaft.

All things considered, it's wrong to celebrate the one — the physical — and ignore the other — the intellectual.

* * *

T he Cubs missed winning their division in 1969 by a full nine games after having a lead of nine games in August. I know most baseball historians say they "blew the pennant" to the Mets, but I believe the Mets took it away from them. That's right. Let's give credit where credit is due. The Mets took it from the Cubs.

When I joined the Cubs in June, Pittsburgh and New York were fighting with Chicago for the top spot in the NL East. I met the Cubs in Steeltown for a big four-game weekend series with the Pirates.

Leo Durocher was still the manager of the Cubs. He'd taken the reins in Chicago back in 1966. He said at the time that the Cubs weren't a eighth place club. They proved him right as they finished 10th in his first year. The next two seasons they climbed into the first division and finished both years in third place behind the pennant-winning St. Louis Cardinals. In 1969 with expansion and the advent of divisional play, just about everybody expected the Cubs to win the National League pennant. After all, they had three of the best pitchers in the league; an All-Star infield in Ernie Banks, Glenn Beckert, Don Kessinger, and Ron Santo; future Hall of Fame outfielder Billy Williams in left; and one of the best catchers in the game at that time in Randy Hundley. They should have won it, but they didn't.

All those guys were still in Chicago when I arrived. Moreover, the Cubs had acquired Johnny Callison over the winter. They also had Jim Hickman who was a late bloomer, having been the only regular to produce down the stretch in 1969. Hickman was in the midst of a career year when I got there.

My first game with the Cubs was another one of those historical events that seemed to be following me around during my career. The Pirates had played at Forbes Field for more than six decades, but they were soon to move into their new park: Three Rivers Stadium. The Pirates played their first game in the old stadium back on June 30, 1909, and the Cubs were their opponent. The great Hall of Fame pitcher Ed Reulbach and the Cubs won that first game, 3-2. I only mention Reulbach because he was born in Detroit and so was I. How's that for an oddity?

Durocher decided to give me my first start in the weekend series with the Pirates because the next series was against the Cardinals and I had a 1-8 lifetime mark against St. Louis. The Cubs were in the midst of a long losing streak at this time. Leo penciled me in to start the second game of a Sunday double-header. The Pirates countered with Jim Nelson, a rookie who'd only been in the big leagues for a couple of weeks. I was rusty, but I was game to start. Hands faced Bob Moose in the opener, and the Pirates extended Chicago's losing streak to nine games, 3-2. The nightcap was the last game to be played at Forbes. The Pirates and that rookie — yes, another unheralded rookie in a long line of unknown rookies who never amounted to a hill of beans — beat me, 4-1, but I pitched decently considering how little mound time I'd had that year.

On July 4th, I got another shot at the Pirates, this time in Chicago. Again I started the second game of a doubleheader, but this time I was opposed by a real veteran in Bob Veale, a great guy and a terrific pitcher. I took the game into the ninth inning, and we won, 7-2, to even my record for the year at 3-3.

My win was the second of the week for the Cubs. Jenkins beat the Cardinals earlier to end the team's losing skein at 12. Then we lost two more before I won. Having lost 14 out of 16 games, the Cubs were under .500 and had slipped to fourth place.

Four days later I moved up in the world when Durocher started me in the first game of a doubleheader against the Expos. I went the distance and beat the Canadian team, 5-1, allowing only seven hits.

Two days after my second win with the Cubs, sportswriter Dick Dozer of the Chicago *Tribune* wrote a piece on me. Dick is one of the good guys in the print media. He raved about my abilities as a pitcher in the article, and he gave the usual background stuff. But he wrote one paragraph that really spoke the truth about my career and my life. Looking back now, I think it speaks for itself.

> *Adversity has been the running mate of Milt Pappas. It's as if a cloud hangs constantly over his head. Pappas has pitched on more good teams in 13 major league seasons, with less to show for it, than anyone in the big leagues.*

I think that's called being poignant.

After the All-Star break, I faced the Astros in Houston, and I was on my game again, beating them, 7-1. I only gave up five hits, and I felt the Cubs and I were headed for a spectacular finish. Anyway, that was my intention. I wanted to pitch the Cubs to the division title, then the pennant, then the World Series championship. I felt I was the missing ingredient on one of the most talented teams ever assembled. Now with three straight wins under my belt, the Cubs were back to .500, and I was certain we were headed to the top of the NL East.

The Reds came to town, and Leo figured I might want a little revenge on those guys. I have to admit I was fired up. They were the "Big Red Machine" from Cincinnati with Johnny Bench, Lee May, Tony Perez, Dave Concepcion, Tommy Helms, Pete Rose, Bobby Tolan, Hal McRae, and Bernie Carbo. They scored runs; lots of them; everyday. Every guy in their lineup could hit it out of any park at almost any time. They were one of the best offensive teams in the history of the game. They hadn't been shut out all year, but on the 23rd of July in Wrigley Field, I held the Reds to five hits and blanked them, 1-0. This was my first shutout since August 30, 1968 and my fourth straight win. My record was now 6-3 for the year, and the Cubs were very much in the race for the pennant.

As a little bonus for winning those games, I received the

weekly "Warren Award." It was a $100 U.S. Savings Bond that was given to the Cubs player of the week by car dealer Warren Ottinger of Warren Buick. He was a good guy. As one of the perks of being a Cub, I got to drive one of his Buicks for free.

The next week those very same Astros that I had handled so easily in Texas banged me around for nine hits and six earned runs in six innings. We lost, 10-4, and my record slipped to 6-4.

At the end of July, the Cubs were only two games behind the first place Mets. Our record was 54-49. Jenkins had a record of 12-12; Hands, 13-8; Holtzman, 11-9; and I was a modest 6-4. I figured we were set for the stretch run and we could pull ahead of the Pirates and Mets to win the division. We had the talent; we just needed a little luck.

We opened August in Cincinnati. I took the mound with the idea of shutting out the Reds for the second time in a row. Now wouldn't that be something? It was really hot that night. We took an early 3-0 lead, and I was sharp. I held the Reds to one hit and no runs for six innings. Then Johnny Bench led off the bottom of the seventh with a single. I got Bernie Carbo to hit a grounder to Willie Smith who was playing first base for us. Willie fielded it cleanly, but his throw to second to double up Bench glanced off Bench's helmet into right field. Bench kept on going to score, and Carbo wound up on second. The next hitter bounced a scratch single into right that barely eluded Glenn Beckert. When I came into the dugout, Leo asked me how I felt, and I told him the truth: I was tired. He pulled me for a pinch-hitter. We scored another run in the eighth to up the lead to 4-2, but the bullpen couldn't hold it. The Reds put four on the board in the bottom of the eighth, and we lost a tough one, 6-4.

That no-decision on the first day of August took a lot out of me. In my next start, the Expos clubbed me, 6-2, in the first game of yet another long doubleheader. I followed that with wins over the Phillies, 4-1, and the Giants, 6-3. I had a triple against Philadelphia and the 17th homer of my career against San Francisco.

Now at 8-5 for the year and 6-3 with the Cubs, I threw what was probably my best game of the year, shutting out the Padres, 7-0. I gave up six hits, but that wasn't why it was a great game. In the bottom of the fourth, San Diego's pitcher Clay Kirby hit me on the right elbow with a pitch. Damn! It really hurt. I went out to the mound in the fifth and pitched gingerly. I got through the inning without any trouble, but I was concerned about the elbow. Then in the bottom of the inning, Ron Santo sort of avenged my being hit by Kirby. He slammed a liner off Kirby's body that knocked him on his butt. Santo was thrown out at first, and to add insult to injury, Kirby stayed in the game to pitch the rest of that inning and the next.

Are ballplayers superstitious? Some are. Me? I don't know. Maybe I am; maybe not. I do know that before my previous start this little Greek lady came up to me and gave me some Greek "worry beads" that were supposed to protect me from harm. Well, I had those "worry beads" in my hip pocket when Kirby hit me, and every inning after that, I stroked those beads. In the bottom of the sixth, I figured I was under their protection, so I threw caution to the wind and returned to pitching the way I normally did. We won.

That win kept us four games behind the first place Pirates with a record of 63-59. The Mets were still ahead of us, but the rest of the division was already looking forward to 1971. I went 3-1 for the month with one hard-luck no-decision. For the year, my record was 9-5 overall and 7-3 with the Cubs.

The Cubs headed west to play the Giants, and I got a start on August 23. Candlestick Park was always a beast for baseball. No matter whether it was day or night, the wind made it seem chilly, and the air there is always damp. This game was no different. I took a 3-2 lead into the bottom of the ninth. The first guy up doubled, then an error by Santo put runners on second and third. Leo pulled me out. In came Phil Regan. A scratch single brought in an unearned run that tied the game. Phil got a strikeout, then Santo gunned down a runner at the plate. That runner reached on me. After another scratch hit that put runners on first and third. Beckert made an error that allowed the winning run to score. We lost, 4-3, and I was charged with the loss. I don't know why, but I was.

Maybe Leo should have pulled me sooner against the Giants, but he didn't. I shook off the loss, and beat the Padres in my next start, 5-1. That gave me a record of 4-2 for August.

We were really in the thick of a three-way race with the Mets and Pirates when September started. Pittsburgh was in first; the Cubs second, a game out; and the Mets in third, a game and a half behind the Bucs. The whole Chicago team was determined not to let happen what had happened the year before. We pressed.

My first start of the month went well. The guys got 17 runs behind me, and I even contributed a homer. That win over the Phillies, 17-2, raised my record to 11-6 for the year and 9-4 with the Cubs. Every win made me recall that telephone conversation with Rick Tally. Not helping the Cubs, Rick? Yeah, right.

Like I said, we were pressing hard not to fold up down the stretch. After being rained out on Sunday, we faced the Pirates on Labor Day, and I got clobbered again, 8-3. I didn't last long on the mound that day, only four and two thirds; so Leo started me again on Thursday. I was much better, beating the Expos, 9-3, in Chicago. We were only a game out of first, but that was my last win of the year.

Leo must have forgotten about my poor record with the Cards because he started me against them when they came to Chicago on September 16. Bob Gibson was my hill opponent. All those banjo hitters played a tune on me, and I was gone in less than four innings. Gibson was sharp, and the Cards won, 8-1. This loss dropped us into a tie with the Mets for second, two games behind Pittsburgh.

We traveled to Montreal to face the Expos. We swept them in a doubleheader, then won the next day. My turn came again on September 20, and we were still only a game and a half behind Pittsburgh. I took a 4-1 lead into the bottom of the seventh. I put a couple of guys on, then Leo pulled me. Regan came in and got the side out but not before a run scored. Phil wasn't so good in the bottom of the eighth, allowing a couple of guys to reach and another run to score. Leo brought in Jenkins who hadn't had a whole lot of time to warm up, and everybody but Leo seemed to know that Fergie needed a good 20 minutes to warm up properly. Jenkins gave up a couple of cheap ground ball singles; you know the kind, the one with eyes that seem to find the holes. Then a lazy grounder eluded Hickman at first and rolled down the right field line. Callison ran over to pick it up and get it back into the infield to hold the runners, but the Montreal ball boy kicked it away from him. The umps didn't see that kid kick the ball, and two runs scored, one of them the winner. Another run came in on another scratch hit, and we lost, 6-4. I had a no-decision, but worse than that, we fell to three games behind Pittsburgh.

However, the race was still on. We had 10 games left to play when we faced the Cardinals again, this time in St. Louis. We dropped a pair of games to them on September 23, both by the score of 2-1. Despite the double-dip loss, we were still only two and a half behind. We weren't out of it yet. Holtzman beat the Cardinals the next night. We had hope.

Then the burden fell on me. The Phillies came to town. I started and went five innings before Leo pulled me for a pinch-hitter. We were down, 2-0. My sub failed, and the rally fizzled. The bullpen gave up two more runs before we could score one in the eighth. Philadelphia posted one more in the ninth, and we put two on the board in the bottom of the inning before the last out was made. We lost, 5-3, and fell to three and a half behind the Pirates with only six games to play. The Phils clubbed us the next day, and Pittsburgh beat the Mets to clinch a tie for the division crown. Jenkins beat the Phillies for his 21st win of the year, but it was to no avail because the Pirates beat New York to wrap up the title.

The Mets got me, 3-1, in my last assignment of the year. We finished five games behind the Pirates who went on to lose the National League Championship Series to Cincinnati.

It wasn't a great year for me, but considering how it started, I'd say it was an okay year. I was looking forward to better things in the future.

* * *

Before Blake Cullen became traveling secretary for the Cubs, he was in the hotel business in Chicago. I met him on a couple of occasions through singer Jerry Vale, who was a mutual friend of ours. Every time I went to Chicago, I'd always see Blake.

One winter when we were visiting my folks in Detroit, Carole and I went to Chicago, and we stayed at the hotel that Blake managed. He was a terrific guy, and he'd always wanted to get into baseball. Finally, the opportunity presented itself, and he became the traveling secretary with the Cubs. He kept talking with Leo Durocher and John Holland and told them they should sign me. He said, "Get Pappas, get Pappas."

Finally, when I was with Atlanta, the Cubs bought my contract. Blake was very proud of me, and I was tickled to death that he liked me that much.

Blake, unfortunately, got a raw deal with the Cubs. He was more or less promised that when John Holland retired that he would become the general manager. Blake was really looking forward to that, and I was hoping he'd get it, too. But it didn't happen. It was too bad. I think if he had become the Cubs general manager, I would have stayed in baseball and worked with him. Unfortunately, Blake got screwed, and he was very disappointed. Blake stayed around a couple of years, then went on to work for the National League Office in public relations and eventually bought a minor league team with Jerry Vale. They later sold it. Blake is now involved with a hockey team. He's done very well for himself, and I'm proud to call him my friend. He's a great guy.

In a way, Blake was like those guys Leo Durocher was referring to when he said, "Nice guys finish last." Maybe I can re-phrase that to read: "Nice guys get screwed." Yeah, that fits what happened to Blake more than Leo's saying.

◆26◆

Twi-nighter:
In the Gloamin'

By the time I got to the Cubs, Major League Baseball had passed up Leo Durocher. He was long past his prime as a manager, and actually, a lot of people thought he should have been fired after his little escapade during the 1969 season that some still say cost the Cubs the NL East title that year.

Leo's little escapade? Okay, maybe that's not the right word for the incident, but whatever it's called, Leo caused a serious morale problem within his club that many say was the primary reason for the Cubs blowing the pennant to the New York Mets in 1969.

What did Leo do? He got married. He left the team to spend a weekend at Lake Geneva, Wisconsin with his new bride. The Chicago players had no problem with him getting married, but they did resent him leaving them in the middle of a pennant race, even if it was only for a few days.

Others argue that the Cubs blew the pennant because Leo played nearly the same lineup nearly every single day. Hundley behind the plate, Banks at first, Beckert at second, Kessinger at shortstop, Santo at third, and Williams in the outfield. With the exception of Beckert who missed part of the season on the injured list and only played in 131 games, each of the others played in a minimum of 150 games, including Hundley who set a record for catching in 151 games that year. If the Cubs had been blessed with the same sort of talent at the other two outfield positions, Leo would have played them just as much as the other regulars. And the pitching staff? Jenkins, Hands, and Holtzman started 122 games between them, and pitched a total of 872 innings.

Whether it was the honeymoon in Wisconsin or the fact that Leo overworked his veteran players, especially the pitching staff, the Cubs came up short when it counted the most.

In 1971, Leo was 66 years old. That's not ancient for most people, but in Leo's case, he was beginning to show some serious signs of age. He hardly seemed to know who any of the younger players were, although we had quite a few that year. He gave most of his attention to the veterans, and he appeared to have very little patience with rookies by this time.

As for the team, we were basically the same club. Hundley was back behind the plate. Joe Pepitone and Jim Hickman would share the first base duties, although Ernie Banks was still around. Glenn Beckert was at second; Don Kessinger, shortstop; and Ron Santo at third to complete the infield. Billy Williams and Johnny Callison roamed in right and left, respectively. But centerfield was again a problem. Brock Davis, a speedy fielder but at best a mediocre hitter, shared time in center with a myriad of other young players as well as Hickman and Pepitone.

The pitching staff still had Ferguson Jenkins who had won 20 games or more for the last four straight years. Bill Hands was back, and so was Ken Holtzman. Hands had won 54 games over the last three years, and Holtzman had chalked up 45 victories. Kenny might have had more, if not for having to put up with military duty every summer, causing him to miss three to five starts each season. This trio had won a total 162 games over those years for an average of 54 wins a year. I figured if I could add my fair share of victories and the boys in the bullpen could hold up their end, then we should win the division and maybe the pennant and World Series. At least, that was the team's attitude while we trained in Scottsdale that spring.

For fun that spring, I played with a red glove. The powers that be in Major League Baseball decided that pitchers could use colored gloves that year. I picked red, and Jenkins tried out a blue one. Black, brown, green, and most other colors were legal, but white, gray or multicolored gloves were still outlawed. When the season opened, I went back to my regular natural leather glove.

For serious work in Scottsdale, I worked on developing a change-up. I called it a slip-pitch. Paul Richards taught it to me, but I hadn't used it very often as an out pitch in my pitching repertoire yet. Basically, I palmed the ball and threw it with the same motion as a fastball except I didn't snap my wrist in the delivery. This slowed it down and threw off the hitter's timing. He'd either swing and miss or hit it weakly for an out. Rarely did a batter get a hit off my change-up, but when one did, it really hurt, especially in the box score where a scratch hit often beat me or at least set me up for a tough slugger who belted one out on me and beat me.

* * *

Our Opening Day lineup was almost the same as it had been the year before. Kessinger led off and played short. Beckert batted second and played second base. Williams hit third and roamed left field. Santo was the clean-up hitter and held down third. Pepitone hit fifth and patrolled center. Hickman was sixth in the order and covered first base. Callison batted seventh and played right. Our catcher was rookie Ken Rudolph because Hundley was still nursing a pair of ailing knees, especially his right one which was sprained in training camp. Jenkins drew the call on the mound for the fifth straight year. Banks missed a starting assignment on Opening Day for the first time since 1954 because he was on the disabled list with arthritis in his knees.

The rest of the roster included veterans Hands, Holtzman, Phil Regan, J.C. Martin, Paul Popovich, and Rusty Torres; and youngsters Bill Bonham, Jose Ortiz, Jim Colborn, Ray Newman, Danny Breeden, Ron Tompkins, Garry Jestadt, Hal Breeden, and Earl Stephenson.

The year got off to a good start when Jenkins beat Bob Gibson, 2-1, in 10 innings. Williams hit a homer in the bottom of the 10th, and he drove in the other run with a triple. The euphoria of winning on Opening Day didn't last though. The Cards won the next day, then the Astros beat us on Thursday.

My first turn came on Friday in Houston. I was up for it. I tossed a three-hit shutout, doubled in a run, and scored another. It took me only 83 pitches, and I still had seven strikeouts. That evened our record at 2-2, but it would be a while before we saw .500 again.

We lost two more to the Astros, then lost the opening game in Los Angeles before my turn to pitch came again. I was cold in the first inning, giving up a pair of runs, but for the rest of the game those Dodger hitters belonged to me. Joe Pepitone hit one out, and we won, 3-2. I was 2-0, but the team was 3-5 and already in fifth place, two and a half games behind the Pirates.

My next start went well except for the fourth inning when I gave up five runs to the Giants in the first game of a double-header. That was all they could get in the game, but we only scored once. So I lost for the first time in 1971. We dropped the second game as the Bay Bombers swept the series from us. The Cubs were now 4-9 and in last place, three and a half games behind Montreal, Pittsburgh, and St. Louis. We weren't exactly getting off to a good start.

After a hard trip to the West Coast, we finally came home to the friendly confines of Wrigley Field. The ivy had yet to green up, but the old ball park still looked good to us. We dropped the first game in a series with the Mets, then I took my turn with them. The guys gave me some good support, and despite giving up a grand slam homer to Tommie Agee, I notched a win, 7-5. This raised my record to 3-1 for the month. I felt I was pitching well, but the other starters were struggling. Jenkins was 2-2; Hands,1-3; and Holtzman, 0-3. We were a combined 6-9. For one of the best starting rotations in both leagues, we stunk. If we didn't turn things around pretty soon, John Holland might carry out the threat we'd heard from owner Philip K. Wrigley and do some house-cleaning.

We won two of the next three, then I faced Chris Short and the Phillies on his turf. We were both superb that day. The difference was home plate umpire Harry Wendelstedt. Maybe that's not exactly fair, but he did contribute to the outcome of the game.

Like I said, Chris and I were both at our best. He was getting out of scrapes, and I was holding my own. In the fifth inning, we loaded the bases on him with only one out. My catcher, Ken Rudolph, came up and hit a weak grounder back to Short, who threw home to get the force out. Then I struck out on three pitches. In the next inning, I thought I had struck out the second man up, but Wendelstedt called it strike two. I thought I already had two strikes on the hitter, but Wendelstedt had called the third pitch a ball, which, evidently, I didn't hear; I thought it was a strike. Not having struck out that batter, I was a little disturbed. I questioned the umpire about the count, and he rudely told me get back on the mound and pay closer attention to the game. This only served to break my concentration. I proceeded to walk two guys to load the bases with two outs before Larry Bowa beat out a grounder to deep short to drive in the only run of the game. I went the distance. So did Short. He won. I lost. That's baseball.

My next start was another quality start, but another loss. This one to the Mets and Nolan Ryan. We left 12 men on base against Ryan, and he beat me, 2-1. This evened my record for the year so far at 3-3, and the Cubs were now 10-15, six games behind the Mets, and in fifth place in the division.

No pitcher is perfect every time out, and I proved this in my next start. I had nothing, and the Expos knew it. They rocked me for six runs on eight hits and a pair of walks in less than five innings. We lost, 7-3, and I was in the throes of a very depressing three-game losing streak. The Cubs as a team weren't much better as they dropped into last place, eight games behind the Mets.

As I wrote before, we had one of the best rotations in either league that year. With that in mind, it was inevitable that we would run off a winning streak, and in the second week of May, we did just that. We won six straight with me winning the fourth game, 3-2, over the Padres in Chicago. Santo hit a homer in the sixth for the margin of victory, and I went the distance. This evened my record again at 4-4, and we climbed out of last place to move to five and a half back of the Mets.

While I was slumping, Jenkins was carrying the club. At this point he was 6-2. He and I had 10 of the team's 16 wins between us, while Holtzman and Hands only had three between them. Everybody felt this wouldn't last, and they were right.

The last time we lost before the streak began I was the pitcher of record. I was also the pitcher of record when the streak came to an end. Trailing the Giants, 2-0, into the sixth, I made a mental error that allowed them to blow the game open. With runners on first and second, Ron Bryant, my mound opponent, came up. He put down a bunt that I fielded. For some reason that still eludes me, I turned to throw to third but didn't when I could have nailed the lead runner. Instead, I turned to throw to first but hesitated for that instant that permitted the slow running Bryant to beat the throw. Bobby Bonds then sent me to the showers with a big hit, and the bullpen gave up two more runs after that. We lost, 7-3.

The Dodgers came to town next. I faced them on the day that Greece celebrates its independence from the Ottoman Empire. With me being Greek, this seemed only appropriate. Some day! In the first inning, Billy Buckner hit a grounder to first. I ran over to cover the bag, took the toss, and got spiked by Buckner. He opened a one-inch cut in my right foot, but after having it attended, I continued pitching. The Dodgers put up two runs in the first, then I shut them down the rest of the way, which wasn't easy considering what happened in the fifth.

Wes Parker lined a real shot off the top of my left foot that ricocheted straight up to hit me in the forehead above my left eye. The ball still had enough behind it to rebound back to my catcher behind the plate. Chris Cannizzaro dropped the ball, and Parker was safe at first. Leo questioned the home plate umpire on whether Parker would have been out if Cannizzaro had held on to the ball, and the ump said he would have been safe anyway because my foot is considered part of the ground. Beats me how they figure that, but that's what he said.

Never mind Parker. I hit the ground, stunned. The trainer stuck some smelling salts under my nose, and I said I was okay. I threw a few practice pitches, then continued the game. I went the distance, and we won, 5-2.

After the game, the reporters asked me why I had stayed in the game after being spiked and then taking that liner off my foot and head. My reply was: "I'm out to prove something. My last two managers didn't think I could pitch more than seven innings. I feel like I'm tough enough to stay in there all the way and that's what I'm trying to do." It's funny, but I'm still trying to prove that I could go more than seven innings.

My last start of the month was in Pittsburgh. I was sharp. I beat them, 4-2, to break the team's four-game losing streak and raise my record to 6-5. I had a good game at the plate, too. I had a pair of singles. We were seven and a half games behind the Cards and feeling optimistic about the coming months.

On May 29, the Cubs sent Jim Colborn to the minors. He had been our union representative. Since I had been a player rep before, I was elected to the post. There was more to it than that, but I'll save that for another chapter.

The next day I came down with the flu or some kind of viral infection. It caused me to miss my next turn on June 2. Leo put me down to pitch on June 5, but I couldn't answer the bell that day either. Two days later he asked for a volunteer to start the game, and like a damn fool, I raised my hand. The wind was blowing out, and the Pirates were in town. I made it through four innings. Willie Stargell, Bob Robertson, and Al Oliver all clobbered homers off me. I was touched for a total of nine runs, six of them earned. We lost, 11-6.

My next start should have been June 13, but I was still sick with that virus. Leo gave me another day of rest, but I still couldn't go. He wanted Jenkins to start, but he also came down sick and had to go to the hospital, he was that ill. Phil Regan started the game, and lo and behold! he beat the Braves, 3-2. Who would have thought that? Not me. Not even Phil.

Finally, I felt well enough to pitch a game. The Cardinals were in town, and Jerry Reuss was my opponent. Reuss was a great guy off the field, but on game day, he was a first class bastard. We'd beaten St. Louis the day before in the bottom of the ninth with a homer, and Reuss set out to let us know that he wasn't about to let us do it to him. I got the Cards out in the first, then Reuss knocked down Kessinger and Brock Davis with high and tight heat in the bottom of the first. In the top of the second, I knocked down Jose Cardenal with a high and tight pitch. When I came up in the bottom of the inning, Reuss nailed me in the ribs and umpire Doug Harvey issued a warning to him. Damn! That really hurt, even if he didn't break any of my bones. I lasted six and a third innings, but I only gave up two runs. In the meantime, we crushed Reuss, and wound up winning, 15-5. This put us over .500 for the year at 33-32, eight games behind the Pirates. I was 7-6.

After the game, the reporters asked me if I'd knocked Cardenal down in retaliation for Reuss doing the same to Davis and Kessinger in the first. I said: "When I pitch, I sit back in the runway. I don't even see us bat. And nobody told me about it (the knockdowns). That was crazy. I hadn't pitched in 10 days. I wasn't sharp. Heck, they hit four liners off me in the first inning. We wanted to pitch Cardenal up and in anyway."

It sounded good then, and it still sounds pretty good. Actually, I almost always sat in the runway and hardly ever watched my team hit. Me knocking down Jose was just a coincidence. Reuss hitting me was quite intentional. He did things like that. Did I do it, too? Yes, but not on that occasion.

When the time comes to raze Candlestick Park, every Cub who ever played a single game there should bring a sledge hammer and give them a hand with the destruction. Check the record. The Cubs have stunk almost every year in that park. And in 1971, we were especially pathetic. We dropped six straight there, and two of them were pinned on me, including the game of June 23 when I lost, 5-2. We left 11 men on base. Either the Giants were that good or we were that bad. Maybe both on that day.

My next start was against the Dodgers in Chicago. I had nothing yet as a pitcher, still feeling puny from that virus. LA rocked me for 12 hits in six innings. They got all six of their runs off me, and we lost, 6-4. This ended our brief three-game winning streak. We were 37-36, in third place, 10½ games behind the Pirates who were taking control of the division.

Leo gave me three more starts before the All-Star Game break. I beat the Pirates at home, 3-1, with a complete game to even my record at 8-8. This win put us three games over .500 and brought us to nine behind Pittsburgh. Then we went out to Los Angeles where I beat the Dodgers again, 6-5, in the first game of doubleheader. I went eight and a third innings. I took a 6-1 lead into the bottom of the ninth, then the roof nearly caved in completely. I gave up a lead-off triple, a sacrifice fly, a homer by Dick Allen, two singles, a wild pitch, and a walk to load the bases and bring up the potential winning run before Leo pulled me. The bullpen allowed a pair of runs to score before sealing down the win. We won the second game to raise our record to 44-38, putting us eight and a half back of Pittsburgh. With half a season left to play, we thought we could still catch the Pirates and take the division.

We played six games in the next four days, but we could only win half of them. I won my start, 2-0, over the Padres in San Diego to give me a won-loss record of 10-8. Our team mark was 47-41, which left us a full 10 games behind the Pirates. Even though Pittsburgh had a double-digit lead on us, we still believed we could do catch them and take the division flag. We still had half a season to go.

* * *

After the All-Star Game, Leo reset the starting rotation back to what it was at the beginning of the year: Jenkins, Hands, Holtzman, and me. At the time, I thought I should have followed Fergie in the rotation because I was having a better season than both Bill and Kenny, but Leo thought differently. Those guys had been together for five seasons, so I guess they had seniority over me. At least with Leo, they did.

My first start after the break was against the Expos at home. I couldn't get through the fifth, but we won anyway to put us eight games over .500, our high water mark so far.

The Mets beat me in my next start when once again I couldn't get through the fifth. I gave up three home runs, two to Tommie Agee, a guy who seemed to have my number. We lost this one.

I got another chance with the Expos, and this time I went the distance to beat them in Montreal, 5-2. This was my ninth complete game of the year. I was beginning to envision a 20-win season for me and a division title for the Cubs.

Then the Mets beat me again; 5-2, this time. Although I went seven innings, we couldn't score on their staff. My record fell to 11-10. In the standings, we were 55-49, 11 games behind first place Pittsburgh, a game and a half back of second place St. Louis, and a half game ahead of the Mets.

I started the home stretch with a shutout of the Padres, 3-0. It was my 37th career shutout and 10th complete game of the year. The Cubs were now 59-50 but still a tough eight and a half behind the Pirates. This game was particularly sweet because my mother was there to see me pitch. I was 5-0 with the Cubs when she watched me pitch, whether in person or on television. Also, I was 5-0 against San Diego in my career at this time.

The Giants came to town the next week, and I mowed them down with a shutout, 8-0, in the nightcap of two. My record was now 13-10, and I had at least 12 starts left. Could I win 20? I thought so. But more important than me winning 20 was a division title for the Cubs. This win raised our mark to 62-51 and moved us to seven back of Pittsburgh. First place was now in sight.

August was hot, and so was I. We went to Cincinnati, and the Reds scored on me in the first inning to snap my scoreless innings streak at 18, but I shut them down the rest of the way as we won again, 3-1. My win would have made headlines in most newspapers across the country if not for Bob Gibson. He picked that night to pitch a no-hitter at the Pirates. Talk about great pitchers. Gibson was one of the best I ever saw. His win put the Cardinals five games behind Pittsburgh with the Cubs a half game behind St. Louis. The race was really getting tight.

From Cincinnati, we went to Atlanta where I threw a complete game, my 13th of the year, for a victory over the Braves, 7-2. It was hot, but I managed to scatter 12 Atlanta hits. Callison was the real hero of the game. He belted a grand slam homer to provide most of our offense.

We went home to face the Astros, and I lost a toughie, 4-3. I wasn't at my best, but we didn't hit either. Even so, we were still in the race. We were in second behind the Pirates by four and a half games. We had 37 games to play. We felt we could do it.

Evidently, Mr. Wrigley thought we weren't trying hard enough to win the division title. On August 26, he issued a public ultimatum to us through the newspapers. "Win or heads will roll." Or some-thing along those lines. Actually, he threatened to trade some of us if we didn't win the division crown. A lot of the guys had things to say about Mr. Wrigley's ultimatum, but they kept their mouths shut. For the time being, anyway. As for me, I hadn't been there long enough to have too much to bitch about. Leo and Holland were treating me fairly well, especially when I compared them to how the Braves handled me.

Anyway, I took Mr. Wrigley's statement seriously. The next day I shut out the Braves, 3-0, in Chicago. It was my fifth of the year and 39th of my career. I had help. The wind was blowing in, and Williams smacked a two-run homer and a triple that drove in the other run. I was now 16-11 with 14 complete games. The Cubs were 70-59, in second place, six games behind the Pirates.

I finished the month with a no-decision against the Expos. I went nine innings, but an unearned run kept me from a win. We scored in the bottom of the 10th for a victory that ended our three-game losing streak. That was my second no-decision of the year.

September started poorly for the Cubs. We lost three of four before I bested Steve Carlton and the Cardinals, 7-5, in St. Louis. I had bronchitis when I pitched that day, so I only lasted six innings. This was my 17th win of the year, and I was ecstatic about it. I'd finally won 17 games in a single season. I felt certain that I could win 20 games for the first time in my career, especially because I had six or even seven starts left.

The worst thing that happened to the Cubs was the loss of Beckert for the remainder of the year. On September 3, he ruptured a tendon in his right thumb when diving for a ball in St. Louis. His was just one of many serious injuries incurred by guys playing on Astroturf. He had to have surgery to correct the problem. Versatile Paul Popovich took over for Beckert at second base. Paul was a solid fielder, but his hitting was nowhere near Glenn's. We lost nothing with his glove, but without Glenn in the batting order, our offense suffered. We went 10-14 without him.

The effects of bronchitis continued to nag at me when I took the mound against the Pirates in Pittsburgh for my next start. I made it through five innings, giving up four runs on four hits and a walk, but Steve Blass was on his game that day. He held us to one run, and our bullpen pitched worse than I did. We lost, 10-1. We weren't quite eliminated from the race yet, but at 13 games behind the Pirates with 20 games to play, it was a fairly good certainty that we weren't going to win the division title. We kidded ourselves that the Pirates could be the second coming of the 1964 Phillies, but deep down we faced the truth of our situation. We were pretty much stranded on the bases with little left to play for except pride and personal statistics.

By the time my next start rolled around, I was feeling much better; the bronchitis was gone and I had energy again. It showed in my performance. I held the Pirates scoreless through six innings before Stargell socked a two-run dinger in the seventh. We had a chance to score in the bottom of the inning, so Leo pulled me for a pinch-hitter. The stratagem failed, then the bullpen failed, allowing three more runs before we finally scored a futile run in the bottom of the ninth. We lost, 5-1. We were now only two games away from being eliminated in the NL East title race.

Having gone two straight starts without a win, the pressure was now on me and on me hard, if I was to be a 20-game winner for the year. I had to win all three of my remaining starts. It was not to be.

My next turn was in the road in Philadelphia, and it was my bad luck to draw Rick Wise as my mound opponent. I went 10 innings and gave up only three runs on 13 hits and three walks. Wise went all the way before his guys put across the winner in the bottom of the 12th. This was my third no-decision of the year.

My record for the year still stood at 17-13, and I only had two starts left. I lost to the Phillies in Chicago, then I faced the Expos on the last day of the season. It was a memorable game because I hit Ron Hunt with a pitch. What's so big about that? It was the 50th time that year Hunt was hit by a pitch. This is still the Major League record. Also, the bullpen blew the lead I left with, and we lost, 6-5. This was my fifth no-decision of the year. Had I won three of those … well, you do the math.

For me, it was still a milestone season with 17 wins for the first time in my career. For the Cubs, it was another winning campaign, but for the fifth year in a row, Chicago was a bridesmaid. Looking back, I can see that I was with the right team at the right time.

◆27◆

Strike:
Painting the Black

O ver the winter between the 1971 and 1972 seasons, the Orioles traded Frank Robinson to the Dodgers for Doyle Alexander and three other guys. The Reds traded him to Baltimore because they thought he was over the hill, and now the O's were doing the same thing. That was an irony that wasn't lost on me. The difference? In 1972, Frank really was in a steady decline as a player.

Robinson coming back to the National League delighted me. That's an understatement. I don't recall jumping up and down with joy exactly, but I was very happy about it. My pleasure found expression when we played the Dodgers in Chicago that June. Before the game, I went to my catcher Randy Hundley and told him I was going to have a little fun with Robinson.

"I'm going to knock him on his butt every time he comes up. I just thought you should know."

Hundley looked at me a little quizzically and said, "What are you talking about?"

I grinned and said, "That's it. That's all I'm telling you." I didn't tell him anymore than that.

The first time up, with the first pitch, I knocked Robinson on his butt with a high inside fastball. The second pitch, I knocked him on his butt again. Three sliders later, I struck him out. He came up the second time, and once again, I knocked him down a couple of times and struck him out again. The third time Frank stepped up to the plate, I knocked him down on the first pitch, and he jumped up just livid. He turned to Hundley and asked, "What in the hell is wrong with this guy? He's trying to kill me.

What in the hell is going on?"

"I don't know, Frank," replied Hundley. "I honestly don't know what in the world he's doing."

Robinson touched me for a single, but the next time up, he popped out. We won the game.

Afterwards, Hundley came up to me and said, "Now, tell me what in the world was going on with you and Frank. Why did you knock him down every time he came up?"

"Well, seven years ago I got traded for him, and he refused to let this photographer take our picture together in spring training."

Hundley just shook his head and walked away.

Looking back, I'm thinking, maybe two wrongs don't make a right; but at the time, I got a lot of personal satisfaction out of it. Since then, the few times that Frank and I have had any contact, we've been civil to each other. He's never mentioned the knockdown pitches, and I've never said anything about the photo incident. He probably doesn't even remember either of those moments in our lives.

* * *

1972 was a really strange year. For starters, Ernie Banks retired; Kenny Holtzman was traded to the Oakland A's for Rick Monday; the Cubs picked up Jose Cardenal from the Milwaukee Brewers for Jim Colborn, Earl Stephenson, and Brock Davis; and Johnny Callison was sent to the New York Yankees in January for the always famous player-to-be-named-later, in this case, much later, May 17, 1972 when the Yankees delivered relief pitcher Jack Aker to the Cubs.

Banks became old for a baseball player. He turned 41 in January that year, so the Cubs made him a coach. Owner Philip K. Wrigley always liked Ernie because he never caused any trouble for the team and he always took the first contract offered to him every year. I'm not saying that Mr. Wrigley was a racist, but whenever other African-American players showed the slightest sign of discontent, they were shipped elsewhere; the first case being Gene Baker who was sent to the Pirates for asking for a little more money one year. Then there was Bill Madlock, a two-time National League batting champ who was only 25 years old; he wanted more money, said so in the papers, and wound up in San Francisco for it. I don't know if this happened to any white players, but if it did, I wish someone would tell me about it so I can give the memory of Mr. Wrigley a better due.

Anyway, Ernie was kept in the employ of the Chicago Cubs after his playing days were behind him.

Holtzman was traded not so much because the Cubs needed a solid centerfielder but because of a conflict. At the middle of the previous season, it became quite apparent that either he would be going elsewhere in the offseason or Leo Durocher would become unemployed. Kenny and Leo were at war in the clubhouse, so one of them had to go. Since Mr. Wrigley was under Leo's spell, Kenny moved on. The deal was announced on November 29, 1971. That same day Leo stated unequivocally to the Chicago press that he would be the Cubs manager in 1972. Actually, he crowed about it because he had won the battle. Afterwards, Kenny had a lot to say about Leo, and none of it was good. This was one case where the team should have kept the player and fired the manager.

Jim Colborn was a rising young star in the Cubs organization, but he was just one of several good arms in the system. Burt Hooton had been signed the year before out of the University of Texas, and it was clear that he had the stuff to pitch in the big leagues. Also, the Cubs had Rick Reuschel on the farm, and he appeared to be ready to make the jump. There were others as well, so Colborn was very expendable. The Brewers needed pitching, and the Cubs needed another solid outfielder. So a deal was done. Colborn went north to Beertown, and Jose Cardenal came south to Chicago. Jose was slated to replace Callison as the regular in left field.

Those moves put a different face on the Cubs for 1972.

Also over the winter, labor negotiations heated up between the owners and the players union. The details about that and the strike that ensued are in another chapter.

Then two weeks before the season was supposed to open I

suffered a real injury. On March 24, we were playing the Angels and I was pitching. I was also batting. The bunt sign was given to me. I squared around to lay one down. Andy Messersmith, California's pitcher, threw a fastball inside. I tried to get out of the way, but I wasn't quick enough. The ball hit the bat anyway. The trouble was, it also hit the little finger on my pitching hand. Actually, the ball kind of mashed it, opening a one-inch cut that needed stitches and breaking the bone in the process. Damn, that hurt! Fortunately, the little finger doesn't have too much to do with throwing the ball. Also, the players' strike gave me a little time to heal.

On a more personal note, my father died on March 10. He'd been fighting stomach cancer. I know I've mentioned this elsewhere in this book, but before he died, I promised him that I would have a great year. This promise had a direct bearing on my season.

* * *

T he Cubs had been contenders for the past five seasons in a row. They finished third in 1967 and 1968 when each league still had 10 teams and no divisions. When expansion created two divisions, they came in second in 1969 and 1970 and third in 1971. In all of those years, they had the same nucleus of players: Randy Hundley, Ernie Banks, Glenn Beckert, Don Kessinger, Ron Santo, Billy Williams, Ferguson Jenkins, Bill Hands, and Kenny Holtzman. Other players came and went, but those guys were the Chicago Cubs.

As already mentioned, Banks and Holtzman were no longer playing for the Cubs when the 1972 season finally began on April 15. Jim Hickman, Joe Pepitone, and Paul Popovich were back. Juan Pizarro and Phil Regan were still around, and so was I. Nearly everybody else was a newcomer. Cardenal and Monday in the outfield and Burt Hooton in the rotation. A few other guys made the team as well. We had a pretty solid roster.

We opened at home against the Phillies and lost, but the next day Hooton threw a no-hitter to put some real pep into the team.

Then we hit the road.

The Pirates were a tough club in the early 1970s. They'd won the division two years running and were World Champions in 1971. I faced them first in 1972. Although I hadn't really pitched in more than three weeks, neither had my mound opponent Bob Moose. I bested him, 6-4, but the real heroes of the game were Billy Williams and Jose Cardenal. Billy hit a three-run homer, and Jose hit a two-run dinger and a sac-fly. I wasn't exactly sharp, giving up nine hits, but a win was a win. I took it.

That was our last win for more than a week. We dropped eight in a row, including a doubleheader with the Mets in New York. I lost the opener, 8-2, when I gave up back-to-back homers to Cleon Jones and Jim Fregosi. I left in the sixth, trailing, 4-2. We finally broke the losing streak when Jenkins beat the Reds, 10-8. He went the distance because our bullpen had been so absolutely atrocious so far.

The next day I faced my old team and lost a heartbreaker to them. I went into the ninth with a 2-1 lead. Johnny Bench led off and did the last thing anybody in the stadium expected; he bunted. Santo and I were caught off guard completely, and Bench beat the throw. Tony Perez followed with a weak grounder that barely eluded Beckert and rolled into right field for a single. That put two runners on with no outs. The Reds brought in a left-handed pinch-hitter; so Leo pulled me out and brought in Dan McGinn. Ted Uhlaender put down a bunt that Santo fielded perfectly. Ron turned and threw to Kessinger who was covering third on the play. Don dropped the ball. It rolled away into foul territory. Bench scored the tying run on the error, and Perez and Uhlaender wound up on third and second, respectively. Two batters later Perez scored the winning run on a ground out. This was my first loss to the Reds since August of 1968.

We were off to a horrible start at 3-10, in last place, six games behind the Mets and Expos. A few more losses and Mr. Wrigley might carry out his threat to make some serious changes in the roster.

Then to make matters worse, Joe Pepitone quit. That's right; he quit. He retired. He said he'd lost his enthusiasm for the game and wanted out. I can't say looking back whether Joe's departure had anything to do with it, but the rest of the team suddenly came to life.

After winning the final game of the Cincinnati series, the Braves came to town and we pounded them three straight by scores of 15-1, 12-1, and 8-0. I pitched the shutout, the 40th of my career. The four-game winning streak didn't gain us much ground on the Mets, but it did get us out of the cellar. When I beat the Reds in Cincinnati, 3-2, with my next start, we had won eight of nine games to climb to 10-11 and were only four games behind the Mets.

We had a pair of postponements before I pitched again. I faced Phil Niekro in Atlanta. We locked up in a real pitchers' duel. The score was tied, 1-1, with one out in the bottom of the ninth when Darrell Evans ended it with a homer off me. This evened my record at 3-3, and the Cubs slipped to five and half games behind the Mets.

My next start came on May 18. I don't know what happened to cause it, but my right forearm was sore. I went out to face the Expos in Montreal, and I couldn't get out of the first inning. I got one guy out, gave up three hits, two walks, and two earned runs. Leo came out after the sixth hitter, and I told him my arm hurt. He pulled me. We wound up winning the game, so I didn't suffer a loss.

Leo passed me over for my next turn because the arm hurt, but he put me back in the rotation when the Expos came to Chicago for a series late in May. I felt fine that day and went the distance as we beat Montreal, 5-2. Besides pitching well, I had two hits and an RBI that day. My record was now 4-3, and the Cubs had climbed into third place with a 20-17 mark but seven games back of the Mets.

That was the good news. The bad news was my arm hurt again. Leo sat me down for my next two starts. I didn't pitch again until the Padres were in town in the middle of June. The arm felt better, but I treated it like it was made of glass. Being too careful cost me. We lost, 4-3. I gave up three earned runs in six innings, and my record fell to a mediocre 4-4 . That was the bad news. The good news was my arm felt good afterwards.

Although my arm felt good, Leo let me go only seven innings

in my next start. The Dodgers and Frank Robinson were in town. The knockdown pitches to Frank didn't affect the rest of the LA team; while I was getting him to swing at air, they were banging out eight hits off me. Fortunately, the guys gave me some very solid support, and we beat the Dodgers, 7-2. I was now 5-4, but more importantly, the Cubs were now 31-22, in third place, three and a half games behind the Pirates who were in first and three games behind the Mets. This was our fourth straight win, and we were in the thick of the pennant race. If only we'd won a few more games in those first two weeks …

We extended the winning streak to seven before I faced the Giants and Ron Bryant at home. Bryant was always tough on the Cubs, and it seemed that whenever he was at his best, I was the opposing pitcher. This game was no different. He beat us, 4-0.

It was about this time that Joe Pepitone announced that he wanted to return to the team. He was supposed to come back to the lineup on June 30.

More bad news for me. My arm was sore again. After beating LA and feeling good after the game, I told reporters that "I even started getting cross at home, and I wondered if whatever was bothering me was mental." Thoughts like that were plaguing me once again. The pain continued, and Leo kept me out of the rotation for the next two weeks. Over that time span, our record dropped from 34-23 to 37-33. Another lousy 3-10 stretch. Take those four weeks of games out of the standings, and we were 31-13. This is proof that it's a long season, and you have to be on top of your game all the time if you expect to win a pennant.

When I did pitch again, it was against the Braves in the second game of a July 4th doubleheader in Atlanta. My mound opponent was the notorious Denny McLain who was making his National League debut. The weather was stormy that evening, and it rained hard on the stadium in the top of the eighth inning. The umpires called it with the score tied, 3-3. A no-decision for me, but my arm felt okay after the game.

We went to Cincinnati from Atlanta, and I got the call for my regular turn. Feeling good and always wanting to beat the Reds because of the way their fans treated me when I was pitching for them, I went the distance as our guys scored 10 runs behind me.

This was the second game of another double-header. Jenkins had shut out the Reds in the opener, 5-0. The twin killing and Pepitone's return seemed to put some life into us again.

We went home to face the Braves. My start against them was going fine until the sixth inning. We were up, 4-2. I gave up a single and a walk around an out. Marty Perez came up and put down a swinging bunt to Beckert. Pepitone charged the ball, but it got by him. Like a fan in the stands, I watched the play instead of covering first base. This loaded the bases. Gil Garrido was the next batter. He hit a doubleplay ball. Force at second, relay to first, inning over, right? Not so said first base umpire Ed Vargo. He called Garrido safe, saying Pepitone had pulled his foot off the bag before the throw got there. A run scored. Joe, Leo, and I charged Vargo and gave him all the verbal abuse that the law allowed. Of course, it was all to no avail. The call stood. I went back to the mound still mad as hell. The inning should have been over, but I was still out there in the hot sun pitching to the guy who should have led off the next inning. I continued to bitch about the call at first. Leo came out to cool me down, but he didn't pull me out. I gave up a hit to let in the tying run. I was still incensed at Vargo. I gave up another single that drove in the leading run. Leo yanked me, but before I left the field, I gave Vargo the finger. He saw it and tossed me out of the game. Leo laughed at Vargo and said, "You forget one thing. I already had him out of there." We wound winning the game, so I had another no-decision.

My last start before the All-Star Game didn't go well. The Reds got the better of me, 6-1. My record was now even again at 6-6, but the team was in the doldrums again. We'd slipped to fourth place, 10 games behind the Pirates.

* * *

It's really easy to second-guess people years after something has happened, but back in 1971, just about everybody except Leo Durocher and Mr. Wrigley said the Cubs needed a new manager. Instead of firing Durocher, Mr. Wrigley told John

Holland to move any disgruntled players. The result was the trade of Ken Holtzman to the Oakland A's for Rick Monday.

Exactly when Mr. Wrigley and Holland realized their mistake in keeping Leo, I don't know, but they fired him at the All-Star break. The move was announced the night before the game and made front page headlines in the Chicago newspapers the next morning. Leo had been the manager of the Cubs for six and a half seasons, and now he was out. To replace him, the Holland hired Carroll "Whitey" Lockman.

Whitey Lockman had played in the Majors, and had even played for Durocher when Leo was the manager of the New York Giants in the early 1950s. His playing career included stops in St. Louis with the Cardinals, Baltimore for a few months in 1959, and finally in Cincinnati. I don't recall too much about him as a teammate with the Orioles because I was still just a kid and he was 15-year veteran by then. As a player, he wasn't exactly a perennial all-star, but he was a steady hitter. He's one of a lot of guys who homered in his first Major League at-bat, and he once hit homers in his first two at-bats in a game. A minor claim to fame for him was the 1951 playoff game between the Giants and Dodgers in the old Polo Grounds in New York. Lockman hit a double off Don Newcomb that sent Newk to the showers and helped set the table for Bobby Thomson's "shot heard round the world" that won the pennant for the Giants.

Lockman had been a minor league manager in the Cubs system and had done fairly well. Beckert and Kessinger had played for him at one time, and both supported his hiring. As for the rest of us, we decided to take a wait-and-see attitude.

* * *

My first start after the All-Star Game was against the Phillies in the city of Brotherly Love. Steve Carlton was my mound opponent. We went through eight innings without either of us giving up a run. In the bottom of the ninth, I gave up a single, then Willie Montañez jerked one out on me to give the Phils the win, 2-0. My record was now 6-7. This game was significant because it was my last loss of the year. Not that I knew that then.

The Cubs started the final two months with a slightly better than average record of 51-46. We were in third place, 10 games behind the Pirates. Could we catch them? The Mets did it in 1969, and the Reds and Cards did it in 1964. We could do it. Or so we told ourselves.

My winning streak got off to an unusual start. We won a rain-shortened game in Montreal, 5-4. The weather preserved my win more than the bullpen did that day.

A sore back made me miss my next turn in the rotation, but I was okay when it came around again. We were home with the Mets in town. I was feeling really good. I threw a three-hitter, but it was my bat that was really hot. I had as many hits as New York had. A double, a two-run homer, and a two-run single. I had four RBIs. The homer was the 19th of my career.

In mid-August, we went to the West Coast for the last time in 1972, and we were still in third place. We weren't exactly making a crazed charge at Pittsburgh, and the Pirates weren't showing any signs of faltering. If we didn't break even on this trip, our hopes of catching the Bucs would be pretty much dashed on the rocks.

I got two starts on the Coast. First, I went up against the Giants, and I came away with a win, 2-1, thanks to Jack Aker who saved the game for us and me. I was sharp, but Jack was perfect when we needed it. Then I faced the Padres in San Diego. I went six innings and gave up four runs. When Lockman took me out, we were ahead, 7-4. The first guys out of the bullpen couldn't hold off the Padres, so Lockman brought in Aker to preserve the win. These two wins raised my record to 10-7 and the Cubs record to 63-56 with six weeks to go in the season.

When we returned to Chicago, I started against the Dodgers and Bill Singer. We had Singer's number. I can't recall exactly how many, but I think we'd beaten him five or six times in a row when I faced him at Wrigley. I made one mistake in nine innings; I gave up a gopher ball to Willie Davis. That was the only run the Dodgers scored, while we put up a pair to win. I went the distance for my 11th win of the year. The five-game personal winning streak was the longest of my career to then.

The win improved our record to 66-57. We were now in second place, but the Pirates still had a lead of 10½ games on us. We could only pray for a total collapse by Pittsburgh. We were also wishing for Hell to freeze over.

* * *

Every pitcher dreams of getting one, including me. On September 2, 1972, I got mine.

The San Diego Padres were in town for a weekend series, the last inter-division games of the year. Lockman put me down to start the second game on only three days rest. Not that this was unusual, but it was the first time in more than a month that I started two games so close together. Even so, I answered the bell.

The Padres were still a very bad team. They'd been in the league for four years, but they still didn't have any stars on their roster. Sure, they had Nate Colbert who hit 38 homers in 1972 and who had a few other decent seasons, but if you say Nate Colbert anywhere except San Diego, most fans will say, "Who?" Nate could hit homers, but he could also be counted on to strikeout once a game. Beyond Colbert, the Padres were pretty much a bunch of hitless blunders.

The first guy up that day was the shortstop Enzo Octavio Hernandez from Valle de Guanape, Venezuela. Hernandez was in his second season in the Majors, both with San Diego. As a rookie, he had hit a "powerful" .222 with 110 singles, nine doubles, three triples, and no homers. In his eight-year career, he homered twice in 2,327 at-bats. I don't know for certain, but that might be the worst home run to at-bats ratio in all of baseball history. He finished his career with a life-time batting average of .224. I got him all three times up that day.

Next in the order was David Wayne Roberts who was born in Lebanon, Oregon back in 1951. Dave was a first class utilityman over a career that spanned 10 years. He could play every infield position and catch a decent game as well. He was a rookie in 1972, and on this day he was playing his primary position of third base. He hit .244 that year, but in this game he went hitless in three trips.

Leftfielder Leron Lee from Bakersfield, California hit third in the lineup in this game. He was in the midst of his career year. The season before he'd hit .264, and he would end up hitting .300 in 1972. He wasn't much of a power-hitter, but his job was to get on base ahead of Nate Colbert. This could explain why he was having a decent year. But not this day. I got him three times.

St. Louis product Nathan Colbert was the cleanup hitter. Nate was in the sixth year of his 10-year Major League career. He'd had three good years in San Diego, having hit 89 homers, including 38 in 1970; but he hadn't had that big RBI year yet, his best to date being 86 the same season as his best homer campaign. The big year would come in 1972 when he would end up with 111 RBIs. None of them would come on this Saturday as no runners reached base ahead of him and he went hitless against me.

Hitting fifth was the rightfielder, Clarence Edwin Gaston, better known as Cito. Like Colbert, expansion gave this San Antonio native the chance to play regularly. His best year was 1970 when he hit .318 with 29 homers and 93 RBIs. He never again approached those numbers in any subsequent season of his 11-year career. He was a great manager after his playing days when he managed the Toronto Blue Jays to four American League East Division titles and two World Series crowns. He wasn't too great this day in September 1972. He had an 0-fer in three trips.

Derrel Osborn Thomas, born in Los Angeles, hit sixth and played second base. He was a highly-touted 21-year-old rookie who had come to San Diego in a trade with the Houston Astros for Dave Roberts, the lefthanded pitcher, not the utilityman. Thomas never lived up to his press clippings. His best season was 1976 when he hit .276 for the Giants. His career average was .249. If he'd gotten a hit off me that day in September, he might have hit .250, but he made three straight outs.

The next guy in the San Diego batting order was John "The Jet" Jeter, the centerfielder. Born in Shreveport, Louisiana, Jeter was a perennial bench-warmer, pinch-hitter, and late-inning defensive replacement. He played in 110 games in 1972, the only year he appeared in more than 100. He drew a starting assignment on this Saturday, and he made three outs in three tries.

Fred Lyn Kendall from Torrance, California hit eighth in the order and played catcher. Fred was a good defensive backstop, but his hitting wasn't anything to brag about. His best year was 1973 when he hit .282 with 10 homers and 59 RBIs, all career highs. He was an easy mark for me, going down three times in three at-bats.

My mound foe was rookie lefty Ralph Michael Caldwell, a true Tarheel from Tarboro, North Carolina. He was 10 years younger than I was. Usually, rookie pitchers seemed to get the best of me. I mean, how many times just in this book have I lamented about losing to some unknown who never amounted to much. Mike Caldwell didn't fit that category because he went on to have some really good years, including winning 22 games for the Milwaukee Brewers in 1978. In fact, his best years were in the American League. Probably because he didn't have to hit there, so he could concentrate on his pitching. In the National League, he couldn't hit decently even for a pitcher, and on this day, I got him twice.

None of these guys will ever make it to the Hall of Fame as players. The San Diego lineup that day was weak, but they were still Major League players. They were exactly the kind of hitters that usually manage to beat a decent pitcher. Who was that guy who seemed to have Steve Carlton's number? Gary Woods. He had a lifetime batting average of .243, but he hit something like .444 against Carlton. Woods was a Major League player, and so were those guys I faced that afternoon in Chicago.

The game started like any other. The Padres went down in order in the first; we scored a pair of runs in the bottom of the inning. The Padres went quietly in the second, and so did we. They continued to go down in order for the next six innings, and we scored six more runs. Leading, 8-0, the question of whether we would win was hardly in doubt as the ninth inning started. Only one question remained to be answered.

So far I'd gotten 24 straight outs, beginning with Enzo Hernandez leading off. John Jeter was the leadoff hitter in the ninth. He hit a routine fly to left center. Billy North, our center-fielder, started back on it with the crack of the bat. Realizing that he needed to move in and to his right, he slammed on the brakes to reverse his direction. Didn't work. He slipped and fell. I could only think one thing. *Shit!*

Then seemingly out of nowhere, but actually out of left field came Billy Williams. He was running at full speed, left arm extended toward the ball which was falling faster than a meteor from the next galaxy. I didn't have time to pray, but something spiritual passed through my mind. I couldn't breathe. My heart stopped on the lub. *Get there, Billy, get there!* Billy stretched; Billy leaned forward; Billy caught the ball. *All right, Billy!* I started breathing again, and my heart hit a heavy dub. Outwardly, I showed little emotion, but inwardly, I thought I'd been brought back from the brink of death.

That brought up Fred Kendall. I had to refocus. I took a deep breath and pitched. He hit a routine grounder to Don Kessinger who scooped it up and made the easy throw to first. *Two outs! Two outs! One to go! Just one!* My heart was really pounding now.

This brought up the pitcher's spot in the order. We'd driven Caldwell from the mound in the eighth inning, so San Diego manager Don Zimmer sent up a pinch-hitter. Larry Floyd Stahl from Belleville, Illinois stepped to the plate to bat for reliever Albert Henry Severinsen. Stahl was a left-handed hitter who was pretty fair as a pinch-batter. In fact, he was so good that 35% of his games in the Majors were as a pinch-hitter. I don't know how many walks he got as a substitute batter, but he did get 52 hits in 252 official at-bats.

Everybody in Wrigley that afternoon knew that I had a perfect game going. How could anyone there not know it? Since the seventh inning, every fan in the place held his breath on every pitch I made, then cheered wildly when the out was made. They went nuts when Williams made that catch of Jeter's fly ball. Years later when the game story was reprinted in the newspapers, Billy was quoted as saying he had made a shoe-string catch of the ball. In the videotape I have, you can see that he made a waist-high catch. I guess making a shoe-string catch sounds more dramatic. I know that's the way I'd tell it if I'd made that catch.

Anyway, the whole joint knew I was working on a perfect game. All 13,000 people in the park and the millions listening on the radio and watching on television knew it, too. Larry Stahl knew it when he stepped up to the plate. He was sweating bullets just like I was. Will he be the guy to break up my no-hitter, my perfect game? He was wondering this, and so was I. He swung and missed the first pitch. Everybody in the park was standing and cheering. The pressure was mounting on me and on Stahl. Something had to give here. He took the second pitch for a ball. It was close, but home plate umpire Bruce Froemming called it outside. The fans groaned. I heaved a sigh. Stahl waggled in the box. Next pitch. *Swing, batter!* He did. And he missed it. The fans cheered me on.

The count was one-and-two. One pitch more. Just one pitch. Just one. Make it a strike. Make him hit my pitch. Strike him out. Either one. Just one more pitch. One more out, and I'd be in the record books. A perfect game. A no-hitter. By me. Me, Milt Pappas. Just one more pitch and — what? — immortality? Yeah! Immortality. In the record books forever. A perfect game. Something that can never be taken away from me. No asterisk. Something nobody can ever beat, only equal. One of the few. The very few. A perfect game. Mine.

Focused? Yes, I was. I looked in for the signal. Randy Hundley, my catcher, called for a slider, my best pitch that day. I wound up and made the delivery. It was right there where I wanted it. Knee-high on the black. *Swing, batter!* Stahl just stood there. Froemming pointed outside and low and called it a ball. *Damn!*

Another signal from Hundley. He wanted another slider. I agreed. I threw a good one. *Got him! Strike three!* Or so I thought. Stahl just stood there and watched it go by. Knee-high on the corner. Froemming pointed outside and low again.

I can't believe it. *What the hell's wrong with him? With both of them? How can Froemming call that a ball and Stahl just stand there? Those pitches were strikes dammit!* Or so I thought.

Hundley called for another pitch. A slider. I nodded. I felt the ball in my hand. I gave it a solid grip, my best. I wound up. I kicked my leg. Left arm out front. Right arm back, then forward. I released it. I watched it all the way into Hundley's glove. It was nearly perfect again. At the knee on the black.

Stahl just stood there.

I grimaced for the call.

Froemming pointed to first base.

Sonofabitch! He called it a ball? How could he call it a ball? It was strike three. It was my perfect game. Damn him! Don Larsen got a call in the 1956 World Series with the whole country watching. Why can't I get a call? Why?

Stahl trotted down to first base.

What did I do? I gave Froemming a few choice words that I won't repeat here, and his reaction was a smirk, as if to say, I showed you, didn't I?

Then I focused once more.

Pat Piper, the public address announcer, told the crowd that Gary Jestadt was pinch-hitting for Hernandez. I went to work and got him to pop out to Carmen Fanzone for the last out of the game.

I had done it. I had pitched a no-hitter. The guys rushed the mound to congratulate me, which probably stopped me from going after Froemming. I was ecstatic with the no-hitter, but it had been made a little hollow by Froemming's refusal to call any of those three pitches to Stahl a strike.

In the postgame interviews, I said a lot of things that were meant strictly for public consumption at the time and to keep me from being fined.

"I wanted that perfect game so badly. But I guess I shouldn't be greedy. The pitches were balls. They were border-line but balls. Froemming called a real good game."

"I can't believe the no-hitter as it is. I've always said I'd rather be lucky than good and I was lucky today. I got away with several hanging sliders and I had three or four real scares."

Both Randy Hundley and I said, "They were so close I don't know how Stahl could take them, but they were balls.

"I was just hoping Froemming might sympathize since it was a perfect game, but he couldn't be expected to do that."

And Froemming had something to say about those pitches. "It

(the perfect game) never entered my mind. They (the pitches) are what they are. It's a ball or a strike. Those three pitches weren't there (in the strike zone).They weren't even borderline at all. They were what we call shoe shiners, well below the knee."

And I capped it off by saying, "Up until recently, this has been a very depressing season."

Later on, I asked Larry Stahl about those pitches. He told me that he had already determined not to swing at any of them once the count was one-and-two. He also said he was surprised that all three were called balls. He'd had lots of pitches that weren't as close as those had been called strikes, but he didn't know why Froemming didn't call any of them a strike.

As for Froemming's remark that the pitches weren't even close, I suggest he look at a videotape of the game. Pictures don't lie. All three were on the outside corner and knee-high.

I suppose I should live by what I said after the game about not being greedy. I did get a no-hitter. Not many pitchers can say that. But I'll know in my heart until my dying day that Bruce Froemming robbed me of a perfect game, and I believe he did it deliberately. I don't think he'll ever admit it, so I don't have to worry about ever forgiving him.

Whatever. On September 2, 1972, I threw a no-hitter at the San Diego Padres, and nobody can ever take that away form me.

* * *

A fter the no-hitter, the rest of the season would have been anti-climactic for most pitchers, but I was on a roll. I'd won six straight decisions, the longest winning streak of my entire career. For all practical purposes, the National League East Division pennant race was over, but I had some personal stats to achieve. For one thing, I was close to 200 career wins. So I still had something to work for.

I missed my next turn because my wife was ill and I had to fly home to be with her. So when I was given my starting assignment I wasn't sharp. The Phillies pounded me for nine hits and three runs in just five innings. Fortunately, we had the lead when

Lockman pulled me for a pinch-hitter, then Jack Aker saved another game for me. This win improved my record to 13-7.

The guys gave me some real support in my next outing when I wasn't sharp again. I gave up three runs to the Mets on seven hits and a pair of walks in eight innings, but we scored nine runs. This broke our three-game losing streak, but it only delayed the eventual outcome of the season.

My mother came to Chicago for my next game because I was going for my 200th career win. She still had a perfect record of seeing me win games. I didn't want to do anything to spoil her streak, so I focused on beating the Expos, 6-3. With this win, I became the very first pitcher in Major League Baseball history to win 200 games in a season without having a 20-win season. Since then, Jerry Reuss, Dennis Martinez, Frank Tanana, and Charlie Hough have joined me in this very exclusive — if not dubious — club. Within the club, Tanana and I have our own chapter as both of us were born and raised in Detroit.

The next day the Cubs were eliminated officially from the NL East Division race when the Pirates beat the Mets.

My next start was in Montreal. The Expos had less to play for than we did, but I had the desire to keep my winning streak alive. I shut them down on four hits, 6-0, to record my 42nd career shutout and raise my record to 16-7.

Lockman gave me one more start that year. I literally faced Jim Bibby and the Cards on the last day of the season. I was still sharp, but Bibby wasn't. I got in five innings of shutout baseball, and we won, 3-0. Why did I leave the game early? Bibby hit me in the face with a pitch. As a precaution, Lockman lifted me. I wanted the complete game shutout, but it wasn't to be. I still got the win. It was my 17th of the year and 11th in a row. Who would have thought that would happen back in August? I know I didn't.

1972 was a Dr. Jekyll and Mr. Hyde season for me. Through the first four months, I couldn't seem to find the groove, but over the last eight weeks, I was the best — and luckiest — pitcher in either league. Maybe that dark cloud that seemed to be haunting me had finally evaporated. I could only pray it had.

◆28◆

Knuckle-Curve: On the Corner

Whitey Lockman was a whole lot different than Leo Durocher as a manager.

Frankly, I preferred Leo. At the very least, he was a jerk to your face when he had a bitch with you. But more than that, he really understood what it meant to be a Major Leaguer. Leo could communicate with the veteran players, but he wasn't much at relating to the younger guys. He delegated a lot of authority and the workload of teaching to his coaches. He was kind of a prima donna as a manager. He would sit on the bench and watch the players train, and when he did come out on the field, he usually just watched and listened as the coaches did all the instructing.

Lockman couldn't relate to the players at all. Also, he was a hands-on manager who didn't delegate much authority at all. He did a lot of teaching himself, but few of the players understood what he was talking about. When it came to pitchers, he didn't have a clue. Only a few guys thought much of him as a good manager. He knew when to bunt, when to run, when to pinch-hit; but he had no idea how to lead. I was in the majority who considered him to be a fish out of water. He knew the game of baseball well enough, but he didn't know men. As a manager, he made a mediocre first base coach — at best.

* * *

The Cubs still had the nucleus of the team that had come close to winning the National League East Division title three of the previous four years. Of the 25 players who had been on the 1969 team, only eight remained. Paul Popovich, Randy Hundley, Jim Hickman, Glenn Beckert, Don Kessinger, Ron Santo, Billy Williams, and Ferguson Jenkins were still on the roster. Bill Hands would have been number nine, but he was traded over the winter to the Minnesota Twins. From the year before, we still had Jose Cardenal and Rick Monday in the outfield; Carmen Fanzone on the bench; and Jack Aker, Burt Hooton, Rick Reuschel, and me on the pitching staff.

The most prominent newcomers on the team were pitchers Bobby Locker, who came to us in a trade with the Oakland A's, and Bill Bonham, who came up through the farm system.

The regular season started on a positive note when Montreal pitcher Mike Marshall walked in the winning run in the bottom of the ninth. For the seventh straight year Jenkins was the Opening Day starting pitcher, but he wasn't around for the finish, having been lifted for a pinch-hitter, which is kind of ironic because Fergie was a first-rate hitter as a pitcher. Locker picked up the win, his first of 10 victories in relief that year.

Lockman sent me out to start the next day. I went seven and a third, leaving with a 2-1 lead a man in scoring position. Aker came in and gave up a hit that allowed the tying run to score. Then he closed the door on the Expos. Santo made a winner of Aker with an RBI single in the bottom of the 10th. With two straight wins, the Cubs were off to a good start in the chase for a flag.

Scheduling and weather put off my next outing to April 13. The Cardinals pounded me for 13 hits in seven innings, and I gave up all six of their runs. It wasn't my day or the team's as we lost, 6-3.

Again the weather interfered with my turn in the rotation, and I didn't start another game until April 22. Once more I wasn't sharp. The Pirates banged out nine hits and six runs on me in five innings, and we lost, 10-4. I was 0-2, but the Cubs were 8-5, in second place, only a game and a half behind Pittsburgh.

My favorite patsies, the San Diego Padres, came to town for a series in late April. I got my regular shot, and I did the usual thing to the Padres. We clubbed them, 10-2. I went six innings and gave up only one run. Locker pitched the last three innings for the save. The victory ended our losing streak at four games and started a winning streak of four games.

We started May just a half game behind the Mets, but we were headed west for a trip to the Coast. I drew the Dodgers in LA, and although I was decent, we still lost, 4-1. I only gave up two runs in six innings, but the bullpen couldn't keep us close.

Lockman had me start the first game of a Sunday double-header in San Francisco. I was lousy, and we lost, 11-9, in 12 innings. I gave up seven runs in less than four innings. We lost the nightcap, then limped back to Chicago after a series with the Padres in San Diego that didn't go well.

I opened the series with the Phillies at Wrigley. We had a 3-0 lead in the top of the sixth when my pitching elbow stiffened up on me. I left with one out and two on. Locker came in and gave up a three-run dinger to Greg Luzinski that tied the game. It was another no-decision for me.

On May 14, the Cubs were in first place by two games over the Mets. I was due to start the next day, but cold weather canceled the game. That was the way things were back then. Today, very few games would be called because of low temperatures. If the thermometer dropped below 40 degrees in the old days, the home team rescheduled the game for a warmer day and a bigger crowd. Now it has to be a blizzard with wind chills below zero to have a game postponed.

When the weather warmed up again, I drew the assignment against the Cardinals in Wrigley Field. I started well, but in the third inning, I fell apart. With one out, I gave up a single to the number eight hitter, walked the pitcher, then was touched for a double by Lou Brock. I gave up three more hits, a walk, and two more runs while getting just one more out. Lockman pulled me with good cause this time. We wound up losing the game, 6-4, but I had a no-decision.

Lockman sat me down for a week to let my arm rest. When I came back, we were in Cincinnati. My arm felt good, and I went six innings without allowing a run to score. Lockman didn't want to risk hurting my arm again, so he pulled me. Aker came in and completed the shutout, 2-0. I got the win to raise my record to a mediocre 2-3. The Cubs were 26-17 now, in first place, three and a half games ahead of the Mets.

My next start was in Chicago against the Astros. I was doing fairly well until the sixth. We were trailing, 2-1. I allowed two runners to reach base with one out, then Lockman yanked me out. Bill Bonham came in, gave up a hit, a walk and a sacrifice fly. Both of the guys I put on scored. We lost, 4-1, but we were still in first place, now four and a half games ahead of the Pirates. I wasn't having any kind of a year so far, but the Cubs seemed headed for a division crown.

June 3 was a red-letter day in my career. I went seven innings against the Braves and held them scoreless. Bobby Locker completed the shutout for us, and we won, 3-0. I had a cold that day and felt lousy, which is why I didn't complete the game. Besides pitching well, though, I hit my 20th career homer, my last career home run. Those "cold pills" I was taking to get me through the day might have done something to jack up my strength. I can't be sure about that so many years later, and I don't recall what brand they were. I only remember that they got me through seven innings against the Braves. This win put my record at 3-4, and the team was now 31-20, still four and a half games ahead of the Pirates.

The Reds were my next opponent. I was still feeling a little weak from the cold, but I went to the hill. I managed to go six innings before Lockman pulled me for a pinch-hitter in the bottom of the inning. We were behind, 5-4, at the time. Monday smacked a two-run homer in the bottom of the seventh, and we held on to win, 6-5.

The Astros were almost as tough on me as the Cardinals were. When I pitched against them in Houston in my next start, they banged me around for nine hits in less than six innings. I was also a little wild that day, walking five batters. I think this may have been the worst game in my career for walks. Whether it was or not, we lost, 6-1.

On June 17, we were in Atlanta for a doubleheader. We won the first game behind Burt Hooton, and I started the second game. The Braves were usually patsies for me. I held them to one run through five innings, and we were ahead, 4-1, to start the bottom of the sixth. I gave up a single, then walked the next hitter. Lockman figured I was tired, so he pulled me in favor of Juan Pizarro. He allowed one of my runners to score before getting out of the inning, but he blew my lead by giving up a two-run homer in the seventh. The Braves went on to win, 8-5, and I had another no-decision. The Cubs were still in first place, five games ahead of Montreal.

A strange thing about Whitey Lockman. Either he didn't care about statistics or he hadn't heard about my poor record against the Cardinals. He sent me out to face them in St. Louis on June 24. I took a deep breath, and started pitching. Nine innings later, we won the game, 2-0. I held those guys to just five hits, while giving up five walks and striking out four. I think being a little wild helped to keep the Cardinal hitters on the loose side. Anyway, it was my 43rd career shutout. It was also my last.

Four days later I beat the Expos, 4-2, in Chicago. I went seven innings, surrendered nine hits and both runs, but I didn't walk anybody. LaRoche saved the game, and Monday banged a pair of homers. His two-run shot in the bottom of the seventh made me the winner. My record was now 5-5. This was the pinnacle of my season. The next day the Cubs reached their peak at 46-31, eight full games ahead of the Cardinals. From this point on, it was downhill for the Cubs and for me.

* * *

July was an absolutely horrible month for the Cubs and for me. As a team, we lost 20 games and won only 10. As a pitcher, I lost five straight, the worst losing streak in my career.

What happened to us? As a team, we quit hitting in the clutch. Our pitching remained steady, although not spectacular. Defensively, guys just weren't doing it. Nobody was diving for balls. Guys weren't putting any zip on their throws. Doubleplays weren't being made like they were before. Most of us had lost our enthusiasm for the game. Why? One word. Or I should say, one name. Lockman. The man didn't have a clue on how to fire up a team. He was not a motivator. Let me explain about Whitey

Lockman, about the kind of leader he was.

San Francisco had a right-handed pitcher by the name of Jim Barr, who was just a nasty guy. Nobody liked him, not even his own teammates. Barr and I were mound opponents in a game in San Francisco that month of July, 1973. He plunked Ron Santo in the top of the seventh.

That year, a new rule had been implemented that if a pitcher throws at a batter, the manager gets ejected. And if you do it again, the pitcher gets thrown out.

Lockman looked at me in the dugout. He was worried.

Of course, I was going to retaliate, and the look on my face said what was on my mind.

"What are you going to do?" he asked. Before I could reply, he added, "Hey, if you do anything, I'm going to get thrown out of the game."

"Yeah, but Barr just nailed Santo. I've got to retaliate. I'm going to go after McCovey or Mays."

Lockman was beginning to show some emotion. "You can't do that. Let 'em sleep. Don't wake 'em up."

"Bullshit. He just nailed Santo, so I have to do something."

"You can't do that," he whined. "You have to wait until Barr gets up there. And don't do that either because I'm going to get my ass tossed out of the game."

Barr just happened to be the leadoff hitter in the bottom of the seventh. He came up, and the first pitch literally lifted his helmet right off his head. He ducked so fast that the ball went between his helmet and his head. That bothered me a little because I never wanted to hit anyone in the head, not even a jerk like Barr.

The umpire walked out toward the mound, turned toward our dugout, pointed a finger, and said, "Lockman, you're gone."

Lockman argued for a few minutes, then started walking away. He looked at me and said, "I told you."

"Well, walk slowly because I'm going to be right behind you."

The next pitch I nailed Barr in the ribs and all hell broke loose. All 50 guys from both teams rushed out onto the field, and a big fight ensued with everybody punching each other. I just laughed my ass off.

Barr got what he deserved, and I was thrown out of the game. We wound up losing, 7-3, but I had defended my teammate. That was my job. Lockman knew that, but he thought of himself before thinking of the team. Durocher would have told me to hit Barr. Paul Richards would have told me to hit him. Just about any good manager would have told me to hit him. That's how baseball is played. If one guy intentionally nails one of your teammates, you retaliate. If you don't …

We had a kid named Bill Bonham on our staff. A nice kid. Too nice.

In a game that summer, Jose Cardenal got hit by a pitch. By the time Jose came back to the dugout, everybody was looking at Bonham and telling him that he has to retaliate. Bill said he couldn't do that because it was against his religion! Everybody stared at him in disbelief as he said again that he couldn't hit anybody because of his religion.

"I don't believe in hitting somebody," he said.

"Bill," I said, "you have to do it to protect your hitter."

But he wouldn't do it. When the first batter came up the next inning, Bonham did nothing. The second hitter came up, and still he did nothing. All of us were waiting for Bonham to hit somebody, but he wouldn't do it.

Jose was playing left field. The third batter came up and hit a medium fly ball to him. Jose patted his glove, moved in toward the infield, and the ball dropped over his head.

Bonham looked out at Jose, who just shrugged his shoulders. On the next pitch, the hitter sent a ground ball between the hole at third and short for a base hit. Jose came charging in with his glove down on the ground, then just as he got to it, he lifted his glove to let the ball roll under it. The ball rolled all the way back to the wall.

When the inning was over and the guys came into the dugout, Jose went up to Bonham and said, "That's why you have to protect your hitters. Any ball that comes out to left field is not going to be caught."

What did Lockman have to say about this incident? Nothing. Absolutely nothing. He acted as if nothing had happened to Jose, and even if it had, he didn't care. That was the kind of leader he was, and that was why we went into that horrible tailspin in July.

* * *

Disaster continued to haunt us in August. Actually, things went from terrible to catastrophic.

On June 29, our record was a very good 46-31. On August 1, it had slipped to 55-51. On August 16, it had plunged to 56-64. We had lost 33 out of 43 games. Most teams would have fired their manager before things had gone that far. For some reason I still don't know, Mr. Wrigley and Mr. Holland let Lockman keep his job. I can only hazzard a guess at this point as to why they kept him around.

For the past few seasons, Mr. Wrigley had been threatening to dump players because the team kept fading in the late going. Halfway through 1972, he fired Leo Durocher as our manager, figuring finally that it wasn't the players that were at fault; it was Leo. When Lockman took the same players that Leo had and won 60% of our remaining games that year then won 57% of our first 77 games the following year, Mr. Wrigley and Mr. Holland must have figured the slump was the fault of the players again. I don't think it ever occurred to them that Lockman had lost our confidence in him as a manager.

Lockman pointed fingers at some of us for our downward spiral in the standings. He demoted me to the bullpen officially on August 7. Why? I had lost five straight decisions and had one no-decision since June. I hadn't pitched that poorly. I was knocked out of the game against the Phillies on July 3, but I left the game on July 7 against the Padres trailing only 2-1 after six innings; Bobby Locker blew that game as we lost, 4-3. July 11 was the infamous brawl game with the Giants that I left with the game tied. July 17 I lost to the Padres in Chicago, 1-0. I didn't start again for 12 days after that, and when I did pitch, I wasn't sharp as the Cardinals knocked me out of the box in the second inning. I started the second game of a twinbill two days later and went five innings, giving up four runs on seven hits but without walking anybody. Larry Gura let that game get away as we lost another one, 6-5.

Other guys were pitching worse than I was or weren't getting any more support than I was, but Lockman didn't demote them to the bullpen. The fact was they were all younger than I was and he was trying to give them experience for the next season.

When I did get another start, it was August 16. Lockman needed a sixth starter in a pinch, and I was it. I pitched six very solid innings against the Braves, holding them scoreless and leading, 2-0. Lockman pulled me because I hadn't pitched more than five innings in a game in a month. Locker and Burris tried to hold the lead, but the Braves hammered them for nine runs in the eighth. We lost, 10-2. I guess that one was my fault, too, for not finishing what I'd started. At least, Lockman made me feel it was my fault.

My next start was against the Reds at Wrigley Field. I wasn't sharp, but I made it through six and two-thirds with the lead. The bullpen held on for me, and I was credited with my sixth win of the year. We were now three and a half games behind the Cards and two in back of the Pirates. We were still in the chase.

Lockman gave me another shot at the Braves in Atlanta. I didn't do well, lasting only three and two-thirds and giving up four runs. We won the game to save me from taking another loss.

We began the final month of the season in third place with a record of 64-69, three and a half games behind St. Louis and two and a half behind Pittsburgh. We prepared for a frantic rush to the finish.

The Expos were usually a team that I handled well, and the game of September 3 was no different. I went six innings and held Montreal to one run on four hits. The trouble was my team-mates couldn't score on them. I left for a pinch-hitter in the top of the seventh with the score 1-0 Expos. The sub failed to get the hit that would have driven in the tying run that would have saved me from another loss and might have gotten me another win. The bullpen allowed Montreal to put up three in the bottom of the inning and another run in the eighth. We rallied for two meaning-less tallies in the ninth. I took the loss.

Now back in the regular rotation I took the mound at home to face the Cardinals. I was on my game. I went seven, surrendered seven hits but only one run, and won. Locker saved the game for me. This was the last win of my career, although I didn't know it would be the last at the time. It was also my 99th career win in the National League. The date was September 8, 1973.

When I toed the rubber next, the Pirates were in town. I fell apart in the second inning giving up three runs and leaving a couple of guys on with two outs. The bullpen got us out of the inning, but we eventually lost, 6-1. This dropped our record to 69-76. We were now in fifth place, but we were only four games out of first. Pittsburgh was on top of the division with St. Louis one out, Montreal one and a half back, and New York three behind. With 16 days left in the regular season, any of us could still win the division title.

Five days the Phillies were in town. Lockman started me in the first game of a doubleheader. I wasn't feeling well. My ribs hurt, but I didn't know why. I didn't say anything to Lockman about it because I wanted to pitch. We were in a pennant race, and I was looking for my 100th win in the National League. I wasn't feeling any better after warming up, but I took the hill anyway. I made it into the seventh inning, but with each frame I felt a little worse. Even so, I was holding the Phillies scoreless, and we had put two runs on the board. After getting the first two guys out, I gave up a double to Greg Luzinski, then a single to Bill Robinson that plated Luzinski. The pain in my ribs was now almost unbearable. That and the pressure of the game situation stepped up my breathing to the point where it was becoming hard to breathe at all. I waved to Lockman in the dugout to come out to the mound. I told him what was wrong, and he told the umpire that I was ill and was being taken out. This allowed Locker to warm up until he was ready to come into the game for me. He got the last out without another run scoring. I went to Northwestern Hospital to be examined. I listened to the remainder of the game on the radio, but this didn't help my condition any. In the top of the eighth, Locker got the first two outs, then induced the next batter to a hit a grounder to first base.

The month before the Cubs and A's had made a trade. Pat Bourque, a decent hitter with power but not-so-decent fielder, was sent to Oakland for Gonzalo Marquez, a decent fielder but not-so-decent hitter with no power. Both played first base. The A's needed a left-handed pinch-hitter for their stretch run at the AL West title, while the Cubs needed a late-inning defensive replacement for their attempt at winning a division crown. Neither guy played much in the Majors. I wouldn't even remember either of them, if not for this one game against the Phillies.

Willie Montañez hit the grounder to Marquez. Locker ran over to cover the bag. Marquez fielded the ball cleanly. Bobby got to first. Marquez threw the ball. He threw it where Locker couldn't catch it. Montañez made it safely to first. The next hitter was Luzinski. Locker was upset by the error. He lost his concentration. Luzinski parked one in the street behind the left field stands to give Philadelphia a 3-2 lead. There went my game, my win, my 100th National League win. The Phillies scored two more and won, 5-2.

This was my last appearance in a regular season game in the Major Leagues. It was my last chance to win 100 games in the National League. Had I won that game, I would have joined a very exclusive club of pitchers who had won 100 games in both leagues. Had I won just one of the games that I left with the lead, then I'd be in that club. But I didn't win any of those games, so I'm not in that club.

By the way, the error that Marquez committed was the only one he made that year in 172 chances.

As for my condition, the doctor diagnosed it as inflamed rib cage cartilage. They gave me some medicine for it, but it took me more than a week to recover.

Back to the Cubs. We won the second game of that doubleheader with the Phillies, then reeled over four more wins to raise our record to 75-79. This was the closest we'd been to .500 in more than six weeks. We entered the final week of the regular season in fifth place yet, but we were only two and a half games behind the now first place Mets. We had three games with the Cardinals and four left with New York. All in Chicago. We won the first game from St. Louis, then the Cards shut us twice in a row, 1-0 and 2-0. Our only hope of winning the division was a sweep of the Mets in five games. That's right five games. If we won all four of the scheduled games over the weekend, we'd only tie the Mets for first. Then we'd have to play one more game on Monday to break the tie. This appeared to be an impossible task that wasn't helped any by the weather. Friday's game was rained out, then Saturday's game was washed out. We had to play two doubleheaders now; one on Sunday and one on Monday. And if we won both, we'd still have to play on Tuesday. We beat New York in the first game on Sunday, but they came back to win the nightcap. This eliminated the Cubs from the pennant chase, but the Cardinals and Pirates still had a mathematical chance if we could sweep the Mets on Monday.

Lockman scheduled me to start the second game. This would the last game of the season and one more chance for me to win my 100th NL game. I never got the chance. The Mets won the opener, 6-4, which made the second game unnecessary. Instead of playing it, the commissioner canceled the contest because it was meaningless to the standings.

But it wasn't meaningless to me.

But that's baseball.

◆29◆

Teamwork:
Around the Horn

P president Abraham Lincoln freed the slaves in the South back in 1863. It took a brave descendant of slaves to bring about the liberation of Major League Baseball players.

Relations between the owners and the Players' Association started to heat up in the late 1960s. With Marvin Miller leading us, some of the player-reps became a little more belligerent in our dealings with management, but the major incident that received a lot of attention was the Curt Flood case.

Curtis Charles Flood was born in Houston, Texas in 1938. He came up to the Majors with the Cincinnati Reds in 1956 for a last month cup of coffee, then got another taste of the big leagues in the final weeks of the following year. The Reds traded him to St. Louis in December that year in one of those transactions that at the time appear to be nothing more than an exercise in business. The Cardinals received Flood and Joe "Cash" Taylor for three pitchers: Marty Kutyna, Ted Wieand, and Willard Schmidt.

Taylor was one of those utility outfielders that get thrown into trades to make them more interesting. He played for the Phillies in 1954 at the end of the year, then came up again with the Reds in 1957. The Cards dealt him to Baltimore in the middle of the 1958 season for the waiver price, and he played one more year with the O's before calling it a career.

Wieand never amounted to anything in the Majors. Kutyna got a shot because of expansion in 1961, but his numbers aren't much either. Schmidt was a veteran reliever who was near the end of his career when he went to Cincinnati.

Only Flood amounted to anything. He played 12 years for the Cardinals. He hit over .300 in six of those seasons and did just about everything asked of him in the outfield. When Lou Brock came to the Cards in 1964, Flood moved down in the batting order without a whimper, then he did his job to help the Cards win the NL flag and the World Series. He was also part of the 1967 World Series Champions and the 1968 team that lost the World Series to Detroit in seven games.

After the Cardinals slipped from the top in 1969, the St. Louis management thought it was time to move some of their veteran players for younger talent. They packaged Flood with catcher Tim McCarver, pitcher Joe Hoerner, and outfielder Byron Browne in a deal with the Phillies for infielders Cookie Rojas and Dick Allen and pitcher Jerry Johnson. This was a big-time trade. All of these guys were regulars at one time or another. Both teams felt they were filling some major holes. The Cards felt certain that Allen would power them to another division title in 1970, while the Phillies figured McCarver and Flood would give them the veteran leadership that their team was missing. It looked like a good deal for both clubs. It might have been, too, if not for one slight problem.

Flood didn't want to be traded. He refused to report to his new team. Instead he chose to challenge Organized Baseball's ironclad reserve clause. Flood believed, given his long tenure with the Cardinals, that he should have the option of being traded to a team of his choice. He asked Commissioner Bowie Kuhn to make him a free agent, but when Kuhn refused, Flood came to the Players' Association and asked for help, wanting to take the issue to court. We gave it to him.

Marvin Miller hired former United States Supreme Court Justice Arthur Goldberg to represent Flood. Goldberg agreed to do it for expenses, which eventually totaled $200,000. The case went to court, and Flood lost. He appealed, and lost the appeal. A further appeal took it to the U.S. Supreme Court.

Our case wasn't helped by the fact that the owners had been exempt for many years from anti-trust laws. We felt that we had amassed a tremendous case against the owners. Many of the points had been brought to the owners' attention before this, but they refused to address them. Flood said that he was little more than a slave to the owners. In the end, after a long battle, the

Supreme Court upheld the decision of the lower courts. The ruling stated that since the owners were exempt from the anti-trust laws by an act of Congress, the Court was powerless to help him.

So, Curt Flood lost his case. I loved Curt Flood, one of the nicest human beings I ever met, who unfortunately has passed away. But even though he didn't win, everyone felt that his case began the changes in baseball. In the end, we were all back where we started from — as far as the reserve clause went. The case took a lot of time and cost a lot of money, but everyone involved felt it was important to take it all the way. Our discontent over the way baseball was perceived by the owners did not go away. The way the owners ran baseball continued as before. However, the case did give the Players' Association a common cause, and down the road, we knew other situations would come, where we would challenge the owners again. The case also enabled the players to rally around Marvin Miller, showing him he would have our support.

* * *

A fter the Flood case, the union kept moving forward. We had to. We actually felt we were getting stronger. Little by little we accomplished a few more things during negotiations, but in 1972 we reached a standstill with the owners on a couple of conditions.

The players wanted arbitration after playing for two years in the Majors. Once again, the issue of free agency was discussed. The union wanted a player who had spent 10 years in the Majors, with the last five of those years being with the same team, to be allowed to become a free agent. But the biggest issue was the pension fund. The owners were getting a lot of the television money from the networks to broadcast the games. The players wanted to share in that money and have it go into their pension fund. Of course, the owners told us to go to hell, so in 1972, we had the first baseball strike.

On March 22, 1972, the owners voted unanimously to oppose

any increase in our pension and health benefit plan. The media reported how greedy we were to want more money for our pension fund and how poor the owners were. The general public bought it. We knew better.

Marvin Miller called a meeting of the player-reps to be held in Dallas about a week before season was to start. Everybody who supposed to be there was there, and so were some guys who didn't have to be there. We discussed all the avenues that were available to us. We had gone almost nowhere in the negotiations with the owners. It was all so frustrating. I was extremely vocal at that meeting, finally getting up and saying, "Gentlemen, we have no choice. We have to strike for what we think is best."

After the meeting, I flew to New Orleans for an exhibition game before the regular season started. Leo Durocher was kind enough to lend me his suite where I called all the players together to take a strike vote. Our guys were unanimous, 28-0. Even Ernie Banks approved of what we did. He couldn't vote because he was now a coach, but he said if he could have voted, he would have voted to strike. That was the only time that I know of that Ernie did or said anything that was in opposition of Phil Wrigley, the Cubs owner.

The strike was approved by the players in both leagues and Major League Baseball had its first-ever work stoppage. Dick Dozer called me "a heavy-handed labor negotiator" in the sports pages of the Chicago *Tribune*. I was quoted in the same paper. "The owners don't want to give in because they want to use this as a lever against us when the basic agreement (a separate contract) runs out a year from tomorrow." Of course, the media thought this was just a lot of crap. They continued to portray the players as a bunch of troublemakers, spoiled kids, and greedy bastards. But did they write anything negative about the owners? Not a word that I ever saw.

The Major League Baseball Players' Association went on strike April 1, 1972. The owners were confident that we'd crack before they did. On April 3, Marvin offered to settle the dispute by accepting the owners' proposal if the owners would give us control of the 6% interest on the money in our pension fund. The owners rejected it. The next day we offered to submit negotiations to an independent arbitrator. The owners said no again. Three days after that Dick Moss, associate counsel for the Players' Association, announced that the union would file an unfair labor practice suit against the owners because three players had lost their jobs because of their union activities. Joel Horlen of the White Sox was one of those players. The next day the owners agreed to meet with us and J. Curtis Counts, a federal mediator, in Washington. We agreed to return to the playing field if the owners would agree to accept binding arbitration. They refused and countered with an offer of their own. They'd give us $400,000 in additional retirement benefits if the players agreed to forfeit their pay for the strike period and play a 162-game schedule. Marvin stated our refusal quite succinctly. "The owners are asking the players to work overtime for nothing." The next day, April 11, the dispute over the pension plan was settled, but now we had a new point of contention: playing a full schedule for less than full play. Both sides won and lost this one when the owners decided to cancel all the games lost by the strike. We made our point about playing for nothing, but we lost our pay for the games that were canceled. The owners kept from paying our full salaries, but they also lost the revenue that they would have made if those games had been made up.

Anyway, we went back to work and the season started late on April 15. When we were afforded arbitration, we felt there had been a move on the owners part.

* * *

T he big bone of contention of our strike was the television revenue. The owners did not want to talk about sharing it by putting some of it in the players' pension plan. They wanted to remove it from the negotiations, but the Players' Association refused to let it go. We got it in, and now it's a big part of the pension.

Around $55 million dollars was pumped into the fund by the owners from television rights in 1997. That enabled former players from the early to late 1960s, who did the groundwork with Marvin Miller, to get the pension to where it is today, to gain a share in some of the financial rewards. Today's players will have a yearly pension of over $100,000 a year when they retire — on top of the millions many of them are already making. But it's rather sad because today's player, who is making so much now and who will have a great pension on retirement, has pretty much turned a deaf ear as to what can be done to enhance our pension.

The Players' Association and the pension plan started in 1946. The men who played in the late 1940s and early 1950s are only drawing $400-$600 dollars a month for their pensions. That's simply criminal. Most of today's players could give a rat's rotten ass about the older ballplayers. But if they would just stop and think about it, those guys and the guys in my generation laid the foundation for their present benefits. When I played, you had to play 20 years to be able to collect the maximum benefits of the pension at the age of 65. You also had to play five years in the Major Leagues to be vested. We managed to lower the vesting eligibility down to four years. However, today it's only one day for vesting! A player with 10 years in the Majors can collect the maximum pension when he turns 67. So, everything that was done earlier has only benefitted the players of today and yet they don't — or won't — take care of us. That really pisses me off.

* * *

Being a player-rep did not help my situation in baseball. Management looked upon player-representatives, back in the 1960s, as trouble.

Management — the owners and their front office people — was not very kind to most player-reps. They greatly resented the player-reps because the owners thought we were doing nothing except alienating the other players from management.

I really did try to solve any problems that arose in the clubhouse before taking them to management. If that didn't work, then I had to take the next step, which was to file a formal written grievance against the team with the Players' Association. Of course, no player-rep wanted to do that. That was the last resort, but a lot of times management gave you no choice. At least, we did have that avenue.

Because I was the player-rep in Cincinnati, I took all the heat and subsequently was traded to Atlanta because of it. It was also a case of the players taking me for granted because they had elected me as player-rep. They really didn't know or care, that I was the one who was taking all the bullshit for them. It's not that I didn't want to do it, but that my teammates never recognized — or maybe cared — what I was doing for them. None of the crap from management was falling on them or affecting them. So why the hell should they care?

And it wasn't happening to just me. It was happening for the other player-reps in baseball. It was just a thankless job.

Of course, management didn't like you because you were a player-rep. They thought you were anti-management. It was just frowned upon. Nobody really wanted to be a player-rep because of all the crap that went with it.

* * *

W hen I was placed on waivers by Atlanta and picked up by the Cubs, the first thing I was asked by the Cub players was to take the job as player-rep. I politely declined, saying that I'd heard the Chicago front office people treated their players all right. I had heard good things from the players about the Wrigleys and general manager John Holland, and I just didn't want to get involved again in a hornets nest.

Here were all these veteran ballplayers. Ernie Banks, Billy Williams, Ron Santo, and many of the other players. They had been with the Cubs for a long time, and none of them really wanted to take the job. Jim Colborn, a young player, was elected player-rep. I was asked to take over, if he would relinquish the job, but I said no.

The following year general manager John Holland asked me to talk to him. The year was 1971. I said to myself, Uh-oh, I guess my days are numbered with the Cubs. I hadn't been there that long, but I was having a decent year, not a great year. I didn't know why he was calling me up to his office, but I went there. He told me to shut the door behind me.

"Yes, sir. What can I do for you?"

"Milt, I need a favor."

"That's a switch. What's the problem?

"Well, I'm not really having a problem, but I'd like you to do me a favor."

"What is it?"

"Well, you know that Jim Colborn is the player-rep, but he's very young and very immature, and I would like you to consider taking the job as player-rep."

I was totally dumbfounded that a general manager of a ball club, who knew my reputation for being a clubhouse lawyer, would ask me to take the job as player-rep.

"Why?" I wasn't quite sure what he said, though I had an idea.

"Because he's young and immature and I have this feeling he'll be up in my office all the time. I don't need that shit. At least, you know what the job is. You went through it. You know it, and you've resolved situations without even coming to management. Please, as a big favor to me and Mr. Wrigley, would you take the job?"

"Well John, this is a first for me, that a general manager has asked me to take a job as player-rep, but yes, I'd be more than happy to do it."

And I did. There was a very mutual understanding between Holland and me. We really didn't have any problems between us. Any problems that came up between the players and management I would try to straighten out before taking them up to Holland. If there were problems I could hammer out with the traveling secretary, I would do it. And most of the time we got it done.

But now the truth about why he asked me to do take the job. Colborn was about to be sent down to the minors, and this way the players would have a veteran to represent them and take care of their problems.

* * *

B ack to that first strike in 1972.

I took a vote of the Cubs players before the strike vote because I wanted to find out their support. I knew a lot of the players had been with the Cubs for a long time. Guys, like Billy Williams, Ron Santo, Glenn Beckert, Don Kessinger, Randy Hundley, Ferguson Jenkins, and Bill Hands had been very, very well treated by the Wrigleys and Holland. The strike was a slap at them. That we would even consider a strike vote, I know hurt them. I told the players it wasn't a personal vendetta against any one owner, but that it was against all of them. All we wanted was the best for all of baseball and the players. I told them that we had to stick together collectively as a team. They were very reluctant to strike against Mr. Wrigley, and I empathized with them. But again, I had to reiterate to the team that they were not doing it against any one owner but against all of them collectively.

It was a very tough situation in Chicago because of the relationship the players had with Holland and Mr. Wrigley. And I must say that Mr. Wrigley was a very fair man.

The year before the strike I won 17 games for the Cubs. When contract time came, I asked for less money than I thought I really deserved. The reason was because President Nixon had come out and asked people not to take big raises in order to help stabilize the nation's economy, so I thought I would do my part. This wasn't what I really wanted to do, but I took to heart what the President had asked the country to do. Obviously, that would give ball clubs an out not to give big raises to their players, even though they may have deserved one.

Anyway, I wasn't asking for the raise I thought I should get, but the Cubs weren't offering me much either. The difference was a couple of thousand dollars. Holland told me he would have to talk to Mr. Wrigley about it, then he'd get back to me. About a week later he told me that Mr. Wrigley had said he'd been more than fair with me concerning the raise he was offering. I said fine and signed my contract.

The next year, the year of the strike, I won 17 games again, including a no-hitter and an 11-game winning streak to close the season that nearly got us into the playoffs. I felt I'd had an even better year than in 1971, and in 1972, President Nixon was making no suggestions on raises. It was basically wide open as to what we could do to negotiate. The Cubs and I were about five thousand dollars apart, which today is just chump change, but back then it was serious money. You either signed the contract or went home. It was as simple as that. We were at an impasse when Holland said to me again, like he did the year before, that he'd have to call Mr. Wrigley to get the contract worked out. This time, though, I asked him if I could use the phone.

"Why? Who are you calling?"

"I'm calling Mr. Wrigley. I want to get this thing straightened out now."

"Go on, get out of here! You've got the five thousand dollar raise."

"Thanks, John. You pulled the wool over my eyes last year, but you're not going to do it this year."

We both laughed like hell. It wasn't Mr. Wrigley who denied me the raise. It was Holland. It's all part of the game, but this time I didn't lose.

That's the way contract negotiations went. A player had no agent. It just wasn't something players did. It was apparently forbidden to have someone else negotiate your contracts. It would have been nice to have someone else do it and put a dollar figure on your head. But that's the way baseball operated then with the general managers trying to get a player as cheaply as possible to show his boss that he did a good job. Of course, the player would try and get as much money as he thought he could. That's the way baseball was run back then. The pendulum always swung to the owners back then. Obviously, today, it's swung drastically the other way.

* * *

Being a player-rep was a job. A lot of things happened in the course of a year, and of course, those problems were reported to the player-representative. When something happened,

I had to find out, like other player-reps, how to handle a certain situation. Some player-reps could take care of it in the clubhouse themselves with just common sense. Others, who were not as experienced, would take issues up with the front office, and many times would make mountains out of mole hills.

It was almost a full time job, but I don't think that it took anything away from my performance as a player. I don't think it ever bothered me to that degree because I knew what I was there for.

Number one, I had to do my job as a baseball player. I had to go out on the mound and try to perform to the best of my ability to get a win for my teammates and me.

Probably the toughest team to be a player-rep for was the Chicago Cubs, and the toughest situation I had to work through was the 1972 strike. I spoke passionately to the 400 or so players that had gathered to take a vote and told them we had not come this far to sit back and let the owners take control and dictate to us everything that they wanted and expected us to do. After the players approved the strike we all went back to our respective hometowns and waited. We were kept informed by Marvin Miller as to what was going on. We also worked out. Three or four of us found a gym in Chicago to keep in shape because it was still a little cold outside. Of course, the media was there everyday, watching and talking to us. I was also in constant contact with Marvin to see if any developments were ready to occur, and I would report back to my teammates. I had all of their phone numbers, and of course, they were calling me all the time.

It was quite a stressful situation to be on strike for the first time ever in the history of the game of baseball, but it was much needed and something we had to do. We weren't proud of it, but we wanted to get our point across that we wanted things to be better for the players, once and for all. Finally, after eight days, the owners did give in on a few things, and we decided to stop the strike and go back to work. It was very traumatic for all of us — especially for the player-reps. Especially for me because I had another situation that it also affected, but that's another chapter in my life.

◆30◆

Swan Song:
Bottom of the Ninth

The Cubs were probably the best organization that I ever worked for.

Philip Wrigley, as I've said before, was very fair and was absolutely great to his players. He took an interest in them, even though we didn't see him because he had stopped coming to the park. That actually happened a few years before I got there because Mr. Wrigley was always being hounded by the press. He did go to the office, and it was amazing because, whenever you would call his office, he would be the one who'd pick up the phone instead of a secretary.

Once I took the family up to Lake Geneva (Wis.) for the three day All-Star break. I figured as long as I was there, I'd talk to my boss. His name was in the phone book, so I called. His lovely wife answered, and after introducing myself and exchanging the usual polite words, she gave the phone to Mr. Wrigley. He invited me to bring the family over to his house, and I accepted. My mother was with us from Detroit. We all went to the Wrigley mansion and had a great time. He was a most hospitable man who treated us with perfect grace for the three or four hours we spent there. He thanked me profusely for coming by to see him.

The next day we had a workout in Chicago. Word had spread to John Holland and Leo Durocher that I had stopped to see Mr. Wrigley. They gave me a hard time, accusing me of "sucking up to the boss." I got a kick out of that.

That wasn't my only experience with Mr. Wrigley. Another occurred the next year in August.

I had been having some difficulty with my wife Carole, who

had a drinking problem. The team was in New York to play the Mets, and I was supposed to pitch that day. Per my custom when I was on the road, I called her from my hotel. She told me she was an alcoholic, finally admitting her problem and saying that she wanted help. Knowing how important this moment was in our lives, I acted. I called Durocher and told him what had happened with Carole, then I said that I wouldn't be pitching that day and that I was going home to be with my wife. Leo said he understood and set things in motion. The traveling secretary made a reservation for me, and I flew home.

A couple of days later, Mr. Wrigley called me at home and to ask how things were going. He was very concerned and asked if there was anything he could do. I told him, no, but thanked him and said — hopefully — everything would get squared away. He told me the next time we had a road trip that he wanted me to take my wife as his guest so I could spend more time with her. Mr. Wrigley told me he would take care of all the expenses and said if we didn't want to fly on the charter to take a different plane. I thought that was an absolutely wonderful gesture by him. I had never been treated like that by any of the other ball clubs I had been with. It was a new experience and a wonderful one. It just seemed like he wanted to do something for the players.

Being with Cubs was more like a family situation.

Mr. Wrigley would help other players out from time to time. Maybe they would have a debt or something and he would lend them the money. He would, of course, take it out of their checks, but that wasn't the point. He wanted to please the players. The Cubs were his team and had been part of the family for many, many years.

I was tickled to death by his generosity and truly enjoyed my time with him, John Holland, and the whole organization. Mr. Wrigley was great to my family and me, and I still really appreciate it. And of course, the fans of Chicago were just unbelievable, and they still are.

Pitching at Wrigley Field was a lot of fun, even when the wind was blowing out. I didn't alter my pitching style because I was pretty much of a low ball pitcher anyway. I had learned how to do that in the American League, whenever I pitched in Fenway

Park in Boston with that short wall — "The Green Monster" — in left field or Yankee Stadium with its short right field fence. You just couldn't alter your pitching because of a ballpark. You had to be more aware, though, as a pitcher, when you pitched in those kind of ballparks, because of the dimensions and the fact that the ball would jump off the bat.

Once when I was pitching against the Mets at Wrigley Field, the bases were loaded. I had walked all three guys, and I was upset about it. I didn't walk too many batters ever, but in that game I walked three in that inning. I think Tommie Agee was the batter. I actually threw him a good slider, down and away, and when he hit the ball, it sounded like he cracked the bat on what I thought was a routine fly ball to center field. Our centerfielder broke in on the ball to make the catch, but all of a sudden, it got in the wind. Then I saw the centerfielder's uniform number as he turned his back to race back after the ball. He could have just stood there because the damn ball carried into the centerfield bleachers for a grand slam home run. Thank God, I won the game!

*   *   *

W|e had some great ballplayers on the Cubs.
Ernie Banks, Mr. Cub, owned the city of Chicago. He still owned it until Sammy Sosa belted out 66 homers in 1998. But Ernie owned it before then. No offense, Michael Jordan. You own the rest of the world, but Ernie owned Chicago.

Ernie was a great ballplayer and had a great career with the Cubs. He was just a funny guy. He was so upbeat all of the time that it really made all of us sick! A lot of times, when some guys would come in from a tough night out, drinking and carousing or whatever they were doing, Ernie would yell, "It's a good day for two!" Everyone would shout back at him, "Shut up, Ernie!" or something like that. He'd laugh, and so would we. He was just a fun guy to be around.

Another great Cub player was Billy Williams. "Sweet" Billy Williams. He was one of the nicest men I've ever met, and man, what a hitter! It seemed like all he did was hit line drives.

Ron Santo was a good third baseman and a hell of a hitter. I really had the good fortune of playing with two of the greatest third basemen of all time. Of course, I broke in when Brooks Robinson was starting to develop into what many people say was the best third baseman the game has ever seen. Then, later to play with Santo, I had another chance to see a superb player. Ron also hit a lot of home runs and drove in a lot of runs. The funny thing about Santo was that he was a hypochondriac. If he walked into the training room and saw somebody being worked on, he would ask the trainer what was wrong with him. If the trainer said the player's back was sore, the next day Santo would come in and say his back was sore. It was funny at the time. The only thing that concerned me about Ron was that when it came to a clutch part of a game and you needed him to drive in that big run from third base, it didn't seem to happen very often. That kind of concerned me a little bit. Other than that, Ron was a darn good third baseman and a good hitter.

(At the time this is being written, Ron is in the hospital having heart bypass surgery. I hope he pulls through and returns to good health. Our prayers are with you, Ron.)

Glenn Beckert really surprised me as far as defense goes. Playing against him, I always thought he was a pretty good second baseman, but it seemed like when I played with him, he made a lot of mistakes in the field. He was a good hitter. One spring training in Arizona, out behind the left field fence was a huge cement truck with some workers were pouring concrete for a foundation for a house. I looked over at it and I started laughing and yelled at Beckert. "Hey, Beck. Look over there behind left field. Do you see that big truck out there?"

He looked at it. "Yeah, so what."

"They're making your glove!" He just looked at me and chuckled and walked away.

Don't get me wrong. Beck was solid player, and he handled the stick with as much finesse as any of the great hitters of our time. What he lacked in the field, he made up for it at the plate.

Don Kessinger, our shortstop, made a lot of great plays behind me. He had good movement and could get to a lot of balls in the hole. I think his basketball prowess really helped because when he'd go in the hole and come up with the ball, he'd jump high in the air and make a throw with good stuff on it to first and a lot of times get the runner. He was a damn good shortstop.

Randy Hundley was one of the best defensive catchers that I ever played with in my career. He took a lot of pride in what he did and knew the hitters very well. We had good discussions before the games on how we wanted to pitch opposing batters. He was very hard-headed, stubborn. Any time I'd shake Randy off, he'd get very upset with me. One time I told him that I really appreciated that he was trying to take care of me, calling the pitches for me and such, but I said there were times I wanted to change and throw what I wanted to throw. I tried to make him feel better by telling him that the next day's paper wouldn't say that Randy Hundley was the losing pitcher. It would my name with "L" next to it. We had a good laugh about that one.

Ferguson Jenkins was a fantastic pitcher. It was amazing that he was able to have so many 20-win seasons pitching in a place like Wrigley Field. He won 20 or more six years in a row! He deserved a purple heart more than he did the Cy Young Award. Fergie was just effortless. He had an easy, fluid motion with good stuff, and he threw the ball exceptionally well. He hit spots, and it seemed he hardly ever broke a sweat when he was on the mound. Plus, it seemed he pitched nine innings every time out. It was just a pleasure to watch Fergie pitch and to be a part of that team.

Bill Hands was a good pitcher. He came from the Giants to the Cubs and was a very good sinker ball pitcher and had all his good years in Chicago.

Ken Holtzman was a good left-handed pitcher but extremely moody. He concentrated a whole lot on pitching. He's a very intelligent guy, and it was a pleasure to be around him. One time the Cubs were in Houston and we went to a professional bowling tournament. I've always been a big bowling fan, since I was about eight or nine years old. I used to set pins in the old days when they didn't have the automatic pinsetters. I personally knew many of them, like Dick Weber, who was a good friend of mine. They knew I was going to be in town, so they called me at the hotel and left me a bunch of tickets. So after the game, we went out. I was pitching the next day, but we went out partying anyway. I got in around three or four in the morning. Of course, I invited Holtzman along, and he was pitching the day after me. After getting in so late, I went out and pitched a two hit shutout with very little rest and was quite proud of what I did. The pro bowlers were in the stands, and they were thrilled to death by the way I had pitched. After the game, they wanted to go out again. I said, great. I'm not going to pitch for another three or four days and I said, "Come on, Kenny. Let's go out and have some more fun."

"Oh, no, I'm pitching tomorrow, and I've got to get some rest."

"You big wimp. You can keep me out until three or four in the morning the night before I'm pitching, but when it's your turn, you have to go back to the hotel and go to bed!"

Joe Pepitone. What can you say about Peppy? He was quite the guy. He was a million dollar talent but unfortunately he hung around with the wrong people and got in trouble. He loved to have a good time and would just party, party, party. I wonder, if he'd ever made up his mind just to play baseball, what kind of career he would have had. Joe was a darn good hitter and was a good defensive first baseman and outfielder and just a natural ballplayer. But unfortunately, he liked to party and stay out late. He used to come in to the ballpark in the morning when we played day games at Wrigley Field and he'd look like death warmed over — maybe not even that good. I'd ask him how much sleep he'd gotten, and he'd just look at me and tell me that he hadn't been to bed yet. What a party animal!

Phil Regan was a relief pitcher with a great sinker. But a lot of the drop in his pitches was due to K-Y Jelly. He would have it on him in a lot of different places, and invariably, every time he'd pitch, the umpire would always check his glove, his hat, and his uniform for the stuff. Because the jelly is transparent, he'd put it on his hair on the back of his head below the cap line and it would look like sweat. Or he'd put it in the crotch of his pants because no ump would ever feel for K-Y jelly in a man's groin!

These guys were players from my school, my era of baseball.

I knew them; I liked them; they were my kind of people. By the middle of the 1970s, almost all of them were gone from the Cubs.

* * *

O ver the offseason of 1973-74, the Cubs made three major deals that changed the whole complexion of the team. The first transaction gave me confidence, but the second put a damper on that. Then the third made me suspicious that my days with the Cubs just might be numbered.

Ferguson Jenkins had been with the Cubs since April 21, 1966 when he came to them from the Phillies with outfielders Adolfo Phillips and John Herrnstein. He had a live fastball and a serious slider, and he was only 22 years old. Over the next seven plus seasons, he became the ace of the staff and the winningest pitcher in baseball with 147 wins. No one was better than Fergie over that time. He won 20 or more for six straight years, 1967-72. Then in 1973, he had his first tough year. He only won 14 games and lost 16, and his ERA ballooned to 3.89. For a lot of pitchers, this was a decent year. For Fergie, it was sub-par.

In October, John Holland traded Fergie to the Texas Rangers for two young infielders: Bill Madlock and Vic Harris. Madlock could hit with anybody, and Harris run like the wind. The Cubs needed speed and hitting to go with the young pitchers that were making up the nucleus of the staff.

The next month Holland sent Glenn Beckert and a throw-in rookie nobody to the San Diego Padres for Jerry Morales, an outfielder who hit well in Wrigley and who could play right field. This allowed the Cubs to move Billy Williams to first base.

At the winter meetings in December, Holland worked a pair of trades that moved two more veterans from the roster.

Randy Hundley was dealt to the Minnesota Twins for George Mitterwald, another catcher. Hundley was only three years senior to George by the calendar, but in body he was a century older. Randy had caught over 600 games in his first four full seasons with the Cubs, and all that kneeling behind the plate had worn out his knees.

Holland followed this up by sending Ron Santo to the White

Sox for right-handed pitcher Steve Stone, left-handed pitchers Ken Frailing and Jim Kremmel, and catcher Steve Swisher. Originally, Holland wanted to move Santo to the Angels, but Ron nixed the deal because his business interests were in Chicago and he didn't want to be far away from them for half the year.

First Holtzman, then Hands. Now Jenkins, Beckert, Hundley, and Santo. All traded. Ernie Banks retired. That left Williams and Don Kessinger of the nine perennial all-stars who had graced the Chicago line-up from 1966 thru 1971. They were the core of the team, the very essence of the Chicago Cubs. Ask Cub fans who were alive during those years what they remember about those guys and every one of them will say the same thing. Those nine men were winners. They might not have won any pennants or division titles, but they were a dynasty of a sort. I just wonder what they might have accomplished if a decent back-up catcher, a regular centerfielder, another solid outfielder in either left or right, and one more first-line starting pitcher — like me — had been on the team with them during those years. Looking back, the Chicago roster was missing one or more of those elements every year, but it didn't have to be that way.

When Leo Durocher took over as manager of the Cubs — and that's what he did: take over the Cubs — in 1966, he knew that to be a strong baseball team the Cubs had to be strong up the middle. They needed a first line catcher who could play defense and handle the pitching staff; if he could hit that was a bonus. They needed a doubleplay combination that covered a lot of ground and could hit .250 or better. And they needed a center-fielder who could play the outfield all by himself and hit .250. That's the old formula: good pitching with speed and defense up the middle and power on the corners. The Cubs had the power on three corners with Banks and Santo on first and third and Williams in right, and they had Beckert and Kessinger at second and short. What was missing? A solid catcher and a speedy centerfielder. Leo and Holland went to work and acquired both in trades. They brought in Hundley from the Giants with Bill Hands over the winter, then the next spring they sent veteran pitchers Larry Jackson and Bob Buhl to the Phillies essentially for Jenkins and Adolfo Phillips, a young centerfielder.

Phillips played for the Cubs for three full years. He didn't hit for average, but he did have some pop in his bat, banging out 46 homers and driving in 139 runs, mostly as a leadoff hitter. Too bad that he also struck out 318 times. He was a decent fielder, but not a great fielder. He frequently misjudged fly balls; mental errors, which errors don't show up in the box scores. When he misjudged one too many in early 1969, he was shipped off to the Montreal Expos for Paul Popovich.

Adolfo's replacement in centerfield was Don Young, a rookie who wasn't any better in the field than Phillips and who was a lot worse at the plate. He struck out more often than Adolfo, and he had less power and less speed on the basepaths.

So why did the Cubs trade Phillips? He got into Durocher's doghouse one time too many.

Durocher made mistakes like that. He allowed his emotions to get the better of him far too often, and his team usually paid the price.

Besides Phillips, Durocher had a strong dislike for Johnny Callison. Why? I never figured that one out, but I saw Leo ride Johnny about some of the most knit-picking things. That was too bad because Johnny was a good guy and solid player.

Durocher inherited Holtzman, Banks, Beckert, Kessinger, Santo, and Williams, then added Hands, Hundley, and Jenkins through trades. Phillips was the only decent centerfielder who played with them, and Johnny Callison was the only decent third outfielder who played with them. Hundley never had a good back-up. The best fourth starter they ever had was me, but I was only with them for the last two years.

I really wonder what they might have accomplished if Leo had kept Phillips in center, gotten me when the Reds wanted to dump me in 1968, and traded for Callison sooner. I just wonder.

* * *

All of the new guys that had been acquired that winter were younger than the four long-time Cub players that were traded. Obviously, Holland and Lockman felt the time had come to rebuild the team.

Only one question troubled my mind. Where did I fit in?

When my contract came in the mail that winter, Holland was offering me a 20% pay cut because I'd had a bad year in 1973. This was understandable, but I didn't think I should have take that big of a cut. I went to see Holland to discuss my contract with him.

Whitey Lockman sat in on our conversation, and I asked them point blank, "What do you intend to do with me? Are you going to trade me, too?" They both assured me that they had no plans at that time to trade me. I told them that I wanted to play out my remaining years with the Cubs, and again they assured me that they had no plans to trade me. I agreed to take a 10% cut in pay and went home to get ready for spring training.

When February came around, I was ready to pitch. I went to Arizona in good shape. I had to be because Burt Hooton, Bill Bonham, Rick Reuschel, and Ray Burris were all younger and sitting higher in Lockman's favor than I was. And how about Steve Stone and Ken Frailing? They were both younger than I was, and Lockman obviously wanted them. So I figured I had my work cut out for me, if I was going to earn a spot in the rotation with these young turks.

Lockman gave me a regular turn at starting, and I thought I did well enough to earn a serious shot at pitching Opening Day. Then he asked me if I'd pitch in long relief once the season started, and I agreed to do that. I did tell them I wanted at least one chance to get my 100th win in the National League, and he assured me that I would.

All through training camp, a lot of the younger pitchers came to me for help at one thing or another. After all, I was a 17-year veteran. Heck, I'd pitched to guys like Ted Williams, Rocky Colavito, Mickey Mantle, Roger Maris, Jackie Jensen, Harvey Kuenn, and I'd pitched against and beaten guys like Whitey Ford, Don Drysdale, Jim Bunning, Billy Pierce, and Early Wynn. Why wouldn't they come to me for advice? I was like an extra pitching coach on the team. I began looking forward to the coming season. Then the roof fell in.

On April 2, Lockman gave me my walking papers. I couldn't

believe it. He and Holland had assured me that I wouldn't be traded. I took them at their word. But neither of them had said anything about being released.

I was furious. I'd been betrayed. I'd been suckered. I'd done everything asked of me and then some. I'd pitched well in every outing. I'd pitched better than some of Lockman's pets.

Reuschel had two good outings — his first two — going three innings both times and holding the other team scoreless. But in the third stint, he gave up 11 hits and nine runs in three innings. In the fourth he was rocked for six runs and seven hits in three and a third innings. He gave up three in five innings the next time, and four in six the time after that.

Bonham had done well, but his only opposition all spring came in "B" games.

Frailing started well, but in his last two outings, he was hit pretty hard for seven runs and seven hits in one game and four runs and nine hits in the other. He didn't go more than four and third in either game.

Hooton did have a good spring. In four outings, he held the other team scoreless three times, but in the fourth, he gave up seven hits and four runs in six innings.

Stone did close to what Hooton did. He allowed only one earned run in his first three stints, then was hammered for nine runs — all earned — and 13 hits in six innings in his fourth.

As for me, I gave one hit in three scoreless innings, one run in three the next time, one earned run on four hits in four my third time out, two runs on three hits in four innings after that, and three runs on six hits in five innings in my last appearance of the spring. I pitched 19 innings and gave up seven earned runs for an ERA of 3.32. That's pretty decent for spring training when veteran pitchers like I was are trying to work on new pitches and their control.

Reuschel's ERA was 6.29; Frailing 4.87; Stone 5.68; Hooton 2.08; Bonham 1.54; and Ray Burris 6.55. I mention Burris with the others because Lockman was touting him as the new Fergie Jenkins. I give their ERAs because of what Lockman told the press after I was released.

"All I know is that Milt wasn't able to make our staff for the opening of the season."

I pitched better than four of his six pets and I "wasn't able to make" the staff for opening day? Dry that out and bag it up and you can sell it to people who want really green lawns.

I went into Holland and demanded to know why I was being released after he and Lockman said I wouldn't be traded. Holland said that his hands were tied; the make-up of the roster belonged to the manager; he couldn't interfere.

To add insult to injury, I lost another job at the same time. I had been a part-time sportscaster with Channel 7 in Chicago. Not any more. They dropped me on the same day, giving me the same brand of fertilizer that Lockman was dropping on the media.

When the newspaper guys questioned his motives for cutting me from the team, Lockman fired back that he and his staff (presumably pitching coach Hank Aguirre) "did not make a judgment based on salary." And, "We couldn't work our staff around a guy trying to win one game."

Now the truth came out. Lockman didn't want me to win that one game with the Cubs. He was still pissed about being thrown out of the San Francisco game the year before when I nailed Jim Barr with a pitch. He'd had it in for me ever since, and on April 2, 1974, he got me.

* * *

"**B**ut I've had 16 good years in this game," I told the press with pride after being released. "I'm walking tall."

And I was. I was within one victory of becoming the third man in the history of the game to win 100 games in both the AL and NL, the first two being Cy Young and Jim Bunning. I'd thrown a no-hitter. I'd thrown 43 shutouts. I'd won 209 games. For guys who pitched only in the 20th Century, I ranked pretty high on the statistical lists. I was proud of that then, and I'm still proud of it.

But I wasn't washed up like Lockman wanted people to believe. I'd had a good spring. The stats proved it. I could still pitch with the best of them. The trouble was the only guy who believed that was Ray Kroc, the owner of the San Diego Padres, chairman of the McDonald's Corporation, and a good friend of mine.

I met Ray through Jim Maros, a Greek friend who owned a few McDonald's restaurants on the south side of Chicago. Jim took me to the McDonald's headquarters one time and introduced me to Ray. We hit it off right away. We ran into each other at one function or another over the years I was with the Cubs and developed a friendship. He tried to buy the Cubs from Mr. Wrigley, but the team wasn't for sale then. Instead, he bought the San Diego Padres.

As soon as I was cut by the Cubs, San Diego general manager Buzzy Bavasi called and made me an offer that was essentially the same as the deal that I'd had with the Cubs. I told him that I couldn't do that because I'd have to rent a place in San Diego for my family for the summer because Carole didn't want to move from Wheaton, where we lived and to do that I needed more money to cover the cost of maintaining two households. Buzzy said he was sorry but he couldn't offer me any more because of the rules back then. Exactly what it was had something to do with the reserve clause, but like most things legal there were ways to get around it.

The Cubs released me because if they had put me on waivers the waiver period would have carried into the regular season. If that had happened, the Cubs would have had to pay me my whole salary for the year, and I could still sign with another club. But since they released me before the season started, the Cubs only had to pay me a third of my salary.

Now any team signing after that would only have to pay me the other two thirds of the salary that my contract with the Cubs called for. That was what Bavasi was offering me, but I wanted more because, after paying for two households over the summer and paying taxes, I'd have nothing left. I asked him for a signing bonus or incentive clause or something that would help cover the extra cost of the second household. Bavasi said he couldn't do that. I said I'd have to pass then.

That's when Ray got involved. He joined the conversation and asked me what the problem was, and I told him. He told me that Buzzy had made me a fair offer. I said I couldn't take it as it was. He told me to sleep on it over night and to get back to him the next day. So I did.

"Ray, I've thought it over. I'll make you an offer. To make it legal, I'll sign with the Padres for $1.00 a year, if you'll give me a McDonald's franchise in the Chicago area."

He laughed. "You're not serious, are you?"

"I'm about as serious as the deal you offered me."

"Look, Milt, it's all we can do."

"You're the owner, Ray. You can overrule him. I'm not asking for the moon here."

"I'm sorry, Milt, but Buzzy's the general manager here. If he says that's the best we can do, then that's the best we can do. I can't overrule him."

I said I'd have to pass then. He wished me luck, and that was that.

I called Roland Hemond who was the general manager of the White Sox. During the winter, I'd talked to him about pitching for the ChiSox if the Cubs should let me go. He said he thought was a good possibility, but when I called him in April, he said that their pitching staff was already set, that they didn't have an opening just then, that he'd have to pass. The truth was he'd already asked about me, and Lockman told him that I was washed up. If they'd had a scout at any of my games, I'm sure he would have given Roland a different report on me.

The Phillies came to Chicago early in the year, and they gave me a look in a workout at Wrigley Field. Nothing came of it.

I tried the Tigers, but they were like the Cubs. They were re-building with youth because all the stars that had taken them to the top in 1968 were past their prime or had already retired. They didn't need a 35-year-old veteran.

Maybe if I'd been one win short of 300 in my career instead of 100 in just the National League, then someone probably would have made me a deal like the one the Indians made Early Wynn. Ol' Early was within one victory of 300 when the White Sox let him go after the 1962 season. He tried to hook on with anybody in 1963, but no team would have him until the Indians decided to give him a shot at winning his 300th. He lost twice before finally getting the one that put him on the list of immortals.

After being snubbed by so many teams, I finally decided to call it a career. I could have signed with a Triple-A team and hoped to be picked up by a Major League team in a pennant drive later in the year, but I considered that beneath me. I didn't need a job that much. Number 100 in the NL just wasn't worth demeaning myself and compromising my integrity. I quit the game and started a new life.

Like I told the media when I was released, "I'm walking tall." I was, too.

Part Five

THE BURBS

◆31◆

Extra Innings:
Pinch-hitters

Baseball was certainly a vehicle that allowed me the opportunity to meet a lot of interesting people over the years. From movie stars to the chairmen of the boards of several large corporations to Presidents of the United States.

I campaigned for John F. Kennedy when he ran for President in 1960. My work for him afforded me the chance to meet him on a number of occasions. I thought he was a very nice man, and Jackie was very gracious to meet. He came to the All-Star Game in 1962, and after the game, he came into the clubhouse to see me. He greeted all the other guys, but he actually sat and talked to me. He was quite a guy, and I enjoyed our relationship very much. Like most Americans, I cried when he was killed.

My friends were not just high-ranking Democrats. As earlier written, I met Spiro Agnew in 1958 in Baltimore through Johnny Wilbanks. At that time, Agnew was an attorney in Baltimore who occasionally would stop in at Johnny's used car lot to talk. That's how I met him. Once when I was in Johnny's office, he told me that he was ashamed to be Greek. I was just furious about that. I couldn't believe that he was ashamed of such a great heritage. From that time on, I didn't have much respect for Agnew at all. The Greek-American people helped Agnew out a lot when he was running for vice-president by raising a lot of money for him and Nixon. There should have been some appreciation from him for that, but I don't think there was. After he became vice-president, he went to Greece to see his homeland and where his relatives were from. When I read about his trip in the newspapers, I just laughed because I was willing to bet that Agnew hated every

minute of his trip home! When he resigned and was later prose-
cuted in Maryland, I had no sympathy for him.

I also had an opportunity to know President Nixon. He was
a big baseball fan. When I was still playing with the Cubs, Bill
Scott was attorney general for the state of Illinois. He took me
once to a big function, where Nixon was speaking. I had a chance
to meet him afterwards. I had to wait in line with a lot of other
people to be introduced to him. Nixon said, "I'm a big fan of
yours, and I like the way you pitch." It was just hard to believe
that the President of the United States was taking time to talk to
me when multi-millionaires and CEO's of giant corporations
were waiting in line behind me. I thought that was pretty funny.
After our meeting, we corresponded. Later, when I was working
on a drug abuse program for Bill Scott, we were both invited to
the White House because of the drug program. It was a very nice
occasion, and I was able to learn a little more about how government worked with drug programs. Nixon was the final speaker
that night, and he talked with everyone. We had a chance to see
the White House. He was a very nice man, and I really liked him.
It's too bad he made some disastrous decisions about the people
around him.

Another political leader that I had the good fortune to meet
— and whom I really liked — was the late Richard Daley, Sr.,
when he was mayor of Chicago. Even though he ruled Chicago
with a so-called iron hand, I thought he did a good job and was
basically a good man. I met Daley through Ed Kelley, a precinct
boss from the North Side who was also in charge of parks and
recreation in Chicago. The mayor and I became friends, and I'd
see him occasionally. Once he asked me if I would help out with
Chicago's city baseball leagues. He wanted me to join him in
talking to the kids, and I said I'd be delighted to do it.

So I took the 35-minute trip into Chicago from my home in
Wheaton to do this with the mayor. I was running a little behind
schedule, and I had a game that day. I stepped on the gas while
driving along the Eisenhower Expressway and was probably
doing about 70 when I was stopped by a Chicago policeman.

"Where do you think you're going in such a hurry?"

"I'm Milt Pappas of the Cubs, and I'm supposed to be

meeting with Mayor Daley to talk to some kids about baseball."

"Yeah, sure you are."

"Well, officer, I guess you have two choices. You can either believe me or give me a ticket. But if you give me a ticket, I'm going to tell the Mayor why I was stopped, and you might have some problems."

The officer didn't know quite what to do. "I'll tell you what. I'll give you an escort down to City Hall."

"Beautiful, because I'm running a little bit late and I don't want to disappoint the Mayor."

The officer gave me a police escort downtown. I pulled up to City Hall, parked my car, and walked inside. I turned and waved at the officer. He waved back and off he went. I guess it pays to know the right people.

* * *

I met Jerry Vale, the singer, in 1960 in Baltimore. Jerry was appearing at a supper club there. Blake Cullen, who was later to become the travelling secretary of the Chicago Cubs and is one of my dear friends, was in the audience. Blake introduced me to Jerry. We became friends and have been ever since.

In 1964, Jerry and his wife Rita came down to spring training in Miami when I was with the Orioles. They stayed at the same complex we were. My mother was down from Detroit. I had an emergency appendectomy while in spring training, so I was on the mend when Jerry and his wife arrived. I wasn't supposed to drive a car, but I went out to the airport to pick them up anyway. A couple of days later Rita got very sick and started to turn white. I told Jerry that he should get her to a hospital because she didn't look very good.

"No, I'll be fine. Don't worry about me," Rita said.

But about 10 minutes later she got worse.

I called for an ambulance, and it came and took Rita to some hospital that I can't recall the name of. She was there for a couple of hours, but they couldn't find anything and released her. She got back to the complex and her complexion hadn't changed. In fact, it was getting worse and I couldn't believe that the hospital couldn't find anything. I had an appendectomy done at Doctor's Hospital in Miami, and I said that was enough. We called for another ambulance and rushed her there this time. They checked her in and found that she was having some problem with her fallopian tubes. She had to have some emergency surgery. The doctor said, if the condition had gone on for another two or three hours, that she would have died. We were all surprised and shocked by the turn of events, but everything worked out all right. Rita survived, but she couldn't have children after that. The Vales later adopted two children.

* * *

Another friend of mine was Audie Murphy, the actor, who was also the most decorated war hero in the history of the United States. He came to a couple of games, and we became friends. I forget exactly how we met, but we became friends and when I came into town, he'd have me over to his house for dinner with his wife and kids.

One thing stands out in my mind about Audie Murphy. Every place he went he always had a gun with him. Once I was at his home before a game. He told me to take his car to the ball park, then we'd meet at a restaurant after the game. I said that would be fine, got in the car, and started to leave. As I was driving away, he yelled at me. "Stop, stop, stop!"

I stopped the car and said, "What's the matter?"

He ran up to the car, opened my door, reached under the front seat, and pulled out a pistol. "I don't want you to be caught with this."

One day I finally said to him, "Audie, why do you carry a gun with you all the time?"

Audie just looked at me. "You know, because of who I am. There's always gonna be some nut out there who's gonna want to shoot me, so he could say 'I killed the great war hero.' "

"And this is the way you live, Audie?"

All of a sudden, I realized what he meant, and I really felt sorry for him.

As for being a hero in World War II, he would very, very seldom ever talk about it. He had such terrible memories about the war and all the killing. He just hated to talk about it, but one day, I commented about his medals, which were never on display.

"Do you really want to see them?" he asked.

"Yeah."

He took me up to the attic to see all the medals, including the Purple Heart and the Congressional Medal of Honor. They were just sitting up there in his attic because they represented such terrible memories. I felt sorry for him because he was such a great human being, but he was so torn up by what happened during the war.

Unfortunately, he was killed in a plane accident, but I just loved going to California and spending time with Audie Murphy. He was a genuine man and just a joy to be around.

* * *

And what can I say about Milton Berle? He's known publicly as Uncle Milty, but in private he prefers to be called Milton because he's proud of his name. He's meant such a great deal to me over the years. We became very good friends when I was playing with the Orioles, and we've been friends ever since. I just love this man. He's one of the nicest people I've ever met. Milton is a great baseball fan.

When the Angels played at Dodger Stadium in the early 1960s, he had a dugout box, which was at ground level. Milton would bring me sandwiches and used to give them to me through the fence. He would bring kosher dill pickles and pastrami sandwiches. It was so funny because, as he was giving me these sandwiches through the fence, I felt like an animal in a zoo. But, man, were they good, and Milton was so nice to me. I just love that man. Any time I had a chance to spend time with him during baseball, I did. Even after baseball, when he was in Chicago, I would go see him. Once I even drove up to Green Bay to say hello. I still call him, and we maintain our friendship.

When I was with the Cubs, he called me after a day game in LA and asked if I wanted to go to a party. I accepted, of course. He picked me up about a half hour later at the hotel, and we drove out to comedian Jan Murray's house in Beverly Hills. When we got there, I just couldn't believe the people that were there. Lucille Ball and her husband Gary Morton, Red Buttons, Don Rickles, Mike Connors, Tina Louise, and the list went on and on. Star upon star. I thought, what in the hell am I doing here? I just couldn't believe the company I was in, and I was thinking, if I had to pay for the talent that was at the house that night, I would have had to have paid about ten million dollars to get all these people on one stage. I remember I had a tremendous evening. Tables were set by the pool for a buffet, and we were being served. I was sitting next to Milton Berle, and Lucille Ball, Gary Morton, and Don Rickles sat across the table from me. All of a sudden Rickles and Murray started throwing barbs at each other and I shut up. Gary Morton got up and started to talk. At that point, Lucille Ball, who was just the epitome of class, tugged at Morton's shoulder and said, "Gary, would you please sit down. You're making an ass out of yourself." I just sat there and laughed until all of a sudden Rickles, whom I had met on one other occasion, started nailing me. Oh, my Lord, here we go.

"Look at Milton Berle," said Rickles. "He's one of the greatest comedians who ever lived He's performed in front of Kings and Queens and Presidents and CEO's of major companies along with people all over the world and on TV every Tuesday night, the biggest star ever on television and who does he bring with him to a party, but some broken down right-handed pitcher! My God, Milty, what's wrong with you? Don't you have any class?" I just roared. It was such a beautiful, beautiful evening.

Milton made it all possible, giving me a chance to meet all these people, and I just had a great time.

* * *

Then there is my very, dear friend, former President George Bush. We met in 1984 in Denver while playing an old-timers game.

I walked into the hotel and saw these guys wearing these strange listening devices that stuck out of one ear, making them look like something out of *Star Wars*. I walked up to one of them, a big African-American guy, and asked him what was going on. He just looked at me and shrugged his shoulders.

"Excuse me for bothering you," I said before walked away. I asked the lady at the front desk what was going on.

"Well, the Vice-President of the United States, George Bush, is staying here."

I thought that was great. I knew he was a baseball fan.

About a half hour later, I got a call in my room, asking me if I could come down and meet the vice president, who wanted to say hello to the ballplayers.

"Sure, I'd love to."

I went downstairs just as he was preparing to give a couple of interviews to the local radio and television people. Then he broke away and came over to see us. In our crowd were Joe DiMaggio, Mickey Mantle, Whitey Ford, Warren Spahn, Billy Martin, and others. The Vice President just looked at all of us.

"Man, this is Walter Mitty night for me," he said. "God, what a great night to be among all of you."

I think he felt just like a little kid as he went on and on, complimenting all of us. He was and is the nicest man.

Later, I was talking to him when I looked him in the eye and said, "Why don't you get away from all of this political bullshit and come out and play in the game tonight?"

The secret service guys were all smiling and saying, "Yeah, do it. Go for it."

Mr. Bush looked at his aides and asked, "What do we have planned tonight?"

"Well, Mr. Vice-President, you have a dinner to attend and I don't know if you're really going to have the time."

I said, "Come on, Mr. Vice-President. Come out and you'll have a great time. You need to have some fun and get away from this stuff."

He said to me, "If we can make it, we will. Thanks for the invitation."

He went his way, and the rest of us went to the ball park.

About an hour before the game, an army of Denver police officers poured into the stadium, and I saw those guys with the odd listening devices sticking out of their ears. A helicopter started buzzing the park, and I started thinking, Hey, the guy is going to come!

It was the top of the second inning, and I was pitching. Mr. Bush had already come into the clubhouse, and he was dressed in a Denver Bears uniform, which I thought was very nice. Denver was a minor league affiliate at that time. He spent some time in the locker room, where Warren Spahn was pitching to him with a whiffle ball, so he could take some batting practice. Then, all of a sudden, this station wagon came out on the field, but no one knew what in the hell was going on. Of course, we suspected the vice-president had come to the game, but we didn't know for certain until he stepped out of the car in front of 49,000 people. I was on the mound, but he had asked Warren Spahn to pitch to him. I was kind of upset about it, but I kept my mouth shut. I went to second base, and Warren took over. Mr. Bush was introduced, and he received a standing ovation. He walked up to the plate, swinging a couple of bats, laughing and having a good time. He took a couple of pitches, then swung at one and popped it up to me at second base. Of course, I dropped it. Then I ran over to first base.

"Mr. Vice President, get back up there and hit again. My God, look at these people. You received a standing ovation. They love you, so get back there and hit again."

"Really?" he asked.

"Yeah, go back up there."

In the meantime, Warren Spahn walked off, so I said great, and took the mound again. On the first pitch I brushed him back and knocked him on his butt. I was thinking, What will I get for this, life imprisonment? After a couple of more pitches, he hit a line drive right back through the middle for a base hit. He really hit the ball great. And he was really happy, standing at first base with the biggest grin on his face and waving to the crowd.

When the inning was over, he went into the dugout and started shaking everybody's hand and telling them what a great night it was. He said it was the thrill of a lifetime.

I walked up to him, threw him a first baseman's glove, and said, "Now, you have to go to work."

"You again," he said.

"Yes, sir. Now you've got to go out there and earn your keep."

"Really?" He had this big smile on his face.

"Yes," I said. "Go out and play first base."

So the vice-president ran out to first base when the inning was over and started throwing ground balls to the infielders. He was having a great time.

I was still pitching. Thank God, the first four or five guys up were right-handed hitters. A couple of men reached base with two outs, bringing up Tony Oliva, who even then, could still swing the bat pretty well. I didn't want to throw him anything inside because I didn't want Mr. Bush to get killed. So I kept throwing pitches on the outside part of the plate, and Oliva kept fouling them off and fouling them off. Tony must have fouled off 10 pitches. I was to the point where I just wanted to get the inning over and get out of there. I threw a ball inside, and Oliva ripped a viscious one-hopper down to first base. Oh, no! But Mr. Bush made a great, fantastic, one- handed pickup. I ran over to cover the bag. Mr. Bush flipped the ball to me for the out, and he ran off the field, threw his glove up in the air, threw his hat up in the air, and yelled, "That's it! I'm done!" He ran off the field, happier than hell with the biggest smile on his face. He had just a tremendous night, and we all were glad for him.

After the game, the players had a party in our suite. Mr. Bush didn't come for some reason, but a lot of the secret service guys did. They got blasted and everybody had a great time. I left about 2:00 a.m. and went to bed. About 7:00 a.m., the phone rang. It was one of the secret service guys.

"The vice-president would like you to come up to his suite and have some coffee. Can you come up?"

"Sure," I said. "I'll be up there in about 20 minutes."

I shaved, dressed, and jumped in the elevator. At 7:30 in the morning, not too many people are floating around, but in the elevator, there was this old man with this real young boy, who I figured was his grandson. Well, I pushed the button for the top floor. When we got there, the door opened. I got out and the old man takes a step out and about five secret service guys converge. They kind of backed up and said, "Can we help you sir?"

He had this sheepish look on his face, backed into the elevator and said, "No, I don't think so."

The young boy who was with him said, "What's the matter, Grandpa?"

"I don't know, but I think we better get out of here."

"Mr. Pappas, could you please come with us?"

I followed them down the hallway and entered the vice-president's suite. When I walked in, I saw the bat that he used the night before, lying on the sofa with the ball that he'd gotten the base hit with.

Mrs. Bush was there, and she came over to me. "I just want to thank you, Milt, for what you did for my husband last night. It was one of the greatest nights he's ever had."

I looked at her and said, "Well, Mrs. Bush. I can tell you that he did a lot for me too."

Mr. Bush walked out of the bedroom. We sat down, had coffee and talked, spending about a half hour together before he thanked me profusely for having such a great evening.

"You don't have to thank me for anything, Mr. Vice-President. Thank you for what you did for me."

After that experience, we became very good friends. Every time he came to Chicago after that, I saw him. I helped campaign for him and President Reagan.

A few years later the Bushes were staying in a suburb of Chicago, close to where I lived. My wife Judi, our daughter Alexandria, Judi's parents, and I went to see them. We were in their suite, talking and taking pictures and having a very, very nice time, when all of a sudden, Alexandria decided to poop her pants. So, it started to smell just a little and Judi excused herself and went into the bedroom to change Alex. Judi had these little bags that all smelled like perfume and she put the poopy bag in there and wrapped it up and she stuck it in her purse. Barbara walked into the bedroom and saw what she was doing and said, "Judi, why are you putting a diaper in your purse?"

"Well, I didn't want to leave it here."

"No, leave it for the maids. I want them to have something to talk about after I leave."

We had a very wonderful afternoon with them.

I also campaigned for George when he ran for President. When he became President, he gave me a lapel pin that gave me access to where he was whenever he came to town.

I just loved being around this guy, and here he was, the most powerful man in the world, but yet so down to earth. The short times that I spent with him over the years, I think, took him away from all of the responsibility that he held on his shoulders for 24 hours a day as President.

Once, I was playing in an old-timers game in Baltimore. I called the White House, said that I would be in town and asked if I could possibly see the President. Arrangements were made for a visit to the White House on a Friday afternoon. I flew in on Thursday and was staying with my dearest friends, Harriett and Elliott Goldberg, in Baltimore. Friday morning, we went to the White House but got a little lost. So, we saw a police car stopped at a corner and we stopped too.

"Officer, we're a little lost. We have a meeting with the President. How do we get to the White House?"

He looked at us with a questioning look, like he thought, Yeah, right, you have an appointment with the President. He finally told us to go two blocks down and turn left.

We got to the White House security gate and stopped. The guard walked out and acknowledged us. "Mr. Pappas and Mr. and Mrs. Goldberg." He went back into the little guardhouse, and a few minutes later came back to the car.

"Mr. Pappas, you're fine. Mr. Goldberg, you're fine. But, Mrs. Goldberg, we have a problem. We haven't gotten the okay on you."

I looked at Harriett. We had been friends for years. "Well Harriett, I guess it's too bad. You're going to have to stay in the car."

"Like hell, I am. If I don't go in, you guys don't go in." She started raising all kinds of holy hell.

Elliott and I remained calm, although we both knew that the

guard was part of a joke on Harriett. The guard came back a few minutes later and said, "Mrs. Goldberg, everything is fine." She calmed down finally. It wasn't until later that we told her it was put up job.

In the meantime, security has this huge mirror and they were underneath the car looking for any explosives. This was standard operating procedure when unsecured cars come to the White House. Satisfied that we weren't part of a terrorist plot, they opened the gate and told us to drive down to the canopy where someone else would take care of us. We followed the directions and came to someone at a desk.

"Mr. Pappas, go down the hallway about 20 feet and you'll see a flight of stairs. You go up there, and someone will take care of you."

We went down the hallway and up the stairs, and when we got there, we were greeted by this beautiful Asian lady, who was in a very small room. "Would you like something to drink?" she asked. We gave her our orders. There were about three tables and six or seven chairs, and secret service guys were at each end of the room. We sat down, and our drinks were brought to us with napkins that had the Presidential Seal on them. A few minutes later, the President's secretary, Patty came in. She's a lovely lady. I'd met her before, so she greeted me with a hug.

"It's great to see you," she said. "The President will be with you in about 10 or 15 minutes."

Before we had gotten to that room, Elliott had asked the secret service if he could take some pictures and they said no. So I asked Patty if Elliott could take some pictures, and she said, "Oh, yes." The secret service guys weren't too friendly after that. Then Patty left down a hallway.

About 10 minutes later, Patty returned to take us to see the President. We walked down the same hall to the door to a little cubicle that had five secret service guys inside. This was Patty's office. She indicated another door and said, "Milt, just go in through that door there, please."

When I opened the door, there was the Oval Office. I was overwhelmed. I thought, Oh, my Lord, I'm here in the Oval Office as a friend of the President of the United States. I'm not a Senator or a Congressman or a National Security Adviser. I'm here as his friend. The room was huge, but there was no President. There was a big, huge desk in the middle and a picture of the Bush family on it.

All of a sudden, way at the other end of the office, a door opened and a voice called out. "Where's Milt?"

"Right here, Mr. President." President Bush walked over and we shook hands and walked over to the desk.

"Say, Milt, look at this." He was laughing and when I looked I saw one of my baseball cards on his desk. I laughed. We sat down and talked, then Elliott and Harriett came in and were introduced. They were awestruck, like most people would be. We took pictures.

I asked the President, "Where do you get your work done?"

"Oh, you really want to know?" We went back to this door where he entered the Oval Office, and here was this little tiny office that was no bigger than six feet by seven feet. There was a telephone and a typewriter on a small desk, and this is where President Bush did a lot of his work. It wasn't in the Oval Office, just a little, tiny room behind the Oval Office. I couldn't help but laugh.

"Now is this the desk Mr. President?

"Oh, do you know about this?" He then took out a tape of the Oak Ridge Boys and put it in. There were speakers built into the desk.

"Yes, they made this for me."

We spent about 20 or 25 minutes with the President in the Oval Office, then he had to go to Camp David.

"Do you want to walk with me out to the helicopter?"

"Sure," I said.

We all walked out with the President to the East Lawn, where the helicopter was. About 200 people were there, including his staff, and they were all waving goodbye. And here I am, walking with the President of the United States up to the helicopter. That was one of the greatest days I've ever had in my life, and I thank George Bush for making that day possible for my friends, the Goldbergs, and me. To this day, Harriett and Elliott still can't get over it.

Postgame Show:
Turn Out the Lights

After I got out of baseball and my son was preparing to go to college, a Greek professor at North Central College in Naperville, Illinois, asked me if I would be interested in coaching college baseball. I hadn't given coaching much thought and told him so.

"Why don't you come over and talk to the athletic director?"

I did, and we took a liking to each other. I figured, since my son was planning to go to North Central in a year or two, that it might be a good challenge and kind of fun. So I took the job.

Trying to put the team together was a very unique experience for me. It was my first try at coaching. It was interesting picking out guys I thought would be the nucleus of a good team. That school was noted primarily for track and field and football, so I was having two-sport guys that were coming out for baseball. They were either a track guy or a football player. Maybe one or two kids that I had were actually there for baseball. The hardest thing I had to overcome being a college coach was the way I looked at everybody. These guys were not performing up to major league capabilities and that was my biggest problem. I had to overlook who I was and what I went through, and instead just look at them as college baseball players. I had to redo my whole way of thinking because these guys weren't professional. I had to restructure my thinking that all these guys wouldn't live up to my expectations. These youngsters weren't Mickey Mantle, Ted Williams or Willie Mays.

Coaching was a big change for me in that I had to come down from a Major League level to the level of a high school or college coach. It was a very difficult transition time for me. But I had to do it, and I had to do it very quickly. Otherwise, I would destroy these kids, and I didn't want to do that.

I coached at North Central for three years in the late 1970s. My son Steve played for me one year. I think it was probably more difficult for my son than for me. He had to put up with the old man, and he had to look up to what the old man did. I told him from a very early age on that his biggest hindrance growing up would be that people would compare him to me, which is very wrong. I said, "Stevie, take what other people say at face value, and don't let it bother you." I enjoyed coaching my son. I had a ball doing it.

We found a tournament down in Florida where we could play two games a day for five days. During spring break, we rented cars and went down there. We spent six days in Florida, playing two games a day. There were teams from all over, but mostly from the Midwest.

I really enjoyed it. The money was absolutely nothing. I got paid $2,000 a year. I was just doing it to see if I liked it, and I did, once I realized I was coaching college kids.

I even got thrown out of a college game by an umpire, so my feelings for umpires didn't change. That philosophy of mine has never changed. I didn't like umpires when I was playing, and it carried over to my college coaching career. When I got tossed, my kids thought it was a blast. They laughed like crazy about it. So my legacy continued.

But after three years, the college decided it wanted a full-time coach who would also be a teacher, so if the kids had questions or problems, they could go to him for help. So my coaching career was pretty short-lived, but I really enjoyed it.

* * *

My first job after baseball was with a neighbor of mine who was in the import-export business of buying and selling grain. I knew nothing much about it, but working with him I got to know a lot about the import-export business. I lasted for about three years. I was inside doing everything by telephone, and being a people person I wanted something other than that.

Then I got involved in the liquor business and became a liquor salesman in Chicago. I enjoyed that because a large number of the restaurants and bars in the Chicago area were either owned or operated by Greeks. Being a Greek, I figured that was the perfect way to get in and do what I had to do. I did that for about three years, and then branched out into the Greek food business, called the gyro. It's a darn good sandwich. I was really just getting started with the gyro business. I was working for a manufacturer and again calling on restaurants. I did that for about three or four years and really enjoyed it.

But it got to a point where I couldn't advance anymore, so I changed occupations and went into the fastener business. For about the last 16 years I've been in the nail and screw business. We're a wholesaler, an importer of nails and screws. We wholesale to lumber yards, home center marts, dry wall distributors and roofing distributors. Itochu Building Products is a Japanese owned company, doing $240 billion worth of business a year. I'm an area wide sales manager.

Back in the era when I played baseball, we weren't afforded the opportunity of making the big money. Obviously, when you have a family to support, you had to get a job. And there aren't many guys I know in my era who did not find a job when they were done with baseball. We all had to go to work.

To go out and find a job after baseball was very, very difficult. Not going to college and not really having any kind of work experience to fall back on made it a little more difficult. Because of the name recognition I had and my ability to relate to people, I felt sales would be a good avenue for me. But interviewing for jobs was just amazing. The mentality of the people that interviewed me was different. Right away, you could see they were wondering why I was interviewing for a job. After all, I had been a Major League pitcher. They all felt that baseball players were making so much money that they didn't have to work, which was totally false. We all had to find jobs when we were done playing. The first question was, "We can't pay you that much money." And I would say, "We haven't even discussed money. I'm here to look for a job. What type of money are you offering?" The reply was, "I can't afford you." And we would never even discuss money. Just about everybody that you talked to thought that you had to make $70,000, $80,000, or $100,000, and that you were asking for that much. That was totally ridiculous because I knew that nobody would offer me the kind of job that would pay me that kind of money. It was very, very difficult to find a place to go to work that really had your well being at heart.

It was very hard to find a job to support my family. I finally did of course, and I've been working ever since.

* * *

T he trials and tribulations that come with being out of baseball are considerable. The number of divorces among guys that I used to play with is incredible. When you're in the limelight all the time, it's tough to make the adjustment.

The wives were also somewhat in the limelight at that time. They were instantly recognized as your wife, even though they were pushed into the background, because everyone wanted to meet the player. I didn't like that. I would always introduce my wife at any function I was at. It was difficult on players' wives, even when you were playing baseball because when you're gone on a two-week road-trip, she would have to be mother and father to your children. She had to take care of the kids and do everything you couldn't do because you weren't there. It was not an easy life for the wives.

Plus, a lot of the wives probably thought that the guys were cheating on them when they're on the road. You always had to answer that question when you came back home. Well, what happened? Did you get involved with anybody? No, I love you. It was a difficult situation.

Once the game is over, you're home all of the time, after not being home for 17 years. Now you're home 24 hours a day. It was even more of a challenge because now you really had to get reacquainted with your wife. Before, you had an idea of who your wife was, but then you were gone two weeks out of every month. You went on the road, and whatever happened at home you really weren't worried about because the wife was there taking care of the family. The broken arms always seemed to happen to your kid when you were on the road. The wife had to take care of that. I felt very, very sorry for the wives of professional athletes because of the role that they had to play, being a mother and a father all of the time you were gone.

Then, when a husband is home all of the time and getting in his wife's hair, it's difficult even to start conversations. It bothers not only the wives, but a lot of the players. It's a very difficult transition.

◆33◆

Shutout:
The Loss Column

C arole, my first wife, had a very tough time with the transition from baseball, but other things that happened in our marital relationship may have — no, probably — led to later problems.

When I was with the Atlanta Braves, I had an affair with a Playboy bunny named Tina. (I have intentionally omitted Tina's last name. She's moved on with her life, just as I have. I see no reason to cause her any grief at this time.) I had my own apartment in Atlanta. I'd had my own place in Cincinnati, too, but I didn't have an affair there. Why? That's hard to say exactly. I was alone much of the time. That's no excuse, but that's what happened. Carole and the kids stayed at our house in Baltimore, just as they had done when I was traded to the Reds. I was lonely there, too, but Cincinnati didn't have a Playboy Club. No, that's not it. Let me back up a bit.

Ballplayers attract women, and women attract ballplayers. I can't speak for football players or basketball players or hockey players, but I do know that baseball players have lots of women available to them just about wherever they go. It was no different for me.

My preference in women was for stewardesses — female flight attendants, as they are now known. They were convenient because they could fly for free to anywhere I went on the road, and many of the ones I met were available. We'd flirt on the plane, and they'd accept my invitation to a game and whatever should happen afterward. Most of them were one-nighters. Sometimes, I would see some of them more than once. This one stew sent me a letter from Boston when she heard that my son had been born. There was no mention of our relationship in the letter; just a friendly note congratulating me on having a son. That could have been a disaster for me, but for all I know, Carole never saw the letter. Therefore, I didn't have to answer any embarrassing questions from her.

It's not like I was the only player who spent road nights with women other than my wife. A lot of guys were doing it. The time was different then. We didn't have AIDS or herpes to worry about, and this was before less than scrupulous women began "shaking down" players after having sex with them. Players of the modern era have to contend with that kind of situation. The only time you hear about something like that is when the guy refuses to pay up and the girl goes screaming to the police that she was raped or taken advantage of or whatever. Whenever I hear about some high-paid athlete being charged with something like that, I thank God the women of my playing days didn't think up such a scam. If they had, either my wallet or my marriage would have been bankrupt.

And I wasn't like a rooster in the henhouse when I was young either. I did practice some form of restraint. I had this theory that I shouldn't have sex the day before I was scheduled to pitch. I practiced this at home as well as on the road. I thought that if I had sex the day before I was to start, then I would have a bad outing. I stuck to my theory until late in my career and I was pitching for the Cubs. This one stewardess flew into Montreal on the day that I was to pitch. We'd known each other before, so I was kind of glad to see her. She said she didn't have much time because she was flying out again that evening. We had sex just a few hours before I took the hill against the Expos, and I threw a two-hitter. So much for my theory.

A couple of incidents when I was chasing around on the road.

I was with the Orioles yet, and Jack Fisher was my roommate on the road. We were out having a good time after a night game, and I returned to our hotel room first. The phone was ringing. Concerned that it might be Carole, I answered it, trying to act like I'd been awakened from sleep. Well, the caller was Carol, Carol Gentile, Jim Gentile's wife. I complained about being awakened, and she said, "Bullshit, Pappas! I've been calling all night long. Is Fisher there?" Trapped, I told the truth that he wasn't, and she said, "Well, tell the sonofabitch his wife had the baby." Oops!

When I was with the Braves, the team was in Cincinnati, playing the Reds. I had a girl in my room when the phone rang. I picked up the phone, and it was my mother on the line. I said it was nice of her to call, and she said she and my brother Perry were in the lobby and could they come up. Oops! Get dressed, baby. Time to go. Now! You never saw a woman get dressed so fast. I hustled her out of the room before my mother and Perry came up.

Whether Carole ever knew about the one-nighters when I was having them, I don't know. It doesn't really make any difference now. If she did know, she never let on about it.

The relationship that Tina the Bunny and I had is what I call an affair — a romance, if you will. She was much more than a one-night-stand.

Tina worked at the Atlanta Playboy Club as a bunny, a waitress. I met her there. She was attractive: dark hair, petite. But the Playboy Club had rules about hitting on the bunnies, and I went along with them. This one night some four or five other players and I went to another bar after the game, and in walked Tina and a few of her friends from the Playboy Club. It was their night off. They knew us, so they joined us for drinks. One thing led to another, and Tina and I went home together.

But why did I have an affair then and not before or after Tina?

When I was traded to the Reds, Carole, the kids, and I went to Florida as usual for spring training. We got a place in Tampa, and all was right with the world. When the season began, Carole decided to go back to Baltimore instead of coming north with me to Cincinnati. I got my own apartment in Cincy, and I got through the year without any attachments. Next year, 1967, and the next went pretty much the same way. But not so in 1969. I wanted my family with me in Atlanta, and I told Carole so. She said she was taking the kids back to Baltimore like she had before because she didn't want to be shuffling them in and out of too many different schools. I said that didn't make any sense because we were taking them out of school in Florida to go back to Maryland. We argued about it, and I lost. She went back to Baltimore with the kids. That didn't set too well with me, and the bitterness hung on for quite a while. I was still angry with Carole when Tina came into my life and began filling the void which I blamed on Carole.

I still don't know how Carole found out about my affair with Tina, but I do know how she verified it. She hired a detective to follow me. Her father paid for the detective, and this guy got the goods on me.

Whenever I was on the road, I called home every day. I was in Philadelphia with the Braves when Carole called me at the hotel. She said she knew about Tina and she wanted a divorce. Hold the phone! I was struck by lightning. Divorce? It all started to come home to me with that one word: D-I-V-O-R-C-E! Panic gnawed at my guts. I started talking and talking fast. About 10 hours later, I promised her that I'd break it off with Tina, and she agreed to call of the divorce.

After I got off the phone, I did some soul-searching and figured out that I loved my wife and my kids more than I wanted to sleep with Tina, so I made the break with my girlfriend. The kids were too young to understand what was happening then, which was good for me because I didn't have to explain anything to them at the time. I wanted to be with my family, and Carole took me back. I gave up Tina but not the one-nighters. Looking back, I wish I'd stopped fooling around as well.

* * *

U nfortunately, Carole started to drink heavily about this time. I was unaware of her problem because she did most of her drinking when I was on the road. It wasn't until much later that I learned about it.

The neighbors in Wheaton, Frank Morgan and Ted Koyzis, knew about Carole's drinking long before I did. They would see Carole trying to maneuver out of the garage with the kids in the car. Frank or Ted would come over and put his car behind hers so she wouldn't be able to back out of the garage. That way she wouldn't drive the car with a chance of killing her and the kids. My kids kept that and more from me, and so did the neighbors until after Carole admitted to me that she was an alcoholic.

Michelle told me later what it was like with Carole when I was away from home, but before I relate Michelle's story, a review of some background on Carole when she was growing up.

Carole was an only child — and a very lonely child. Helen, her mother, had a miscarriage before she became pregnant with Carole, and Helen lost hearing in one ear at the same time. The doctor told her that the hearing loss was due to the miscarriage. Whether that can happen or not, I don't know; I'm not a doctor. But Carole's mother thought she would lose the hearing in her other ear because she was pregnant again. I'm sure, if abortions had been legal back then, that Helen would have gotten one and Carole would never have been born. So even before she came into this world, Carole had one strike against her.

After she was born, Carole's parents lavished her with gifts every Christmas, but for the remaining 364 days of the year, they ignored her. Her father, Oliver Tragge, operated a tool-and-die company, and he was a slave to his business. Her mother was a housewife, but she also worked at the business as a bookkeeper. They never showed Carole any love or affection — nothing that you would call nurturing. That was strike two.

I've already told you about strike three.

The point is Carole wasn't abused as a child that I know of, but she was neglected. She didn't grow up in the same kind of loving atmosphere that I did, and she didn't have anything near what people would call a good parenting example to follow like I did. For that, she was always jealous of my family situation.

Now back to Michelle's story.

Whenever Carole would get drunk, she would deliberately take the kids with her when she left the house in the car. Unhappy over this, Michelle would turn her face to the side window and stare out until Carole would grab her by the hair and jerk her head around to face the road ahead. Then she'd slap Michelle and tell her to watch the road so when they crashed she'd know they would be killed. She'd actually say that to Michelle. What a horror that was for her!

And for Steve. He told me how he would unhook the battery cables on Carole's car whenever I was gone just so she couldn't drive. He mentioned this one time when I was away picking up Michelle from college at Illinois Wesleyan, and he came home to find his mother in such a stupor that he had to take her to the hospital. I'd forgotten about that night. I'm surprised he remembered it because he's blocked a lot of the bad stuff out his memory.

Like I said before, I would call home every day when I was on the road. Often the kids would answer the phone. I would ask for their mother, and they'd lie to me and say she was out at the store or something. The truth was Carole was passed out on the bed, too drunk to do anything.

Now this is not to say that Carole was a bad person. She was a good mother to both our children up until the time she started to drink heavily. I say heavily because she drank before my affair with Tina, but it was always casual drinking at a meal or some social function. And it was never in the daytime. I guess the booze did things to her. The really sad part was she did most of the bad things to Michelle.

Another incident happened when Michelle turned 16. We had been planning a "Sweet 16" dinner party for Michelle. This was a very special occasion, and I asked Carole not to drink that day. She did anyway. An hour and a half before we were supposed to leave she was so sloshed that I had to put her to bed to sleep it off. I took Michelle out by myself. The next morning Carole was remorseful about the night before, but I was still upset with her. Carole pleaded that she just couldn't handle Michelle turning 16, and I told her that was a load of bullshit. She whined some more, but I stuck to my tough stance. I don't know if that helped her or made things worse in her mind.

When I asked Michelle and Steve and the neighbors, Frank and Ted, why they didn't tell me about Carole sooner, they gave me the same basic answer. They didn't want to upset me and maybe hurt my career in baseball. I know they meant well, that their intentions were good, but the road to Hell is …

* * *

I t was late in my career when I was with the Cubs. We were in New York, and I was scheduled to pitch a night game. Carole called and told me she was a drunk. She was scared about it and said she needed me at home. I went to our manager, Leo Durocher, and told him what the problem was. Say what you will about Leo, but he did the right thing by me. He told me to go to her — to get dressed and jump on the next plane home. I did.

Carole admitted again that she was an alcoholic, then she promised me that she would do everything to right herself. I believed her, and I tried to help her as best as I could. It was very difficult, but we both tried. She joined Alcoholics Anonymous, and I went to Al-Anon meetings to get an insight on alcoholics. AA gave her a sponsor to help, and the sponsor did the best she could — whenever Carole would let her.

After I left baseball, I was home all the time like a regular guy with a regular job, but this situation was even more difficult on both of us. I missed baseball, and Carole was unaccustomed to having me around so much. We got on each other's nerves. She tried to get sober, but she wouldn't make it. She'd start drinking again — on the sly. Why? Pressure. Stress. Pressure from me, more than anything, I suppose. It was a very, very difficult time for me because I couldn't stand the fact that my wife was an alcoholic. I compensated for her condition by taking out my anger on her. My mind would imagine all sorts of bad things. The worst of those was that she could get in the car with my kids and have an accident and kill somebody — her, the kids, some stranger, anybody. I even got so that I didn't want to come home from work because I was afraid she'd be drunk again. Looking back, I'm somewhat surprised that I didn't over compensate by becoming an alcoholic myself.

Someone along the way during those years suggested that I should divorce Carole because she was an alcoholic. Believe me, I thought about it, but the process of even filing for a divorce hurt. I couldn't divorce her, not when she needed someone the most. Besides, I loved her deeply. Maybe that's why I didn't become a drunk as well.

How much of an alcoholic was Carole? Let me give you this

piece as an illustration. Carole was arrested for shoplifting once. It's not the act of stealing that is of concern here; it's what she stole. She was caught taking a bottle of vanilla extract. She paid the fine and never told me about it. For some reason, she kept a receipt for the fine in a safety deposit box, and I didn't find it until years later.

I stuck it out — her alcoholism. I put enough time in to where I thought I could help, but nothing was really helping her. I tried. The sponsor tried. The kids tried. Everybody tried to help. All to no avail.

* * *

On Saturday mornings, Carole normally went to the beauty shop and to the store, then came right home about one or two o'clock. It was a regular routine. Then one Saturday the routine was interrupted.

The date was September 11, 1982. Carole and I were alone then. Steve and Michelle were in college at North Central College in Naperville and living elsewhere in the Chicago area.

Carole left to go about her usual chores, and I started cutting the grass. It was warm that day. Around 1:30 in the afternoon I started getting a little dizzy from the heat, so I stopped mowing and went inside to lay down for a while. As soon as I felt a little better, I jumped into the shower to clean up. By the time I was done with that, it was 3:00 or so, and it occurred to me that Carole wasn't home yet. My first reaction was anger that she was late, but that quickly turned to concern when I began thinking about why she might be late.

Around 6:00 in the evening, I called Steve and Michelle to ask them if they'd seen their mother, and both said no. They were familiar with Carole's routine, so they quickly became as concerned as I was. They came over to the house. I decided to call the police.

We lived in Wheaton, Illinois at that time. The officer at the Wheaton police department that I spoke with said there was nothing they could do for 24 hours as far as filing a missing person report.

"That's ridiculous! My wife's not home, and she's usually home by one or two o'clock in the afternoon. It's eight o'clock at night, and she's not here."

"We're sorry, Mr. Pappas. There's nothing we can do at this time."

Our apprehension was growing by the minute, but there was nothing we could do except wait and wait and wait. The time dragged slowly. We sat together that night. No sleep. No phone call. No nothing.

Of course, your mind starts to wander at times like these, and you begin imagining all sorts of things that could have happened. Did she run away? Was she in an accident? If it was an accident, why hadn't I been contacted by the police? Was she drinking again? If she was drinking, was she somewhere sleeping it off?

That's about the time that something else occurred to me.

Carole had been at the dentist the day before to have some surgery done on her gums. The dentist prescribed something with codeine in it for the pain. When I thought about that, I checked the bottle to see if any pills were left. Much to my relief most of them were there, which meant she hadn't overdosed on them or something like that.

The kids and I slept very little that night.

The next day I filed a missing person report. The Wheaton police sent a patrol officer out to take my statement. I gave it to him, then said I wanted to go public at that time. The police told me, "No, you don't want to do that."

"Why wouldn't I want to do that? I can gather instant publicity because of who I am. If somebody knows where my wife is at and what happened to her, I'd like to know."

The police said, "Well, we don't think that's a good idea because 80 percent of all the missing persons come back."

"Wait a minute. You can take your statistics and stick them up you butt because you don't know my wife. I've known my wife for over 20 years. She's never done anything like this. I'm very concerned."

Well, they wouldn't let me go to the press. For a couple of days, the only person I contacted was my employer. I told him what was happening, and I stayed home hoping to hear something either from Carole or the police or a kidnaper or whatever; just something or someone.

The only person outside of the Wheaton police that I told about Carole's disappearance was Jose Cardenal, who was one of my best friends. He said, "What are you doing about it?"

"I'm not doing anything."

"Well, man, you have to say something."

"Well, they won't let me."

Again, my wife had disappeared on Saturday, and this was a Wednesday. Jose took it upon himself to call Johnny Morris, a Chicago sportscaster. Jose told Morris the story, and Johnny broke it on the air that my wife was missing.

Instantly, I was inundated with the press about my wife's disappearance. It was local and national news. The nightmare was just beginning.

◆34◆

Collision:
Out at Home

The kids and I continued the vigil on Sunday. I wanted to
call all the places that I knew Carole was supposed to go,
but none of them were open. I had to wait until Monday to call,
and that made Sunday absolute torture for me and the kids.

Carole was supposed to go to the beauty shop, dry cleaners,
and grocery store. I'd also given her some bills to mail. She could
have gone to the post office or she might have dropped them at
a mail box. The visit to the beauty shop was a regular Saturday
ritual with Carole. She had a standing appointment there. The
cleaners was a usual stop, but not an every Saturday thing. The
grocery store slipped my mind until the following Wednesday.

I called both the beauty shop and the dry cleaners first thing
Monday morning. Carole had been at the beauty shop right on
time, and she left after they finished her hair. The women there
said she seemed quite normal, quite sober. At the cleaners, they
said the same thing. She came in, picked up our laundry and dry-
cleaning, then left. She appeared to be fine and sober. I didn't
bother to call the post office because she usually didn't go there
except to buy stamps; however, the bills had been mailed, which
was something that I verified later.

The police checked the same leads and turned up the same
answers. When I told them about the grocery store a few days
later, they spoke with the clerks who were working there on
Saturday. A couple of them recognized a photograph of Carole,
but none of them could recall seeing her on Saturday.

Carole was now missing for more than 48 hours, but this
wasn't the first time that she didn't come home on time. She'd

done something like this before, which was why we held out the hope that she would come home at any time soon.

Oliver Tragge, Carole's father, had died the year before after a long illness. Carole went alone to see him in Detroit while he was sick. When she was coming back to Wheaton, a snowstorm struck the Midwest. We worried about her driving alone in the storm, but our concern turned to panic when she was late arriving home. A whole night passed without any word from her. When she did show up the next day, she gave me a feeble excuse about being too scared to stop and call. She said that she'd stopped on the side of the highway because the snow was falling too hard to see the road. A trucker stopped to see if she was okay. When she told him what was what, he said she should follow him down the highway because the rear lights of his truck would be visible to her through the snow. They drove very slowly through the storm, and finally made it to Chicago early the next morning. She managed to find her way from there and got home in the early hours of the morning.

I was angry with her for not calling, and she seemed rather sheepish about it. Why? I don't know, and I certainly don't want to speculate here about it. Her story was quite plausible because my friend Larry Names had pretty much the same thing happen to him out in Idaho once. He drove into a blinding snowstorm at night that slowed him down to a crawl until a trucker came by. The 18-wheeler pulled in front of him, blinked his rear lights as a signal that Larry took to mean that he should follow the truck. Larry stayed on that truck's tail until they passed out of the storm at the Utah line at which point the trucker put the pedal to the metal and left him far behind in the night. He never got to thank that trucker, and I never got to thank the guy who helped Carole that night.

* * *

The media can be merciless. They can be your friend, or they can be your worst enemy. It just depends on which side of the law that they perceive you to be.

When Jose Cardenal called Johnny Morris to tell him that Carole was missing, Johnny called me to verify the story. Johnny was an old friend, and he's half Greek. He asked me why the story hadn't broken before this, and I told him that the Wheaton police wanted a lid kept on it because they feared the publicity would taint their investigation. Johnny said he planned to air the story on the 10 o'clock news, and I told him to run with it. He did.

The next morning all hell broke loose. When I got up after another fitful night in bed, I found television news cameras, radio sound trucks, and newspaper reporters camped on my lawn like a school of sharks waiting to start a feeding frenzy with me as the main course. The police weren't happy with me, but I gave the media all the details as I knew them to that point. Every station in town was already running the same information that Johnny had telecast the night before, but now they had tape and sound bites to punctuate the basic information.

Within hours, the police started getting phone calls about sightings of my wife. Only one proved worth anything.

A sales person called from the Marshall Field's store in Carol Stream, which is just north and west of Wheaton. She said, "Mrs. Pappas was here. She was exchanging a pair of hose. Something was wrong with her and I said, 'Can I help you? Can I call somebody to come and get you?' And she said, 'No, no. I'll make it home all right.' She wobbled out of the store."

This information confirmed my suspicions that Carole had gotten drunk that morning. This was also when I told the police about Carole's drinking problem. They raised their eyebrows at me, but that was all there was to it.

The days started turning into weeks, and the weeks became a month. About then, I called the credit card companies to see if any of her cards had been used since the day disappeared. No, none of them had been used. At about this same time, my canceled checks came from the bank. That's when it was confirmed that Carole had gone to the grocery store that Saturday morning. The check she had written to the Jewel store was a handwriting nightmare. This was one more confirmation that she had been drinking that morning.

Sometimes when people disappear and want to take on a new identity, they try to change their social security number. I called the Social Security Office in Baltimore to see if there was any movement on her number, and they said no.

It was about this time that the police approached me to take a lie detector test. The media had been asking them persistently if I was a suspect in Carole's disappearance. Some of them were hinting that I had murdered my wife. Others were hinting that I had hired someone to kill her. All sorts of rumors were flying around about Carole's disappearance, and most of them had me being part of some foul play. When the Wheaton police asked me to take a lie detector test, I agreed to do it without hesitation.

It was Columbus Day, October 12, 1982 when I took the test. My lawyer went with me. They asked me all the questions that I had to answer with a yes or no. Was my name Milt Pappas? Did I live in Wheaton? Was Carole my wife? All that until they asked the big question: Did I kill my wife? No. Did I have anything to do with her disappearance? No.

Commander Terry Mee of the Wheaton Police Department will tell you that I passed the test with flying colors. They didn't have me under suspicion for anything because they had neither evidence or testimony against me. All they had to support me taking the test was the constant pressure from the media that demanded to know if I was a suspect. Now that the test had been administered and I had passed, they could tell the press that I was not a suspect and never had been one.

Of course, the media didn't like this because they had no-where to go now. They couldn't assassinate my character in the newspapers with innuendo and hearsay. Now they had to take me off their list of suspects and put me at the top of their list of victims. Before this, only Stevie and Michelle were considered to be victims.

Like I said, the media can be your friend or they can be your worst nightmare.

About two months after her disappearance, I came to the conclusion that Carole was dead, even though I didn't have any proof. My kids were just heart broken. They said that Mom was alive and that nothing had happened to her. I said that something had happened because she had never done this before. She'd always called us, if she was in trouble. The fact that she was an alcoholic compounded my feelings that something terrible had happened to her.

* * *

After the publicity came out, the sales lady called from Marshall Field's. That was the last place that we knew for certain that Carole had been. She never made it home from there. So our search — mine and the one being done by the Wheaton police — focused on the route from the shopping center in Carol Stream to our house. I looked for possible places where she might have stopped, and the police did the same. We all failed to turn up anything.

What had happened to Carole? The question remained unanswered. I thought somebody kidnaped and killed her. That was my thought process from the second month on; she was dead somewhere; somebody got her and killed her; pulled her out of the parking lot or something. Something terrible. Something too horrible to think about.

But there were absolutely no leads. No solid leads. Just all kinds of bullshit that came from every direction. "Oh, we saw her here in Wisconsin." Or, "We saw her here in Minnesota." Or she was seen in Timbuktu. The police could never put anything together. Everything that came in they pursued. No matter how wild it was, the Wheaton Police Department pursued it until it dried out. I think they would have chased down a report that she'd been abducted by aliens from outer space, if one had come in, but nothing that absurd was reported.

Only one lead led to anything. Four men who were abducting, raping, torturing, and murdering women — primarily prostitutes — were captured. They would grab a woman, throw her in a van, tie her up with wire, then rape and torture her until she died. The police caught them because one of the prostitutes escaped and gave them a description of the van. They traced it to two men who lived out by me.

A deputy sheriff was part of the investigation team. I asked him if these men were involved in Carole's disappearance. The police took five pictures of women, including Carole, and laid them on the table in front of these two suspects. One of them picked out my wife. He said that they grabbed her in the shopping center where she was last seen. He said that they grabbed her, took her in the van, and one of the other guys drove her car. They said that they took her out to the woods, tortured her, and killed her. He told them where the spot was, but when they went out there, nothing was found.

Once I heard that story, all of my focus was on those guys. I believed that they had killed her and had done something with the car. Even the deputy sheriff said, "I know they did it. I know they killed her." But the police couldn't find Carole's body, and without a body, they had no case.

* * *

The months became years. Five years, in fact. Until 1987. In the interim, my mother-in-law hounded me with calls accusing me of having murdered Carole. She called at all times of the day and night. Sometimes she was drunk when she called. She called Stevie and Michelle and told them that I had killed their mother. This went on and on.

Other rumors floated around. I'm still hearing new ones. Two of the most recent are real beauties. The mob killed her to punish me for some bad gambling debts, and the mob killed her because of my affiliation with Jimmy Hoffa. Another one said the Major League Baseball owners conspired to kill her to punish me for my part in building up the players union. Remember that baseball had a strike in 1981, then football had one in 1982.

On and on it went. I killed her and dumped her and the car in Lake Michigan. I had her killed and her body disposed of. On and on and on.

My son Stevie even consulted a psychic, Irene Hughes. She told him to bring her something that had belonged to Carole. He did. She felt it and said, "Your mother's in water." She said other things, but none of them were as precise as that one statement.

Between the time of her disappearance and the summer of 1987, I was a guest on a few television shows. I appeared on the Phil Donahue show in Chicago, then was on the "Today Show" with Byrant Gumbel interviewing me.

In 1983, Harriett Goldberg appeared on Oprah Winfrey's show in Baltimore. This was before Oprah moved to Chicago.

Carole was gone, and I was sure she would never come back. I was certain she was dead. My life needed to go on. The kids were gone, and I was living alone. I was lonely, and I didn't like it. Then I met Judi, who would later become my second wife, and the loneliness left. The time went by easier, then Judi and I had a daughter. We named her Alexandria. I was settling into a new life, and I liked it. I was ready to put the past behind me. Forever.

Then the big shock came.

The day was August 7, a Thursday, around 5:00 p.m.. While driving home from work, I wanted to stop at a convenience store to buy a pack of cigarettes. For some reason, I was taking a different route home, one that went by the local fire station, which was only four blocks from my house. The place was just teeming with cars and people — and helicopters, which I found peculiar. I couldn't figure out what was going on, so I attempted to stop to see what was happening. When I couldn't find a place to park, I decided to go to another store and get my cigarettes, then go back and find out what was going on. I got the cigarettes and went back to the fire station, but I still couldn't find a place to park.

I couldn't wait to get home to tell Judi that something was going on at the fire station. When I pulled into my driveway, another car was in my parking spot. This irritated me, so I blew my horn. Out of my house walked the detective from the Wheaton Police Department. He came up to me as I was getting out of my car and said, "We found your wife."

My reaction was instant. "Where?"

"Four blocks away. She was still in the car in the pond next to the fire station."

"I was just there. How long have you known this?"

"About three hours."

"Three hours?" My anger shot through the roof. "And you never bothered calling me at work to tell me that you found her in the car? I almost stopped there to see what was happening. Can you imagine if I would've gotten out of the car to walk up there? What an ass I would've looked like coming there and finding my wife dead inside an automobile! You guys have bungled this case from day number one. Why in the hell wouldn't you have called me so at least I could have called my kids so they wouldn't have to hear about it on the radio coming home from work, that their mother was found dead? What the hell's the matter with you guys?"

I walked into the house to find the chief of police making a statement on television, and I still hadn't been officially notified. I was livid. I just couldn't imagine that this police department didn't have the courtesy of calling me three hours before to tell me they had found my wife dead. I said, "Why?"

"We don't know."

"Well, how did you find her?"

"There's a pond next to the fire station."

"Yes, I know that."

They said that one of the firemen was out there with his remote control boat, and it got stuck in the middle of the pond. When he went out to free the boat, he found it sitting on top of a car. When he dove down, he pulled off the license plate. He called the police with the plate number, and it turned out to be from my wife's car.

Divers were brought in from the forest preserve. They went down to look inside the car, and they found Carole's body there.

Why did they find the car at this time? In the years since her disappearance, the area around the fire station had built up considerably. A lot of people were visiting the retention pond for one reason or another. The city of Wheaton decided to make it more like a park. To do that, they had to improve the shoreline, and to improve the shoreline, they had to lower the water level. That's what they were doing when the fireman's remote-control boat got hung up on Carole's car. Even if he hadn't been sailing that boat on the pond, her car would still have been found once the water level went low enough.

To this day, nobody can tell me for certain how Carole and her car wound up in the middle of that pond. The coroner ruled it an accidental drowning. I made sure to ask them if there were gun shot wounds or knife wounds or anything out of the ordinary on the body, and he said no. He said that the water was cold and there were no fish in there, so the body actually was in pretty good shape. I told them to make sure to check the car to see if anybody rammed the car into the pond. They did all that and then some, but they never uncovered anything. The final analysis was accidental drowning.

The car was in the middle of the pond, the deepest part. How it got there is still a mystery, but there is one logical theory. It slowly slid there over the years. How could that be? How could Carole have gotten the car in the pond in the first place? That's a question that will never be answered. Even the police won't speculate on that one.

No matter how the car got there, when the police found it, the gear shift was in the park position, the ignition was turned off, the air-conditioner was in the on position, all the doors except the driver's door were locked, and all the windows except Carole's were completely closed. Only the driver's window was half open.

During the course of the morning, Carole started drinking. She became disoriented, then lost; then somehow she ended up in the pond. How she got there, nobody knows for sure because nobody saw her go in. It was a mystery in 1982, a mystery in 1987, and it's still a mystery.

◆35◆

Low Bridge:
When to Duck

I built up a barrier throughout the course of my adult life because of what happened to me at an early age with my teammates on the Baltimore Orioles. That barrier cost me my second marriage.

What was the barrier? I was always instigating things and looking for things that were wrong, that shouldn't have been, instead of communicating. I was always pointing a finger at anything that was wrong instead of looking at things that were right.

In the early 1990s, I started seeing a psycho-analyst because my second marriage was breaking up and I couldn't understand why. I was so intimidating that I was always putting the finger of blame on everybody but myself. I would pass it off like nothing was wrong, even though I had hurt the person that I loved. With the thought of the divorce and not knowing why, I came to the realization that maybe the fault was with me. I sought help. It was too late to save my marriage, but I finally saw myself in the light that I thought I was in before.

The way I was brought up by my Greek family — to love people, to honor people, not to be a phony person, to be yourself, to be real — were all of the things that I thought I was. I was that to everybody else except my own family. That realization, when it came out in the analysis, hurt me, that I would do this to the people I love. I was a great person to everybody on the perimeter, but not to the people I loved. I was always pointing the finger of blame at everybody but myself, which was the wrong way of living. It took my going to see a doctor to realize that I had that problem.

Did my personality quirk affect Carole? Probably. Was that why she drank? It may have been a contributing factor, but as I've revealed before, it was my promiscuity that started her drinking. Did my promiscuity continue after I left baseball? No, it had ended long before I quit the game. So why did Carole continue to drink after I quit playing around? Alcoholism is a disease that not everybody can conquer. As hard as Carole tried to beat it, she just couldn't, and that was that.

My personal problem broke up my marriage with Judi, but before we parted, we brought a beautiful girl into the world. Alex is one of the few children to have the privilege of attending her parents' wedding. She's been the joy of my life these last years.

* * *

A few months ago I celebrated my 60th birthday. Celebrated gives the idea that happiness was involved. I'm not so sure about that when it comes to milestone birthdays like number 50 or number 60.

Looking back over the years, I see a lot of accomplishments in my life. Three of the greatest ones are my children: Steve, Michelle, and Alex. My achievements in baseball are elsewhere in these pages.

My one big regret — besides losing Carole — is not being in the Baseball Hall of Fame. I believe I deserve to be there as much as a lot of guys who are there. My numbers either match theirs or surpass them. I don't feel the need to make specific comparisons here; I'll leave that up to the people of SABR (Society of American Baseball Researchers). But in addition to what I did on the field, I did a lot off the field for the players with the work I did as a player-rep in the union. Ironically, it's that very work that probably kept me off the ballot in the first place. I know I didn't make a lot of friends among the sportswriters — the guys who do the voting for the Hall of Fame — when I was working to make things better for the players. But maybe the players who make up the old-timers committee might see me in a different light, maybe they'll consider what I did for them and our peers and vote me into the Hall.

I also regret not accepting the contract with the San Diego Padres in 1974. If I had pitched that year, I would certainly have won my 100th game in the National League. And if I'd had a good year in San Diego, maybe I would have been traded to a better team or maybe I would have elevated San Diego to a contender for the NL West title. Maybe I would've stuck around baseball long enough to cash in on some of that big money that I helped the guys start making in the late 1970s. Who knows what might have happened?

That's it for regrets. At least the major ones. Like anybody else, I've got some small ones, but none of them are really worth mentioning here.

On the positive side, I've had a pretty good job for the last 14 years. I'm a sales rep for Primesource Building Products, which is a subsidiary of Itochu, a Japanese company. And just this past summer, I got into broadcasting. I do the color analysis for the Cook County Cheetahs, a minor league team in the independent Frontier League. My partner on WJOB radio out of Hammond, Indiana is Steve Dull. I'm also assistant pitching coach for the team.

What more can I say about my life? Only this: Maybe I've had more than my share of triumphs, but I think I've paid for them with more than my share of tragedies.

* * *

T hank you for reading my book. I hope my story helps to keep you or someone you love from making the same mistakes that I made, and at the same time, I wish you all the happiness that I've had.

◆INDEX◆

~A~

Aaron, Hank - 124, 137, 142, 152, 180, 192, 198, 202-204, 220
Abernathy, Ted - 181, 184, 188
Adair, Jerry - 67, 116, 125
Adair, Jimmy - 4, 93
Adcock, Joe - 124
Agee, Tommie - 234, 239, 286
Agnew, Spiro - 59, 301
Aguirre, Hank - 295
Aker, Jack - 244, 252, 259, 262-263
Alexander, Doyle - 243
Allen, Richard Anthony "Richie" "Dick" - 138, 180, 238, 274
Allison, Bob - 69
Alou, Felipe - 180, 198, 220
Alou, Jesus - 180
Alou, Matty - 180
Alston, Walter - 183
American Association - 145-146
American Baseball Guild - 146
American Federation of Labor (AFL-CIO) - 150
American Legion baseball - 17, 21, 23, 27
Anaheim, CA - 86
Anaheim Angels - 66, 79-80, 82, 86-87, 95-97, 104, 118, 120-121, 125-129, 135, 187, 197, 245-246, 291, 305
Anson, Adrian "Cap" - 222
Aparicio, Luis - 54, 115-116, 119, 125, 135
Arrigo, Jerry - 187
Aspromonte, Bob - 198
Atlanta, GA - 172, 184, 191-193, 197, 200-201, 240, 248-249, 264, 269, 319, 321
Atlanta Braves - 68, 80, 97, 124, 142, 155, 172, 174, 181, 183-185, 188, 190-192, 195, 197-198, 203-204, 207, 212, 219-221, 230, 237, 240-241, 248-250, 264-265, 269, 279, 319, 321-322
Augusta, GA - 48
Autry, Gene - 86

~B~

Babe Ruth League - 17, 20
Baker, Gene - 245
Bakersfield, CA - 253
Baldschun, Jack - 169
Ball, Lucille - 306
Baltimore, MD - 2, 31-34, 37-39, 43-45, 48-50, 58-65, 71, 73, 77, 82, 84, 90, 93-95, 97, 101, 103-14, 106, 109-110, 120, 122, 124-126, 128, 133, 135-137, 139-141, 151, 158, 168-169, 174, 178, 190, 198, 200, 202, 208, 212, 214-216, 221-222, 301, 303, 311, 319, 321-322, 332

Baltimore Bullets - 202, 214
Baltimore Clippers - 214
Baltimore Colts - 202
Baltimore Orioles - 1, 4-6, 22-28, 31-35, 37-40, 47, 51-52, 58-60, 62, 64, 66-67, 69-70, 73, 78-79, 82, 85, 87, 91-92, 99, 110, 114-117, 122-127, 130, 132, 142, 148, 151-152, 154-156, 158, 164, 167, 169, 176, 178, 184, 187, 197-198, 202, 204, 207-208, 213, 215, 243, 251, 273, 303, 305, 320, 338
Baltimore *Sun* - 37
Banks, Ernie - 68, 180, 193, 220, 223, 231-233, 244-246, 276, 279, 286, 291-292
Barber, Steve - 47, 68, 74, 81, 91-92, 116-117, 120, 125, 127, 130, 132-133, 167-168
Barker, Raymond "Buddy" - 135
Barr, Jim - 266-267, 295
Baseball Players' Fraternity - 146
Batsakes, George - 170
Batsakes, Stella - 170
Bauer, Hank - 35-36, 85, 123-127, 130, 132-134, 139, 167-168
Bavasi, Buzzy - 296-297
Beckert, Glenn - 223, 226-227, 231-233, 241, 246-247, 250-251, 262, 281, 287, 290-292
Bell, Gary - 48, 54
Belleville, IL - 256
Bench, Johnny - 184-185, 188, 194, 225-226, 247
Berberet, Lou - 41, 49
Berle, Milton - 305-306
Berra, Larry "Yogi" - 2, 35-36, 52-53, 69, 73, 75, 134, 137, 152
Beverly Hills, CA - 306
Bibby, Jim - 260
Blair, Paul - 132
Blanchard, John - 121
Blass, Steve - 193, 241
Blefary, Curt - 132
Bloomington, MN - 94, 121, 126-128, 137
Bolin, Bobby - 175
Bolling, Frank - 69
Bonds, Bobby - 236
Bonham, Bill - 233, 262, 264, 267, 293-294
Boros, Steve - 26
Boston, MA - 1, 41, 52, 56, 82, 90, 104, 120, 122, 139, 221, 285, 320
Boston Braves - see Atlanta Braves
Boston Celtics - 82
Boston Red Sox - 6, 25-26, 32, 41, 43-44, 48, 50-52, 54, 56, 74, 80, 85, 93, 114, 120-122, 126-127, 133, 136, 139, 160, 163, 185, 197
Bourque, Pat - 270

Bouton, Jim - 125
Bowa, Larry - 235
Bowens, Sam - 124-125, 128
Boyd, Bob - 32, 40, 48
Boyer, Clete - 73, 198, 220
Bragan, Bobby - 45, 198
Brandt, Jackie - 82, 93, 116, 125, 135, 169
Brecheen, Harry "The Cat" - 2, 4, 27, 124
Breeden, Danny - 233
Breeden, Hal - 233
Breeding, Marv - 67, 93, 99
Bressooud, Ed - 120
Brickhouse, Jack - 90
Briggs, Spike - 163
Briggs Stadium (Detroit, MI) - 22, 24
Bristol, Dave - 174-177, 181-183, 187-189, 198
Britton, Jim - 198-199
Brock, Lou - 134, 180, 263, 273
Brooklyn, NY - 162
Brooklyn Dodgers - see Los Angeles Dodgers
Brown, Hector Harold "Hal" "Skinny" - 33, 40, 47, 50, 74, 81, 93, 96
Brown, Richard "Dick" - 116, 125
Browne, Byron - 274
Bryant, Ron - 236, 249
Buckner, Bill - 236
Buhl, Bob - 181, 291
Bunker, Wally -125, 130, 132
Bunning, Jim - 49, 54, 74, 95, 148, 152, 173, 293, 295
Burris, Ray - 269, 293-294
Busby, Jim - 32, 40, 62
Busch, August - 164, 197
Bush, Barbara - 310-311
Bush, President George - 306-311, 313
Buttons, Red - 306

~C~

Caldwell, Ralph Michael - 255-256
California Angels - see Anaheim Angels
Callison, Johnny - 180, 223, 228, 232-233, 240, 244-245, 292
Camp David, MD- 313
Candlestick Park (San Francisco, CA) - 227, 238
Canelos, Ann - 62
Canelos, Jimmy - 62
Canelos, Mary - 62-63
Cannizzaro, Chris - 236
Cannon, Judge Robert - 143, 148-149, 150
Carbo, Bernie - 225-226
Cardenal, Jose - 237-238, 244-247, 262, 267, 328, 331
Cardenas, Leo - 170, 175, 178, 180

Cardwell, Don - 173
Carlton, Steve - 179, 241, 251, 255
Carnel, Herb - 66
Carol Stream, IL - 331, 333
Carrasquel, Chico - 48
Carroll, Clay - 191
Carty, Rico - 180, 198, 204, 220
Cash, Norm - 69, 82, 122
Castleman, Foster - 40
Catalinas, Ed - 26, 27
Cepeda, Orlando - 39, 180, 198, 200, 220
Cerv, Bob - 54, 79
Cey, Ron - 118
Chance, Dean - 57-58, 118
Chandler, A.B. "Happy" - 147
Chapman, Mark David - 210
Chapman, Ray - 118
Charlotte, NC - 36, 61
Cheney, Tom - 98, 99-100
Chicago, IL - 10, 50, 58, 71, 77-78, 86, 90, 104, 125-127, 133-134, 140, 197, 210, 221, 223-224, 228-230, 235, 238, 241-243, 245, 248, 251-252, 255, 260,263-265, 268, 271, 281, 283, 284-286, 288, 291, 295-297, 302, 305, 310, 316, 326, 328, 330, 335
Chicago Cubs - 26, 39, 56, 90, 113-114, 131, 134, 138, 161, 163-164, 171-175, 181, 183, 185, 188, 193, 195, 197, 201, 207-210, 220-221, 223-232, 235, 237-242, 244-246, 248-249, 251, 260-265, 270-272, 276, 279, 281-286, 288, 290-293, 295-297, 302-303, 306, 320, 325
Chicago *Tribune* - 63, 225, 276
Chicago White Sox - 6, 32-33, 40-42, 44-45, 47, 50-54, 57, 69, 71-74, 81, 95-96, 98, 115, 117, 120-121, 126-129, 133, 136-138, 140, 163, 185, 197-198, 277, 290, 297
Chicago White Stockings - 144-145
China - 9
Cincinnati, OH - 169-170, 172, 174, 176, 180, 185, 188-189, 191, 193-195, 215, 226, 229, 240, 248-249, 251, 263, 319, 321
Cincinnati Reds - 24, 26, 40, 73, 129-130, 164, 168-169, 171-173, 175, 178, 178-179, 181, 184, 186-187, 189-192, 197-198, 207, 212, 225-226, 240, 243, 247-250, 252, 264, 269, 273, 279, 292, 321
Clarke, Horace - 135
Clarkson, John - 222
Clemente, Roberto - 1, 76, 180, 182
Cleveland, OH - 48-49, 51, 70, 74, 95, 121, 148
Cleveland Indians - 6, 23, 32, 40, 44-45, 48-49, 51, 53-54, 69-72, 74, 79-80, 96-98, 117-118, 121, 126, 128-130, 133, 136, 138, 187, 197-198, 297

Cloninger, Tony - 191
Cobb, Ty - 22
Cody High School (Detroit, MI) - 22
Cohen, Max - 216
Coker, Jimmie - 116
Colavito, Rocco "Rocky" - 49, 54, 70, 72, 95-96, 111-112, 293
Colbert, Nate - 253-254
Colborn, Jim - 233, 237, 244-245, 279-280
Coleman, Ed - 82
Coleman, Gordy - 180-181
Coleman, Jerry - 36
Collins, Joe - 35-36
Columbia Broadcasting System (CBS) - 66, 163
Comiskey, Charles, Sr. "The Old Roman" - 163
Comiskey Park (Chicago, IL) - 45, 55
Concepcion, Davy - 225
Conigliaro, Tony - 136
Conley, Gene - 82
Conlon, Jocko - 111, 113
Connors, Mike - 306
Cook County Cheetahs - 340
Cooley High School (Detroit, MI) - 14, 17, 19, 23-24
Cosell, Howard - 66, 89
Counts, J. Curtis - 277
Courtney, Clint -41, 67-68, 70, 123
Cronin, Joe - 152
Cullen, Blake - 220, 229-230, 303
Cullen, Jack - 140
Culver, George - 187
Cuyler, Ki Ki - 21

~D~

Daley, Bud - 40, 125
Daley, Richard, Sr. - 302-303
Dallas, TX - 276
Dalton, Harry -168
D'Annunzio, Lou - 17, 24-25, 27-28, 31, 110
Davidson, Donald - 203
Davidson, Ted - 188, 191
Davis, Brock - 232, 237-238, 244
Davis, Tommy - 57, 180
Davis, Willie - 252
Dean, Dizzy - 66
Delock, Ike - 54
Denver, CO - 306, 308
Denver Bears - 308
Detroit, MI - 2, 4-5, 8-10, 13-14-15, 17-18, 22-23, 26-28, 34, 37-38, 46, 57, 59-60, 63-64, 70, 74, 82, 95, 97, 102, 103, 129-130, 139, 142, 224, 230, 260, 284, 303, 330
Detroit Amateur Baseball Federation - 17, 22-23

Detroit *News* - 27
Detroit Tigers - 6, 13, 21-22, 24-26, 32-33, 35, 42-44, 49-50, 52, 54, 57, 66-67, 69-70, 72, 74, 80-83, 95, 97, 116, 121-122, 126, 129-130, 133, 135-136, 163, 173, 185, 197-198, 202, 274, 297
DeWitt, William - 164
Dickey, Bill - 52
Didier, Bob - 198, 204
DiMaggio, Joe - 52, 123, 307
Ditmar, Art - 72-73, 75
Doby, Larry - 40, 54
Doctor's Hospital (Miami, FL) - 304
Dodger Stadium - 119, 162
Donahue, Phil - 335
Donovan, Dick - 54, 98
Dozer, Dick - 225, 276
Dropo, Walt - 70
Drysdale, Don - 24, 155, 171, 179, 183-184, 293
Dull, Steve - 340
Durocher, Leo "The Lip" - 113, 172, 181, 223-232, 236-239, 241-242, 245, 247-251, 261, 267-268, 276, 284-285, 291-292, 325
Dykes, Jimmy - 198

~E~

Edison, Thomas A. - 222
Edwards, Johnny - 170, 180-181, 194
Eisenhower, President Dwight D. - 48
Eliowitz, Abe - 17, 26
Ellis Island, NY - 8-9
Ellis, Sammy - 170, 175, 178, 180, 186-187
Estrada, Chuck - 47, 67, 72-73, 75, 91-92, 97, 116, 125, 132
Evans, Darrell - 248

~F~

Fairly, Ron - 180
Fanzone, Carmen - 258, 262
Fenway Park (Boston, MA) - 42, 52, 56, 76, 285
Ferrarese, Don - 40
Fidrych, Mark - 54
Finley, Charles - 164
Fisher, Jack - 47, 68, 73, 75-76, 85, 87, 91-92, 116, 132, 187, 212, 320-321
Fisher, Judy - 187, 321
Fitzgerald, Ed - 48
Flood, Curtis Charles - 273-275
Forbes Field (Pittsburgh, PA) - 224
Ford, Whitey - 35, 52-53, 57, 72-74, 80-81, 97, 117, 120, 127, 134-135, 140-141, 293, 307
Fox, Nellie - 54
Foytack, Paul - 44, 54
Frailing, Ken - 291, 293-294

Francona, Tito - 32, 40, 51, 121, 198
Fregosi, Jim - 247
Frick, Ford - 84, 85
Froemming, Bruce - 111, 257-259

~G~

Galbreath, - 163
Garagiola, Joe - 66
Gardner, Billy - 32, 40, 48, 54
Garrido, Gil - 198, 250
Gaston, Clarence Edwin "Cito" - 254
Gates, Bill - 222
Gehrig, Lou - 52, 123
Gentile, Carol - 320-321
Gentile, Jim - 67, 69, 77-78, 82, 92-93, 116, 119, 124, 212-213, 320
Gibson, Bob - 179, 228, 233, 240
Giggie, Bob - 97, 100
Giles, Warren - 152
Gilliam, Junior - 124, 174
Ginsberg, Joe - 27, 67
Goldberg, Arthur - 274
Goldberg, Elliott - 213-215, 311-313
Goldberg, Harriett Scherr - 213-216, 311-313, 335
Goldberg, Wilbert - 215
Gonzalez, Tony - 180, 198, 220
Goodman, Billy -32, 40
Gussage, Goose - 118
Gowdy, Curt - 66
Grant, Jim "Mudcat" - 54, 121, 138
Grba, Eli - 79
Greece - 8-9, 13, 236, 301
Greek Orthodox Church - 10
Green Bay ,WI -305
Griffith, Calvin - 163
Griffith Stadium (Washington, DC) - 46
Gumbel ,Bryant - 335
Gura, Larry - 269

~H~

Haddix, Harvey "The Kitten" - 80, 124-125, 127
Hadley, Kent - 123
Hale, Bob - 32, 35, 49
Hall, Dick - 84, 93, 99, 125, 128, 139, 212
Hammond, IN - 340
Hands, Bill - 221, 224, 226, 231-235,239, 246, 262, 281, 288, 291-292
Hansen, Ron - 62, 68, 115
Harper, Tommy - 170, 180-181, 187-188
Harris, Luman - 4, 82, 85, 92, 191-192, 198-201, 220
Harris, Vic - 290

Harshman, Jack - 40-42, 47
Hart, Jim Ray - 180
Harvey, Doug - 237
Harwell, Ernie - 66
Heenan, Tom - 22
Heffner, Don "The Jeep" - 171, 174, 176
Held, Woodie - 44, 51
Helms, Tommy - 170, 180-181, 225
Hemon, Russ - 40
Hemond, Roland - 297
Hernandez, Enzo Octavio - 253, 255, 258
Herrnstein, John - 290
Hershey, Barbara - 210
Herzog, Whitey - 49, 71, 93, 116
Hickman, Jim - 223-224, 228, 232-233, 246, 262
Hinton, Chuck - 98
Hitchcock, Billy - 85, 92, 95-96, 98, 123, 156, 198, 214
Hodges, Gil - 136
Hoerner, Joe - 274
Hoeft, Billy - 54, 93, 116
Hoffa, Jimmy - 15, 334
Hoffa, Jimmy, Jr. - 15, 142
Holdredge, NE - 79
Holland, John - 220, 230, 234, 241, 250-251, 268, 279-282, 284-285, 290-293, 295
Holtzman, Jerome - 222
Holtzman, Ken - 221, 226, 229, 231-235, 239, 244, 246, 250, 288-289, 291-292
Honochick, Jim - 114
Hooton, Burt - 245-246, 262, 264, 293-294
Horlen, Joel - 277
Hough, Charlie - 260
Houston, TX - 183, 199, 225, 233, 273, 288
Houston Astros (nee Colt .45's) - 85, 87, 160, 174-175, 181-183, 188, 192-193, 197-200, 225-226, 233-234, 240, 254, 264
Houston Colt .45's - see Houston Astros
Howard, Elston - 53, 134
Howsam, Bob - 189-190
Hriniak, Walt - 5, 36-37
Hughes, Irene - 334
Hulbert, William - 144-145
Hundley, Randy - 223, 231-233, 243-244, 246, 257-258, 262, 281, 288, 290-292
Hunt, Ron - 242
Hurley, Ed - 49, 73, 86-87, 111, 113
Hurwitz, Don - 215-216

~I-J~

Illinois Wesleyan College - 324
Internal Revenue Service - 23

Jackson, Larry - 181, 291
Jay, Joey - 180
Jackson, Sonny - 198, 220
Jarvis, Pat - 195, 198-199, 204, 220
Jenkins, Ferguson - 173, 179, 181, 221, 224, 226, 228-229, 231-235, 237, 239, 246-247, 249, 262, 281, 288, 290, 292, 294
Jensen, Jackie - 42, 52, 54, 293
Jestadt, Gary - 233, 258
Jeter, John "The Jet" - 254-256
Johnson City, TN - 19
Johnson, Alex - 187-188
Johnson, Bob - 135, 191
Johnson, Connie - 32, 40
Johnson, Deron - 170, 178, 180-181
Johnson, Jerry - 274
Johnson, Walter - 97
Jones, Cleon - 247
Jordan, Michael - 286

~K~
Kaline, Al - 22, 25, 52, 54, 58, 72, 83, 129
Kansas City, MO - 50, 54, 74, 139, 197
Kansas City Athletics - see Oakland Athletics
Kansas City Royals - 197
Keane, Johnny - 134
Kekich, Mike - 192
Kell, George - 32
Kelley, Ed - 302
Kelly, Mike - 222
Kelso, Bill - 187
Kendall, Fred Lyn - 255-256
Kennedy, Jackie - see Jackie Onassis
Kennedy, John - 174
Kennedy, President John F. - 188, 208, 301
Kennedy, Robert - 189
Kessinger, Don - 223, 231-233, 237-238, 246-247, 251, 256, 262, 281, 287, 291
Key Biscayne, FL - 167-168
Killebrew, Harmon - 53, 69, 127, 138-139
King, Jim - 136
King, Rev. Martin Luther, Jr. - 188
Kirby, Clay - 226-227
Kirkpatrick, Ed - 119, 125
Kluszewski, Ted - 72, 73, 79
Knoxville, TN - 4-5, 36, 60
Knoxville Smokies - 5, 31-32, 36, 60
Koosman, Jerry - 192
Koufax, Sandy - 24, 138, 155, 171, 179
Koyzis, Ted - 322, 324
Kremmel, Jim - 291
Kroc, Ray - 296-297
Kubek, Tony - 36, 53, 66, 73

Kucks, Johnny - 50, 71
Kuenn, Harvey - 43, 54, 293
Kuhn, Bowie - 189, 274
Kutyna, Marty - 273

~L~
Lake Geneva, WI - 231, 284
Landis, Jim - 54
Landrith, Hobie - 58, 93
LaRoche, Dave - 265
Larsen, Don - 45, 123, 258
Lary, Frank - 54
Lau, Charlie - 93, 96, 98
League Protective Players' Association - 146
Lebanon, OR - 253
Lee, Bob -135
Lee, Leron - 253
LeFebvre, Jim - 157
Lehman, Ken - 33, 40
Lemon, Bob - 44, 55
Lemon, Jim - 53
Lennon, John - 210
Lewis, J. Norman - 148
Lile, Jerry - 23
Lincoln, President Abraham - 273
Little League - 16-17, 20
Locker, Bobby - 262-264, 268-271
Lockman, Carroll "Whitey" - 251-253, 259-270, 272, 292-295, 297
Loes, Billy - 33, 40, 47, 49
Lollar, Sherman - 45, 54
Lombardi, Vince - 183
Lopez, Al "*El Señor*" - 32, 53, 73, 137-138, 140
Lopez, Hector - 54, 74
Los Angeles, CA - 6, 78, 86, 97, 104, 118, 125, 128, 135, 162, 173, 182-184, 189, 192, 234, 238, 254, 263, 306
Los Angeles Angels - see Anaheim Angels
Los Angeles Dodgers - 24, 33, 86, 124, 137, 156, 161-163, 171-172, 174, 176, 179-180-182, 188, 193, 197, 199-200, 234, 236, 238, 243, 248-249, 251-252, 263, 305
Louise, Tina - 306
Lown, Turk - 54
Lum, Mike - 198
Lumpe, Jerry -36, 71
Lutherville, MD - 101
Luzinski, Greg - 263, 270-271

~M~
Madlock, Bill - 245, 290
Major League Baseball Players' Association - 142-144, 148-155, 157, 159, 207, 273-278

Malden, Karl - 42

Maloney, Jim - 138, 170, 178, 180, 188, 195

Malzone, Frank - 42, 44, 52, 54

Mantle, Mickey - 1-3, 35-36, 46, 52-53, 69, 72-73, 75-76, 79, 83-84, 93, 117, 120, 123, 134, 293, 307, 314

Marichal, Juan - 137-138, 175, 179

Maris, Roger - 44, 50, 54, 69, 73-74, 76, 83-85, 93, 134, 293

Maros, Jim - 296

Marquez, Gonzalo - 271

Marshall, Jim - 40

Marshall, Mike - 262

Martin, Billy - 307

Martin, J.C. - 233

Martinez, Dennis - 260

Mathewson, Christy - 97

Matlack, Jon - 56

Maxwell, Charlie - 70, 72

May, Lee- 181, 225

Mays, Willie - 1, 39, 137, 152, 172, 174, 180, 192, 266, 314

Mazzoni, Joyce - 19

McAuliffe, Dick - 122, 138

McCarver, Tim - 211, 274

McCool, Bill - 174, 180

McCormick, Mike - 116, 142, 148, 152

McCovey, Willie - 1, 171-172, 174, 177, 180, 192, 266

McDaniel, Lindy - 26

McDaniel, Von - 26

McDougal, Gil - 69

McDowell, Sam - 138

McGinn, Dan - 247

McGwire, Mark - 85, 222

McHale, John - 26-27

McLain, Denny - 249

McNally, Dave - 116, 125, 132

McPhail, Larry - 163

McPhail, Lee - 124, 125, 155, 167-168, 204-205

McQueen, Steve - 168

McRae, Hal - 225

Mediterranean Sea - 8

Mee, Terry - 332

Mejias, Roman - 120

Memorial Stadium (Baltimore, MD) - 2, 62, 114

Messersmith, Andy - 245

Metropolitan League - 21-22

Metropolitan Stadium (Bloomington, MN) - 137

Mexico - 9, 15

Miami, FL - 101, 104, 167-168, 303-304

Millan, Felix - 198, 220

Miller, Marvin - 149, 152, 158-160, 163, 190, 207, 273-278, 283

Miller, Norm - 192

Miller, Stu - 45, 91, 115-116, 121, 125, 127, 136

Miltiades - 8

Milwaukee Braves - see Atlanta Braves

Milwaukee Brewers - 244-245, 255

Mincher, Don - 94, 128, 139

Minneapolis, MN - 6

Minnesota Twins - 55, 77-78, 80, 82, 94, 96-97, 117, 121, 128, 136-139, 141, 163, 185, 197, 262, 290

Minoso, Orestes "Minnie" - 54

Miranda, Willie - 3, 32, 40

Misiakoulis, Eudoxia (Eva Pappas) - 8

Mitchell, Eva - 8

Mitchell, John - 9

Mitchell, Magdeline ("Ya-Ya") - 9, 12, 20

Mitchell, Tom - 9

Mitterwald, George - 290

Molitor, Paul - 57

Monday, Rick - 244, 246, 250, 262, 265

Montañez, Willie - 251, 271

Montreal, CAN - 228, 239, 248, 252, 260, 320

Montreal Expos - 197, 199, 224, 226, 228-229, 234-235, 239, 241-242, 247-248, 260, 262, 265, 269-270, 292, 320

Moore, Ray - 32, 36, 40

Moose, Bob - 224, 247

Morales, Jerry - 290

Morgan, Frank - 322, 324

Morgan, Joe - 180, 192

Morris, Johnny -328, 331

Morton, Gary - 306

Moss, Dick - 277

Murphy, Audie - 304-305

Murphy, Robert - 146-147

Murray, Jan - 306

~N~

Names, Larry - 116, 330

Naperville, IL -314, 326

Nash, Jim - 220

National Broadcasting Company (NBC) - 66

National Brotherhood of Professional baseball Players - 146

National Labor Relations Board - 146

Nelson, Jim - 224

Newhouser, Hal - 21, 25, 28, 31, 59

Newman, Fred - 135

New Orleans, LA - 276

New York, NY - 2-4, 36, 51, 64-65, 72, 81, 85, 89-90, 93, 95, 104, 117, 127, 130, 134, 140, 173, 175, 182, 189, 194, 201-202, 207, 221, 247, 251,

271, 284, 325
  New York Giants - 91, 251
  New York Jets - 202
  New York Knicks - 202
  New York Mets - 56, 130, 173, 182, 188, 193, 197, 201-202, 204, 223, 226-229, 234-235, 239-240, 247-249, 252, 260, 263-264, 270-272, 285-286
  New York Yankees - 2-3, 6, 19, 25, 32, 35-36, 40-41, 45-47, 50-53, 57, 68-75, 80-84, 86, 93-98, 117, 119-123, 125-132, 134-138, 140, 152, 158, 163, 197, 201, 213, 244
    Newcomb, Don - 251
    Newman, Ray - 233
    Nicholson, Dave - 96, 115
    Niekro, Phil - 198-199, 204, 220, 248
    Nieman, Bob - 32, 40, 48, 142
    Nixon, President Richard M. - 48, 140, 281-282, 301 302
    Nolan, Gary - 181, 188
    North, Billy - 256
    NorthCentral Illinois Colelge (Naperville, IL) - 314-315, 326
      Northwestern High School (Detroit, MI) - 13, 15
      Northwestern Hospital (Chicago, IL) - 270
      Nuxhall, Joe - 172, 178, 180, 186, 211

~O~
  Oakland, Athletics - 2-3, 6, 32, 37, 43-44, 47-51, 54, 69-72, 80, 82, 94, 96-97, 117-118, 120-124, 135, 139, 164, 197-198, 220, 244, 250, 262, 270-271
    Oakridge Boys - 313
    O'Dell, Billy -40, 47, 51, 54
    Oliva, Tony - 1, 75, 309
    Oliver, Al - 237
    O'Malley, Peter - 163
    Onassis, Jackie Kennedy - 301
    Oosterberg, Carol - 60
    Orsino, John - 116, 125, 135
    Ortiz, Jose - 233
    Osinski, Dan - 126
    Osteen, Claude - 171, 174
    Ottinger, Warren - 226
    Ottoman Empire - 236

~P~
  Palmer, Jim - 125, 133
  Panama Canal - 8
  Papastedgios, Stedious (Steve Pappas) - 8
  Pappas, Alexandria - 310, 339
  Pappas, Carole Tragge - 58, 60-61, 63, 78, 101-104, 106-107, 109, 167-168, 187, 209, 212-213,

215-21℃ 230, 284-285, 296, 319-337, 339
  Pappas, Eva - 8, 10, 13, 15, 17, 19-20, 60-61, 63, 260, 303, 321
  Pappas, Judi - 310, 335, 339
  Pappas, Kosta "Gus" - 10, 17-19, 61
  Pappas, Michelle Anne - 107, 212, 323-324, 326, 332, 334
  Pappas, Pericles "Perry" - 10, 17-19, 61, 321
  Pappas, Steve - 8, 10, 17, 19-20, 63
  Pappas, Steven John - 101, 104, 107, 212, 315, 324, 326, 332, 334
  Paris, TX - 79
  Parker, Wes - 157, 236
  Pascual, Camilo - 53
  Pavletich, Don - 180-181
  Pearson, Albie - 49
  Pepitone, Joe - 135, 195-196, 232-234, 246-247, 249-250, 289
  Pepsi-Cola - 15
  Perez, Marty - 250
  Perez, Tony - 170, 180-181, 225, 247
  Perkins, Anthony - 42
  Perry, Gaylord - 179
  Perry, Jim - 74
  Peters, Gary - 140
  Philadelphia, PA - 173, 194, 201, 242, 251, 322
  Philadelphia A's - see Oakland A's
  Philadelphia Phillies - 23, 25, 92, 116, 129-130, 171, 173, 175, 181-184, 188, 193, 197, 199, 201, 210, 226, 228-229, 234, 242, 246, 251, 259, 263, 268, 270-271, 273-274, 290-291, 297
  Philippines, The - 15
  Philley, Dave -74, 82
  Phillips, Adolfo - 290-292
  Pierce, Billy - 54, 57-58, 71, 293
  Piersall, Jim - 41-42, 52, 54
  Pilarcik, Al - 32, 40, 59
  Pinson, Vada - 170, 178, 180-181
  Piper, Pat - 258
  Pipp, Wally - 123
  Pittsburgh, PA - 175, 237, 241, 252
  Pittsburgh Pirates - 24, 124, 146-147, 163, 171, 173, 176, 182-184, 188, 192-193, 197, 200, 223-224, 226-229, 234, 237-242, 245-246, 249, 252-253, 260, 262, 269-270, 272
  Pizarro, Juan - 126, 128, 246, 265
  Players League - 146
  Podres, Johnny - 171
  Poland - 9
  Polo Grounds (New York, NY) - 251
  Popovich, Paul - 233, 241, 246, 262, 292
  Portacarrero, Arnold - 49, 70
  Powell, Boog - 92-93, 95-96, 116, 125, 133-134,

139
    Power, Vic - 44, 54
    Preuss, Paul - 27
    Puertp Rico - 15, 216

~Q-R~
Queen, Mel - 180-181, 187
Rakow, Ed - 129
Ramos, Pedro - 48, 53, 55-56, 82
Raymond, Claude - 192
Reagan, President Ronald - 310
Redford, Robert - 210
Reed, Ron - 198, 199, 204, 220
Reese, Pee Wee - 66
Regan, Phil - 227-228, 233, 237, 246, 289
Reulbach, Ed - 224
Reuschel, Rick - 245, 262, 293-294
Reuss, Jerry - 237-238, 260
Richards, Paul - 2-5, 27-28, 33-36, 38-40, 42-
45, 47-49, 51, 54-56, 62, 65, 67-72, 80, 82, 85-87,
92, 113, 151, 183, 198, 204, 232, 267
Richardson, Bobby - 53, 71, 135
Richert, Pete - 138
Rickles, Don - 306
Roberts, Dave - 254
Roberts, David Wayne - 253
Roberts, Robin - 92, 96, 116, 125, 148
Robertson, Bob - 237
Robinson, Bill - 270
Robinson, Brooks - 3, 32, 40, 48, 54, 62-65, 67,
71, 77, 82, 93, 116, 125, 202, 212, 287
Robinson, Connie - 78
Robinson, Earl - 82
Robinson, Floyd - 73
Robinson, Frank - 164, 169-170, 176, 178, 243-
244, 248
Rojas, Cookie - 274
Roman, Bob - 23
Rose, Pete - 170, 175, 178, 180-181, 194-196,
225
Roseboro, John - 137
Rudolph, Ken - 233-234
Runge, Paul - 48-49, 111-112
Runnels, Pete - 54
Ruth, Babe - 52, 83-84, 141, 222
Ryan, Nolan - 235

~S~
Sadecki, Ray - 183-184
St. Louis, MO 139, 193, 197, 199, 241, 251, 254,
265
St. Louis Browns - 33, 82
St. Louis Cardinals - 124, 129-130, 134, 164,

171, 174, 179, 182-185, 187-189, 191, 193, 197,
199, 201, 204, 223-224, 228-229, 233-234, 237,
240-241, 251-252, 260, 262-265, 268-274
    St. Paul, MN - 6
    Sally League - 31, 36
    San Antonio, TX - 254
    San Diego, CA - 219, 239, 252, 254, 263, 296
    San Diego Padres - 197, 226-227, 235, 239-240,
248, 252-256, 262-263, 268, 290, 296, 340
    San Francisco, CA - 115-116, 174, 192, 219,
245, 263, 266
    San Francisco Giants - 39, 113, 116, 137, 157,
168, 171, 175-177, 183-184, 191-192, 197-200,
226-227, 234, 236, 238, 240, 252, 254, 266, 268,
288, 295
    Santo, Ron - 138, 172, 180, 211, 223, 227, 231-
233, 235, 246-247, 249, 262, 266, 279, 281, 287,
290-292
    Santo Domingo - 15
    Scherr, Harriett - see Harriett Goldberg
    Scherr, Robert - 213
    Scherr, Stanley - 213-215
    Scherr, Sylvia - 213
    Schmidt, Willard - 273
    Schwall, Don - 56, 80
    Score, Herb - 71
    Scott, Bill - 302
    Scottsdale, AZ - 232
    Seattle, WA - 197
    Seattle Pilots - 197
    Seaver, Tom - 179, 193
    Severinsen, Albert Henry - 256
    Shamsky, Art - 180
    Shantz, Bobby - 36, 53
    Sheffing, Bob - 82
    Short, Chris - 234-235
    Shreveport, LA - 254
    Siebern, Norm - 53, 123-125, 169
    Sievers, Roy - 53
    Simpson, Dick - 169
    Singer, Bill - 252
    Sinks, Mickey - 23
    Sisler, Dick - 171
    Skowron, Bill "Moose" - 2, 35-36, 46, 53, 73, 140
    Slaughter, Enos - 2, 35-36
    Smith, Al - 54, 115-116
    Smith, Willie - 226
    Snyder, Mack - 214-215
    Snyder, Russ - 93, 99, 125
    Sosa, Sammy - 85, 286
    Spahn, Warren - 179, 307-308
    Spearman, Nancy - 18
    Stafford, Bill - 73, 94, 98

Stahl, Larry Floyd - 256-259
Staley, Jerry - 45, 54-55
Stallard, Tracy - 85
Stargell, Willie - 137-138, 180, 237, 242
Staub, Rusty - 180, 192
Stedman, John - 66, 94
Steinhagen, Ruth Ann - 210
Stengel, Casey "The Ol' Perfessor" - 46, 173
Stephenson, Earl - 233, 244
Stephenson, Gene - 74
Stewart, James - 22
Stillwell, Curt - 98
Stillwell, Roy - 98, 100
Stingley, Daryl - 118
Stock, Wes - 47
Stone, George - 198-199, 204, 220
Stone, Steve - 290, 293-294
Stottlemyre, Mel - 127
Stuart, Dick - 114, 120
Sturdivant, Tom - 46, 57
Sullivan, Frank - 54
Sutton, Don - 171-172
Swisher, Steve - 291

~T~

Tally, Rick - 221, 228
Tampa, FL - 321
Tanana, Frank - 260
Tarboro, NC - 255
Tasby, Willie - 48
Tatum, Jack - 118
Taylor, Joe "Cash" - 273
Temple, Johnny - 93
Terre Haute, IN - 79
Terry, Ralph - 51, 54, 75, 97, 137
Texas, Univ. of - 245
Texas Rangers - 290
Thomas, Derrel Osborn - 254
Thomson, Bobby - 251
Three Rivers Stadium (Pittsburgh, PA) - 224
Throneberry, Marv - 123
Tillman, Bob - 198, 204, 220
Timonium, MD -212
Tolan, Bobby - 225
Tomanek, Dick "Bones" - 44
Tomkins, Ron - 233
Torgeson, Earl - 73
Toronto Blue Jays - 254
Torrance, CA - 255
Torre, Joe - 138, 204
Torres, Rusty - 233
Tragge, Carole - see Carole Pappas
Tragge, Helen - 102-103, 323

Tragge, Oliver - 61, 102-103, 323, 330
Tresh, Tom - 135, 140-141
Triandos, Gus - 2, 32, 40, 45, 48-49, 54, 67, 80, 92-93, 116, 212-213
Turley, Bob - 35-36, 53, 75
Tuttle, Bill - 71

~U-V~

Uhlaender, Ted - 247
Union Association - 146
United Auto Workers - 161
Upshaw, Cecil - 198, 204, 219-220
Vale, Jerry - 229-230, 303
Vale, Rita - 303-304
Valle de Guanape, Venzuela - 253
Vargo, Ed - 111, 250
Veale, Bob - 171, 224
Veeck, William, Sr. - 164
Veeck, William "Bill" Jr., - 33, 164
Venezuela - 15, 253
Verdi, Bob - 222
Versalles, Zoilo - 128

~W~

Wagner, Dick - 189-190
Wagner, Leon - 137
Waitkus, Eddie - 210
Walker, Jerry - 33-34, 40, 47, 50, 62-63, 72, 91, 125, 132
Ward, Pete - 115
Ward, Preston - 44
Washburn, Ray - 182, 184
Washington, DC - 48, 50, 77-79, 128, 136, 189, 277
Washington Senators (old) - 2, 6, 37, 40-41, 47-48, 51, 53, 68-70, 72, 74, 163
Washington Senators (new) - 78-80, 82, 98-99, 117, 120-121, 126, 128, 130, 136, 138-140, 148, 197
Waxahachie, TX - 85
Weaver, Earl - 85
Weber, Dick - 288
Wendelstedt, Harry - 234-235
Wert, Don - 122
Westrum, Wes - 173
WGN-TV (Chicago, IL) - 90
Wheaton, IL - 296, 302, 322, 326-328
Whitfield, Fred - 187
Wieand, Ted - 273
Wight, Bill - 33, 40
Wilbanks, Johnny - 59-60, 213, 301
Wilhelm, Hoyt - 45, 47-48, 68-70, 72-73, 81, 84, 91-94, 115-116, 204, 220

Williams, Billy - 180, 223, 231-233, 241, 246-247, 256, 262, 279, 281, 286, 290-292

Williams, Dick - 40, 93, 99

Williams, Ted - 1, 42, 50, 52, 54, 75-76, 90, 197, 293, 314

Wills, Maury - 157, 180

Wilson, Jim - 54

Wilson, Red - 70

Winfrey, Oprah - 335

Wise, Rick - 242

Woodeschick, Hal - 70

Woodling, Gene - 40, 48, 54, 79, 142

Woodward, Woddy - 191

Woods, Gary - 255

Wooster, OH - 58

Wright, George - 222

Wrigley Field (Chicago, IL) - 77, 86, 161, 164, 225, 234, 252, 256, 263, 269, 285-286, 288-290, 297

Wrigley Field (Los Angeles, CA) - 86

Wrigley, Philip K. - 163, 197, 234, 240-241, 244-245, 247, 250, 268, 276, 279- 282, 284-285, 296

Wynn, Early - 50, 54, 293, 297

Wynn, Jimmy - 180, 192

~X-Y~

Yankee Stadium (New York, NY) - 36, 52, 85, 93, 124, 141, 207, 286

Yawkey, Tom - 163

Yazstremski, Carl - 82

Yost, Ed - 41, 53

Young, Cy - 97, 295

~Z~

Zauchin, Norbert - 41

Zimmer, Don - 256

Zipfel, Marion Sylvester "Bud" - 98-100

Zuverink, George - 2, 33, 40